CITY POWER

CITY POWER

*URBAN GOVERNANCE
IN A GLOBAL AGE*

RICHARD SCHRAGGER

OXFORD
UNIVERSITY PRESS

OXFORD
UNIVERSITY PRESS

Oxford University Press is a department of the University of Oxford. It furthers
the University's objective of excellence in research, scholarship, and education
by publishing worldwide. Oxford is a registered trade mark of Oxford University
Press in the UK and certain other countries.

Published in the United States of America by Oxford University Press
198 Madison Avenue, New York, NY 10016, United States of America.

Library of Congress Cataloging-in-Publication Data
Names: Schragger, Richard, 1970– author.
Title: City power : urban governance in a global age / Richard Schragger.
Description: New York, NY : Oxford University Press, 2016. |
Description based on print version record and
CIP data provided by publisher; resource not viewed.
Identifiers: LCCN 2016021497 (print) | LCCN 2016009577 (ebook) |
ISBN 9780190246679 (E-book) | ISBN 9780190246686 (E-book) |
ISBN 9780190246662 (hardback)
Subjects: LCSH: Municipal government—Economic aspects. |
Municipal government—Social aspects. | Urban policy. |
Income distribution—Government policy. | Living wage movement. |
BISAC: POLITICAL SCIENCE / Public Policy / City Planning & Urban Development. |
POLITICAL SCIENCE / Economic Conditions. |
POLITICAL SCIENCE / Government / Local.
Classification: LCC HT321 (print) | LCC HT321 .S36 2016 (ebook) |
DDC 307.76—dc23
LC record available at https://lccn.loc.gov/2016021497

3 5 7 9 8 6 4 2
Printed by Sheridan Books, Inc., United States of America

For Risa, Eliana, and Solomon

Distrust of democracy has inspired much of the literature on the city.

—FREDERIC HOWE, 1905

Is it too much to hope that we might be on the verge of . . . the age of the democratic city within the democratic nation-state?

—ROBERT DAHL, 1967

CONTENTS

ACKNOWLEDGMENTS

IN JANUARY 2010, I WAS sitting in a hotel lobby in Philadelphia talking with Jerry Frug when he told me I should be writing a book. It took a number of years for me to believe him. Jerry was my local government law professor at Harvard Law School, and he has continued to quietly prod me along, including by reading in draft what eventually became that book and providing excellent suggestions.

Other friends and colleagues have also been remarkably generous. Two tremendous scholars of cities, Bill Lucy and John Henry Schlegel, read early drafts and forced me to explain what I was doing and why. Nathaniel Popkin, my oldest friend and a great champion of Philadelphia and all things urban—did so as well. Lee Anne Fennell and David Barron—two giants in the field of local government law—provided insightful comments, as did my colleague Mike Gilbert, who read every page with his characteristic attention to detail. Darien Shanske provided a thorough and excellent read of the manuscript for Oxford University Press, as did a second anonymous reader, whose suggestions for improving the manuscript were spot-on. Fred Schauer and Debbie Hellman read my introduction to make sure it made sense. Elisha Cooper, Jon Cannon, Ken Abraham, John Setear, Leslie Kendrick, Christian McMillen, and Stephanie Tatel all provided support and advice when it mattered.

My colleagues at Virginia have listened to me talk about cities for almost fifteen years, mostly without complaint. Micah Schwartzman gave me time off from our joint writing on religion to finish this manuscript—and complained only a little. Their support, the support of numerous other colleagues and friends, and the support of two exceptional deans, John Jeffries and Paul Mahoney, has sustained me in my work.

The students at Virginia have inspired me, and many have worked on this book over the years as research assistants, including, most prominently, Lyle Kossis, Zach Croft, Katherine Maxwell, Antonio Elias, and Ashley Williams. My spring 2016 Urban Law and Policy students cheerfully read the manuscript and offered helpful comments. The law librarians at Virginia all deserve enormous thanks, especially Leslie Ashbrook and Kent Olson, who seemed to know what research I needed even before I did and made sure the manuscript met the highest standards. David McBride, my editor at Oxford, was always excited about this book and shepherded it ably through the publication process.

As always, many people who did not suffer through reading drafts of the book nevertheless inspired or supported my endeavor. I am lucky to have so many friends—here in Charlottesville and elsewhere—who actually wanted an honest answer when they asked how the book was going. My parents, Fred and Arlene Schragger, have always been an inspiration. My scholarly interest in municipal law and government can be traced back to my father's and grandfather's legal practices in Trenton, New Jersey, which taught me more than one would expect about zoning, municipal finance, and the relationship between cities and suburbs. My in-laws, Hal and Linda Goluboff, are avid fans. My children, Eliana and Solomon, continue to amaze me every day with their insight, wisdom, and sense of humor. They only occasionally asked me if the book was done yet.

On the other hand, I often asked Risa Goluboff if I was done yet, and she always gave me an honest answer. Despite writing her own award-winning books (and more recently becoming a law school dean) she has read and edited every line of everything I have ever written, and has made it immeasurably better. I am lucky that we live in the same house. She is, it must be said, the author of my life.

I have been working on the relationship between cities and law for almost fifteen years, and some of the ideas in this book were first rehearsed in law review articles. Chapters 1 and 7 more fully develop the arguments first made in "Rethinking the Theory and Practice of Local Economic Development," 77 Chicago Law Review 311 (2010). An early version of chapter 2 appeared as "Decentralization and Development," 96 Virginia Law Review 1837 (2010). Chapter 3 develops the claims first made in "Can Strong Mayors Empower Weak Cities? On the Power of Local Executives in a Federal System," 115 Yale Law Journal 2542 (2006). Chapter 4 is a much revised version of "Cities, Economic Development, and the Free Trade Constitution," 94 Virginia Law Review 1091 (2008). Chapters 5 and 6 expand on a section of "Mobile Capital, Local Economic Regulation, and the Democratic City," 123 Harvard Law Review 482 (2009), and chapter 8 fully develops an argument first formulated in "Democracy and Debt," 121 Yale Law Journal 860 (2012). Finally, my conclusion echoes some ideas I developed in "Is a Progressive City Possible? Reviving Urban Liberalism for the Twenty-First Century," 7 Harvard Law and Policy Review 231 (2013).

CITY POWER

Introduction

Cities, Capital, and Constitutions

THIS BOOK EXAMINES THE nature of city power in the United States. By power, I mean the city's *formal authority* to engage in particular activities—to decide whether to enforce a minimum wage, for instance, or to adopt campaign finance laws, to protect the environment, to regulate land use, to ban sugary soft drinks, or to operate or own businesses. These things are sometimes within a city's power and sometimes not. The question of whether cities or some other level of government should do them is a question of how institutions are structured—and more generally a question about the possibility and desirability of legal and political decentralization.

By power, however, I also mean the city's *actual capacity* to govern—its ability through its policies to improve the material well-being of its citizens. That kind of power is obviously related to the city's capacity to foster economic growth and avoid economic decline. When we ask whether cities can govern, we are often asking whether the city can weather economic booms and busts, encourage development, foster employment, provide basic services, and adopt effective rules and regulations that are responsive to its citizens' desires. We often act as if cities can do at least *some* of these things. But it is not obvious that cities can do *any* of them, and scholarship on cities has often vacillated between treating cities as powerless to act and blaming them for their failures.

Consider Detroit, a city that recently emerged from the largest municipal bankruptcy in U.S. history. Detroit's demise has often been blamed on bad governance. It has also been blamed on macroeconomic factors like the changing nature of the automotive industry—a singular instance of the larger phenomenon of deindustrialization. Consider also Pittsburgh, another industrial city, but one that seems to have had more success recently. Its decline had been less pronounced than Detroit's—a fact that is sometimes attributed to Pittsburgh's better governance, or the presence of anchoring educational and medical institutions, or to its leaders' wise development policies. Cities live, die, thrive, stagnate, and change. We sometimes attribute city success and city failure to good city policies. But how much of a city's economic health is or can be attributed to the decisions made by city leaders is quite uncertain.

Of course, city agency does not have to be all or nothing. Models of the city's capacities tend to ascribe a certain *kind* of agency to cities, while denying cities other kinds of agency. The conventional view is that territorially limited local jurisdictions—and the citizens that live in them—can only weakly counter large-scale processes like deindustrialization, suburbanization, and globalization. Plant closings, the movement of manufacturing to the south or overseas, the movement of persons out of old, cold cities to new, warm ones, or out of certain cities into others, while potentially painful, are unavoidable consequences of relatively open economic markets. Nevertheless, according to this view, cities can influence their economic fates by attracting and retaining desirable mobile factors—highly educated persons and investment capital. At a minimum, cities must be development-friendly and business-friendly. Cities have to be careful not to regulate or tax mobile capital to such an extent that it flees. Social welfare redistribution and other efforts to address economic inequality must therefore by necessity take place at a higher level of government.[1]

Indeed, much of the literature on urban law and policy revolves around three interlocking ideas that reinforce this particular view of city agency. The first idea is that cities are operating in a worldwide location market and are in continuous competition to attract and retain high-value persons and businesses. The second idea, closely related to the first, is that cities can improve their economic prospects by adopting good policies—namely minimal redistributive taxation, relatively low levels of economic regulation, and polices that attract and subsidize mobile capital. And the third idea is that politics in the city is "limited" to issues involving economic development and that policies addressing economic inequality must be made by central governments.[2]

This book challenges this set of ideas and a number of others that flow from them. First, I argue that the competitive paradigm—which treats cities as products that can be improved in the "location services market"—is mistaken and misleading. Second, I claim that so-called good policies—many of which are deregulatory to some degree—have much less to do with good economic outcomes than is often assumed. If developmental policies do not readily induce growth and welfarist policies do not readily induce decline, then choosing to pursue one or the other is a political choice, not an economic necessity. And third, I argue that cities can both do more of the things that conventional wisdom thinks they cannot do and less of the things that conventional wisdom sometimes thinks they can. Namely, they can engage in more social welfare spending than conventional wisdom predicts but less economic development.

These claims contradict much received wisdom, which predicts that cities will invariably converge on the same development-friendly policies.[3] The standard model assumes that cities are at the mercy of mobility, specifically the mobility of skilled workers, corporate investment, and finance. Cities have little choice but to chase mobile capital.

But cities are not merely vessels to be filled with desirable people or investments. And the relationship between economic prosperity and policy is not straightforward. Consider, for example, the living wage movement, which has had considerable success in cities throughout the country. A number of the largest U.S. cities—Los Angeles, Chicago, Seattle—have now adopted wage floors that are significantly higher than the wage floors of their states—a handful are almost double the national wage floor. On the standard view, a local minimum wage is economically foolhardy and should be politically unpopular. Businesses and residents will put up with some of the higher costs of living in the city, but not costs that redistribute significantly. A local business facing higher labor costs will simply move across the border.

To assert that a local minimum wage or any municipal regulation that raises costs for business will produce capital flight, however, one has to assume that city growth and decline are highly susceptible to local municipal fiscal or regulatory policy. But there does not seem to be a direct relationship between local minimum wages and economic growth in the places that have adopted them, and certainly not the negative relationship that conventional theories would predict. And this illustrates a larger point: the reasons cities form, grow, and decline are not at all obvious. Tying growth or decline to any particular policy is a hazardous business.

Unsurprisingly, city leaders tend to take credit when cities are booming and deflect blame when they bust. Theorists also often give highly confident accounts of why cities rise and fall. Yet neither local officials nor urban theorists are very good at predicting the trajectory of any given city. At mid-century, few people would have predicted the dramatic fall of Detroit and the other Rustbelt cities that were the engines of American industrial might; nor would they likely have imagined the rise of then-provincial places like San Antonio or Las Vegas. The more recent resurgence of some old-line cities—consider Pittsburgh, Philadelphia, and Washington, D.C.—has been amply described, but again, these reversals came as something of a surprise. The urban resurgence of the last quarter-century was not appreciated except in hindsight.

All of which is to say that we should be modest about asserting particular causes for urban growth and decline. Indeed, there is no reason to believe that cities *can do* development any more than there is reason to believe that cities *cannot do* social welfare redistribution. The common assumption that cities grow or decline because city officials have acted in ways that either attract or repel business investment is questionable.

Nevertheless, the notion that cities can do little else but make themselves attractive to mobile capital underwrites a political claim about the limited capacity for cities to govern well. Conservative reformers charge that cities need to be prevented from over-taxing and over-spending. Liberal reformers assert that cities are beholden to developer interests and corporate capital. The expectation of municipal political failure provides a reason to privatize government services or to shift power away from the city to the states or the federal government. State oversight of city decision-making is commonplace and easily justified.[4] Michigan's appointment of a receiver to govern failing Detroit is a dramatic example, but it is entirely consistent with the modern history of city powerlessness in the United States.

That history shows how city power has been regularly viewed with skepticism—in some cases, because city power was used by private interests to pursue private gain; in other cases, because empowering the city meant empowering the ethnic or racial minorities living there. Conventional economic wisdom asserts that cities cannot do very much. Conventional political wisdom asserts that they *should* not be doing very much. In both cases, city governance is understood as relatively marginal. At its best, it is ineffectual. At its worst, it is corrupt and unattractive.

This book rejects these claims. I argue that cities *can* govern, but not because macroeconomic forces ultimately exert any less influence on city welfare. Rather, it is because the imperative of growth—which limits city choices—is misplaced. City growth and decline are *not* primarily a function of particular policies and thus city leaders are not limited to doing what will make the city marginally more attractive to global capital. Our institutions have been designed to encourage cities to compete in an intergovernmental marketplace for mobile capital. But they should instead be designed to enable cities to help their citizens manage the inevitable cycles of economic growth and decline. How and why our institutions do the former and not the latter—and how we should change our approach to city power in order to better do the latter is the main subject of this book.

The other theme of this book is the *desirability* of city power. In the United States, we are often ambivalent about the exercise of local, participatory democracy—especially when it comes in an urban form. American cities are usually viewed as relatively inconsequential political units, the poor stepchildren of states and the nation. The city's lower status is driven by assumptions about its limited capabilities, but also by skepticism about the content of municipal politics.

I argue that we should *want* cities to govern. The justification for limiting U.S. cities politically has been that they should pursue certain narrow ends—the development of their local economies most centrally—and that when cities fail to do so, it is a political failure that requires state or federal intervention. But the pursuit of growth need not be the city's primary purpose, and local democratic politics can aim toward goals other than making the city a more effective market participant in a hypothetical global marketplace.

When we ask whether cities should have the authority to pass a minimum wage, regulate predatory lending, adopt environmental standards, condemn private property, subsidize incoming development, build hospitals, provide schools, guarantee health care, or do any of the other myriad things that governments do, we are asking about the appropriate scale for government action. How power is distributed between municipal government and the state and federal governments turns in part on what we think cities can do and how much we trust them to achieve certain ends. The possibility and desirability of the exercise of decentralized political power thus has to begin, as I do, with an inquiry into the city's capacities.

Private Capital and Public Power

The city's capacities cannot be understood in the abstract, however, for they are a function of legal and political institutions that distribute power between two different sets of actors: the state and the market and governments in a system of governments. A book about the city is really about the relationship between local economies and legal institutions.[5]

That is because the city is an economic phenomenon and a legal one; an agglomeration of persons, goods, and capital, as well as a political jurisdiction; a marketplace and a constitutional entity. In a market economy, the well-being of citizens turns on the choices of individuals, firms, and institutions to invest, locate, and participate in the city. The city does not exist independently of the private asset-holders who build, work, and reside there. The city develops in tandem with private investment, commercial activity, and capital formation; with the in-migration of people and investment; and with the multiplication of work. The city itself exists because the proximity of people in space generates economic gains. The city is thus the economy made spatial—geographical. Its rise and fall in three-dimensional space is analogous to the business cycle's rise and fall in time.

As this description suggests, the urban process—the growth or decline of a city—turns on the mostly uncoordinated activities of hundreds, thousands, and sometimes millions of individuals. The highly decentralized nature of city formation and development presents a difficulty for city leaders. That is because resources, investment, residents, and labor—in short, "capital" of whatever kind—cannot be compelled. The capital—human and otherwise—that makes up the city resides in individual actors and investment, and importantly in the smaller- and larger-scale associational and corporate entities that they have created.

It is no surprise, then, that the city's law and politics are preoccupied with the management of the relationship between private economic activity and the exercise of public power. This relationship is so central because the city is both the aggregate activity of individual economic actors and what makes that aggregate activity possible. The city is both an outcome of private wealth creation and a mechanism for it.

In this way, the city resists our usual distinctions between market and state, private and public, business and government.[6] It is why we talk about cities as if they were businesses, when that is not what cities are at all. It is why we often treat the success or failure of the private actors within cities as the success or failure of the city itself. And it is why we often assert (fairly or not) that a thriving city is doing its economic work well and that a declining city is not.

It is also why we struggle with the city's legal and political authority, for much of what a city does as a policy or legal matter enhances private wealth or detracts from it. The city is sometimes a promoter of private economic activity and sometimes a threat to it—sometimes passive in the face of private power and sometimes aggressive in its deployment. These tensions are apparent in the language we use to talk about the city and the laws we use to regulate it. The very term "municipal corporation" captures this duality.[7]

Economically minded theorists sometimes assume that markets drive cities and can explain all. But lawyers know that markets are creatures of law. The city always exercises power in relation to some other entity or institution: Markets are one such institution; the state and federal governments are another; unions and corporations could be others. Even as the lines between these institutions seem organic or obvious, they are not—legal work is required to keep them separate, and that work requires judgment about where the lines should be drawn.

Consider "green" cities. Cities are usually empowered to adopt land-use and building codes that encourage or mandate carbon-reducing practices. But they are generally not permitted to establish fuel economy standards, control emissions from coal-fired electricity plants, or regulate greenhouse gases more broadly. We take for granted that cities are limited in their regulatory authority, for we know that federal or state law often preempts local law in these areas.

Consider also what kinds of profit-making ventures the city can operate, what conditions the city can require when it contracts with private providers, and what kinds of duties the city can impose on developers. These activities are often regulated by state law, not municipal law. Courts often have to decide whether a specific exercise of municipal power is allowed by the state's statutory grant of authority.

The legal effort to separate markets and state, to draw lines between the city as a neutral platform for investment and a promoter of it, helps us to understand how cities have been and are currently treated as a legal and constitutional matter. In the U.S., the scope of the city's legal authority and the division of authority between cities, states, and the federal government—what constitutional theorists call *federalism*—are best understood as a reaction to the political pathologies that arise from the city-business relationship. Those pathologies reflect our political ambivalence about the inevitable intermixing of public and private power. Local political power has often been viewed as corrupt, understood broadly as the use of public monies for private ends. Even as the public subsidization of private activity has become commonplace, we have not resolved our nagging concerns about this intermixing.

This is understandable, for it is often impossible to disentangle where the "public" city ends and the "private" interests begin. The history of the development of the city and the law's attempts to regulate it show a fairly clear-eyed understanding that business and the city are interdependent—that capital uses the city to promote private agendas and that the city uses capital to promote public ones.

The result has been judicial vacillation—a legal structure that privileges private economic ordering but is ambivalent about how public power should be used to promote, develop, and otherwise attract economic resources. The city is not allowed to favor local or city-owned enterprises, but must open its doors to global capital, even when certain investments might be contrary to the city's long-term economic stability. State-imposed limitations on the city's taxing, debt, and spending powers coincide with tax abatements and other forms of tax expenditures that cities are encouraged to use to attract investment. Cities attempt to promote development with the strategic use of eminent domain, but then are accused of giving too much away to transnational corporations and of violating the rights of private property owners. The city is charged with providing for the basic needs of its citizens, but its revenue-raising capacity is limited by the restricted scope of its taxing authority. Meanwhile, city officials are told that their electoral success turns on the success of their growth program, but the politics that results—dominated as it is by the construction trades, local business groups, and real estate interests—is viewed as venal or even worse.

The economic discourse and the legal discourse tend to be skeptical of the exercise of city power. City power smacks of corruption. And limiting city power is seen as a means of protecting vulnerable property owners. But the vulnerability runs in the other direction as well. The city is dependent on market processes, on the choices made by private-side investors to locate inside the jurisdiction. The local democratic public is thus as vulnerable to the exercise of private power as private actors are vulnerable to the exercise of public power.

In this way, the economic problem of mobile capital drives the political problem of how to divide up government authority. This is a—perhaps *the*—constitutional problem, as we will see. When lawyers debate the distribution of powers between cities, states, and the federal government, they rarely see that distribution as a proxy for regulating the relationship between private capital and public power. At the same time, those urban theorists who begin with the assumption that cities are severely limited by the economics of capital flight often forget that capital flight is itself a feature of law. The structure of local legal power is a response to and reflects the city's dependence on private investment.

City Power thus addresses a series of conceptual issues that are of central concern to theorists of the city and theorists of democracy, to urban policymakers and constitutional lawyers. Once one dispenses with the notion that economic markets arise out of nature, that the state and the market operate independently, and that the line between the public and private is apolitical, one is faced with deep questions about how to preserve individual as well as collective political choice despite the interpenetration of private investment and government. In the modern social welfare state, when the government has taken a primary role in advancing the material welfare of its populace, how the problems of government-market relations are worked out is paramount. These problems are worked out in the city.

Growth, Agency, and Institutions

The structure of this book reflects its three preoccupations: the mechanics of local economic growth, the scope of city agency, and the role that legal institutions play in shaping both. Chapter 1 begins with an argument first made by the great urbanist Jane Jacobs that has now been echoed by other theorists: that cities are the primary drivers of economic growth in nations. After a half-century of retreat, the city—at least in some places—seems to be once again at the center of economic activity and increasingly at the center of economic theory as well.

That being said, how we think about what a city *is* alters what we think the city can do—any theory of city growth and decline implies a theory of city power. The city is often described either as a *byproduct* of technological, economic, or social forces well beyond its control or as a *product* to be bought and sold in a competitive local government marketplace. The first account is obviously highly deterministic. The second attributes to city leaders the capacity to improve. Neither account seems quite right. Cities are themselves economic and social phenomena, not merely the outcome of those phenomena. And cities are always in the process of being formed, of growing or declining, so to treat them as products suggests too static a vision.

I treat the city as an economic and social process in itself—neither wholly explainable by technology nor the predictable result of large-scale economic forces like capitalism (as some Marxian theories do). That does not mean that the city is conjured up out of thin air, an invention without any context, past, or future. The city is an ongoing spatial economic *process*, not a product that can jostle for market share. In chapter 1, I describe what that means in an attempt to thread the needle between determinism and agency.

More needs to be said about the ubiquitous claim that competitive inter-jurisdictional settings encourage economic growth, however. The *city-as-product* is a very powerful idea, for it suggests that city growth and decline can be explained by the success or failure of the city in a hypothetical marketplace for location. And it underwrites the further assertion that our institutions can and should be structured to encourage cities to compete for investment. Chapter 2 challenges this *decentralization-growth thesis*—the idea that federal constitutional regimes are more amenable to economic growth than unitary ones.

Leading theorists of this view like to present U.S. nineteenth-century, state-based federalism as the chief example. The problem with this historical claim, however, is that states were not the chief sites for economic development in the nineteenth-century industrializing United States—*cities* were. And the history of municipal power does not support a causal connection between institutionalized legal autonomy and economic growth. Indeed, what that history shows instead is that the city's prosperity usually *preceded* institutional change, not the other way around.

The lack of a causal link between the city's formal legal autonomy and its economic growth matters because the decentralization-growth thesis serves as a justification for a whole range of deregulatory and market-favoring policies. Without a growth-related justification, those policies become significantly less attractive, and cities become less constrained to abide by them. Challenging the connection between growth and inter-local competition thus liberates cities to engage in policies that are responsive to values other than economic development. And it casts further skepticism on the notion that cities can improve if they can just get their pro-market policies right.

The next two chapters move from the general theory to the particular, examining how state-based federalism as practiced in the United States *actually* affects city power. If the decentralization-growth thesis is not proven, then we are that much closer to deemphasizing growth as the central preoccupation for municipal policy. Cities can pursue *other ends* with less concern for their effects on the city's alleged "competitive position."

As I argue in chapters 3 and 4, however, cities operate within a federal regime that limits the city's capacity to achieve those ends. Chapter 3 argues that U.S.-style state-based federalism creates politically marginal cities, in large part because state and federal officials are in political competition with local officials, but need not take direct responsibility for local economic conditions. Even as U.S. cities often exercise significant formal authority, city leaders' ability to influence state and federal governments—the governments with access to the most resources—is often slight. The vertical separation of powers between cities, states, and the federal government does not promote city power; it limits it. If one favors decentralization, federalism as practiced in the U.S. is not the way to get it.

Chapter 4 pivots from the vertical relationship between governments in the U.S. to their horizontal relationship and comes to a similar conclusion. The rules of horizontal federalism govern how states and cities within states interact—in particular how and under what circumstances subnational governments can favor their own residents, impose barriers to trade, or subsidize the flow of capital into their jurisdictions. And though the legal doctrines that govern interstate relations are not designed with cities in mind, those legal rules significantly undermine the capacity for the city to adjust to economic cycles. The rules of U.S. horizontal federalism are supposed to maintain a national common market—and they certainly do so to some extent. But they also encourage the local chase for mobile capital, with richer local jurisdictions seeking to exclude poor in-migrants while poorer local jurisdictions engage in desperate strategies to attract investment. This combination of exclusions and enticements often favors suburban jurisdictions over urban ones, but not always. Declining suburban jurisdictions also suffer from a legal structure that in the main encourages local governments to pursue investment capital above all.

What should cities be doing instead? One possibility—overlooked by the conventional theory of the city's capacities—is social welfare spending. Conventional theory asserts that inter-local competition will discipline cities because capital will flee efforts to regulate it. But that is not what has happened. Despite a constitutional structure that limits local officials' political influence and encourages their pursuit of mobile factors, cities have in fact engaged in the kinds of regulation that conventional wisdom thinks is impossible. This is the subject of the next two chapters, which examine the potential scope of cities' capabilities in light of the institutional constraints under which they operate.

Chapter 5 turns to the minimum wage and other forms of municipal regulation that are often thought to be the provenance of national or state governments. As I have observed, the conventional model asserts that redistribution cannot take place on the local level or capital will flee. This assumption is the foundational premise of the decentralization-growth thesis: Growth will follow if subnational governments are disciplined by the threat of capital exit. Yet cities are providing a great deal of social welfare and regulating incoming development and investment in other ways. The fact that municipalities are making efforts to address economic inequality necessitates a further rethinking of the assumptions underlying the conventional theory of inter-municipal competition.

These efforts also require rethinking the supposed dominance of development politics in the city. City-business relations are rightly at the heart of the municipal political economy. But the privileging of developmental policies over social welfarist ones is not foreordained. Chapter 6 describes the emergence of the "regulatory city"—a strand of social welfarist local politics that undergirds the policies described in chapter 5. That there can be a politics of municipal redistribution at all flies in the face of longstanding urban literature that assumes cities will converge on similar developmental policies. It also undermines the claim that growth in cities is a function of market-enhancing policies.

The final two chapters of the book use the coincidence of urban resurgence and urban crisis to reinforce this last point. Chapter 7 examines the relatively recent rise in urban popularity—not in order to provide a definitive account of a complex phenomenon—but to illustrate the tenuous connection between specific policy recommendations and urban outcomes. If it is correct that local fiscal policies matter and that cities should favor business-friendly, anti-redistributive policies, then we should have an explanation for why some cities are doing well and some cities are doing poorly.

An examination of the urban resurgence of the last quarter-century, however, reveals that cities have not made great changes to their existing policies. Cities have not significantly improved their services, decreased taxes, or added infrastructure. Central cities and certain neighborhoods in certain cities seem to be more attractive to residents and firms, but there is no evidence that intercity competition or pro-development policies had anything to do with it. Any claim that cities have transformed themselves through improved policies of capital attraction and retention is seriously overstated. That does not mean that urban policies do not matter along numerous dimensions, but only that conventional explanations for city economic success or failure cannot explain what we see in the world. The relationship between growth and power has to be rethought.

Chapter 8 discusses urban fiscal crises. While it is true that many central cities are doing much better and that many old-line suburbs are doing worse, the deep problem of concentrated, racialized, urban poverty persists. Consider Detroit again. Detroit's 2013 filing of the largest municipal bankruptcy in U.S. history was merely the endpoint of a long historical decline. Formerly industrial cities are often blamed for their failures—the coincidence of urban resurgence and urban decline leads politicians and policymakers to the conclusion that rising cities are doing something right and failing cities are doing something wrong. Further, it suggests that the city's political failure is at the root of the city's fiscal failure.

The sorry state of many poor, minority neighborhoods in U.S. cities *is* in fact a political failure, but it is not a failure of any particular city's economic development policy. It is well known that U.S. metropolitan areas continue to be heavily segregated and economic opportunities are unequally distributed, both within cities and within regions. State and national policies have historically reinforced and exacerbated this socioeconomic and racial segregation. The fact that cities sometimes grow and sometimes decline is not a direct result of those policies. That poor minorities are disproportionately trapped in declining cities, however, *is*.

One of the themes of this book is that the city's legal status is often manipulated for political ends. Municipal fiscal crises provoke a standard reaction from state officials and policymakers: Attribute to cities more agency then they have, take formal power away from locally elected officials when they fail, and criticize them when the rebound does not materialize. Race certainly plays a role in this dynamic. Urban democratic politics has always been viewed skeptically by elites, who in previous eras sought to dilute, limit, or eliminate altogether the electoral power of the ethnic or racial "mobs"—whether they were Irish, Jewish, Italian, or African American. That state officials limit the power of cities by narrowing the formal powers of local elected officials or by eliminating local elected officials altogether is not new. The city's vulnerability is perfected: Shorn of electoral politics, the city as a democratic entity disappears altogether.

City Power

We thus circle back to the possibilities for, and desirability of, city power. What is a city that has no locally elected government and that is ruled by appointed state officials, who decide how monies will be raised and spent and which services will be provided? We might call such an entity an administrative unit, a prefecture. The boundaries and governance of such an entity likely would not concern us very much. Special-purpose governments are like this: Most people take little notice of the regional water and sewer authority. Even as these entities often exercise a great deal of power, their governance goes mostly unremarked. And we could easily organize the provision of such services differently. Homeowners associations provide much of what local governments provide, and they are increasingly places where people live.[8]

This would be a real loss. Cities are different. They too are administrative units, service providers, and political jurisdictions, but they are not *just* those things. Indeed, one difficulty in writing about cities is that readers with different reference points and disciplinary lenses are likely to have many different conceptions of what constitutes a "city."

My own conception of the city is grounded in its public role: the city as a site for individual and collective economic and political development. Like all cities, that city is an abstraction. Municipalities have political boundaries, but cities have sociological, economic, and spatial ones too—and municipal boundaries do not usually capture those. There is always a mismatch between the economic and cultural city and the territorial city. The city and its legal jurisdiction are not the same thing.

As I refer to cities in the chapters that follow, I will attempt to be clear about what the term means and, in those cases where it matters, which parts of the metropolitan area I am discussing. I use the generic "city" sometimes as a synonym for local government in a three-tiered federal system, sometimes to contrast the core city with its surrounding suburbs, sometimes to refer to the traditional industrial city, and sometimes as a proxy for the economic benefits of proximity or the political benefits of smaller-scaled democracy. Sprawling Los Angeles, compact Manhattan, expansive Atlanta, low-density Detroit, Pittsburgh, Charlotte, Minneapolis, Trenton, Camden, New London—these and other places are cities even if they do not all look like one another.

This book is about the power (or lack thereof) exercised by these kinds of places because I believe that cities are in many ways more economically and politically relevant than states or nation-states. Economic theorists are beginning to recognize that cities are the central engines of economic activity here and throughout the world. Despite predictions that the rise of distance-compressing technologies would be the death of the city, location *matters*, and being in particular cities seems to matter a great deal.[9]

Meanwhile, the increased power of large-scale, transnational capital has led some to question the regulatory capacities of the nation-state. Decision-making appears to be migrating away from democratic institutions to global markets, leaving many to ask whether citizens have any role to play in the governance of their political communities.[10] City politics can provide an answer. As when the industrial city boomed at the beginning of the twentieth century, the new urban age presents an opportunity: the possibility of an urban democracy that promotes individuals' participation in economic and political life on terms of equality.

The American city has not often been viewed as such a vehicle. Thomas Jefferson thought city life unfit for a free republican people. The Victorians tried to reform the city. In the twentieth century, architects tried to flatten it, planners tried to rationalize it, and the political elites tried to disempower it.[11] Oftentimes, they were successful, for better and (much more often) for worse. In many cases, reformers believed that their schemes were improving the city. That remains true today, though our ambitions have become increasingly chastened. Cities are most often seen as problems of management, preoccupied with attracting the right people or the right businesses, obsessed with economic development, and only incidentally concerned with the improvement and uplift of a free and democratic people.

Urban-based political movements like the ones I describe in chapters 5 and 6 can help to redefine the city's goals, for there is more room than is commonly appreciated for an expansive municipal politics. The adoption of municipal minimum wage laws and local ordinances in areas like labor, health care, and environmental law suggests that cities might be able to pursue policies that are less biased toward mobile capital. This is encouraging, for it suggests that locals may be able to adopt policies that are responsive to values other than economic growth, that cities may be able to regulate markets to reduce their vulnerability to economic booms and busts, and that those citizens who are normally marginalized by a politics of capital attraction can still assert influence over economic policy.

This enlarged realm of possibility collectively challenges the general assumptions about the limits of city power. No doubt, the national government is still the main site for income redistribution. Nevertheless, the reemergence of a progressive decentralist strand in our political economy represents a renegotiation of the terms of both capital dependence and national supremacy. The city's subservience to markets and the nation-state is not inevitable (even if it may be politically expedient).

The current wisdom about city powers and policies gives far too much weight to capital and competition. But the legal and constitutional status of the city in the American democratic order is a function of decisions to privilege some kinds of social and economic ordering over others. The result has often been the political infantilization of the city. In 1967, Robert Dahl wrote that "city building is one of the most obvious incapacities of Americans."[12] It does not have to be.

I

What Is the City?

I BEGIN BY PUTTING cities in their rightful place at the center of our economic and constitutional thinking. The reasons to do so are so obvious that they are often taken for granted. First, urbanization: The city is *the* primary fact of human civilization. Cities are the chief economic engines in their regions, states, and nations. And as we have been recently told, the world is now an urban place. More people on this planet live in cities than outside of them. Second, agglomeration: Increasing evidence links economic growth to physical proximity. Cities have always been productive places; they exist when propinquity generates economic gains. The effect of people and firms being near one another helps explain why cities are not simply a result of economic development but also a primary cause. Third, trade: City influence extends well beyond its immediate borders, for cities are the nodes through which persons, goods, and capital flow. As barriers to trade between nations have fallen, cities' interaction and economic influence have grown. It is unfortunate that so much of our attention has focused on the relationship between nations when the connections between cities, between cities and suburbs within metropolitan areas, and between metropolitan areas are so important.[1]

These are themes that I will return to throughout the book. In this chapter, I want to elaborate upon them to make two points. The first point is that cities are relevant economic concepts in ways that nations are not—a claim that will undoubtedly provoke some resistance. As Peter Taylor has argued, "social science is endemically state-centric: the 'national' is taken-for-granted, sometimes even treated as 'natural.'"[2] At least since Adam Smith's *The Wealth of Nations*, the nation-state has been the basic unit of economic analysis—its welfare the central obsession of policymakers. And especially during the twentieth century, as bureaucratic, centralized governments surged, and—later—as the large industrial cities declined, the city seemed increasingly irrelevant and even obsolete.

But the urban resurgence of the last few decades has been accompanied by a renewed scholarly appreciation for cities, and particularly for the role that cities play in fostering economic innovation.[3] Here I rehearse those arguments, starting with a claim Jane Jacobs made in *Cities and the Wealth of Nations* some 30 years ago. Jacobs argued that cities are foremost economic units, and not merely political ones. And she claimed that cities are engines of economic growth, and not merely the products of it.

The second point is that policymakers, local officials, and local residents often use a relatively narrow conception of what a city is and how it grows and declines when thinking about policy. The view espoused in much of the literature on cities is that local government jurisdictions—whether they be cities, small towns, or suburbs—are in competition with one another for residents and firms, and that this competition is not so different from the competition between other producers of goods and services in the marketplace.

This image of the city as a *product* that can be improved in the local government marketplace can be contrasted with two other conceptions of the city. The first understands the city as a *byproduct* of large-scale social forces. For some, those forces might be a technology, such as the automobile, that makes urbanization more or less productive or appealing. For Marxian theorists, global capitalism is the force that produces our existing forms of urbanization.[4]

The second views the city as a *process*—an ongoing manifestation of growth or decline not dissimilar to other kinds of biological phenomena. This is how Jacobs conceived of the city, as a problem more akin to biology than engineering, a problem of—as she put it—"organized complexity." While at least some policymakers have come to accept Jacobs's point about the economic centrality of cities, they have sometimes missed her point about the organic nature of city formation, rise, and fall.

Building Blocks of Economic Life

I start with the reemergence of the city as a driver of economic development. Observers of the city have always appreciated the city's central role in cultural, political, and economic life. But the city *qua* city has not conventionally been treated as a core economic concept. The nation-state has tended to be the dominant unit of economic analysis.

If there is a conventional wisdom, Jane Jacobs will challenge it. And in *Cities and the Wealth of Nations*, Jacobs does just that by attacking the economic primacy of the nation-state. She writes:

> Nations are political and military entities, and so are blocs of nations. But it doesn't necessarily follow from this that they are also the basic, salient entities of economic life or that they are particularly useful for probing the mysteries of economic structure, the reasons for rise and decline of wealth.... Once we ... try looking at the real economic world in its own right rather than as a dependent artifact of politics, we can't avoid seeing that most nations are composed of collections or grab bags of very different economies, rich regions and poor ones within the same nation.... We can't avoid seeing, too, that among all the various types of economies, cities are unique in their abilities to shape and reshape the economies of other settlements, including those far removed from them geographically.[5]

Jacobs goes on to argue that the wealth of nations is actually generated by particular places inside nations—the "grab bags of very different economies." And so, for Jacobs, management of the "potpourris we call national economies" is really the management of a collection of city economies, even if some are rising and some are falling.[6] Cities are the generators of new economic activity because, first, they contain producers who can build upon their existing skills, and second, city markets—for consumers or producers—are both diverse and concentrated. Moreover, cities influence far-flung non-city economies—changing the nature of rural areas, small towns, and villages—by their needs. Nation-states that are not working economically have cities that are not working economically.

There is an important debate within the urban economics literature about whether cities generate growth for a national economy or merely capture and concentrate it.[7] The evidence is overwhelming that within nations, cities account for a disproportionate share of gross domestic product and income. And also within nations, there is a strong correlation between city size and wealth. But the fact that there is a high rate of urbanization or a lot of big cities in a particular nation does not mean that nation will be wealthy. Urban economists continue to debate the role of cities in national and global economic development.[8]

Whether cities create or capture growth is in some ways the wrong question, however, for it assumes that the city preexists its own (and the nation's) economy. To hold this view is to assume that the city exists independently of the economic processes that produce it.

Whatever the merits of the debate, then, many urban economists have come to share the view that cities are at least a *necessary* (even if not sufficient) condition for economic growth. And many of Jacobs's insights about the linkages between economic growth and urbanization have been embraced. Indeed, over the last decade or so, we have witnessed what Edward Soja calls "the rediscovery of the generative power of cities."[9]

Three sets of ideas have contributed to this renewed appreciation for the connections between cities and economies. First and foremost is the development and diffusion of sophisticated approaches to the geography of economic activity. The economics literature now recognizes the spatial quality of economic activity—the fact that the bulk of economic activity happens in particular places. Jacobs's insight that nations do not have one economy but many turns out to be prescient.

The central insight of economic geography is that "the world is not flat."[10] Maps of the density of economic activity show it concentrated in very specific places: in cities first; in regions within nations second; and in particular nations within the world third. Economic activity seems to exhibit a particular structure, whereby development happens mostly in particular regions and not at all in others.[11] The industrial belt of the United States and the Ruhr Valley in Germany are examples. Another example is the concentration of finance, accounting, and law firms in places like New York and London. That cities or regions exist at all is itself a reflection of the fact that economic activity happens in territorial clumps.

Economic geographers have argued for some time that there is a spatial regularity to economic processes.[12] That regularity manifests itself in the distribution of economic activity in space—in the necessary fact that some places have more economic activity and some have less. Indeed, a person's location is the central determinant of economic opportunity, and it has become a primary focus for those who think about economic development. As the *2009 World Development Report* observes, urbanization and economic production tend to run in tandem. Economic production concentrates; it does not spread evenly across space. How geography influences economic opportunity is thus the central question for economic policymakers; formerly "mere undercurrents in policy," "space and place" have now become a "major focus."[13]

Second, much regional economic literature recognizes that "cross-border economic processes—flows of capital, labor, goods, raw materials, travelers" are now dominated by cities and regions.[14] Those "global cities" that dominate the international financial markets—New York, London, Tokyo—are particularly relevant. But these cities are only the most obvious examples of how certain places have far-flung economic influence. The city has always exerted power over other economies either in the immediate hinterlands of the city or farther afield— through its demands for goods, its generative capacity, and its diverse and incessantly mobile population.

Theorists attribute the more recent rise of cities and regions to the globalization of the economy, the lifting of interstate trade restrictions, the rise of the transnational business corporation, and the emergence of high-technology regions.[15] There was a moment when globalization, the lowering of barriers to entry, and the decreasing costs of transportation and communication seemed to suggest the end of the city. What was the purpose of a city in an era of instant communication, when workers could work from anywhere and goods could be purchased and delivered to anywhere? But cities have not disappeared, and many in fact are more robust than ever before. Productive enterprises have to be *somewhere*, they want to be in particular places, and they now have increased access to those places as national borders have become less salient. The change from nation-state-dominated trade flows to city-dominated trade flows is understood as a significant shift in the global economy. As barriers to trade between nations have fallen, cities' interactions and economic influence have grown.

Third, and relatedly, many scholars have drawn a connection between cities and economic innovation. Much of this work emphasizes the benefits of physical proximity for the sharing of knowledge within and across industries, for providing large and diverse sources of labor, and for generating specialized industries. These are what economists call "economies of agglomeration." Proximity or co-location is both a product of and a source for a set of effects that are said to foster innovation, increase productivity, and generate growth.

Agglomeration economies come in three basic flavors. The first form of agglomeration is what firms do when they expand in their current location. This is the familiar traditional economies of scale, where expanding production at some given site lowers a firm's unit costs and allows it to operate at greater efficiency. The industrial plant is an example.

A second form of agglomeration exists where there are benefits to businesses in one industry for locating in the same place. Co-location might be a benefit because shoppers want to minimize the costs of shopping trips and maximize the benefits of choice. The shopping mall is an example. Clustering of industries or businesses is also beneficial because it can encourage specialization. When firms cluster together, they can share inputs among themselves, which allows suppliers to tailor their products to a specific industry and provide better access to them. Los Angeles's fashion district and New York's publishing industry are examples.

Further, workers with industry-specific skills will be attracted to a place with lots of different firms operating in the same industry. When firms within an industry are clustered together, it benefits both the businesses and employees because search costs for jobs for both employees and employers are low, and laid-off employees can quickly obtain employment at a similar firm.[16]

There also may be learning across a single industry when it is concentrated in one place. Economists, following classic work by Michael Porter and AnnaLee Saxenian in the 1990s, emphasize the role that business clusters play in stimulating innovation, as businesses benefit from the technological and creative spillover of other knowledgeable and productive persons within their community.[17] Silicon Valley, with its concentration of technology firms, is the classic example of a single industry agglomeration.

A third form of agglomeration exists when businesses from different industries gain from locating in the same place. Here we start to see how a full-fledged city—which is again both the product of and the source for these economic gains—takes shape. The gains to having many different kinds of business activities in the same place include the benefits to consumers and customers of having multiple retailers and suppliers in close proximity, the benefits to businesses of specialization, the benefits to employees and employers of deep labor pools, and the benefits that come when knowledge is shared across different businesses and activities.

The city is an "urban warehouse" that allows businesses to specialize in their production since they do not need to provide all required services to the area's population.[18] The proximity of firms to suppliers and customers also reduces shipping costs, which in turn encourages more trade and innovation among the city's businesses and leads to the creation of new kinds of work. And by locating in an urban area, businesses can take advantage of public infrastructure like good highways and well-functioning public utilities.[19]

In the best case, these benefits are all enhanced by the knowledge and technological and creative sharing that occurs across industries, activities, and businesses in close proximity. These spillovers across different kinds of industries and businesses are sometimes referred to as "Jane Jacobs's externalities," for it was Jacobs who articulated the relationship between local diversity and economic innovation.

Indeed, as Jacobs saw intuitively, innovation is both what creates cities and what cities in turn *do*:

> Cities are places where adding new work to older work proceeds vigorously. Indeed, any settlement where this happens becomes a city. Because of this process city economies are more complicated and diverse than the economies of villages, towns, and farms, as well as being larger.[20]

This process is one of invention—"Economic life develops by grace of innovating." Thus, as Jacobs famously points out, Mrs. Ida Rosenthal, a custom seamstress, realizes that her customers need better undergarments so that her dresses fit them better. After experimenting with brassieres on the side, she invents a new industry in 1920s New York: brassiere-making. The new industry results from the coincidence of customers, existing technology, and the availability of new technology—all of which occurs in the city. Urban economies expand "by adding new kinds of work."[21]

There have been efforts to test the connection between urbanization and cross-industry innovation. One important study appears to show a link between urban variety and higher employment growth, especially in cities with smaller businesses.[22] Studies on the location of patent applications suggest that more invention is going on in cities or large metropolitan areas. And many theorists have noted a connection between cities and creative enterprises, driven by the interchange of ideas face-to-face. "As Jacobs rightly emphasized," Robert Lucas writes, "much of economic life is creative ... what can people be paying Manhattan or downtown Chicago rents *for*, if not for being near other people?"[23]

Whatever the form that the agglomeration benefit takes in the city, it has been cited as the reason for why city workers are more highly educated and enjoy higher incomes than those outside the city, and why specialized industries are more readily found in urban rather than rural areas. Industrial expertise and specialization occur most readily within cities. Cities in turn trade with each other on that comparative advantage. A nation's economy is thus the combined production and trade of a network of cities. Without intercity trade, there is very little economic production at all.

These agglomeration effects explain the salience of cities and other geographical agglomerations (like Silicon Valley) in a technological era that seems—at first glance—to have overcome the costs of transportation and the need for physical proximity. Indeed, as Mario Polèse observes, "[o]ne of the paradoxes of the IT revolution" is that firms and individuals still place high value on proximity to big cities.[24] "The more the world shrinks, the more *place* matters. In a completely flat world with no barriers to trade or interaction, what matters is access to the right places with the right people."[25]

Some economists have also hypothesized that agglomeration economies have a self-reinforcing, positive feedback quality. Larger markets lead to more customers; this makes the location more attractive to firms, which leads to more firms and more jobs; the market then grows larger, which leads to even higher profits as the cycle repeats. The city grows! Agglomeration economies explain why cities become more important, not less, when one considers the mechanisms for economic growth.

It thus should not be a surprise that urbanization is the salient fact of American demographic and political life.[26] The twentieth century witnessed monumental shifts in Americans' work and living patterns, including the great migration into the industrial cities, a later movement out of central cities into the suburbs, and the development of increasingly large and dense metropolitan areas.[27] In 1860, less than 20% of the population lived in urban areas; in 2000, close to 80% did.[28] The story of nineteenth- and twentieth-century economic development is the story of the industrial city and the rise of the greater metropolitan region.[29] In the last quarter-century, that has been followed by the repopulation of certain city cores. Urbanism—with its characteristic density, division of labor, and social interaction—is the norm now, not the exception.

Of course, even when North America was mostly rural and the continent's economy was agriculturally based, cities were the ports of entry and the chief sites of interstate and international trade.[30] Cities have been trading centers from the beginning of civilization; this was no different in early America, and it is no different now. American cities developed along the coasts or at the mouths of rivers for maximum access to trans-Atlantic trade.[31] Later, with the development of canals and the building of the railroads, trade moved into the center of the country.

For example, it was Chicago that drove the engine of midwestern agricultural and industrial development in the mid-1800s. As William Cronon shows in *Nature's Metropolis*—his now-iconic story of Chicago's rise—the economies of scale that could be achieved in the city made it possible to produce and then to move resources—wheat, wood, cattle, pigs—out of the hinterlands. The city literally created "commodities" by generating the infrastructure needed to trade them in large quantities, and in so doing unalterably shaped the rural and agricultural landscape.[32] Trade and capital flows moved between the great cities, and between Chicago and the smaller cities of the Midwest. Resources and material moved into Chicago to be bundled; capital flowed back from the East.[33]

The late nineteenth and early twentieth centuries saw the rise of the industrial cities. Migrants flowed into cities like Detroit, Pittsburgh, and Buffalo to provide labor for the expanding industrial economy. Cities grew at an increasing pace: Between 1900 and 1920, Detroit grew from 285,704 to 993,078; New York from 3,437,202 to 5,620,048; San Francisco from 342,782 to 506,676; Chicago from 1,698,575 to 2,701,705; Buffalo grew 43.8%; Pittsburgh grew 82.9%.[34] The great migration of African Americans began with World War I, when millions began moving out of the South and eventually into the large cities of the West, Midwest, and Northeast.[35] Meanwhile, immigrants from Europe were pouring into American cities. Between 1900 and 1920, close to fifteen million immigrants entered the United States, many of whom settled in industrial cities.[36]

The Great Depression and wartime economy accelerated the migration to the cities, though at a time when the urban industrial age was starting to decline. Industry and persons began to move out to the suburbs and to the urbanizing South and West. Central city populations began to experience population losses in the 1950s, and then more rapidly through the '60s, '70s, and '80s.[37] Since the mid-twentieth century, old, cold cities have lost ground to newer Sunbelt cities, though urbanization itself has increased. The eastern corridor between Boston and Washington constitutes a massive metropolitan area of fifty-five million people.[38] The population of the region spanning from Los Angeles to San Diego in California is approaching twenty million people. The economic and urbanized region of Chicago and its environs arguably sprawls from Kenosha, Wisconsin, in the north, to Joliet, Illinois, in the south.[39] The Texas cities of Houston and Dallas and their regional areas constitute 47% of the state's population. Denver and its massive metropolitan area constitute 60% of the state's population. The Atlanta metropolitan statistical area (MSA) contributes 50% of the population of Georgia.

Of course, there is an important distinction between central cities and MSAs—this difference is often submerged under the general rubric of "urbanization." That the concept of urbanization includes the densest parts of midtown Manhattan, sprawling Los Angeles, and suburban Phoenix makes the concept somewhat less useful when talking about intra-metropolitan relationships. The form that urbanization takes in any given metropolitan area is obviously extremely important, as is the relationship between any given central city, its suburbs, or the other cities within its regional orbit.

Moreover, there are important distinctions that any general account of "the city" will leave out: distinctions between small, medium, and large cities; cities with hinterlands and cities that are mostly self-contained; cities with a recognizable urban core and cities without, or cities with multiple cores. The distinction between cities and suburbs itself may not hold in particular metropolitan areas. That distinction—so dominant in the twentieth-century writings on cities—has eroded as low-density sunbelt cities have sprawled and relatively dense and economically active places with no identifiable core have developed in otherwise suburban settings. The sociological and economic line between cities and suburbs has also eroded. Metropolitan-area racial and income segregation has not tracked the city-suburb line for some time.[40]

One also has to be attentive to scale. Agglomeration effects occur at different distances depending on their form. Knowledge spillovers that require face-to-face contact may be highly localized; one might have to be located in lower Manhattan to obtain the benefits of Wall Street's financial agglomeration. The benefits of agglomeration for consumers also can be obtained only at relatively close range: in the shopping mall or on the main street. Labor and talent pools, however, will likely operate on a metropolitan scale as long as transportation costs are not prohibitive. Distance will be felt differently depending on the type of spillover. And the multiple parts of a city and the wider metropolitan region will be affected by different agglomerations operating at different scales.

Nevertheless, the "rediscovery of the generative power of cities" encompasses both a renewed attention to the benefits of a dense and economically robust urban core *and* the emergence of the city-region as a central economic unit. For my purposes, the important point is that nations and states are secondary in importance to metropolitan regions and often to specific cities within those regions.[41]

And for good reason. Urban areas generate the bulk of economic development in the United States. Cities are the largest economic entities in their states, regions, and nations. The top ten metropolitan regions in the world account for 2.6% of the global population but over 20% of global economic activity.[42] Phoenix generates 70% of Arizona's total economic output and 71% of the state's employment.[43] Cleveland's metropolitan economy is bigger than Ireland's.[44] Six American metropolitan areas—New York City, Los Angeles, Chicago, Washington, D.C., Dallas, Philadelphia—rank among the thirty largest economies in the world. The gross metropolitan product of the top ten metropolitan areas in the country exceeds the total gross domestic product of thirty-four states and the District of Columbia combined. New York's metropolitan-area economy is the tenth largest economy in the world. The Los Angeles metropolitan-area economy is the eighteenth largest. Though the United States began as an agricultural and rural nation, it is now indisputably an urban one. Thus, when one speaks about the economy, one is mostly speaking about inter- and intra-metropolitan trade.[45] To talk about the national economy is to talk mostly about urban-based development and urban-based trade flows.[46]

Byproducts and Products

Predictably, the rediscovery of the city's generative capacity has led to efforts to harness that capacity through policy. To what extent we believe that local policy can affect local economic outcomes, however, depends importantly on our account of how a city grows and declines. If the city is a *byproduct* of economic forces, then government policy plays little role in its rise or fall. If the city is instead a *product* that can be improved in the local government marketplace, then what cities do as a matter of policy should matter a lot.

The city-as-byproduct theory assumes that cities are mostly the result of changing technologies or large-scale social forces. The conventional historical story of the economic rise and fall of the great industrial cities, for example, seems mostly devoid of local agency. These stories often begin with agricultural surpluses.[47] In explaining the great industrial cities, narratives of city formation start with trading and transportation nodes. Cities came into existence at the confluence of goods and services, the termini of ports or railheads, or along stagecoach lines, where raw materials could be transformed into goods to be shipped, or provided to a large local market. There too the legal, financial, and governance expertise necessary to coordinate these large entities and provide them with capital developed. With the advent of the automobile, the subsequent extraordinary decline in transport costs, and the lessening importance of coal-fired plants, the industrial city of the nineteenth and early twentieth centuries lost its technological reason for being.

Thus, as Douglas Rae argues in his important study of New Haven, the urbanism of the industrial city was a happy accident, a result of a coincidence of emerging technologies and delays in the emergence of others.[48] Rae argues that six factors created the industrial city in the mid-to-late-nineteenth-century United States. The first four factors are affirmative: the rise of steam-driven manufacturing, an agricultural revolution that made possible ever-larger urban centers, the emergence of national markets made possible by an integrated railroad system, and a relatively open immigration system. The remaining two are a matter of timing: Rae argues that these four events occurred before the invention of the automobile and the wide diffusion of alternating current electricity—both of which eventually permitted the development of less dense patterns of settlement. These six factors involved government policy to be sure, but not purposeful government policy. "Nobody planned this concatenation of events, and very few saw it unfold with the lucidity afforded by a century of hindsight."[49] Rae is quite specific about this: Industrial cities were essentially *byproducts* of distance-changing technologies, "accidents of urban creation."

It is quite common to think of cities in this way. Indeed, one could conceive of the rise and decline of all human forms of settlement as a function of technological or environmental change. Prominent accounts of the development of civilization often emphasize the technological basis for development, the happenstance of particular environmental conditions, and the contingency of existing patterns of political and social organization. Jared Diamond's *Guns, Germs, and Steel* is an example.

Nevertheless, this relatively deterministic narrative sits somewhat uneasily alongside a different conception of what a city is and how it grows and declines: the notion that cities are products that one can understand in terms of the supply and demand for urban space (and for particular urban spaces).[50] On this account, individuals and firms choose city space (versus other kinds of space) and choose among cities based on various costs and benefits—say, the costs of transport and congestion balanced against local amenities, or balanced against the gains of propinquity to customers, other firms, labor markets, and raw materials.[51]

The supply-and-demand story does not have to be at odds with the technological story. In fact, those stories are often told in tandem. Urban space can be understood as a commodity that rises and falls in value depending on its usefulness. A dense urban core is more useful (and thus more valuable) if employees need to live close to factories or if factories need to be near rail lines or suppliers. A dense urban core is less valuable once technologies unrelated to urbanism make it possible to shift production to a far-flung plant in the suburbs. On this account, the value of city space is still wholly determined by distance-changing technologies.

But often the supply-and-demand story suggests something else: that cities can control the factors that make them desirable in the spatial supply-and-demand market. This conception of the city emphasizes the importance of human-made institutions and policies in city formation, growth, and decline. Once one posits a market in urban space, it is not a difficult conceptual leap to the idea that cities are like *products*, and that they "compete" with one another to attract persons, goods, and capital. Indeed, the rhetoric of "competition" follows somewhat easily.

That rhetoric can be seen most clearly in Charles Tiebout's famous construct of a market in local government. Tiebout's article "A Pure Theory of Local Expenditures" has been wildly influential. In seeking to solve the problem of public goods provision, Tiebout posited a market in which citizen consumers are mobile and local government jurisdictions provide identifiable bundles of goods and tax policies. Citizens "vote with their feet" by moving into jurisdictions with their preferred tax and spending bundle. In this way, Tieboutian governments "compete" to provide services to residents. The marketplace in local governments does all the work of a market in goods or services, establishing appropriate supply and demand, and setting prices.[52]

It is important to note that, though Tiebout was addressing the problem of the provision of public goods, he seems to conceive of local governments as mostly passive providers of goods and services. One of his examples is a local beach—a natural resource that local governments cannot generally "choose" to provide. The quality of the local weather—another amenity that appears to strongly drive residential choice—is similarly not under the control of local governments. The city's average temperature in mid-January is not a matter of local policy.

Nevertheless, Tiebout has also been understood to apply to those government services over which cities appear to have some control, namely tax and spending bundles. If cities are in competition, then this competition must be *for something*. If the demand for city space (and for a particular city's space) was outside the control of any particular city, then the language of competition would make little sense. Competition implies some level of agency, an ability to improve the product being offered. So we arrive at the notion that cities compete to provide amenities to firms and residents, that this competition disciplines local governments so that they provide efficient public services, and that this competition further encourages salutary innovation.[53]

I will address these kinds of claims further in chapter 2. For now, it is enough to point out that the competitive model suggests that cities can do something about economic growth and decline if they have good management. Moreover, good management often (though not always) means adopting a business model of the city that keeps costs down while keeping quality up. Thus, a conventional view is that cities can do well by keeping their fiscal houses in order, keeping taxes relatively low, not redistributing monies from rich people to poor people, keeping crime down, and by otherwise providing an environment conducive to capital attraction and retention, either with policies that attract skilled labor or with policies that attract firms that will employ skilled labor.[54]

Of course, many urban scholars argue that local managerial competence is not sufficient. A popular view among reformist local government scholars is that cities are not well positioned to help themselves.[55] Thus, policymakers argue that cities should have more legal authority so that they can innovate, that they should be able to annex suburban land so that they can capture economic growth, or that there should be legal rules that make it more difficult for richer jurisdictions to avoid their own responsibilities for the regional poor.[56]

Competition can be positive insofar as it encourages cities to provide good services at a low cost or invest in infrastructure and innovate in order to attract economic resources. Competition can be negative to the extent that it leads to races to the bottom—the lowering of taxes or regulation below an optimum, the poaching of neighbors' productive enterprises, the intra-metropolitan fight for tax base. The underlying notion here is that certain legal and political structures make cities more or less able to affect their own outcomes, and that these structures can be reformed, thus placing cities in a position to pursue prosperity unconstrained.

What both the competitive account and its reformist critique share is an emphasis on city agency, however. Whether one believes that local governments currently have too little, enough, or (in some cases) too much power, the assumption is that city, suburban, and—more generally—regional policies have consequences for local economic growth and decline. One can assume that there is a fairly full-fledged market in location because of the mobility of residents and firms, and that this market is, on the whole, a positive one (for the same reasons that all markets are good).[57] This is the stance of many Tiebout-inspired public choice scholars. One can assume, more cautiously, that there is something of a market in location, in the sense that some residents and firms are mobile, but that it is shaped to a significant extent by government policy. This is the stance of many reformist local government scholars. In either case, jurisdictional competition remains. Either cities themselves are to blame for their decline or the policies that circumscribe cities are to blame.

As I have noted, these kinds of claims sit uneasily alongside technological accounts of the city. In fact, many stories of city rise and decline partake of both highly deterministic accounts of city development and highly purposeful ones—between city-as-byproduct and city-as-product. For technology-minded theorists, specific local (and even national) policies may be minor players when compared to the invention of the steam locomotive, alternating current, or the internal combustion engine. How these technologies are deployed is, of course, often a matter of policy. But if the technology story is correct, the scope of any potential intercity competition is going to be quite narrow.

On the other hand, theorists who emphasize the importance of the quality of local governing institutions argue that economic development crucially depends on background institutions like the rule of law or property rights. Some of this literature looks at the rise of cities, arguing that cities are more likely to develop and prosper in relatively open societies, where trade is encouraged and predation by despots is limited, and where there is a relatively stable legal regime.[58] In these accounts, the quality of government—an institution over which policymakers exert a great deal of control—matters a lot.

We should be cautious about these accounts. First, there is a causal problem: It is far from clear that stable political and legal institutions are preconditions for urban life or that urban life generates stable political and legal institutions.[59] Histories of the rise and fall of cities (and civilizations) often emphasize the rising city's relative political stability and the declining city's relative political corruption. But these may be an effect, not a cause. Jacobs repeatedly points out the fallacy of mistaking the results of economic development for its preconditions. The claim that stable legal institutions are a precondition for growth has been criticized for the same reason. Indeed, cities do not usually come into being *after* the establishment of cultural, legal, and political institutions. The development of the city might in fact be a necessary precondition for those institutions.[60]

Second, urbanization is occurring in the absence of good institutions. The mega-cities of the developing world are growing dramatically, often despite the absence of stable political institutions or formal property rights, let alone the provision of basic municipal services.[61] To say that the worldwide process of urbanization represents intercity competition for providing urban amenities seems, at the least, overstated. Urbanization is occurring, but it is simply not plausible to describe it as the outcome of a market in local governments or to claim that some cities are winning in a kind of good governance race.

That does not mean that cities are wholly accidents, however. Though the city exists against the backdrop of existing technology, it is as much a result of human ingenuity and institution-building as it is an accidental efflorescence of some other human activity. And indeed, the city's reason for being is not only technological but also associational, cultural, and political. The determinism of the technological account does not quite square with our understanding of cities as affirmatively founded, chosen, and—most importantly—governed by human beings. The city-as-product seems to overstate this intentionality, while the city-as-byproduct seems to understate it.

The City as a Process

A third approach to the city is to understand it as a *process*. This brings us back to Jane Jacobs and the economic geographers. "Why think about processes?" asks Jacobs,

[o]bjects in cities—whether they are buildings, streets, parks, districts, landmarks, or anything else—can have radically different effects, depending upon the circumstances and contexts in which they exist. Thus, for instance, almost nothing useful can be understood or can be done about improving city dwellings if these are considered in the abstract as "housing." City dwellings—either existing or potential—are *specific* and particularized buildings *always involved in differing, specific processes* . . . . [62]

The focus on processes of change reflects a certain methodological orientation—one that is attentive to the ecology of places.[63] In *The Death and Life of Great American Cities*, Jacobs shows how a safe street emerges from tiny interactions among hundreds of independent and uncoordinated actors, how an urban economy emerges from small-scale production and invention, and how small changes at the street or neighborhood level can cause catastrophic changes in the urban landscape. These urban phenomena are complex, but they are not random (and in fact, scientists of complexity have recently sought to put numbers to the city's "emerging natural structure"). Jacobs takes it for granted that "the cities of human beings are as natural, being a product of one form of nature, as are the colonies of prairie dogs or the beds of oysters."[64]

A more mathematically inclined version of this approach can be seen in the new economic geography (NEG)—for which Paul Krugman won a Nobel Prize in 2008. The NEG approaches cities as "self-organizing" systems: "systems that, even when they start from an almost homogeneous or almost random state, spontaneously form large-scale patterns."[65] The NEG holds that, given particular parameters, urban systems will exhibit certain spatial regularities—seemingly natural development patterns that emerge from a set of basic assumptions. A growing city, on this account, is more "like a developing embryo" than it is like a widget that is produced and sold in the marketplace.[66]

Thinking about cities as processes rather than products highlights the role of both contingency and path dependence in city growth and decline. And it does so without relying on technological determinism. It thus steers a middle path between predestination and agency.

What the NEG seeks to show is why agglomeration happens (i.e., how cities, business districts, and regional and local industrial clusters occur). Krugman starts with some basic assumptions—namely, that there are forces encouraging people and businesses to clump together, and that there are forces encouraging people and businesses to disperse. He then models how a city might form under these circumstances even if individuals and firms begin by being relatively uniformly distributed throughout a particular geographical space.[67] He also shows how an initially almost-uniform distribution of business within a metropolitan region "evolves spontaneously" into a highly structured metropolis with two concentrated business districts.[68] Change the parameters a little bit, and one will generate a metropolis with four business districts—the so-called edge cities that Joel Garreau describes in his book of the same name.[69]

A key insight in all of these models is that small differences in initial conditions or small perturbations in an otherwise stable equilibrium can lead to dramatically different outcomes; that once growth or decline starts, it does so explosively or catastrophically; and that the spatial order that emerges may have little to do with individuals' or firms' preferences understood in isolation. There was nothing particularly unique about the geographical place that became Silicon Valley—given slightly different initial conditions, such an agglomeration of high-tech firms could have arisen elsewhere. Nevertheless, once one sets certain initial conditions, one can make some predictions about where such agglomerations will arise.[70]

Similarly, the development of a regional economic core and a less economically developed periphery in a particular nation is not a function of the innate characteristics of those geographic places, but rather the result of historical accident. Nevertheless, that the industrial belt developed where it did in the northeast United States at the turn of the century was predictable considering the initial starting points and the self-reinforcing effects of economic development.[71] Cities—spatial agglomerations—are both contingent and path dependent.

The idea that order arises from chance is not unfamiliar to economists or urban theorists. Krugman notes that his account of city formation is inspired by Thomas Schelling's famous model of how a racially segregated metropolis can emerge even when individual preferences would be consistent with full integration.[72] As Schelling showed, the integrated distribution of persons in space is unstable; add an almost imperceptible change in the initial distribution of persons, and the equilibrium completely unravels, resulting in a spatial order that is almost entirely segregated.[73] Such cascades were familiar to Jacobs. She argues that making small changes in a neighborhood—replacing a store with a parking lot, building a road, closing a local grocery—could lead to a neighborhood's rapid failure. She also notes how small improvements—the opening of a store, the influx of a few new residents—could result in cascades in the other direction.[74]

The emergence of regularity from randomness seems to be at work at the most basic level of economic geography. Consider Zipf's law of city size. As numerous theorists have pointed out, cities in a particular urban system often exhibit a striking regularity: The population of a given city is inversely proportional to its rank.[75] Thus, in most countries, we tend to see a distribution of city sizes in which the number-two city has half the population of the largest city, the number-three city has one-third the population of the largest city, and so on. This "rank-size" rule has remained fairly consistent in the United States since at least 1890; a universal law of city size seems to be at work.[76]

One can see immediately how difficult it might be to reconcile Zipf's law with the conception of the city as a product. One would predict a much different distribution of population if in fact cities were competing for firms and residents by providing particular services, goods, or amenities. Unless individuals' and firms' preferences for location exactly tracked the rank-size rule, cities would arguably fall within relatively similar size ranges. Zipf's law implies that cities exist in an urban system: Population increases and decreases operate across the urban system, not solely at the level of a particular city or metropolitan area. Something about the ways in which cities form, become populated, and develop or decline is geographical—that is to say, a reflection of an emergent economic-spatial order.[77]

This self-organization happens at all scales. Thus, we see a core-periphery structure within metropolitan areas, within nations, and across global regions.[78] Importantly, these patterns often result from small differences in initial conditions. Those initial conditions generate feedback effects that are self-reinforcing and create an equilibrium that is quite lopsided.[79] These feedback effects mean that locations—cities, regions, and nations—with almost identical initial endowments might end up in diametrically opposite economic circumstances. Indeed, one region's initial success might limit other regions' potential.

Economic geographers predict this kind of development pattern, arguing that because economic growth is self-reinforcing, the gap between economic leaders and laggards will increase dramatically before it decreases.[80] They have also shown—at least on the international level—that the distance from the core of economic activity is negatively correlated with economic growth.[81] Rich places tend to get richer; poor places tend to remain poor. Space and distance matter.

How do geographically poor laggards and rich leaders come to be? Contingency is at work, but also path dependence. As I have already noted, because small initial differences can have huge consequences over the longer term, luck and happenstance play a large role. If Hewlett Packard had initially settled in Oakland instead of Silicon Valley, Oakland might now be the global center of technological innovation. This possibility is consistent with economic geographers' assertion that historical accident may lead to long-run differences in economic outcomes. Firms are willing to pay to be closer to other firms and larger markets; labor desires the added value that comes with density.[82]

Once a city or other location has established a virtuous cycle, whereby economic development reinforces additional economic development, path dependence kicks in. Economic activity tends to follow existing economic activity.[83] This fact may explain the persistence of urban and national economic hierarchies.[84] It may also explain why economic laggards have a hard time catching up while economic leaders remain leaders even when exposed to significant external shocks. Moreover, path dependence explains why the economic integration of lagging and leading areas (through free trade regimes) will not necessarily promote development in the lagging areas. What might happen instead is that economic activity will flow even faster into leading areas, causing lagging areas to do worse as trade and labor barriers fall.[85] Those disparities might eventually be smoothed out, but the initial result would be an increase in inequality.

Historical accident, path dependence, spatial persistence: These features of economic geography suggest that geographically uneven economic development is not an aberration but rather a salient feature of economic life. Indeed, if the city is a spatial economy, then we might expect its ups and downs to be cyclical. And, in fact, the NEG treats spatial economic phenomena the same as temporal economic phenomena.[86] Thus, in the same way that temporal economic busts follow booms, so do spatial economic busts follow booms. The urban cycle might be caused by the very processes unleashed by an urban boom in the first place.

These features also suggest that chance and very small perturbations in an existing equilibrium can make a big difference for outcomes. It turns out that mobility across geographic space—toward or away from the city—is not the same kind of mobility that characterizes purchases of consumer goods. Mobility in geographical space is "lumpy" and prone to all the characteristics of self-organizing systems: interdependence, cascades up or down, and feedback loops.[87] Economic growth does not start from a clean slate whereby each political jurisdiction can act to ensure its own prosperity. Geography is not incidental to economy. It is a key feature of economy.

Does all this mean that cities cannot do anything about their economic development, as the technological account of city development suggests? Not necessarily. City self-organization grants a large role to both historical accident and the self-reinforcing effects of economic development. Luck matters because small random events (David Packard and William Hewlett begin their business in Silicon Valley) can produce large consequences (once HP was there, other firms wanted to be there).

Thus, cities might be able to intervene in the local economy in such a way as to nudge the process forward. Clustering of people and firms is the chief characteristic of city space and the central economic benefit for which some firms and residents are willing to pay higher rents. Thus, if firms believe that other firms are going to settle in (for example) Chicago, then the city becomes a self-fulfilling prophecy.[88] Chicago is able to beat St. Louis at the start of the urban race for no reason other than firms' beliefs that other firms will want to be there. Indeed, the original city boosters believed that the city was really the *promise* of the city. They might have been right.

Nevertheless, it may be very hard to tell what the effects of any particular policy intervention will be over the long term.[89] Certainly, Chicago would do well to set itself up as the gatekeeper to the West by building railroads; in an era in which railroads drive the economy, a city would do well to have as many lines running through it as possible.[90]

Yet the reason that Chicago beat St. Louis, Cincinnati, and Milwaukee to become the leading metropolis of the West had as much to do with luck as with any set of policies. During the first third of the nineteenth century, each of those cities (and many with names less well known) were aggressively pursuing infrastructure development, gathering capital, and positioning themselves to control regional trade. Many of these cities started out with similar geographical, social, infrastructural, and economic attributes—or at least attributes that offset one another.[91] Indeed, in the antebellum period, St. Louis seemed to be better positioned than Chicago, having a larger population and a seemingly firm grip on the Mississippi trade.[92] The rapid emergence of an urban hierarchy with Chicago at the top is a result of the dramatic instability of the urban system during the mid-nineteenth century.[93] It could have been otherwise.

At a minimum, we should be very cautious about attributing any given city's outcome to a particular factor, policy, or institution. Jacobs makes just this point in *The Economy of Cities*. In a section titled "Specious 'Causes' of City Growth," she observes that Britain has numerous excellent natural ports, all at points that have never become cities. She also notes that settlements along rail lines in the United States only occasionally grew into cities. And finally she tells the story of Jersey City—which was better positioned than New York in relation to the Erie Canal and the Atlantic Ocean, so much so that Alexander Hamilton predicted it would become "the metropolis of the world." But, as Jacobs observes:

> Cities simply cannot be "explained" by their locations or other given resources. Their existence as cities and the sources of their growth lie within themselves, in the processes and growth systems that go on within them. Cities are not ordained; they are wholly existential. To say that a city grew "because" it was located at a good site for trading is, in the view of what we can see in the real world, absurd. Few resources in this world are more common than good sites for trading but most of the settlements that form at these good sites do not become cities.[94]

How then do we explain city outcomes? The problem is one of hindsight. Many of the narratives written about successful economies over the long term read like "just so" stories: By picking a particular time period (during which growth occurs), and ignoring others (in which growth stagnates), one can make claims about the impact of certain factors on city development.[95] But without knowing exactly what set the economic ball rolling and when, the correspondence of economic development and particular factors can easily be coincidence.[96]

Consider again New Haven and Douglas Rae's story about the end of industrial-era urbanism. While many cities experienced the decline that accompanied the rise of distance-compressing technologies, some other cities expanded. Sunbelt cities grew during the second half of the twentieth century. Some attribute this growth to the rise of inexpensive air conditioning, but here again, cause and effect are easy to conflate. Chicago's summers are awfully hot. Air conditioning cannot explain the rise and fall of literally hundreds of cities that are not in particularly temperate regions.

Better adaptation to the car culture might be an explanation for why these newer cities grew while older cities declined. But here again, the automobile's rise and the industrial cities' decline is too neat. Detroit— a sprawling, low-rise city that was fairly amenable to the car—also declined in the latter half of the twentieth century. To be sure, it is true that federal highway funds subsidized low-rise development, and Cold War military budgets led to industrial expansion in certain southern and western places. Money was moving into new settlements across the country—but that is what it had always done. Northern money was also moving to the South, but in fits and starts, as the economic and social integration of that region paralleled the trajectory of the civil rights struggle.

Nevertheless, northern industrial cities were often perfectly well placed to take advantage of federal Cold War monies, highway funds, and the changing industrial landscape. While in hindsight, the decline of northern industrial cities looks obvious, it wasn't. In 1960, as Michael Storper observes, few commentators

were worried about the decline of dozens of major metropolitan areas in the Manufacturing Belt, and the average resident of Detroit gave nary a thought to the idea that their metropolitan region would be considered the poster child of failure several decades hence. Nor would many have imagined that Houston and Las Vegas would be considered big success stories soon thereafter.[97]

Conclusion: Mystery and Modesty

The idea that luck, path dependence, or some other feature of the spatial economy might play an outsize role in city fortunes is likely to be resisted by both theorists who lean toward technological explanations and those who prefer to attribute city growth and decline to policy or governance. A sophisticated urbanist probably would concede that the causes of city rise and fall are complex and multifaceted, even as she also argues that they are in the main knowable. One of the reasons for thinking about cities as spatial economic processes, however, is to resist that certainty—to highlight the limits of our knowledge. That does not mean that we cannot say something about city governance and its relation to growth. It just means that confident predictions that economic growth is attainable if city leaders would just get with the program are seriously oversold.

I will say more about the relationship between institutions and growth in the next chapter, and about the relationship between specific municipal policies and urban resurgence in chapter 7. Predictably, I am skeptical that we can say anything definitive about the factors that generate urban growth and decline. I am not claiming, however, that large-scale structural economic forces simply dictate city outcomes or that local policies never matter.

I am instead concerned with advancing a certain methodological orientation—one that emphasizes the ecological nature of human settlement, the coexistence of contingency and path dependence, and the cyclical nature of urban development—in other words, the complexity of urban systems. That complexity does not preclude city agency. Indeed, it allows for more agency than a technologically deterministic account of city development. Nevertheless, any claim that a specific policy will foster growth or decline should be treated with a great deal of caution.[98] Certainly, a city is not merely abstract space waiting to be filled with desirable residents or standing passively as desirable residents go elsewhere. Citizens and city leaders make decisions, adopt policies, and govern. But those decisions cannot be assessed unless one has a plausible and defensible account of how cities form, grow, and decline—and that account will always be incomplete.

Jacobs treats city growth and decline as a fundamentally biological process. Cities cannot be fully explained by good harbors, enlightened governance, or the accidents of technological timing. Nor are cities the result of choices made by consumers in a preexisting market for location. Indeed, prior to the existence of a system of cities, no such market exists. The city is self-generating. Like all networked goods, the resident-consumer of the city is both a consumer of city life and a producer of it. She and her fellow citizens *are* the city. Describing city decline as a "failure to compete" is thus a conclusion, not a cause.

That is not to say that municipal governments are not competing in some limited sense. Certainly cities, towns, and suburbs do *experience* themselves as engaged in governmental races against other jurisdictions. And, no doubt, some residents and firms make decisions about where to locate based on the existence of quality urban infrastructure, good schools, or a low tax environment. But cities also emerge without any infrastructure whatsoever, and prosper in places with notably poor schools and high taxes—the infrastructure and good schools come later, after people and businesses have flocked there. Why people flock there, however, is often a mystery.

That mystery should induce modesty. In particular, it should make us wary of causal claims concerning the relationship between city agency, legal institutions, and economic growth. The next chapter turns to a specific claim of this kind—the argument that competitive interjurisdictional systems of government foster growth.

2

Decentralization and Development

IF IT IS TRUE that cities are spatial economic processes, that cities exist in a system of cities with some growing and some declining, and that spatial economies generally have the cycling features of temporal economies, then urging cities to do things to "compete" for economic growth seems to miss the point entirely. Our urban policies and the institutions governing city power would be better directed toward doing something other than seeking economic growth.

And yet for many theorists and policymakers, economic development seems to be the primary point of the city—both what preoccupies its leaders and what is often identified as the city's main goal. One reason for this has already been mentioned: Thinking about the city as a competitor in a global marketplace for location encourages the notion that cities have no choice but to compete, or, for some, that cities *should* be competing in this way.[1]

The *"should"* is the target of this chapter, for more needs to be said about the relationship between city agency, intercity competition, and economic growth. I have already argued that city growth and decline are not directly susceptible to policy in the ways we sometimes assume. But to the extent that one is unconvinced or believes that cities have some (even if small) policy space to influence economic outcomes, then we have to address the question of how the exercise of city power or city agency might affect the city's economic development.

Specifically, this chapter challenges a particularly powerful justification for creating a competitive inter-jurisdictional system of government: that federal or more decentralized political systems generate economic growth. The *decentralization-growth* thesis is a theory of economic growth coupled with a theory of power. It asserts that giving fiscal power to local jurisdictions promotes more growth—at least if institutions are structured so that subnational governments have to compete for mobile investment.[2] Economic growth is thus a justification for decentralizing fiscal powers to subnational governments, including cities and other local governments.[3]

There are two big reasons to be skeptical about this claim, however. First, economic growth is not really a justification for empowering cities, but rather an argument for *limiting* city power. The decentralization-growth thesis posits that subnational governments are in a salutary competition for capital that will lead them invariably to adopt "market-friendly" policies conducive to growth. The asserted connection between decentralization and growth thus tends to justify market-favoring, often anti-regulatory policy prescriptions: minimal redistributive taxation, capital attraction and subsidization, and the rejection of revenue sharing or regional consolidation. Further, the asserted connection between decentralization and growth predicts that all cities will ultimately converge on similar capital-favoring, developmental, and non-redistributive policies. Legal decentralization as it is deployed in this context is intended to *discipline* cities—the form that discipline takes is the threat of capital flight.

Second, the history of local government law in the states provides *little evidence* for the asserted link between formal legal decentralization and economic growth. The history of local government law is important because theoretical accounts of the relationship between decentralization and growth assume that the vertical distribution of powers makes a difference in economic outcomes.[4] In support of the decentralization-growth thesis, economic historians often invoke nineteenth-century American federalism, arguing that states competed to create economically favorable conditions in the nascent industrializing United States.[5]

The problem with this approach is that *cities* were the chief engines of economic development in the late nineteenth- and early twentieth-century U.S., as they continue to be around the world. If the decentralization-growth thesis is correct, then the history of local government law in the states should reflect a relatively robust and stable form of institutionalized political decentralization over the course of the nineteenth and twentieth centuries. And economic growth should be a recognizable consequence of legal decentralization.

Neither appears to be true. Throughout the nineteenth century and into the twentieth, we have seen a highly contingent and politically unstable division of authority between states and localities. And there seems to be no causal connection between relative city power and economic growth—indeed, institutional reforms granting power to cities seemed to *follow* economic growth, not *precede* it.

If the decentralization-growth thesis is correct, it should be able to explain why some cities do well and why some do poorly. But the relative degree of municipal fiscal autonomy does not seem to play any role in economic development. States grant varying degrees of autonomy to their local governments, but economic growth and decline do not appear to respect jurisdictional lines—those tend to occur across large regions of the country or across metropolitan regions that do not abide by state boundaries.

If municipal fiscal autonomy is not doing any work, then the pro-market policies that theorists predict will be a result of inter-local competition are not likely doing much work either. Indeed, it would be surprising if the reasons that some cities are doing better and some are doing worse were attributable to their relative legal autonomy.

That does not mean that we should oppose the decentralization of power to cities. As should already be clear, I am in favor of city power. But the competitive local government marketplace is understood as a way of enhancing *markets*—not promoting robust local democratic decision-making. And the form that such decentralization takes—with its emphasis on municipal fiscal autonomy—means that cities are often left to struggle on their own during economic downturns. If there is no connection between formal legal power and growth, however, then "disciplining" cities serves no real purpose. Cities can reject the current obsession with economic development and focus their energies on something else. The theoretical demands of growth are a false constraint on the city's policy choices.

Competition and Growth

I should start by observing that how we define "federalism" or "decentralization" or "local autonomy" makes a big difference in determining their effects. Accounts of the relationship between federalism and growth, for instance, have to explain what is common among the United States, Switzerland, China, and Russia—all of which have been described as federal political systems. Real-world descriptions of government institutions often fail for lack of agreement concerning basic criteria. A decentralized system of government need not be federal, and federalism may hamper decentralization rather than promote it.

Local government theorists have long faced this problem. It is very difficult to compare relative municipal autonomy across states in the United States, let alone compare it across countries. Some features of a decentralized system can be ascertained: whether municipal leaders are locally elected or appointed centrally, whether the city enjoys an independent taxing and spending power—and the like. But these kinds of criteria can be misleading. A city can have the authority to spend, for instance, but have few resources, in which case its relative formal authority is a fiction. A city that reliably receives monies from the central government, however, might exercise more policy autonomy, even if its formal authority to tax is more limited. (I will say more about this in the next chapter.)

Theoretical models of the benefits of competitive decentralization do not need to wrestle with messy definitional problems, so I will start with those. Generally, two kinds of arguments are made in asserting a link between competitive inter-jurisdictional constitutional arrangements and economic growth. The first set of arguments can be characterized as *disciplinary*: In a decentralized system, cities will be forced to adopt capital-favorable policies because if they do not, they will be punished by capital flight. Cities therefore will generally converge on similar market-friendly policies.

The second set of arguments can be characterized as *preference-fulfilling*: Decentralized local government provides for the efficient provision of local public goods by matching citizens to the tax and spending bundles they desire. This is the Tiebout hypothesis, already discussed in chapter 1, which holds that citizens "vote with their feet" by selecting the local jurisdiction that meets their preferences. Extending Tiebout, proponents of competitive decentralization argue that the provision of local public services through a roughly competitive inter-local marketplace enhances economic growth.

Competition for Capital: Disciplinary Decentralization

The disciplinary argument is quite common, but it depends substantially on a controversial account of why government officials act as they do. A central tenet of competitive federalism is that the existence of subnational governments induces inter-jurisdictional competition, and "inter-jurisdictional competition provides political officials with strong fiscal incentives to pursue policies that provide for a healthy local economy." Among these policies is the efficient (i.e., non-corrupt) provision of public goods. As Barry Weingast argues, "[m]arket-preserving federalism limits the exercise of corruption, predation, and rent-seeking by all levels of government."[6]

But why a healthy economy is a goal of local political officials, and what officials can do to foster such an economy is often left unspecified. As Roderick Hills has observed, the competitive federalism literature assumes that "subnational officials want to maximize the land values, revenues, or tax base of their jurisdiction,"[7] but it often fails to tell us why they would want to do so, how they can do it, or for whom.

Consider first that the motives of local officials, who have to respond to a local electorate, might be quite complicated. Local elites (such as landowners) may have different policy interests than local workers; local employers will have different preferences than local employees; and local residents may have very different policy desires than transnational firms. Assuming that local officials seek to maximize their electoral fortunes, local revenue enhancement may not be their sole or even driving concern.

Indeed, local officials may not see any real political gains from an increase in a locality's economic activity. Economic activity brings in outsiders, induces competition, and dilutes local monopolies. A local official's political power may turn on keeping outsiders at bay, fostering local monopolies, and preventing new firms from competing with existing ones. Local political officials are often hostile to entrepreneurial capital, favoring established firms and businesses over newcomers or startups.[8]

Weber famously asserted that the medieval cities of Europe helped foster economic growth by providing a political and territorial space to promote commerce free from the greedy reach of princes.[9] But local autonomy does not always have a growth valence. The autonomous cities protected the guilds from rapacious princes in medieval Europe, but they also permitted medieval city merchants to erect barriers to entry, thus arguably reducing economic growth over the long run, as David Stasavage has recently argued.[10] The closed city corporations of some early American cities are better understood as cartels that limited opportunity than free communities that enabled it. The lesson here is that local power (under conditions of capital mobility) has no particular growth valence. It can point in both directions.

This leads to another puzzle: Even if local officials can be encouraged to pursue growth-related policies, how do we recognize what those policies are? Mobile capital's "disciplining" power might in fact be quite detrimental over the long term. Under pressure to pursue growth at all costs, local officials may pursue short-term gains at the expense of long-term economic stability. As we shall see in the next part, over-investment in growth-related infrastructure was the problem for nineteenth-century cities, not under-investment. Limitations on local power were one legal result. The problem of competitive races to the bottom has been the primary hobgoblin of competitive federalism. A damaging race is often only realized in retrospect.

Proponents of competitive federalism sometimes argue that subnational governments will more likely pursue innovative new policies than will a central government. Competition for mobile capital is said to promote policy experimentation because entrepreneurial government officials find it more conducive to try new things at the subnational scale where the risks of failure are lower and the gains of success are higher.

But this assumption is also questionable. As Susan Rose-Ackerman has argued, local officials may have a strong political incentive to play it safe. A local official has little incentive to depart from the current menu of options and lots of incentives to wait and adopt only those policies that turn out to be successful. Risk-averse local actors may not want to deviate from the bundle of services that other jurisdictions are already providing. Because there is limited advantage to being the first mover, and a substantial risk of failure, subnational governments may produce little innovation.[11]

It is, moreover, almost impossible to distinguish at the outset between an "innovative" policy (with its positive connotations) and a policy meant to reward political supporters or obtain financial spoils. Consider the range of possible policy choices local officials might contemplate. Is it innovative to heavily subsidize a new industrial plant, to build a stadium with public monies, to create business incubators in certain fields, to issue bonds for a new airport, to condemn land for economic development purposes, to adopt a living wage ordinance, to favor municipal unions in contract negotiations, or to fully fund a pre-K education program?

Innovation is not a meaningful concept without some idea of what actually works and for whom, at which point there is no need for local officials to implement it because state or federal officials will do just as well. Indeed, "experimentation" of a certain sort is exactly what good government reformers in the nineteenth century sought to discourage—as one might expect. State officials will have substantive disagreements about what works and will have political incentives to protect their constituents from failure. But state officials will also have political incentives to quash local experimentation when it benefits local officials who are in political competition with them—or to allow experimentation when locals can be set up to take the political fall.

Consider Sebastian Heilmann's description of how decentralized experimentation by Chinese local governments "minimized the risks and costs to central policymakers by placing the burden on local governments and providing welcome scapegoats in case of failure."[12] China in the 1990s is often considered a model for the decentralization-growth thesis. But as Heilmann points out, because local experimenters had strong incentives to overstate their results, "ill-conceived and impracticable experiments" were detected only after the fact. The oversupply of local infrastructure and the huge debt of Chinese local governments have been the result.[13]

The final difficulty with disciplinary decentralization is that it assumes that capital flight is what drives local market-favorable policy decisions. It is worth pointing out that this reflects a particularly jaundiced view of the local political process, for it relies almost wholly on the threat of exit as a mechanism for holding city officials accountable.

The risk of capital flight creates incentives for local officials to pursue prosperity-enhancing policies.

But, of course, local officials also respond to local voters and other political constituencies. Exiting is not the only—or even the most conventional way—to express one's policy preferences. Voting, lobbying, and other forms of "voice" (to use Albert Hirschman's famous term) are also obviously important. If voice is more powerful and exit is limited—as is often the case—then local officials are not constrained in the ways that the competitive model assumes (though they may be constrained in other ways). All of which is to say that the threat of capital flight might not be doing any work that is not already being done by local politics. As we know, powerful local actors can already achieve a great deal politically without having a credible threat to flee. And government officials will have incentives to act independently of capital flight.

More importantly, capital flight might not produce the incentives that market-enhancing decentralists want. As Hongbin Cai and Daniel Treisman have shown, under conditions of capital mobility, governments that are well behind in the capital attraction race are more likely to give up than to try to compete. That is because any investment the government makes will be unlikely to shift the needle of growth significantly away from the better-endowed cities or regions. As I observed in chapter 1, economic geographers have realized that rich places tend to get richer while poor places tend to get poorer. Better-off regions can always out-compete the poorer ones, and capital in the poorer region will almost always seek the higher returns possible in the better-endowed region.[14]

The assumption has been that competition to attract mobile capital disciplines governments toward business-friendly investments. But why invest when capital will invariably flee? As Cai and Treisman observe: "Knowing they cannot compete, governments in poorly endowed units will give up on pro-business policies and focus instead on either predation or satisfying the demands of local citizens."[15] In this way, capital mobility in a decentralized political system exacerbates economic differences among subregional units. It does not ameliorate them. This would explain why we continue to see divergence in economic outcomes between regions instead of the convergence that the competitive account predicts.

Local Government Markets: Preference-Fulfilling Decentralization

Disciplinary decentralization relies on a theory of how local officials will respond to capital mobility, namely the mobility of residents and firms seeking out congenial places to locate. And as we have seen, public officials might not respond to capital mobility in the ways that the competitive decentralists assume.

But even if public officials *do* respond to the desires of mobile firms and residents, theorists have to show that there is a connection between fulfilling location preferences and economic growth—between the outcomes of a hypothetical market in local governments and economic activity. That connection turns out to be difficult to establish. First, there is not an obvious link between the efficient provision of municipal services in a local government marketplace and economic growth. And second, even if there is a connection, it could well be *negative*. The sorting of residents and firms into their preferred jurisdictions might in fact *retard* economic growth.

There are a great many problems with the Tieboutian theory of public goods sorting—especially with its unrealistic assumptions about the mobility of individual households.[16] But let's start by assuming that Tiebout is right, and that the efficient delivery of public goods and government services is an outcome of a market in local governments.[17] How does that turn into economic growth? One possibility is that the efficient targeting of infrastructure investment could raise an economy's growth rate. It seems sensible that infrastructure and human capital policies that are responsive to local or regional conditions will be more effective in encouraging economic development than centrally determined policies that ignore geographical differences.[18] Because a competitive, decentralized system of local government goods provision would be more tailored to local conditions than a centralized one, one would expect economic development to follow.

There is a deep intuition here—that more attentive local government will result in more economic development. But how plausible is that intuition? In fact, it is not at all clear that the efficient provision of public goods has anything to do with economic growth. Tieboutian public goods sorting is not (and was never presented as) a theory of regional growth. Indeed, Tiebout's original model does not contemplate that local officials will modify their behavior because of competitive capital flight or budget pressures.[19]

To get from efficient public goods to growth requires something else, and the difficulty in formulating the relationship is that one has to make claims about how public finance affects private activities, innovation, and investment decisions. Those effects can be quite indirect.

Consider, for instance, Jan Brueckner's theoretical claim that more efficient local government might affect private individuals' incentives to save. This savings, he argues, gets plowed into increased individual investments in human capital, which in turn leads to economic growth.[20] Whether this is plausible or not depends on many factors: Better, more targeted provision of public goods leads to individual savings that are spent on education, which in turn leads to higher economic growth. One can immediately see how tenuous the connection is between the provision of local public goods and economic growth. If education is the driver of economic development (as many theorists now believe), why not provide it directly, evenly, and universally? In other words, why adopt the local and differential provision of education if you already know that it is a potent source of economic growth?

There is a more profound difficulty with the link between preference-fulfillment and growth, however: Efficiency and growth do not have to correspond at the local level. Remember that, in a Tieboutian scheme, citizen preferences are matched to local governments. There is nothing at all that assures that citizens will prefer policies that encourage economic growth over policies that do not. In Tieboutian terms, it would be entirely efficient for many (or all) citizens to choose a local government that is dominated by antigrowth forces. But those choices might retard economic development in the whole if too many citizens prefer policies that limit economic development.

Indeed, those who advocate regional government or expanding the city's annexation authority have long argued that inter-municipal competition for tax base has resulted in the under-provision of necessary infrastructure that would otherwise enhance the regional economy. Local governments' competition for tax base causes them to under-invest in education, resist providing workforce housing that might enhance the local labor force, and reject regionally necessary land uses, like airports, public transit, landfills, and industrial plants. Instead of cooperating to create regionally beneficial infrastructure, each locality puts up barriers to entry, hoping to free ride on the economic benefits generated by the productive or necessary infrastructure next door. For instance, evidence shows that highly productive coastal regions in the U.S. often deploy land use restrictions that significantly raise housing costs. These "anti-growth" policies limit relocations into highly productive metropolitan areas, forcing development to go elsewhere—a big problem from the perspective of growth economists.

Nevertheless, this is a predictable outcome in a region where many communities are willing to pay a high price (in terms of taxes foregone) to keep out housing for families with children, or industrial, commercial, retail, and other facilities. Economic growth is always being balanced against congestion or other negative effects. If local governments have to internalize the costs and benefits of economic growth, then they might make the appropriate tradeoff—though some localities would certainly disfavor growth. The problem is that local governments never fully internalize the costs and benefits of their local economic policies. One therefore has to explain why in a competitive system of governments in which each government is trying to obtain the benefits of growth without the attendant costs, the system as a whole will favor growth. One might equally predict that such a system would instead promote the opposite.

In fact, the sorting of residents into the particular local governments that meet their individual preferences can easily undermine an important engine of economic growth. Recall that one of the chief advantages of the city is the beneficial knowledge, consumption, and labor spillovers that occur when firms and residents locate in relatively close proximity. As we saw in chapter 1, economists have come to the realization that being close together generates economic benefits. These agglomeration effects are increasingly seen as an important mechanism for economic growth.

Relatively high-density urbanization is necessary to obtain the gains of agglomeration. But there are costs to living close together, and many individual consumer-voters might prefer to reside in low-density suburbs, where congestion and compromise costs are lower and services are provided more cheaply.

From the perspective of agglomeration, however, this is a problem. For purposes of economic growth, we would prefer residents to live and work in close proximity. Yet the proximity necessary to obtain the benefits of agglomeration is probably inefficient from the perspective of fulfilling residents' public goods preferences. Lower-density suburbs are less expensive and might be more congenial from a public goods standpoint, even if not from a productivity standpoint. As the distance between firms and residents increases, the benefits of agglomeration are lost. In this way, the efficient provision of public goods in a competitive inter-jurisdictional marketplace is not just unproven as a means for generating economic growth; it is affirmatively contrary to it.[21]

In fact, residential sorting of the type contemplated by competitive decentralists often forces a choice between productivity and public goods. Moving to opportunity—from an economically depressed rural community to an economically vibrant urban one, for example—is beneficial for individuals and for the economy as a whole. Individuals become more productive and reap the individual benefits of that productivity; society reaps the collective benefits. But the differential provision of public goods in a highly fragmented metropolitan region might induce households not to move for productivity but simply to move to access better public goods. Moving for this reason is, from the perspective of growth, detrimental: Moving to access better public goods does not necessarily generate a gain in productivity and might in fact reduce productivity.

Consider a move from the city to the suburbs to gain access to safer streets. This move may be efficient from a public goods perspective: Households' preference for public safety is better met in the suburbs than in the city. But fulfilling this preference also could (and often does) result in a change in employment that reduces households' total productivity. We want people to move when it will improve their life opportunities, and sometimes accessing better public goods (like education) will do so. But there is a significant societal tradeoff if that location decision constrains the household's labor opportunities or increases the costs associated with accessing those opportunities. Consider the significant social costs of many metropolitan-area commutes.[22]

One could conclude from all this that significant disparities in service provision among localities—as we commonly see between American central cities and wealthy suburbs—is actually *bad* for economic growth. Such disparities will induce individuals to move for the *wrong* reasons—not because they are gaining through increased economic productivity, but because they are trying to access services that they cannot access in their home jurisdiction. Even if a move to better services generates an individual welfare improvement, it does not foster economic development. Indeed, it strongly suggests that competition between decentralized governments in providing basic public goods is not a route toward economic growth.[23]

We know this intuitively. The tradeoff between city and suburb can often be understood as one between productivity and efficiency. Large cities, unlike smaller places, are unable to provide local public services that are as personally tailored to residents. There are simply more people with different tastes to satisfy, and congestion costs will be unavoidably higher. And yet we would never confuse the efficient provision of public services in a small town with the economic vitality offered by a large city. We know instinctively that efficiency and productivity do not run in parallel and are often at odds.

Jane Jacobs, as usual, already developed this idea. She spends a chapter in *The Economy of Cities* describing the "valuable inefficiencies and impracticalities of cities." As she acknowledges, the most routine and ordinary activities "absorb ridiculous amounts of energy, time, and money in cities, as compared to towns and villages."[24] But these congestion and transaction costs are not just unfortunate byproducts of agglomeration; they are integral to the process of making new work. That is because the production of new work requires multiple, redundant, repeated experimentation, chance encounters, diverse and overlapping firms and businesses, and social and economic intermixing. Economic development is synonymous with a big and diverse (and inherently inefficient) city. Metropolitan-area public goods sorting of the Tieboutian variety could very well be inimical to this process. Competitive theories of city growth mistake a theory of public goods provision for a theory of economic development. These are not the same things.

The Historic Vulnerability of City Status

Despite the flaws in the decentralization-growth hypothesis, it continues to be influential. Some cross-national studies comparing federal and nonfederal constitutional systems purport to show a link between federalism and growth. Other studies dispute this. Historically minded scholars often point to the nineteenth-century United States as a model instead, arguing that development in the industrializing U.S. was fostered in large part by competition between states.

In the nineteenth and early twentieth centuries, however, big, noisy, congested (and often corrupt) cities were the generators of economic growth in the industrializing United States (as they are today in China and other developing economies). If some form of institutionalized legal decentralization *causes* growth, then the history of local government law in the states should reflect a relatively robust and stable form of institutionalized political decentralization over the course of the nineteenth and twentieth centuries—when the industrial cities were growing their fastest.

In local government law, however, we see something quite different— an oft-changing, arguably cyclical battle between political interests (often "reformers" and "machines") that results in a grab-bag of institutional constraints, some favoring city power and some disfavoring it. City power is forever contested, and shifts between local and state power do not often *precede* growth but instead seem to *follow* it.

The Public-Private Distinction

Indeed, the history of local government law in the states has been an ongoing effort to redefine, control, and *limit* city power, not expand it. For nineteenth-century reformers witnessing the birth of the modern city and the development of modern local government law, the primary effort was to define the city as *public* as a way of cabining its activities to that sphere. To do so required that cities withdraw from their active participation in the market and limit their powers to those that could be derived from the state legislature.

This "public" city, separate from the private market, is a creature of law. The city originally *was* the corporation—an assembler, promoter, regulator, and developer of capital itself. The early Anglo-American municipal corporation controlled almost all aspects of the market: It determined who could be admitted into the various trades of the city, what prices those tradesmen could demand for their goods or commodities, which goods and commodities met certain quality standards, where those goods and commodities could be sold, at what times and under what circumstances. As Jon Teaford has observed, "Commerce, not residence, defined membership in the commercial community, and thus a man acted his political role not where he ate or slept but where he produced and traded." The privilege of operating a trade in the city was the privilege of the freeman. Admission was controlled by a closed corporation governed by self-appointed aldermen, who "sought to apportion vocational opportunity, guarantee equitable dealing, and maintain commercial facilities with the hope of ensuring present solvency and future prosperity."[25]

The chartered city's power and authority to control the local economy were a medieval, and later, colonial political phenomenon—these were the privileges of the merchant class protected and defended against royal invasion. But the eighteenth and nineteenth centuries witnessed a new bifurcation of political and commercial life, state and market. First, facing both political and economic resistance, the city began to lose its commercial monopoly, slowly withdrawing from its regulation of vocations, its control of city markets, its oversight of quality, and, eventually, its regulation of prices. Second, the city began to rely less on property ownership, fees, and licenses for income, and increasingly on taxes. Third, the city became more democratic, moving from a closed, autocratic oligopoly toward universal manhood suffrage. And fourth, the municipal corporation began to provide new public services, increasingly abandoning the regulation of trade and turning its attention to the provision of sewers, clean water, paved and lighted streets, fire protection, policing, parks, and other urban infrastructure. Over the course of a century, the municipal corporation evolved from a territorially based trading corporation designed to protect the member merchants' and tradesmen's prerogatives to a political jurisdiction charged with protecting and advancing the health, safety, and welfare of its populace.[26]

Scholars have told a number of different stories about this dramatic shift. Republican ideology plays a role—the medieval and early colonial municipal corporation was vulnerable to the same political winds that produced the American Revolution. The city, like other hierarchical, aristocratic, and nondemocratic institutions, was not immune to republican challenge. The new economic thinking of Adam Smith and the developing notion of free markets also influenced the change, as did the far longer historical movement from status to contract and the rise of the liberal legal order. The shift away from collectivism toward individual autonomy, with its language of human rights, required a reconfiguring of those institutions that were neither state nor individual.[27]

There was also the simple fact of urbanization itself. It was not possible for a limited government to control the economic enterprise of the increasing numbers of city-dwellers. Technological change and the pace of urbanization had generated a more sophisticated and complex society. The economic chokepoints of the city could not be maintained.

Once the city got out of the business of controlling the capital that sustained it through its direct monopoly on trade, vocations, and the selling and buying of goods, it had to establish a new relationship with commercial activity. In the United States, the bulk of that work was done by classical jurists and reformers concerned about the relationship between legislatures and economic favoritism more broadly.[28] Late-nineteenth-century legal thinkers worried that legislatures were inclined to favor certain groups in the marketplace over others. Judicial oversight was necessary to ensure that legislation was in the public interest. Limits on municipal power were also necessary to protect the fundamental right of all free persons to enter into markets or participate in avocations on an equal basis. In the arena of municipal law, cities were actively engaged in what classical legal thinkers saw as economic favoritism—the distribution of exclusive franchises and monopolies and the use of public power to promote private gain.[29]

As legal historians have shown, the curtailment of local power occurred along a number of dimensions. First, city officials began to look to the state legislature for confirmation of their authority. The colonial city was an independent corporation, often a chartered entity, with the privileges and duties of all private corporations. It was conceptually autonomous in the ways that all private property owners are conceptually autonomous. But relatively early on, the city became subject to the dictates of the state legislature. Indeed, the city's subordination to the state legislature is of a piece with republican political theory, which could not countenance the existence of corporate bodies not subject to democratic will. Classical ideology condemned corporate privilege, and to the extent that cities were corporate bodies, they were targets of control by the late eighteenth- and nineteenth-century state legislatures. This transformation expressed itself in both subtle and not-so-subtle ways.

Local political actors began to seek "permission" from the state legislature to support actions they may have previously undertaken without seeking such a grant. Meanwhile, state legislatures began to assert their authority over city charters, property, services, and boundaries.[30]

In his seminal book on New York City, Hendrik Hartog shows how the city was transformed from "a government insistent on governing through its personal, private estate, to one dedicated to using a public bureaucracy to provide public goods for public consumption." Eighteenth-century New York City was, by definition, a private corporation. Hartog describes how the city's charter created a system of blurred property and governmental rights as it granted the city government property in fee simple absolute with no restrictions on how the property could be used. During this period, the city sold land grants to private parties as a means of shaping, controlling, and profiting from the city's development—again a mix of private and public purposes. By the beginning of the nineteenth century, however, distrust of the corporation had caused New York City to transform into a public institution, largely resembling the modern municipal corporation of New York City today. The institution became largely dependent on public tax revenues, rather than the proceeds from the sale of land grants, for funding of public welfare projects. And in stark contrast to the independence enjoyed by the corporation during the eighteenth century, the municipal agency's fundraising actions required prior authorization by the State of New York.[31]

Regulating the Early City

We are the inheritors of this late eighteenth- and early nineteenth-century legal conception of the city as public and governmental as opposed to private and corporate. Maintenance of that distinction required and requires ongoing legal work, however. The development of the concept of the municipal corporation has always entailed determining what powers it should enjoy.

It should be emphasized again that the initial nineteenth-century inclination was to limit city power. As cities lost the character of autonomous corporations, they became entirely subject to state control for purposes of constitutional doctrine. Early industrializing cities had no formal constitutional status under the federal constitution—indeed, they still do not. They were and are, as the Court stated in *Hunter v. Pittsburgh*, a 1907 case: "political subdivisions of the State, created as convenient agencies for exercising such of the governmental powers of the State as may be entrusted to them." Further,

> [t]he number, nature, and duration of the powers conferred upon these corporations and the territory over which they shall be exercised rests in the absolute discretion of the State. . . . The State, therefore, at its pleasure may modify or withdraw all such powers, may take without compensation such property, hold it itself, or vest it in other agencies, expand or contract the territorial area, unite the whole or a part of it with another municipality. . . . In all these respects the State is supreme, and its legislative body . . . may do as it will, unrestrained by any provision of the Constitution of the United States.[32]

City power was further constrained through Dillon's Rule, an interpretive command that requires the strict construction of state grants of municipal authority. The rule was formulated by jurist and treatise writer John Dillon in the 1870s. Adopted by almost all the states in the nineteenth century, Dillon's Rule asserts that municipal corporations can exercise only those powers expressly granted by the state legislature and essential to the purposes of the corporation, and that "[a]ny . . . doubt concerning the existence of power is resolved by the courts against the corporation, and the power is denied."[33]

The original animating purpose of Dillon's Rule was to prevent the city from overinvesting in private enterprise, privileging certain private enterprises over others, or distributing franchises or monopolies to particular "insider" commercial interests. State constitutional debt limitations, restrictions on local taxing authority, and especially judicial oversight of local regulation became mechanisms to prevent the use of city monies for private gain. For Dillon, "what corruption meant was the mingling of the private sector's profit motive with the business of the state."[34] Defining the appropriate sphere for government and business was an overriding concern of municipal reformers. This concern was consistent with classical legal thought generally, which sought to police the line between private and public by limiting government interference in the market.

Dillon's Rule is a nice example of how institutional design *follows* economic development—the impulse to limit city authority came *after* economic growth; it did not precede it. The disempowerment of the cities happened in response to local economic and political behavior brought about by the newly wealthy or wealth-seeking municipalities. Those municipalities were providing many new services that cities had not provided before: sewer and water systems, roads, sanitation, ports, parks, schools, electricity, streetcars, street lights, and public buildings. Those services had to be funded, and franchises for provision of those services had to be granted—thus opening the way for local officials to engage in self-dealing and for transportation and utility interests to line their pockets.

Indeed, Dillon's Rule was meant to prevent cities and states from engaging in competitive developmental races—the exact opposite of what a competitive inter-jurisdictional system encourages. Thus, on the heels of the Crédit Mobilier scandal in 1872, E.L. Godkin of the *Nation* declared,

> The remedy is simple. The Government must get out of the "protective" business and the "subsidy" business and the "improvement" and the "development" business. It must let trade, and commerce, and manufactures, and steamboats, and railroads, and telegraphs alone. It cannot touch them without breeding corruption.35

Dillon's Rule thus "sought to protect private property not only against abuse by democracy but also against abuse by private economic power."36 Predation was a rampant problem: The initial and still enduring solution was to move power *up* the scale of government, not *down* it.

The home rule movement that followed was also a response to this perceived problem. Home rule ostensibly returned power to the cities. Under Dillon's Rule, cities had to seek permission from the state legislature for even the most uncontroversial and mundane tasks of government. As urban governance became more complex, the Dillon's Rule structure made local administration too cumbersome. But home rule was also intended to protect the city from the state legislature, which had shown itself to be as susceptible to the siren call of private gain as locally elected mayors and city aldermen. Thomas Cooley, another jurist of the classical period, blamed state legislatures for corporate give-aways and thus argued for an inherent right of local self-government intended to insulate municipalities from avaricious state legislators.[37]

But this battle over the relative formal powers of cities was again joined at the moment when urbanization and industrialization were concentrating enormous wealth in the cities. It was in the late nine-teenth and early twentieth centuries that the great industrial cities were growing rapidly, and it was at this moment that the old institutional regime was seen to be deficient. Why? Because the state legislature and other state political actors were eagerly expropriating the wealth that was being generated in the cities: "The large rewards which lay in cities' of-fices, their contracts, and the franchises in their streets became the mark of the political spoilsman in the state legislature."[38] Institutional reforms meant to limit the center's intervention into local affairs were a direct result of this grasping for wealth; they were not a *cause* of the wealth.

Moreover, the shift from Dillon's Rule to home rule, in those states that adopted it, did not change the fundamental relationship of subor-dination between cities and their states. It certainly did not produce the equivalent of a federal system—with its notion of dual sovereignty—within the states that adopted it. Nor did it substantially alter the basic framework of state legislative supremacy.

Indeed, to think of home rule efforts as taking power away from the state and giving it to the city would be a mistake. Often city officials and the city's state legislative delegation represented one political ma-chine or competing machines, pursuing in parallel the economic inter-ests of particular urban constituencies. To talk about city versus state, or decentralized versus centralized power, thus misstates the political dynamic. Home rule was not an effort to shift power to the represen-tatives of the local government; it was oftentimes instead an effort to limit the law-making role of the city's state legislative delegation, which was (according to reformers) responding too readily to every costly demand of their urban constituents.[39] Urbanization and industrializa-tion created equal opportunities for corruption at different levels of government, but mostly it created opportunities for politicians who represented city districts, whether those politicians served on the city council or in the state legislature.

Moreover, though home rule reforms appeared to return power to city officials, reformers also created numerous institutions that took power *away* from them, in the form of state-led expert boards and administrations. The turn of the century witnessed the rise of state boards of health, water, sewage, and schools—the beginnings of state administrative law. These reforms were of a piece with the Progressive Era emphasis on technical and expert administration, data collection, and efficiency. A new corps of inspectors, auditors, and engineers, governed by independent professional norms, began to oversee municipal work. Moreover, by the end of the first quarter of the twentieth century, numerous states had adopted state utility and rate-making commissions in response to the corrupt awarding of municipal contracts for gas, electric, streetcar, and telephone services. Angered by giveaways of municipal contracts and the poor service provided by irresponsible utilities, turn-of-the-century reformers advocated municipal ownership of public utilities, and in some places, cities took over local provision. The utility companies preferred state regulation to municipal control, however, as did many good government reformers, who were skeptical of local ability or inclination to regulate the utility magnates. State commissions ultimately prevailed.[40]

As utilities regulation illustrates, some of the support for "reforming" municipal government came from pro-business conservatives, who opposed the expanded role of municipal government more generally. For those who believed that the ethnic rulers of the turn-of-the-century city were incompetent and irresponsible, that redistribution to the poor was not a task for government, or that government regulation of industry and business of any kind was improper, public works and the taxes needed to fund them were anathema. The rush to adopt expert boards or limit altogether the authority of elected officials (whether state or local) was animated in part by a more general antigovernment (and perhaps anti-city) sentiment; it was animated less by respect for municipal governance and its reformist capability than by a concern that municipal government was overreaching.[41]

The Progressive Era institutional landscape of local-central relations in the states was thus quite complicated and improvisational. Some states continued with Dillon's Rule as a rule of construction (and a number have some version of it to this day). There were also widespread popular movements to adopt home rule grants and constitutional bans on special legislation. But these grants of local prerogative were often part of a package of state constitutional reforms that also limited local power.[42]

For example, constitutional public purpose requirements limited the government's authority to engage in economic development activities that privileged private entities; constitutional debt limitations restricted the borrowing capacity of local (and state) governments; city charter reforms transferred important local government functions to nonpolitical professional city managers; and states shifted power away from locally elected officials to state regulatory bodies and administrative professionals. Bans on special legislation that only applied to certain cities arguably reduced city power, for they limited the city legislative delegation's ability to push through city-specific laws in the legislature. Now all laws would have to be "general" in nature.

Good Government and Growth

Importantly, institutional efforts to protect some sphere of local autonomy were not driven by the belief that decentralization per se led to economic growth. Good government groups regularly asserted that better government would promote prosperity, but there was no particular relationship between good government and decentralization, and certainly not a relationship that viewed inter-jurisdictional competition as the engine of government efficiency. Indeed, "good government" often meant spending less on services demanded by urban constituents. Sometimes good government could be obtained by granting cities more power; sometimes it could be obtained by granting them less.

In fact, the connection between governance and growth in nineteenth-century American cities was quite tenuous. The decentralization-growth thesis asserts that good government will help foster growth and that intercity competition will generate good government; neither seemed to be true in the industrializing United States.

Indeed, at the peak of their economic prowess, the great industrial cities were often beset by some of the worst political pathologies. Observers of late nineteenth-century urban government could declare city governance a "conspicuous failure" even as the country's urban centers grew dramatically.[43]

Did municipal corruption indicate a lack of economic growth? This question matters because, as we have seen, a central claim made on behalf of competitive federalism is that it reduces corruption. Competitive forces produce cleaner municipal government, and cleaner municipal government fosters economic growth.

The nineteenth-century industrializing cities of the U.S., however, appear to be a counterexample—and a dramatic one. As Rebecca Menes notes, between 1880 and 1930, "the dominant economic feature of American cities was growth."[44] Menes also observes, however, that urban corruption was at its height during this period. Jon Teaford's *Unheralded Triumph*—his classic treatment of city government in the late nineteenth century—contains its thesis in its title: Municipal government was disrespected, both at the time and in retrospect. Nevertheless, late-nineteenth-century industrializing cities grew rapidly, wealth was generated, infrastructure was built, and services were provided to an expanding urban constituency. Today, we see something similar in China, where massive urbanization and massive corruption also coexist.

If not clean government, then perhaps intercity fiscal and political competition played a significant role in this enormous growth rate? Certainly, city boosterism was a part of the industrial and urban landscape in the nineteenth and early twentieth centuries, and the rhetoric of intercity competition has always been a feature of local government. Perhaps competition to become the "best" or "largest" or "fastest-growing" city fostered a political atmosphere that induced locals to adopt policies that favored growth.

We should be cautious about how such competition worked, however. An initial question is one of causation: Did local investments in infrastructure foster growth, or were they a response to it? To be sure, in some cases, investment in municipal services may have preceded the great influx of people into certain places. For example, small settlements competed to be blessed by a stop on a railway line. In those cases, supply created demand. Nevertheless, it would be a mistake to think that municipal investment in infrastructure always or usually preceded growth. Urbanization and industrialization were occurring at a rapid

pace. Some kinds of infrastructure investment may have made a difference as to where development would happen, but most municipal services were a result of demand: In-migrants needed and demanded street
paving and lighting, water works, sewers, parks, and utilities. And these
large projects were possible because cities or private providers could
access the increasing wealth being generated in place.

Certainly there is an element of circular causation here—cities grow,
which leads to the construction of municipal services, which allows
them to grow more. But the urban infrastructure that arose as rural-
urban migration accelerated is better understood as an outcome of
growth, rather than impetus for it. Communities were growing and
urban infrastructure had to grow with it.

Moreover, one should take note of how institutional reformers
viewed intercity competition. For legal thinkers like Dillon (as well as
the home rule advocates who came after him), intercity competition
did not promote good economic practices, but rather quite detrimental
ones. Competition did not promote efficiency, but rather corruption.
Competitive pressures brought about races-to-the-bottom that had to
be solved with better institutional checks, many of which took power
away from local jurisdictions and gave it to state-led administrative
boards.

We should also be clear about whose interests were being advanced
by the rhetoric of intercity competition. Presumably, locals would be
interested in pursuing their own prosperity whether or not it reflected
well on their city or region. But in pursuing their private economic
interests, urban elites, speculators, and industrialists often deployed the
rhetoric of local civic patriotism, and for good reason. Appeals to the
city's interests (in becoming the "biggest" or the "best") were effective
tools used by those with direct interests in the railroad, streetcar, utility,
and real estate industries. As it is today, city boosterism was a potent
justification for subsidizing favored development, granting particular
franchises, or providing advantageous land-use and regulatory treatment to specific elites.

This rhetoric of civic populism had little to do with economic
growth generally. Local landowners or businessmen were interested
in their own economic advancement, only incidentally interested in
the economic growth in their jurisdiction, and not at all interested in

economic growth in the state or nation as a whole. Competition was arguably zero-sum. The railroad had to go somewhere—that it ended up in Chicago rather than some other place did not mean that the national economy would grow more, just that it would grow in a different place.

Indeed, it is notable that city boosters did not favor a competitive inter-jurisdictional economy when it came to their own regions. Metropolitan-area jurisdictional fragmentation and a Tieboutian market in local governments were emphatically *not* on city boosters' agendas. Instead, the nineteenth- and early twentieth-century boosters' vision was for ever-larger cities. New York grew by joining with Brooklyn—then the fourth-largest city in the country. Chicago, Philadelphia, St. Louis—all these cities (and hundreds of others) grew by annexing miles and miles of territory. The big city, not the decentralized one, was the goal of local development forces. And, in fact, nineteenth-century economic growth fostered ever-larger political jurisdictions, the equivalent at the time of the mega-cities of the twenty-first century.

Finally, even if intercity competition did motivate city officials to act, their range of powers was quite unstable. The city had no constitutionally protected right of self-government, no sovereignty, and was only minimally protected from state government intervention. Moreover, municipal reform was a continual business. Before home rule reforms, the city's powers were adjusted on an almost yearly basis. But even after the adoption of home rule charters, the impetus to adjust institutions continued. As Teaford observes, constitutional home rule movements in Missouri and California "ended the [state legislative] practice of perpetual tinkering," thus creating a more rigid and permanent structure for state-local relations:

> Yet the social and economic currents of change continued to propel the cities of Saint Louis and San Francisco inexorably onward. Populations soared, demands for new services increased, expectations rose, and fads in municipal reform appeared and disappeared. But whereas the needs and desires of many of the city's residents changed, the home-rule system of municipal government proved inflexible. Thus during the 1880s and 1890s some of the very citizens who had demanded an end to legislative interference found themselves

yearning for additional flexibility. . . . By 1900 some viewed the previously desired permanence as a form of paralysis, and realized that
in a changing world stability was a close cousin of stagnation.[45]

Institutional reforms were thus cyclical, partial, and reactive. During
economic shocks, when economic downturns revealed the vulnerability of local governments to boom and bust, we see the imposition of
constraints on certain local actors. When that form of centralization
showed itself to be as corrupt as the more local-favoring regime before
it, institutions were adjusted to protect some local autonomy while
maintaining restrictions on city power in other areas. Institutional
design mostly responded to perceived policy crises, and those designs
represented the outcomes of politics, not some durable institutional
scheme. Meanwhile, the "economic currents of change continued to
propel [the city] inexorably onward."[46]

Selective Localism in the Twentieth Century

Indeed, the institutional changes of the nineteenth and early twentieth
centuries turned out to be quite manipulable only a few decades later.
First, the legal doctrines that set the terms of local-central relations
during the Progressive Era have been easily changed in response to perceived policy needs. The supposed institutional settlement is never settled. Second, in the twentieth and into the early twenty-first centuries,
municipal autonomy has been severely restricted by state constitutional
and statutory limitations on local taxing, debt, and spending. These
provisions were meant to limit the influence of private capital, but the
result has often been the opposite.

As to the first point, the manipulation of "settled" institutions began
almost immediately in the twentieth century. Home rule itself has
turned into less of a bulwark against state intervention than a mechanism to *restrict* local power. Courts tend to interpret state constitutional
home rule grants as limitations on local power—cities have authority
under state constitutional grants only to the limits of their home rule
powers, and those home rule powers are restricted to matters of "local
concern." Issues of "statewide concern" are entrusted to the state legislature and—because most issues can be understood as having statewide
effects—the exception tends to swallow the rule. It is relatively easy for

states to legislate in areas of traditional local concern as long as there is some minimally rational justification for it. Even the prohibition on "special legislation" has become diluted, as courts defer to state legislatures when they regulate classes of cities, even if the "class" includes only one municipality.[47]

These decisions suggest that courts and legislatures are not at all interested in defending some entrenched form of intergovernmental relations. Legislative actions are driven by political need and fiscal expediency. And courts tend to defer to legislatures in large part because of the judges' inability to settle on nonpolitical principles for dividing up authority. As at the federal level, where battles over state-national relations continue to be highly politicized, conflicts over state-municipal authority are proxies for political fights that have nothing to do with the pros and cons of decentralization.

More recent institutional innovations are also a product of political battles that have little to do with intergovernmental relations per se. Consider one of the most important developments in local government finance in the last fifty years—state constitutional taxation and spending limitations. Starting with Proposition 13 in California, adopted in 1978, many states began to severely limit local governments' ability to tax and spend. In the California case, these limits were arguably spurred by rapid rises in property values as newcomers found their way to California in the 1970s. Again, an institutional reaction appeared to *follow* economic growth—California was growing rapidly and existing residents were concerned about the fiscal effects brought about by the influx of in-migrants.[48] Colorado's Taxpayer Bill of Rights (TABOR), adopted in 1992, also appears to have been in part a reaction to rising tax rates brought about by increasing service demands of increasing populations.

The combination of debt, taxing, and spending limitations in state constitutions bears further attention, as these provisions starkly illustrate how fiscal control has been increasingly centralized in state legislatures, and also how ad hoc that process has been. These limitations in the states are a product of a nineteenth-century reaction to state and municipal debt and a twentieth-century movement to restrict taxation. The resulting state constitutional arrangements are entirely uncoordinated—historically, logically, and conceptually. They were and are political responses to the perceived crises of the day. But their constitutionalization severely affects states' and localities' capacity to respond to changes in economic circumstances, while inducing forms of government financing that are less transparent and more expensive—an issue I return to in later chapters. States and localities have to fund their services, and they will often find indirect ways to do so.[49]

In fact, current state tax and spending limitations tend to reinforce the kind of private-public intermixing that generated consternation in the nineteenth century. Constraints on municipal revenue-raising increase the city's dependence on private-public partnerships. The selling of municipal infrastructure or the contracting out of municipal services is an example. Another example is the popularity of tax increment financing, which essentially trades public tax dollars for private development. These forms of privatization would have elicited protests from conservative reformers like John Dillon as well as the progressive reformers who came after him.

The relatively easy ability to govern from the legislature, to amend local charters, to adjust state constitutions, and to engage in proposition-driven government means that local-central relations in the states are not particularly institutionally embedded. Those relations often reflect politics in its rawest form and can be explained by the tension between existing residents and future ones, anti-tax sentiment, the city-suburban divide, the power of land-based elites or business interests, or the reality of racial conflict.

This should come as no surprise. Demographic and economic shifts tend to precede shifts in the contours of municipal power. Thus, as wealth and power moved out of industrial cities to suburbs in the mid-twentieth century, the form that local power took changed as well. Industrial-era cities exercised certain powers that would be unthinkable today. For example, forcible annexation was the rule in most states prior to the mid-twentieth century. Cities could take unincorporated—and some incorporated—territory at will, despite objections from residents of the annexed land. Early twentieth-century cities also more routinely engaged in extraterritorial regulation and exercised the power of eminent domain outside their boundaries. Again, in an era of the ascendant city, these powers were uncontroversial; that fewer cities can exercise them now reflects a shift in the city's economic and political salience.[50]

That the economic power of the suburbs is reflected in a different form of state-local relations, one that privileges suburban jurisdictions over urban ones, has been a common complaint of urban scholars for some time. Local "autonomy" in the suburban form means preserving suburbanites' land-use powers—their ability to zone out low-income households; it means preventing city annexation and expansion; it involves restricting local taxing capacity generally so that municipalities are encouraged to favor low-tax growth; and finally it means limiting schools to local residents, so that suburbanites can preserve their public service advantage and limit it to only those who can afford to live in the jurisdiction. This strategy continues to work for many wealthier suburban jurisdictions, though it is working less well for old-line, declining ones.[51]

Central cities, on the other hand, have conventionally struggled with limited fiscal capacity since the middle of the twentieth century. Their "local autonomy" is more of a curse than a blessing because it means that they are responsible for providing services to a relatively needy population, their fiscal resources are limited, and state intervention is selective. State legislators—in many cases dominated by suburban interests—are unwilling to share their economic largesse with the cities. But they are more than willing to limit the city's taxing capacity, and are also willing to intervene to prevent cities from accessing new revenue sources—like taxes on commuters or high-income earners—that would help offset urban costs. This selective localism does not reflect a rational division of authority between states and cities. Rather, the division of authority is an outcome of political contests between interests in the metropolitan region, and it reflects those interests' relative economic and political power. As some central cities begin to gain a larger share of metropolitan-area wealth, we might expect to see shifts in the relative political status of cities and suburbs.

The larger point is that the dramatically and constantly changing institutional status of cities—both in the nineteenth and twentieth centuries—should make us skeptical of the decentralization-growth thesis. First, state-local relations have gone through spates of centralization and decentralization. This cycling does not represent the rational evolution of a well-working fiscal division of labor. It is ad hoc, contingent, and political. Institutional movements to centralize or decentralize political power in the states have always served particular political interests. Sometimes those political interests desire growth and sometimes they do not. There is no reason to believe that growth-related political interests will desire or reinforce decentralization; to the contrary, they will often pursue centralization. The best that can be said is that there has not been a particularly robust institutional settlement one way or another.

Second, economic growth seems to have *preceded* institution-making. In particular, the boom and bust cycles of the 1800s drove much of the reform in American state-local relations in the nineteenth century, while suburbanization drove intergovernmental relations in the second half of the twentieth.

And third, it should be emphasized that institutional settlements in dividing up local and state power are never settled. As Joan Williams has pointed out, local government's legal status is easily manipulated in the service of other aims. The shifting of powers up and down the scale of government is a proxy for political battles that have nothing to do with central-local relations, growth, or the efficient provision of public services.[52]

What Does Decentralization Do?

That the history of local government law in the states does not support a connection between formal legal autonomy and economic growth should not be surprising. Current trajectories of city growth and decline do not appear to track relative local fiscal autonomy either. There are fifty different state-municipal regimes within the United States. If decentralization matters, then states with a more decentralized constitutional regime should be outperforming states with a less decentralized constitutional regime.

There seems to be little or no correlation when one compares local fiscal and political autonomy with statewide growth rates, however. And anecdotally, such state-to-state differences seem unlikely. In the United States, the Sunbelt cities have grown and the Rustbelt cities have generally declined. These patterns seem to be regional as opposed to state-specific and explainable by many factors other than a state's relative decentralization or even the efficacy of local government.

The few internal national studies of American local government are at best inconclusive and suffer from the difficulties attendant to all efforts to isolate one cause of economic growth.[53] Consider a recent study by George Hammond and Mehmet Tosun. As a proxy for decentralization, the authors rely on the numbers of local governments in a particular region, which is actually a measure of metropolitan-area fragmentation, not local autonomy. They find different effects depending on whether they are measuring population, employment, or income growth, and depending on whether a given county is part of a larger metropolitan area or is in a nonmetropolitan setting. And they conclude, as they must, that policymakers "should be wary of claims that any and all forms of fiscal decentralization will enhance growth."[54]

Indeed, there is evidence that municipal fragmentation *reduces* regional economic health. Andrew Haughwout and Robert Inman have claimed that a fiscally weak central city with high rates of poverty depresses both the city's and the surrounding suburbs' private economies.[55] Fragmented, highly decentralized government can easily be antigrowth to the extent that it is anti-city, impoverishes human capital, limits mobility, or increases the distance between workers and employers—all of which are criticisms of our current metropolitan-area organization.[56]

The problem runs deeper, however, and its source goes back to the assumptions made about the causes of city growth and decline. If the city is a product that can be improved in the global marketplace for location, then competition is an unalloyed good—it lifts all boats as long as it is properly managed. In this way, a theory of growth suggests a theory of power. If growth is a function of competition, then distributing formal powers downward is an obviously correct strategy. The decentralization-growth thesis requires that subnational governments be created and further assumes their agency (i.e., that they be capable of implementing policies that improve their economic prospects), otherwise the competition between them serves no growth-related purpose.

But as I have been arguing, the city is not a product but an economic and spatial process, and the causal relationship between good governance and city economic health is not at all self-evident. I have already noted how turn-of-the-century cities were growing rapidly at the moment when they were arguably the most corrupt. Longer-term growth or decline also seems somewhat impervious to good institutions.

As Rebecca Menes points out, Detroit, Buffalo, and Cleveland all had relatively clean governments at the turn of the century, and they adopted significant institutional reforms during the Progressive Era that remain in place. However, those reforms did not stem those cities' postindustrial declines.[57]

In truth, no one really knows exactly what kinds of policies are best in generating new growth. Competitive federalists talk about how decentralization will induce the provision of "market-enhancing public goods"—but it is not entirely clear which goods will produce economic gains. While infrastructure investments are a favorite example of proponents of the decentralization-growth thesis, many economists now attribute growth to investments in human capital, like education. But many local governments are notoriously bad at providing education, in part because intergovernmental market pressures tend to undermine long-term human capital investments.

That too is unsurprising. Inter-jurisdictional competition for growth can and does lead to potentially misplaced investments—stadiums instead of schools, highways instead of health care. There is nothing intrinsic about the market in jurisdictions that ensures that it will produce the right kind of spending, even if we knew what that spending was.

Conclusion: Freeing Cities from a False Constraint

My conclusion about the relationship between decentralization and development echoes Daniel Treisman's, who has argued that "to decentralize, in most settings, requires a leap of faith rather than an application of science."[58] The reference to "faith" in the context of intercity competition is apropos. Treisman argues that decentralization's appeal comes partly from the attraction to market-based theories of government. Though Tiebout did not draw any growth consequences from his market in public goods, the image of cities competing for households has remained alluring for those who evince a preference for markets over governments.

Here then we see how the city is subordinated to the market—how the city's fiscal autonomy is deployed in the service of capital's mobility. Though described in devolutionary terms, the theory of competitive decentralization is intended to *limit* cities, not empower them. That is because the asserted theoretical requirements of growth in the global marketplace for location put a fairly rigorous outer bound on the range of plausible local policies. Cities have no choice but to converge on development- or market-friendly efforts in order to remain competitive. Fiscal decentralization is thereby presented as a "neutral" institutional technology, necessary for the development of those institutions and policies that will lead to economic development.

This is a kind of false necessity.[59] On its own terms, competitive decentralization relies on a set of questionable presuppositions about the expected behavior of local government officials and the assumed causes of growth. The claim that a particular set of laws or a particular institutional arrangement causes development also assumes a distinction between the market and the state—private and public—that is always under construction. The decentralization-growth literature assumes that markets can be preserved or fostered by governments, but it does not tell us how to distinguish between these two realms. As the history of the nineteenth-century city shows, these categories are not natural. They have to be *made*. The city's identity as a "municipal corporation" is an example.

Moreover, the causal claim might be exactly backward. The fluctuating legal authority of cities in the nineteenth and twentieth centuries is a good illustration. As I have argued, the city's formal powers shifted *in response* to newly created wealth, not the other way around. Indeed, suburban interests have conventionally been and are still often aided by the current form of local autonomy that is most common in the United States. That is no surprise—wealth and population have been moving to the suburbs over the last century. Nonetheless, many suburban jurisdictions have seen their fortunes decline in the past few decades. It is thus possible for political power to shift and for institutional arrangements to change. We should in fact expect them to.

The history of state-based federalism in the United States does not prove otherwise. The happy narrative of nineteenth-century American competitive federalism—which holds that federalism helped cause economic growth in the newly industrializing U.S.—entirely forgets that the cities that made the industrial United States were not protected by a robust legal or political autonomy. There is little evidence that the ascendance and decline of the great American industrial cities over the last 150 years or so can be attributed to legal decentralization—those cities' relative formal legal autonomy or legal subordination.

That does not mean that city power is undesirable; only that it should be desired for the right reasons. My goal in challenging the decentralization-growth thesis is not to attack city power but to free cities from a false constraint—to move away from decentralization in the service of markets and toward decentralization in the service of other goals.

One can favor a robust, democratically responsive, politically autonomous city. The argument that such cities will generate growth, however, is more often a claim about the benefits of a market-friendly, non-redistributive, minimalist regulatory government wherever it occurs. We can debate whether such a government actually promotes economic growth. But invoking decentralization as a means to this end simply proves the vulnerability of city status: The city's powers are frequently manipulated in the pursuit of particular substantive ideological and policy goals. Economic growth provides a potent justification for a certain kind of city *powerlessness*. Without that justification, we can more easily think about the other goals a city might pursue and how existing institutions facilitate or obstruct those goals.

3

Vertical Federalism: Making Weak Cities

IF THE DECENTRALIZATION-GROWTH THESIS is unproven, then we are closer to shifting the emphasis of city policy away from pursuing growth and toward pursuing other ends. Whether those ends are achievable, however, turns on the city's power relative to other institutions. The previous chapter argued that the theoretical demands of economic growth are a false constraint on the city's policy choices. The next two chapters turn to a *real* constraint on those choices: U.S.-style, state-based federalism.

My argument in the previous chapter was that the formal institutional division of authority between cities and the state and federal governments has little causal relationship with economic growth. That institutional division of authority, however, *does* affect the city's ability to achieve its other potential goals. U.S.-style, state-based federalism makes for weak cities, though not because cities do not normally exercise a wide range of formal powers. The problem for American cities is that while they exercise power within their sphere, they exercise little political influence outside it. And because states and the federal government exert so much control over the policies and resources that matter to cities, the city's political influence is more important than its formal authority. U.S. cities are not always powerless, but they are politically marginal.

This argument may be somewhat counterintuitive. The United States is often presented as an example of a highly decentralized state. In comparative studies of relative legal decentralization, we find that

American cities often enjoy more formal powers than cities in other countries. U.S. cities generally have the power to elect local leaders, to tax and spend, and to make basic budgeting decisions. Nevertheless, U.S. cities—individually and collectively—do not appear to exercise significant political influence *as* cities. Their ability to achieve the goals that are important to their citizens is often highly constrained.

Some commentators have attributed this lack of influence to the fact that cities are not formally recognized in the U.S. Constitution. In the U.S., as I have noted, federalism is the institutional arrangement that embeds state power, and as a constitutional matter, states exercise plenary power over their political subdivisions. Certainly, the absence of formal recognition means that cities cannot raise a constitutional objection if a state interferes with local governance or even eliminates it altogether. There is no individual federal constitutional right to an elective municipal government—or to any local government at all.

Yet despite their constitutional subordination, cities in the United States still exercise a great deal of legal authority under their own state constitutions and as a matter of the political practice of federalism. Local government constitutes a legitimate third rung of government in the United States; it is well entrenched.

That entrenchment does not necessarily translate into political power, however. For the leaders of the American city, the gap between formal authority and political influence is the arena in which much relevant policy is made. As I argue below, two features of American federalism—the formal separation of functions between the federal, state, and local governments and the vertical competition between government officials—sharply limit local officials' political influence vis-à-vis state and federal officials. Despite the fact that local governments are well-established features of our federal system, state-based federalism does not promote city power. Indeed, the city's formal autonomy masks the city's constitutional marginalization.

That marginalization is reflected in the relative political weakness of city officials. Consider the status of the U.S. mayoralty. As a legal matter, American mayors often govern cities that enjoy significant legal powers—at least as compared with their European counterparts. But mayors also need significant cooperation from state and federal officials to effectuate policy. And though mayors have experienced periods of influence in national policymaking, they tend not to be serious players in national politics, and any political influence they do wield is normally outstripped by state and federal officials.

The weak mayoralty helps illustrate a number of features of American political organization as it is practiced: an elite skepticism of democracy, a belief in technocracy as a solution to political failures, and, importantly, an emphasis on formal, legal decentralization over informal, political decentralization. This last feature is implied by the competitive model of economic growth. Formally defining the relative powers of subnational governments and then preventing interventions that might muddy the distinctions between inter-jurisdictional competitors is viewed as necessary for a functioning intergovernmental marketplace.

As we have already seen, this commitment to formal localism just as easily *limits* city power as it grants it. The irony of localism in the United States is that we are so rhetorically, legally, and ideologically committed to it. Yet, as I conclude below, the exercise of *actual* city power is often treated as highly suspect.

Legal Autonomy and Political Influence

One of the challenges in assessing the relative power of cities in the United States is the sometimes divergent legal status of local governments. As I observed in the previous chapter, under the U.S. Constitution, local governments are convenient agencies of their states, not independent polities. As a formal matter then, there is no constitutional law of local government per se. Doctrinally speaking, the Constitution has little to say about how the states exercise power over their cities.

There are exceptions. The Supreme Court has sometimes treated local governments as constitutionally significant for certain purposes, and it has even occasionally sided with a local government against its state when vindicating some other interest. But these cases represent a kind of "shadow" constitutional law.[1] If one squints, one can discern the vague outlines of a constitutional law of local government, but that law is incidental to and parasitic on some other judicial interest. The bottom line is that, as a general matter, cities are constitutionally subordinate to states, and thus states are mostly unrestrained by U.S. constitutional law in limiting cities' formal powers.

At the same time, however, in most states, cities do enjoy some degree of local autonomy—as we have seen—sometimes as a matter of foundational state statute or more often as a matter of state constitutional grants of home rule. These grants mimic (though are not identical to) the national-state federal relationship. And so, as a matter of state constitutional law, local governments can enjoy significant formal authority, at least on paper. So too, as an administrative matter, local governments in the U.S. are entrenched. And thus, while the U.S. federal system is formally two-tiered, it is as a matter of practice three-tiered: The federal, state, and local governments are conceptually and administratively independent, even if not always and not for all purposes.

The city thus enjoys a somewhat contradictory legal status: It is an instrumentality of the state, but it is also politically autonomous within its sphere—it is an administrative unit as well as a mini-sovereign. These conceptual and descriptive accounts of local power can coexist. As a formal matter, cities in the United States enjoy a significant amount of legal authority, at least when compared with cities in some other western democracies. Local governments usually have taxing authority (though it is limited) and are thus not entirely dependent on grants from higher-level governments. And local governments can generally make decisions about what to spend monies on (though again, the state requires certain kinds of expenditures, like public pension contributions).[2]

Moreover, state home rule or statutory grants of local authority give cities significant authority over local land-use decisions, zoning, condemnation, and urban redevelopment, and over basic local services. State and federal authorities generally do not interfere with local budgeting or fiscal decisions until a city is well into insolvency. And cities are generally politically autonomous. Local officials are elected locally. Except in rare circumstances, the choice of local officials is generally not dictated by the winning political party at the state or national level. And municipal officials can (and do) disagree vociferously with the policy preferences of the party that exercises power statewide or nationally.

That cities enjoy some amount of legal and political autonomy, however, does not mean that city leaders exercise influence over those policies that are in fact most important to their constituents. Indeed, U.S. state-based federalism operates not primarily by formally limiting local legal authority, but by formally endorsing it. The very existence and character of local municipal autonomy tend to limit the city's political influence rather than extend it. In other words, local autonomy and local power are not the same things. The vertical distribution of powers can be a tool of constraint, not empowerment.[3]

As a number of commentators have pointed out, the mere existence of a federal system does not itself guarantee political decentralization. A system in which local governments are wholly dependent on funds from a central government, but in which the central government is entirely responsive to powerful local officials, might have a high degree of political power despite its low degree of legal autonomy. Conversely, local governments that have the formal power to tax and spend may have little power to influence state and national policies that make it difficult for them to operate on a sound fiscal basis. These localities may experience a low degree of political power despite their relatively high degree of legal autonomy. The question, as Sidney Tarrow famously put it, is whether the center moves the periphery or the periphery moves the center.[4]

Federalism and City Power

In the context of American cities at the turn of the twenty-first century, the center appears to dominate. In our federalism, overlapping political authority is the norm, and therefore the city's formal authority tells us very little about the political influence of its elected leaders. That influence is limited. First, because of the existence of three separate governments, each with its own administrative apparatus, local leaders are relatively unimportant when it comes to implementing important state and federal objectives. Second, because locally elected officials are not the only officials who represent "local" interests, the city's political power qua city is easily diluted.

Separate Spheres

I start with a discussion of the first point: the effects of the formal distribution of powers on the city's policy influence. In the United States, formal legal autonomy tends to be equated with the exercise of decentralized power. The assumption is that political power flows from legal authority. This is the essence of categorical or "separate spheres" federalism, according to which the division of political power—the actual exercise of influence over policy outcomes—is assumed to follow from the formal or legal separation of functions.

But, of course, there is no necessary relationship between the formal decentralization of power and the actual exercise of political influence, between "legal localism" and "political localism,"[5] between autonomy and power.

Consider the relative powers of French cities. France has a highly centralized government—it is a "unitary" state in the language of comparative constitutionalism. For most of the twentieth century, financial power and legal authority in France were officially concentrated in the hands of the central state, with localities merely fulfilling state mandates.[6]

But as Walter Nicholls points out, "the ability of the central state to achieve its goals depend[ed] upon the active consent and cooperation of local elected officials." And in the twentieth century, the French mayor became the "territorial gatekeeper," controlling the downward flow of state resources and funneling those resources into urban growth beneficial to the city.[7] Central city mayors exercised power by developing personal relations with central administrators, by lobbying state ministries, and by influencing policy through their representation in parliament and in other national-level councils.

The key element to French mayoral power, however, was the dependence of central authorities on local cooperation to accomplish state ends. The French mayor's power was derived in significant part by his ability to exert political control over national directives. In other words, the mayor exercised significant power because he operated within a highly centralized constitutional system, not in spite of doing so. Mike Goldsmith has described local power in terms of access. As he has observed, cities with limited functional responsibilities or discretion may have more access to the center than do cities that have greater functional responsibilities and discretion.[8]

For those who are steeped in the ideology of American federalism, the robustness of local influence in an otherwise-unitary constitutional system might seem anomalous. And indeed the Supreme Court's federalism doctrine assumes that political power follows from legal power.

Consider *Printz v. United States*, which involved a challenge to a federal gun-control law that required local law enforcement officials to conduct background checks on gun buyers. By a 5-4 majority, the U.S. Supreme Court held that the federal law unconstitutionally "commandeered" state officials in contravention of the states' sovereignty. The Court held that respect for the distinction between state and national power limits the federal government's ability to use local officials when pursuing federal goals. If the federal government wants to perform background checks, it must do so itself.[9] It should be noted at the outset that the *Printz* challenge was brought by local sheriffs, not state officials. But the U.S. Supreme Court did not view such a distinction as relevant, at least not for purposes of its federalism decisions—which treat local officials as state appointees for constitutional purposes. The Court has stated that the Constitution requires the drawing of boundaries between what is "truly national and what is truly local."[10] But what the Court means is that the Constitution requires a distinction between states—no matter how large and centralized—and the federal government. Localism and federalism are not the same thing, though the Court often treats them as if they are.

Printz is also notable for its fairly rigid and formalistic approach to central-local relations. Writing for the dissenters, Justice John Paul Stevens pointed out the irony of the majority's constitutional logic. As he noted, the federal government could avoid "commandeering" state officials by using federal officials to do the same work. But, as Justice Stephen Breyer observed, "[w]hy, or how, would what the majority sees as a constitutional alternative—the creation of a new federal gun law bureaucracy, or the expansion of an existing federal bureaucracy—better promote either state sovereignty or individual liberty?"[11]

Breyer went on to question the theoretical connection between formal legal authority and political influence. As Breyer argued, a constitutional system that creates rigid obstacles to intergovernmental cooperation by treating sub-federal governments as bureaucratically (and formally) autonomous does not necessarily lead to increased local power. In many European federal democracies, Breyer noted, constitutionalists believe that the assignment of centrally mandated duties to local authorities "interferes less not more" with the authority of local government.[12]

Preventing the central government from ever requiring local governments to implement federal directives in fact reduces local control by mandating the creation of a centralized implementation bureaucracy, independent from and unaccountable to local authorities. The formal separation of powers maintains the locality's legal autonomy, preventing interference by central authorities in some (limited number of) cases. But the formal separation of powers also means that local officials might have little influence over policy when central governments do intervene or in cases in which the locality would otherwise desire intervention.

In fact, federalism may be contrary to decentralization. In *Printz*, the Court was debating how to protect state power from central encroachment. Both the majority and dissenters assumed that federalism—rightly implemented—would foster political decentralization. But some scholars have argued that federalism and decentralization are themselves at odds—that federal political systems impede the actual exercise of *truly* local power.

Frank Cross, for example, has argued that federal regimes are generally *less* decentralized than unitary ones, citing a number of empirical studies including one that found that larger states in the U.S. are more decentralized than smaller ones. Other scholars have also persuasively argued that the American form of federalism always impedes significant decentralization to local governments.[13]

There are two commonsense arguments for why federal regimes might be less amenable to the exercise of municipal power. First, larger organizations are generally more decentralized than smaller ones, for obvious reasons: Implementation and monitoring are costly in big organizations. We might therefore expect a large, unitary government to devolve significant powers to smaller-scaled entities, many of them smaller than American states. The power of French cities in a unitary state is an example.

Second, in a federal system, regional or state governments will often take up the policy and fiscal space that would otherwise be occupied by local governments in a unitary system. Cross and others have argued that federalism always impedes localism, because it interposes a regional government between the center and the periphery. The intuition is that a middle tier of government will reduce the political power of local officials.

This may have real-world consequences for the provision of municipal services. Some studies have argued that federal systems are more corrupt and less effective at delivering government services than unitary ones. The interposition of a third layer of government might understandably increase the number of officials who need to be bribed and the number of bureaucracies that need to be fed.[14]

This finding is consistent with studies that show that local officials compete with state and federal officials for policymaking space. Elisabeth Gerber and Daniel Hopkins have argued, for example, that city policy outcomes differ when "local actors are less constrained by political actors at other levels of the U.S. federal system."[15] The political science literature has debated the question of whether local public officials' political preferences play any role in the making of local policy. A significant literature has asserted, for example, that city leaders from one political party do not appear to govern very differently from city leaders from a different political party.

What Gerber and Hopkins find, however, is that municipal policy outcomes appear to depend on the policy at issue, and specifically on the degree of shared authority between cities, states, and the federal government for that policy. In areas of shared authority, city policy tends to be homogeneous despite differences in local officials' political ideologies. In areas of less shared authority, cities appear to diverge along partisan lines. The conclusion seems fairly obvious in retrospect: When state and federal officials share authority for policymaking, city leaders are going to be less politically autonomous.

The problem is not just overlapping authority and a concomitant inability for local leaders to influence the center, however. Cities are also hampered by the particular *form* that decentralization takes: a combination of formal legal autonomy and local political subservience.

For American cities, the problem is not that states fail to devolve significant powers and responsibilities to local governments, but rather that the ideological and formal commitment to localism is selective. State officials intervene fairly regularly in local affairs, but rarely to take on the baseline social welfare responsibilities of tax base-dependent local governments. They are quick to intervene to counter local decisions they disagree with, but slow to intervene to take on the responsibility for providing basic municipal services. Cities thus may have significant responsibilities, but insufficient resources to meet them.[16]

For example, even in states whose cities enjoy constitutional grants of home rule authority, the regulatory authority that cities exercise is almost always contingent on grants of authority from the state or subject to revision by the state, often through regular legislation. State legislatures have been aggressive in overruling local decisions with which they do not agree. Recent attempts by cities to regulate predatory lending, adopt minimum wage laws, or ban hydraulic fracking have often been rejected or overruled by state legislatures. In a number of high-profile cases, state legislatures preempted city ordinances that had extended anti-discrimination protections to gays, lesbians, and transgender individuals.[17]

States have also been aggressive in preventing cities from taxing their own citizens for local services, and have adopted statewide tax and spending restrictions that often hit cities particularly hard. For purposes of state intervention, the city is treated like a subordinate state agency; the city's range of action is quite limited.

This state interference with local decision-making does not alter the city's responsibility to provide basic services to its citizens, however. Cities are primarily responsible for the basic health, safety, and welfare needs of the populace. State and federal elected officials can thus pick and choose when and under what circumstances to intervene. And because the provision of basic municipal services is understood to be a local responsibility, the variations among localities in that provision normally do not concern the state.[18] This works well for localities that are resource-rich; it tends to work less well for those that are not. The well-documented gap between cities and suburbs over the course of the twentieth century is in part a product of this formal division of responsibilities.

Moreover, cities are deeply affected by the decisions made by neighboring jurisdictions and by state and national tax, spending, immigration, labor, and industrial policies. Regional or macroeconomic forces are not easily susceptible to policies that can be pursued by municipalities acting alone. In a highly fragmented metropolitan region, there are often hundreds of local governments, each asserting control over its portion of regional development, but none able to manage it. Cities cannot print money, engage in countercyclical spending, or enter into trade agreements. Much of what city leaders need requires the assistance of higher-level governments. Indeed, formal localism often checks central interference where it would do certain localities the most good—for example, in redistributing monies from richer jurisdictions to poorer ones.

Consider again the federal gun-control legislation at issue in the *Printz* case. It is notable that the majority of large cities where urban gun violence is most pressing supported, and continue to support, federal background checks implemented by local officials. The background checks assist cities in their ongoing struggle with illegal guns; the lack of a national program undermines local efforts, as guns purchased illegally in one city can easily end up in another.

As *Printz* illustrates, honoring the dignity of states may undermine the policy preferences of cities. Indeed, the constitutional status of states means that when the federal government seeks to intervene on behalf of cities, state-based dignitary interests can trump. State sovereignty can interpose a significant barrier to achieving joint federal-local aims.

There is certainly no guarantee that federal officials will be more responsive to cities than are state officials. That being said, the dynamics of state legislative and U.S. congressional politics can be very different. As to the former, we might expect state legislative battles to result in significant geographic-specific winners and losers. State politics often involves intrastate conflicts between, for example, upstate and downstate interests, cities and suburbs, rural and urban.

In contrast, geographical battles might be less particular in the national legislature. To be sure, the U.S. Congress has its geographic conflicts. But it is also more likely to adopt large, cross-geographical programs that assist all cities or rural areas or suburbs across all states. As Cross points out, "much of the supplementary funding for local governments comes directly from the federal government, rather than the states."[19] Consider also that many statewide leaders have been willing to reject federal health care monies under Medicaid—something the Court has held that they have the right to do—while many cities in those states would gladly accept federal funds.

Health care is not the only example of the conflicting priorities between states and cities. Despite formal decentralization, at the turn of the twenty-first century, the urban "periphery" in the United States appears to have limited ability to move the center. Consider some dramatic examples: New Orleans is reduced to begging for state and federal assistance in the aftermath of Hurricane Katrina; Philadelphia's school district (one of the largest in the country) is forced to the brink of insolvency by the state's refusal to fully fund it; Detroit is taken over by the governor's hand-picked receiver after the state refuses to come to the city's financial aid.

Much of local leaders' weakness may be attributable to "politics." It may be that the difficulties of urban mayors stem from the disjuncture between Republican legislatures and governors and Democratic and black-dominated cities, aided and abetted by political gerrymanders that limit urban influence in state legislatures and the U.S. Congress. The fact that the U.S. Senate favors rural states over urban ones is also a factor. The increasing "nationalization" of state politics and the con-comitant polarization of state legislatures play a role too.

But also important is that the formal independence of the local, state, and federal governments means that state and federal govern-ments rarely need the direct cooperation or assistance of local officials to achieve state or national aims. And where states decide to govern, municipalities are going to be constrained. Thus, whatever the merits of unitary versus federal regimes in the abstract, as implemented, U.S. state-based constitutional federalism does not advance cities' interests.

Political Redundancy

For local officials attempting to influence policy, the problem of verti-cal departmentalism is compounded by a second feature of U.S.-style federalism: vertical redundancy. City leaders do not have a monopoly on local representation. Aside from other city officials, there are sig-nificant numbers of state and federal elected officials—namely, state representatives and members of Congress—who represent "local" con-stituents. All of these officials are in competition for political credit and spoils. All are also nominally responsive to local constituencies, but not directly to the city as a whole. The result is a political competi-tion for influence and money in which local officials are at a distinct disadvantage.

The most mundane form of competition is the direct competition to take credit and avoid blame. State and national elected officials have incentives to take popular positions on state and national matters and push any negative consequences onto lower-level officials. State and federal tax "relief" (which often merely pushes the cost of providing essential services onto localities) is an example of this phenomenon, as are unfunded mandates. National and state politicians want credit both for providing services and for cutting taxes; they can do both by adopting laws that shift costs to local governments. The No Child Left Behind Act—a federal enactment that requires states and localities to hew to national education targets—is a primary example of this occurrence.[20]

The turn of the twentieth century saw a more venal example of this competition, as state legislators co-opted the spoils systems of urban political machines. As I have previously observed, state-level corruption explains in part why Progressive-Era political reformers sought to insulate municipal government from state legislative interference through adoption of constitutional home rule guarantees. One of the reformers' concerns was that state legislatures—dominated as they were by representatives of rural areas—were generally hostile to city interests. But another fear was the corrupt inclination of those legislators who actually represented districts within the city. If state legislators could adopt laws regulating all aspects of municipal government, as they did on a relatively regular basis in the late 1800s and early 1900s, reform control of municipal government would accomplish little as long as the city's state legislative delegation or the wider state apparatus was controlled by the political machine. Reformers wanted to insulate city government from state government and then work on the political problem of electing local pro-reform candidates within the city.[21]

In addition to their interest in seeking political credit, state and national officials—though locally elected—often have other widely divergent interests from city officials, in part because they have to be responsive to larger state and national interest groups and in part because they are accountable to a different local electorate. Because state legislative districts and U.S. congressional districts are normally not coextensive with municipal boundaries, the city qua city is not "represented" at these levels of government. State and national elected officials have strong incentives to inject themselves into city politics, often on behalf of their relevant local electorate, but only incidentally on behalf of the local polity.

As noted, the conventional story is that state legislatures, dominated as they are by rural and suburban interests, are hostile to big cities, and there seems to be some truth to that standard view. But what seems more in evidence, as Gerald Gamm and Thad Kousser have argued, is that big-city bills fail in the state legislature in large numbers because of disagreements within the city's own legislative delegation.[22]

Even in home rule states, local governments often must obtain legislative authorization to regulate in wholly municipal matters that will only or primarily affect that locality. Normally, one might expect nonlocal state legislators to defer to the stated interests of the local legislative delegation—and indeed, that is often the case. But the failure rate for big-city bills is significantly higher than for bills that pertain to smaller cities and towns across the state, which signals that deference is not occurring. The heterogeneity of big-city interest groups and the disparate interests of state legislators representing districts from the same city appear to explain that result.

It is no surprise that state officials might be responding to different constituencies than local officials. Consider some high-profile political battles between the mayor of New York City, Bill de Blasio, and the governor of New York State, Andrew Cuomo. Though both are Democrats, de Blasio was elected as a populist and progressive, with plans to expand the city's social welfare policy footprint. His proposals for universal citywide pre-K programs, limitations on charter schools, and a minimum wage increase in New York City, however, were opposed by the governor. In particular, the governor objected to de Blasio's proposal to tax the city's highest earners to fund the pre-K plan. Cuomo also objected to de Blasio's proposed restrictions on charter schools. In both cases, Cuomo was responding to significant and vocal city-based constituencies: wealthy taxpayers and proponents of charter schools. Though he did get the legislature to adopt universal pre-K, de Blasio lost on the tax, as well as the limitations on charter schools and the minimum wage increase. Shortly after vetoing de Blasio's proposal for a higher, expansive minimum wage ordinance, however, Cuomo proposed his own statewide minimum wage increase. Though Cuomo's proposal was much more limited in scope, as well as in dollar amount, he effectively co-opted de Blasio's idea while simultaneously limiting its impact on his pro-business constituents.[23]

As for many mayors throughout the country, dependence on state (and sometimes federal) officials is the current policy and political reality for the mayor of New York City. Despite his formal authority, much if not most of the mayor's important initiatives (and even many not-so-important ones) have to be approved by the state legislature. As noted in the *New York Times*:

> As long as he is mayor, Mr. de Blasio is beholden to the murky mechanics of Albany, whose permission he requires for even the most minimal changes to city policy. On Monday, Mr. de Blasio signed a bill lowering the city's speed limit to 25 miles per hour, a measure he first had to negotiate with Mr. Cuomo earlier this year, when the mayor needed approval from the state legislature. . . . Mr. de Blasio has ambitious policy plans in store. . . . Few of those plans will materialize without Mr. Cuomo's help.[24]

The previous mayor of New York, Michael Bloomberg, also required the cooperation of the governor and the state legislature to achieve his more significant aims. Bloomberg's proposal to develop a stadium on the West Side in an effort to attract both the Olympics and a professional football team to New York City was resisted by the then-speaker of the state assembly, Sheldon Silver. Before his conviction on federal corruption charges, Silver represented the Sixty-Fifth Assembly District, which includes portions of lower Manhattan. As speaker of the assembly, Silver was one of three officials on the Public Authorities Control Board, which also included the senate majority leader and the governor. To obtain state financing for the stadium, Bloomberg had to obtain board approval for the issuance of state bonds. But Bloomberg could not convince Silver, who wanted to focus on downtown redevelopment in his district, to support a stadium on the West Side.[25]

Consider also how the mayor's influence over redevelopment at the former site of the World Trade Center was mediated by state and federal agencies and thus indirectly by state and federal elected officials. The commission nominally in charge of the redevelopment effort is the Lower Manhattan Development Corporation (LMDC), which is governed by a sixteen-member board, half of which is appointed by the governor of New York and half by the mayor. Thus, the mayor has some influence on the LMDC, though no more than the governor. The LMDC is a subsidiary of the Empire State Development Corporation, whose nine members and chair are appointed by the governor. Another agency, the Port Authority of New York and New Jersey, whose members are appointed by the governors of New York and New Jersey, owns the World Trade Center site. And finally, the LMDC is funded by a Community Development Block Grant administered and regulated by the Department of Housing and Urban Development, a federal agency. The mayor's competitors for influence are thus formidable, and include the governor, state legislators, and the congressional delegation from New York City, including New York's two U.S. senators. All of them were arguably as influential, or more influential, than the mayor in the rebuilding of the World Trade Center site.

The rebuilding of lower Manhattan was unusual in its scope and national visibility. Nevertheless, it is indicative of the ways in which state and national officials influence local decisions.[26] These officials often operate through state-created public authorities that control important aspects of city policy. Specialized agencies, created by both state governments and the federal government, undermine mayoral authority. Moreover, the intergovernmental grants that fund such agencies often contribute to the competition for political credit.

Unlike many other developed industrial nations that use block grants or generalized revenue-sharing to help fund local governments, the United States tends to use a system of program-specific or selective grants. This style of intergovernmental fund transfer increases state and federal politicians' involvement in local affairs, for it makes every grant a potential political investment and a battleground for conflicting local interests.

Because state and national funds are both necessary to achieve many city ends and often program-specific, the city must obtain the cooperation of state and federal elected officials if it is to engage in large-scale public works projects, fund health, education, and welfare services, or provide housing or other basic amenities to its citizens. Those state and federal officials' political interests are not always or even usually aligned

with the mayor's. And those officials regularly broker relationships between local constituents and state and federal agencies. They influence
the direction and flow of funds to organizations and groups in their
districts. And they seek political credit for the results.

Mayors thus approach the state and federal governments as suppli-
cants. Mayors come to Washington to lobby for aid or assistance, but
they tend not to have ongoing relationships with federal elected officials or bureaucracies. Instead of being direct participants in state and
federal policymaking, they are outsiders to it, only as influential as any
other representative of a group or institution seeking government aid
might be.

Local elected officials are thus often preoccupied with lobbying state
and national government officials, a task that they have undertaken
with mixed results. At the height of the New Deal, mayors had a significant voice in national affairs through the United States Conference
of Mayors (USCM), which was established in the early 1930s and was
an important political component of the New Deal coalition. Fiorello
LaGuardia, the fifth president of the USCM, was a friend of Roosevelt's,
and that connection meant that the cities exercised influence in the administration of New Deal programs and the flow of federal resources
to the cities. Postwar mayors, like Richard Lee of New Haven, also had
some success in directing the flow of federal resources to their cities,
especially during the War on Poverty in the 1960s and early '70s. And
when mayors controlled the local Democratic machine, as Richard
Daley did in Chicago, they had a significant voice in party politics even
at the national level.[27]

In all of these instances, mayoral influence tended to turn on the
mayor's ability to turn out the vote for state and national politicians. But
these urban political coalitions were often short-lived. After LaGuardia
(and by the end of the New Deal), the USCM never regained its stat-
ure in Washington. And while the War on Poverty brought significant
federal funds to cities, those programs often bypassed local politicians.
Indeed, federal government programs were often designed to avoid the
mayor's office altogether by mandating the creation of independent
local agencies to handle federal funds.

More importantly, suburbanization and the declining strength of
local and national political parties reduced the importance of mayors

as vote-getters. As Margaret Weir has argued, interest groups have replaced parties as the leading instruments of legislation at the state level. Before the dominance of interest groups, Weir notes, cities had the ability to make legislative deals by playing rural or suburban interests against one another. But in an era of reduced party influence and increased suburbanization, legislators are less responsive to local interests, and the urban mayoralty has lost much of its influence in the state and national political marketplaces.[28]

Indeed, the relative political invisibility of American mayors is indicative of their relatively limited political influence. Most mayors—even those in big cities—have little name recognition outside their cities. Moreover, the very departmentalization of local, state, and national government has effects on politicians' career trajectories. In unitary systems, it might not be uncommon for politicians to begin their careers at the local level and work their way up through regional administrations, culminating in a career in the central administration.[29] In the United States, the local, regional, and federal units of government are constitutionally distinct, and often politically distinct as well. Local office is not a prerequisite for state or national office, and it may even be a detriment. As one observer of the New York mayoralty noted, "[w]hat [mayors] must do to get elected and re-elected are the very things that prevent them from ever moving on to higher office."[30]

In fact, except in unusual circumstances, the mayoralty in the United States tends not to be a precursor to higher political visibility, state or national executive authority, or even a position in the national legislature. Very few of those who have served in the U.S. House of Representatives or the U.S. Senate have ever had experience as a local elected official. Only three presidents began their careers as mayors, and few who obtained significant posts in the federal administration did so because they performed admirably as a mayor. Local officials have experienced periods of influence in national policymaking, but, except in rare circumstances, local officials are not serious players in national politics and rarely use the mayoralty as a stepping stone to national political prominence. The mayoralty is both a thankless job and often a dead-end one.[31]

This political reality reflects a structural one. Mayors tend to be politically salient in constitutional systems that permit cities to be represented at higher levels of government, as in Germany or Russia. In the United States, cities are not represented in state or national councils, and one need not hold local office to represent local interests. This is not to say that local political officials cannot influence national and state policy. In some states with large cities and few other population centers, cities can dominate the political landscape.

Nevertheless, the layering of political influence in the U.S. federal system tends to fracture the city as a polity and thus reduce the influence of any one political leader or of the city as a whole. The city's vertical political fragmentation limits the ability of its leaders to effectuate public policy; the mayor's status is a reflection of this political reality. It is notable that since the late 1970s, federal aid to local governments and to programs that serve urban populations has declined significantly and continuously.[32] It is further worth noting that Michael Bloomberg may be able to exercise more influence on national policy—in particular gun-control and immigration policy—as the current leader of a very well-funded political action committee than he did as the mayor of the largest and arguably the most important city in the country.

Technocracy versus Democracy

The weak mayor is not only a function of a federal system that fragments city power. It is also a product of a political culture that treats the city mostly as a problem of administration, rather than as a robust site for the exercise of popular political energy. Market-based theories of local economic growth reinforce this conception. Local autonomy is favored to the extent that it is deployed in service of the competition for investment and the efficient provision of local services. The exercise of local democratic preferences that might depart from those two imperatives, however, is often highly suspect. The city's formal authority but limited political influence reflects this bifurcation.

The city as convenient administrative unit and the city as sovereign point to two conceptions of city policymaking: the technocratic and the democratic. The former is consistent with the notion that the city's primary goal is to promote economic development: The city should both be an instrument of business and be "run like a business." Conceiving of the city as an administrative entity also serves the interests of political actors at the state and national level—it heightens their own political influence. The city emerges as a political force and a site for robust democratic participation only intermittently.

Indeed, the technocratic conception of municipal government is so dominant that departures from it often seem quite subversive (and sometimes are). Because cities are so often viewed as problems of administration, local forays into social and redistributive economic policy are widely regarded with suspicion.

A nice example is the municipal foray into the same-sex marriage debate. In February of 2004, when he was mayor of San Francisco, Gavin Newsom argued that he was required by the California and U.S. Constitutions to order the City of San Francisco to issue marriage licenses to same-sex couples. Newsom argued that state and federal guarantees of equal protection required his city to provide marriage licenses on a gender-neutral basis. (He turned out to be right, but it took until 2015 for the U.S. Supreme Court to decide the issue.[33]) Following San Francisco's lead, a number of other cities throughout the country began to issue same-sex marriage licenses as well.

The mayors' actions elicited a predictable response. State officials sued the mayors, demanding that they comply with state statutes. And most courts sided with the states. In California, the state supreme court issued a strongly worded ruling that voided all the marriages performed for same-sex couples in San Francisco.[34]

The opinion is notable for its rhetorical reining-in of wayward local public officials. The city was asking for a determination on the merits (i.e., whether it was acting unconstitutionally in denying same-sex couples marriage licenses), but the court viewed the city's issuance of licenses as akin to civil disobedience. "[T]he scope of authority entrusted to our public officials," stated the court, "involves the determination of a fundamental question that lies at the heart of our political system: the role of the rule of law in a society that justly prides itself on being 'a government of laws, and not of men' (or women)." Rule of law values dictate that a local public official charged with a ministerial duty cannot be "free to make up his or her own mind whether a statute is constitutional and whether it must be obeyed."[35]

Whether a local official must always comply with a state statute that is arguably unconstitutional is a tougher legal question than the majority opinion indicates. At least one of the California court's dissenters expressed concern about the breadth of the majority's ruling. What is noteworthy about the majority opinion, however, is its disinclination to view the mayoralty as anything other than an inferior ministerial office. Mayor Newsom's actions were subversive because he challenged the subordinate posture of cities. He not only laid claim to a role in interpreting the state and federal constitutions (thus challenging the authority of the judiciary), but he also asserted a populist vision of the mayoralty that did not accept its relatively weak constitutional status. That departure was viewed as quite threatening, even by a California Supreme Court that was otherwise sympathetic to same-sex marriage.

This is not to say that the California Supreme Court would have treated other public officials with any more deference. What was unique about Newsom's actions, however, is that he challenged the conventional division of authority between state and city, asserting a power to act on behalf of the city and its residents despite the clear limits of his legal authority.

In the last decade, Newsom's more aggressive attitude has become more common. Cities have become more willing to regulate individual rights and social welfare, and adopt other measures viewed as being well outside the city's purview. Mayor Bill de Blasio's efforts in New York City are again a good example. De Blasio's numerous policy campaigns— universal pre-K education and a living wage are two examples—reflect the increasing effort, taken up by mayors in cities elsewhere as well, to fill in gaps in social welfare provision. In an era in which state and national governments are increasingly at political stalemate, or, at best, are retreating from serious urban policy and social welfarist agendas, some cities have sought to respond to both the substantive and participatory demands of their constituencies.

Nevertheless, managerial competence and business-friendliness have become so closely associated that policies considered hostile to business are understood as lacking sophistication or technocratic expertise. De Blasio's critics have sounded a great deal like the progressive technocrats of the Progressive Era. The mayor, these critics argue, will scare off wealthy taxpayers, overcompensate the unions, overregulate business, undermine public safety, and otherwise destroy the city's fiscal health.[36]

That the exercise of mayoral power would invoke such fears is predictable considering the historic American ambivalence toward the exercise of urban power. The weak mayor is an ongoing trope. Indeed, the most conspicuous characteristic of the office of the modern American mayoralty is how rare it is. A unified municipal executive—akin to the American presidency—has generally been disfavored except for a brief period at the turn of the twentieth century. Few cities have it and few reformers want it.

This was not always so. In the late 1800s, an era in which city government was characterized by many as a "conspicuous failure," the mayoralty seemed to hold promise as a possible instrument for reform. Early progressive reformers like Frank Goodnow, John Bullitt, and Frederic Howe advocated a strong mayoralty, arguing that centralizing power in the executive would promote accountability, transparency, and democracy.[37] The reformers had in mind a mayoralty that could act directly for the people, untarnished by the city machines, uncorrupted by the ward leaders and the parochialism of the city councils, and independent of big business interests.

Frederic Howe's 1905 *The City: The Hope of Democracy* captures the tenor of the times, at least among some subset of progressive urbanists. Howe, a reformer and author who served in the Ohio Senate and the Cleveland City Council and later in the Roosevelt administration, argued that urban reformers had "voted democracy a failure." Instead of deploying democracy to the benefit of good government, they had convinced themselves that "mass government will not work in municipal affairs." Reformers sought to address corruption by treating the city as a "business concern" and by putting the city's affairs "in the hands of commissions or experts." As Howe pointed out, "A businessman's government is their highest ideal."[38]

It was not Howe's. Municipal reformers' inclination to suppress urban democracy by fragmenting executive power and placing authority in boards and commissions was driven by the reality of municipal corruption, but it was also driven by the notion that urban democracy was potentially lawless. For Howe and other decentralist progressives, however, the real threat to good government was not the democratic mobs, but state and local elites who suppressed local democratic will. The attraction of the strong mayor for these early reformers was not efficiency. Municipal government was to be designed to promote democratic energy, to foster cities that could lead a revolution in good government from the bottom up.

The strong mayoralty offered two benefits to the democrat that a more diffuse structure could not: accountability and the possibility of dynamism. "The boss," Howe argued, "appears under any system, whether the government be lodged with the mayor, the council, with boards, or commissions."[39] But under a strong mayor, the exercise of power is easily identified: "Attention can be focussed on a single official, whereas it is difficult to follow boards, commissions, or a large council, each member of which is seeking to shift the burden of responsibility on to someone else."[40] An elected, centralized executive with complete authority over appointments and city departments was endorsed by the National Municipal League in its first Model City Charter, adopted in 1900.[41] An elected city council would serve as the legislative branch, with an independent civil service commission operating to counter the old spoils system.

In fact, power was shifting to the executive just as urban governance became more complicated and executive administration became more necessary. As cities began to engage in significant infrastructure investments related to the burgeoning urban population—waterworks, libraries, parks, sewer systems—professional administration was replacing layperson stewardship. In the late nineteenth century, mayors began to take the reins of city government from the city fathers—the aldermen, city councilmen, and selectmen—who had been the amateur governors of the antebellum city. The role of the mayor was greater than it had been previously because the role of municipal government was greater than it had been previously.

But the mayor's official ascendancy was short-lived, for competing power bases were emerging—specifically, special-purpose districts and state-created authorities, sometimes responsive to the mayor and sometimes not. A spate of charter activity resulted in the interposition of boards and commissions between the executive and city departments as a means of insulating the departments from cronyism and corruption. The complicated layering of municipal bodies began almost immediately and mocked the first Model City Charter's efforts to centralize power in an executive.[42]

By 1915, when the National Municipal League published its second Model City Charter, the strong mayor had been completely excised. In 1900, Galveston, Texas, turned governance over to a special commission charged with responding to the flooding of the city. Subsequently, commission government became popular among municipal reformers. A number of pioneering cities combined the commission form with a professional city manager, analogizing the municipal corporation to the private business corporation.[43]

The council-manager plan, in which an elected council placed administrative powers and responsibilities in the hands of an appointed, professional city manager, appealed to business-minded city fathers. As reformer John Patterson argued, "[a] city is a great business enterprise whose stockholders are the people.... Our municipal affairs would be placed upon a strict business basis and directed, not by partisans either Republican or Democratic, but by men who are skilled in business management and social science...."[44]

The council-manager also dovetailed nicely with Progressive-Era reformers' faith in expert administration. And it reflected elite opposition grounded in paternalistic and nativist sentiments. The council-manager plan distanced the administration of the city from politics. Reformers assumed that council members would serve part-time and most municipal undertakings would be committed to a nonpartisan professional answerable to the council but not directly to the voters. The council-manager plan became the Municipal League's dominant model.

Howe's strong mayor in the democratic city has thus been mostly repressed. In six subsequent Model City Charters, including the most recent 2003 edition, the Municipal League has advocated a council-manager structure. That structure was and continues to be attractive, as evinced by the steady increase in the number of cities that have adopted the council-manager plan.[45]

Indeed, the office of the mayoralty does not exist or exists only for ceremonial purposes in a significant percentage of cities. And to the extent that it does exist, the mayoralty is often limited by numerous boards and commissions mandated by state and local law: Budget authority may be administrative; department heads or commission boards may be insulated from mayoral control by set terms of office; other executive officials may be elected citywide; unions may have charter-protected rights;

or significant power may be vested in a chief administrative officer who is answerable only indirectly to the mayor. To be sure, there have been some recent movements in a few larger cities to place local schools under mayoral control. But as Gerald Frug and David Barron have shown, generally, mayors exercise fairly limited control over school administration, local land-use decisions, and the city's transportation, sewer, water, or electric services.[46]

In this regime, the mayor is normally a figurehead, and political power is purposefully fragmented. In most cities, this reformist vision of expert administration, insulated from democratic control and independent of political power, has dominated.

This "professionalization" of city administration provides a comforting image of governance in which executive power (in fact, the exercise of political power of any kind) is submerged and repressed. Weak-mayor charters and the dominance of the council-manager model reflect the widespread notion that municipal government is mainly administrative in nature.

This notion reinforces the dominant conception of the city as a product that can be improved in the local government marketplace. The rhetoric of competition, the idea of the city as a business, and the ideology of municipal technocracy all cabin city power and importantly enhance the power of state and federal officials. Treating the city as a business concern also reflects and reinforces, as one commentator on the weak mayor put it, "the persistence of elite ambivalence toward democratic politics."[47]

Conclusion: "Things Could Be Worse. I Could Be a Mayor."

Lyndon Johnson famously quipped that "[things] could be worse. I could be a mayor."[48] City leaders exist in a system that demands they meet their responsibilities, but often without the power to do so. The mayor is a "little Caesar"—the head of a municipal bureaucracy that is politically and formally separate from the state and federal bureaucracies. Within her sphere, the mayor may be able to exercise significant authority, but that sphere is limited, and she exercises relatively little influence outside of it.[49]

As I observed in the previous chapter, such an intergovernmental system is justified by a competitive model of city growth and decline—one that emphasizes the provision of efficient government services by fiscally autonomous subnational jurisdictions. If one adopts such a view, then it is relatively easy to assume that municipal success or failure is primarily a problem of management. Competing visions of the mayoralty preoccupy city charter reformers in large part because municipal government has historically been understood as requiring a tradeoff between democratic responsiveness and managerial competence. The mayoralty has often been suspect because it seems to pose the starkest choice between democracy and good government.

Thus, like the city it represents, the mayoralty embodies the ambivalences of the democratic experiment: the simultaneous attraction and revulsion toward the exercise of political power, the professed allegiance to—and deep skepticism of—local self-government. The rhetorical commitment to federalism—as if it were a bulwark for local self-government when it is often contrary to it—is evidence of this ambivalence. The very commitment to the vertical division of authority produces American cities that are "constitutionally" parochial.

Whether a city *can* govern depends in large part on whether we *want* the city to govern. While we pay lip service to the idea of political decentralization, the specific features of American-style state-based federalism tend to undermine city power. The city's formal powers are often restricted by states, for state officials are in competition with local officials to gain political credit and avoid political blame. But more importantly, even when cities exercise significant formal legal autonomy, the political influence of city officials over the policies emanating from the center is limited. As I have argued, state-based federalism does not foster growth in cities. But it does, contrary to conventional wisdom, undermine city power.

4

Horizontal Federalism: Encouraging Footloose Capital

THE VERTICAL DISTRIBUTION OF authority between cities, states, and the federal government is a real constraint on city power. This chapter now turns to the horizontal aspects of U.S.-based federalism and comes to a similar conclusion. The rules of horizontal federalism govern how states and cities within states interact—in particular how and under what circumstances sub-federal governments can favor their own residents, impose barriers to trade, or subsidize the flow of capital into the jurisdiction. In other words, the horizontal aspects of U.S. federalism determine how legally salient the borders between states and between cities will be.

This is important, for cities are defined by their jurisdictional borders, and so any account of city power has to contend with how those borders are created and defended, and to whose advantage. The previous chapter addressed the division of political authority between local, state, and federal governments. This chapter addresses the formal and informal rules that govern the political boundaries between states and between local governments in the metropolitan area.

There are good reasons to examine the constitutional rules that govern metropolitan-area borders from the perspective of the city. The conventional wisdom is that cities have no choice but to chase mobile capital around the globe, but the truth is that much of what matters to cities occurs within metropolitan areas. Borders within metropolitan areas matter—a lot. Indeed, the jurisdictional boundaries between local governments in a metropolitan area often determine a city's fate. The city's borders establish its taxable real estate, its economic, civic, and social assets, and its jurisdictional and regulatory reach. More importantly, those borders establish a significant separation between any given city and the local government jurisdictions on the other side of the line. This separation makes an enormous difference to the city's residents, as one's access to public services is normally a function of where one resides. Empirical research has established what is already well known: that where one resides has significant effects on one's life chances.[1]

Moreover, as I observed in chapter 1, the cross-border movements of persons, goods, and capital are importantly local. Though we tend to talk about interstate or international trade and labor flows, it is more accurate to talk about the movement of persons, goods, and capital between and among metropolitan areas. Persons, goods, and capital do not flow indiscriminately across state lines; they follow identifiable inter-metropolitan patterns—say, between New York and Chicago or San Francisco and Boston. As urban theorists have pointed out, the flow of goods and services among metropolitan areas "is comparable to trade flows between nations."[2] And despite the increasing pace of global trade, much economic activity still takes place within metropolitan areas, among consumers who live relatively near one another.[3] Indeed, as I have noted, the gross metropolitan product of the largest U.S. regions dwarfs many countries and vastly exceeds the combined gross domestic product of many states. The U.S. economy is dominated by intra- and inter-metropolitan trade and labor flows. An account of the American common market that emphasizes interstate cross-border relationships can therefore only be partial.

Metropolitan areas—like the nation as a whole—are obviously common markets in the most essential ways. There is no question that inter-local relations in the United States have the basic features of a free trade regime: Cities (like states) do not exercise control over their own currency, they do not have formal immigration controls, and they cannot directly restrict the import of goods through the imposition of tariffs. These features are commonly understood as prerequisites for economic integration and are the basic building blocks of the American economic and political union.

Significantly, however, the extent and degree of inter-municipal openness is contingent on legal rules. And an examination of those rules introduces an important qualification to the conventional assumption of fluid city borders. Local governments, unlike states, often use land-use regulations to control the location of productive enterprises and particularly the flow of persons across local borders.

This form of border control generates an important asymmetry. Local governments that want to close their borders to outside investment, enterprises, and persons can often do so, in some dramatic and in some more limited ways. Cities that desire to prevent the flight of investment, persons, or goods, however, normally cannot. Cities are preoccupied with controlling the cross-border flow of resources and persons. They cannot use tariffs, engage in currency manipulations, or adopt restrictive immigration policies, but they can and do use land use as a means of regulating their borders.

These kinds of border-manipulating activities are often justified on the grounds that they generate economic growth, but there is little evidence that they do so. As I have been emphasizing, economic growth in cities is not simply a matter of improving the "product" offered by a particular local government jurisdiction. And while subsidizing desirable entrants may have short-term effects on a city's tax base, it appears unlikely to alter a city's long-term growth trajectory.

The fact that metropolitan-area borders are so important legally, however, does have serious consequences for the distribution of wealth across the metropolitan region. Whether in traditionally urban or suburban areas, poorer and often minority jurisdictions are seriously disadvantaged by the proliferation of metropolitan-area borders. Highly mobile individuals and businesses benefit from these borders—and the inter-municipal tax-base competition that is the result of them. Highly immobile cities (and relatively immobile citizens) do not.

Inter-Municipal Border Controls

Metro-Area Mobility

We should start first by observing that the internal borders of the U.S. are *not supposed* to act as barriers to cross-border mobility. The general rule is that subnational jurisdictions in the United States cannot have an immigration policy. States are presumed to be open to all members of the polity on equal terms—indeed, the Supreme Court has stated that the ideal of a national polity depends upon it.[4]

This mobility guarantee is grounded in a number of federal constitutional provisions. As early as 1823, in *Corfield v. Coryell*, the Court found that citizens enjoyed a right to travel located in the Privileges and Immunities Clause of Article IV of the Constitution.[5] In *Edwards v. California*, a 1941 case dealing with Depression-Era restrictions on mobility, the Court grounded the right in the Commerce Clause. *Edwards* invalidated a state law that criminalized the bringing of indigent persons into California.[6] In *Shapiro v. Thompson*, in 1969, the Equal Protection Clause was used to strike down a state welfare waiting-period law that was motivated by a similar concern about indigent in-migration.[7] The law in that case discouraged indigents from crossing state borders by imposing a waiting period on newly arrived citizens before they could receive welfare benefits.

More recently, in *Saenz v. Roe*, decided in 1999, the Court used the Privileges or Immunities Clause of the Fourteenth Amendment to strike down another welfare restriction aimed at discouraging the interstate migration of indigents. In *Saenz*, the Court held that California cannot limit new residents, for the first year that they live in the state, to the welfare benefits they would have received in their state of origin.[8]

In these cases, the Court has insisted that states cannot close their borders to persons in an effort to defend in-state economic interests, either by limiting out-of-state labor competition or by protecting local tax rolls from welfare-seeking outsiders. In *Edwards*, the Court observed that no state could attempt to "isolate itself from difficulties common to all of them by restraining the transportation of persons and property" across state lines.[9] This language is repeated in *Shapiro* and *Saenz*, where the Court declares unequivocally that states cannot "inhibit migration by needy persons. . . ."[10] The Fourteenth Amendment in particular protects the right of the "newly arrived citizen to the same privileges and immunities enjoyed by other citizens of the same State."[11] Interstate migration is seen as both a personal right of individuals as citizens of the United States and a necessity of the federal union and the common market. Interstate internal migration controls are anathema.[12]

But consider how U.S. constitutional law treats the cross-border movement of persons for residency in a given *local government* jurisdiction. Though the Court has declared that a citizen of the United States has an individual right to become a resident of any state, it has not declared that a citizen of the United States has an individual right to become a resident of any particular *city*. Cities cannot do directly what the Constitution forbids the states from doing. Thus, local governments cannot explicitly identify a set of people and prevent them from entering the jurisdiction or treat them as second-class citizens once they arrive. But cities can do so indirectly in a way that is unavailable to states, often through land-use regulations.

Starting with *Euclid v. Ambler Realty*, decided in 1926, land-use laws have been used consistently to restrict the housing options available to certain income classes.[13] The *Euclid* ordinance—which ushered in the era of Euclidean zoning—made it impossible for a landowner to build anything but single-family detached homes. The district court understood very well the purpose of the ordinance: "In the last analysis, the result to be accomplished is to classify the population and segregate them according to their income or situation in life."[14]

A series of later Supreme Court decisions affirmed the legitimacy of such zoning, making it difficult for potential low-income renters or homebuyers to challenge restrictive ordinances under the Equal Protection Clause. In *Warth v. Seldin* and other cases decided in the 1970s, the Court held that low- and moderate-income persons who desired and intended to seek housing in an exclusive suburb did not have standing to challenge the suburb's zoning ordinance because they could not show that a change in the ordinance would benefit them directly.[15] And the Supreme Court explicitly rejected a right-to-travel claim in *Village of Belle Terre v. Boraas*, a case that upheld a town-wide restriction targeting students that limited the number of unrelated individuals who could live together in a household to two.[16]

Restrictions on inter-local residential mobility have not gone unnoticed by litigators or commentators. Litigators brought right-to-travel challenges to restrictive zoning ordinances in the 1970s, but those challenges failed. Commentators too have noted that local governments differ from states in that local governments have the legal ability to "select" their residents by preventing the construction of certain types of housing.[17] This restriction on inter-local mobility has led a few state courts—most prominently the New Jersey Supreme Court in the *Mount Laurel* decisions[18]—to hold that the exercise of the zoning power to select certain kinds of residents and bar others from the local jurisdiction violates their respective state constitutions.

As the New Jersey Supreme Court observed, local governments use zoning to control for the economic characteristics of incomers, to ensure that only those who contribute to the local tax base can afford to live in the jurisdiction.[19] This use of zoning for fiscal purposes has become commonplace. Indeed, most local governments have been given a free pass to control the movement of newcomers across their borders. Localities may and do adopt restrictive zoning laws that severely limit the supply of land, increase property values for those who already own land in the jurisdiction, exclude certain kinds of land uses altogether, extract exactions or impact fees from new entrants (thus raising their costs relative to existing residents or businesses), and effectively set minimum prices of entry for those who would become residents.[20]

While the courts have imposed some limitations on the ability of cities to charge landowners for development, they have not generally been willing to treat municipal land-use regimes as local border controls. And even in New Jersey and the few other states that have barred the use of zoning for fiscal purposes, efforts to limit suburban border controls have mostly failed. In part, that is because zoning laws are usually facially neutral. They do not discriminate against outsiders but apply to residents and nonresidents alike. In addition, zoning laws usually have a plausible non-protectionist or fiscal purpose, and so they can be justified on grounds of aesthetics, traffic congestion, or the preservation of property values. Courts cannot easily distinguish between legitimate land-use concerns and illegitimate protectionist ones.

Nevertheless, that land-use restrictions have mostly received little judicial scrutiny is notable considering that the cumulative impact of local zoning ordinances generates significant distortions in the regional and national market for land. As numerous scholars have observed, in many places, entry into the local housing market will be dictated less by supply and demand than it is by local regulations. In virtually every locality in the country, the "free market" in land is only provisionally

so. As commentators have long noted, local zoning regimes often operate as cartels.[21]

Moreover, because zoning laws inform the siting choices of every
business and residence in a jurisdiction, those rules invariably alter the
provision of goods and services in a given metropolitan area. As William
Bogart has observed, land is a factor in production. Restrictions on the
supply of land raise the cost of goods and services by forcing location
decisions that do not comport with the actual costs of transport. Classic
Euclidean zoning literally shapes the geographic-economic landscape
by foreclosing business and residence location decisions that would
otherwise be economically advantageous.[22]

Residency Requirements

Land-use-based economic regulation is driven by the fiscal structure of
local governments. The incentive to deflect certain types of development and favor other types is a function of the connections between
residency, municipal services, and local taxes. It is often taken for
granted that municipal services are generally paid for and provided to
the people who reside in the jurisdiction. While certain services must
be provided on equal terms to all comers—for example, access to public
roads—many very important government services are provided only to
legal residents. Among those are forms of social welfare, local housing,
health care, and, importantly, schools.

Residence-based provision of basic government services is generally
unremarkable. But residence requirements become more problematic
when there are dramatic differences in local taxing and spending capacity, and when those differences are exacerbated by the widespread use
of land-use-based entrance controls.

Consider schools. Education spending is often the largest item in a
local government budget. Schools are expensive, and educating more
and poorer students is even more expensive. Local officials are thus
singularly preoccupied with the number and socioeconomic makeup of
their school-age population.

Here too, local borders have been made constitutionally significant. In
San Antonio v. Rodriguez, the Supreme Court held that neighboring local
school districts may spend significantly different amounts per pupil on

education without implicating the strictures of the federal Constitution's Equal Protection Clause. The *Rodriguez* Court rejected a challenge to Texas's use of local school districts to provide education services even as those districts enjoyed vastly different taxable property wealth. In asserting that these differences were not constitutionally significant, the Court held that linking residence, local property wealth, and education provision was not merely a reasonable way for the state to provide primary and secondary education, but that it was also laudable.[23]

Similarly, in *Milliken v. Bradley*, the Court held that federal desegregation remedies could not be applied across local school district boundaries absent some showing of intentional discrimination. The Court rejected a desegregation order that required the consolidation of Detroit's overwhelmingly black school district with neighboring overwhelmingly white suburban districts. Because the white districts had not engaged in intentional discrimination, they could not be included in the desegregation of Detroit's schools.[24]

Milliken and *Rodriguez* obviously permit and encourage local governments to attempt to control their school-age populations—indeed, to control the characteristics of their populations more generally. As Myron Orfield has observed, "In *Milliken*, the Supreme Court had in effect told whites that it was safe to flee and that it would protect them."[25] Closing the border to lower-income residents (or all new residents) is a strategy for controlling costs and managing a locality's fiscal health.[26] Avoiding low-taxpaying residents with high service needs and attracting high-taxpaying residents with low service needs is the municipality's fiscal goal. This is so much the case that residency requirements are enforced by the criminal law, as one parent who falsified her address to get her children in a better school district found out.

The contrast with the rhetoric of the cases rejecting border controls at the state level is stark, however. The purpose of the California law struck down in *Saenz* was to prevent lower-income residents from flowing into California for generous welfare benefits. The Court rejected this strategy at the state level but has not applied the same reasoning to local land-use and school-residency regimes that accomplish the same goal.[27]

In part, there is a formal difference between these kinds of laws. The law in *Saenz* discouraged cross-border movement. But residency restrictions do not facially prevent cross-border movement. It is the combination of residency requirements and restrictive land-use ordinances that does the work. It is not that the courts cannot recognize when cities are acting for protectionist reasons. It is just that land-use regimes that have the effect of closing borders are not viewed in the same way as local rules that facially differentiate between insiders and outsiders.

Consider, for example, the contrast between the Court's tolerance of residency requirements for accessing municipal services with its intolerance for residency requirements that relate to employment. The *Corfield* case asserted a right to travel based in part on the concept of free labor. The right to pursue a common calling on equal terms as others is an aspect of personal liberty that the classical-era courts revived as substantive due process. The right to enter any state or city for work is now thought of as a component of the common market—necessary to prevent subnational governments from putting up barriers to entry. Thus, while the Court has not subjected local limits on residential mobility to scrutiny, it has been more skeptical of local limits on labor's mobility. Even after the demise of economic substantive due process, the insistence on labor mobility has survived.

The general rule is that individuals have a right to enter a state and engage in trade on equal terms as others in that state. The pursuit of a common calling, the Court has stated, is "one of the most fundamental" privileges protected by the privileges and immunities clause of Article IV. In *United Building & Construction Trades Council of Camden County v. Camden*, the Court extended this nondiscrimination rule to municipal governments. The city of Camden, New Jersey, had adopted an ordinance requiring that at least 40% of the employees of contractors or subcontractors working on municipal construction projects be Camden residents. The restriction encouraged contractors to hire local residents, favoring them over nonresidents.[28]

Camden accepted that a statewide residency preference rule would be constitutionally suspect, but argued (and Justice Blackmun, writing in dissent, agreed) that a city residency preference should not be treated as protectionist. Camden argued that it was only incidentally discriminating against out-of-state workers because its rule applied to non-Camden New Jerseyans too. Because there was an in-state political constituency that could represent the interests of out-of-state residents,

Camden's discrimination could be remedied by the political process without need for judicial intervention. Intercity discrimination was thus different from interstate discrimination because the former supplied a political remedy that was unavailable to the latter. If the state of New Jersey, representing non-Camden residents, determined that Camden's residency preference was troubling, it could easily overturn it.

The Court rejected that argument and held that state and municipal labor residency requirements should be treated the same. The majority opinion noted that the protection afforded by the in-state political processes to out-of-state residents was too "uncertain" to be relied upon.[29] And while the Court did not hold that residency preferences could never be justified, it raised a bar to their constitutionality. The principle is clear: One has a right to pursue a common calling not just in the state, but also in the city of one's choice.

Despite the Court's decision in *Camden*, cities do attempt to funnel work to local residents in two ways. First, the Court has allowed municipalities to require that some of their own government employees reside in the jurisdiction.[30] These residency requirements are often justified for specific policy reasons. For example, localities argue that first responders such as firefighters and police officers need to live in the jurisdiction in order to be available on short notice. These kinds of justifications are not particularly persuasive, however. The real reason for residency requirements for municipal employees is often to keep taxpayers (and their tax dollars) in the jurisdiction.

Second, when the government acts as a market participant and not a regulator—when it acts in its "proprietary" capacity and not in its "regulatory" capacity—the Court has held that the government can favor in-jurisdiction contractors over outsider contractors. This means that cities are permitted to take into account any of the myriad characteristics of a good or service (including where it is produced) when they make purchasing decisions and thus act as participants in the private market. As long as the government is not regulating or taxing the good or service, they can favor their own industries and discriminate against nonlocal goods or services by "buying locally." To the extent that a municipal government is the primary purchaser of particular classes of goods, local purchasing regimes are seen as a way to benefit local economies. Those requirements are still subject to the limits imposed by the *Camden* case—cities cannot favor contractors on the basis that they employ local workers except in unusual circumstances—but directing purchasing to in-jurisdiction firms has become a commonplace strategy.

Both residency requirements for (some) municipal workers and local purchasing regimes are important exemptions to *Camden*. But they tend to operate at the margins of a local economy. The Court will almost always strike down direct regulations of or taxes on the private sector economy that attempt to favor or privilege local workers or local firms over nonlocal workers or nonlocal firms. Even local laws that are not facially discriminatory but impose an undue burden on interstate commerce will be struck down if those burdens exceed the benefits to the jurisdiction and the state could have achieved its ends in a less burdensome way.[31]

In other words, when the city acts in its regulatory capacity—as a government—its power over capital (its own and others) is limited. It cannot favor its own citizens or firms over outsiders. In contrast, when the city acts in its proprietary capacity—as a private citizen or firm—it has much more room to maneuver. It can choose to spend its money how it wishes, and this includes favoring its own industries and citizens—at least in a limited way—over outsiders.

It should be noted that this difference is not tied to how subsidies to local firms actually operate. The city that directs municipal purchasing decisions only to in-city firms is acting no differently than the city that discriminates against out-of-city firms through discriminatory taxation or regulation. The former is permissible, but the latter is not. The difference is how we conceive of the city in those two situations. In the first, the city is using its private property as any private actor is permitted to do. In the second, the city is using its regulatory authority to put a thumb on the scale, thus exercising a power that elicits concerns about unfairness and protectionism. The proprietary doctrine thus reinforces the conceptual primacy of private-side property rights. Those rights are paramount. Indeed, they can even be enjoyed in limited ways by "public" governments.

That governments can act in a proprietary capacity illustrates the deep connection between the public/private distinction and city power. The city's scope of permissible action turns on a conceptual and legal idea in which private ownership is a protected right and public regulation is an exercise of power. In the rare cases when the city falls on the "rights" side of the line, it too gets to make decisions that only "private" actors get to make. On the public side, however, the city cannot constitutionally prevent the entry or exit of labor without a very good reason.

Barriers to Economic Integration

What emerges then is a fairly inconsistent picture of the American common market at the metropolitan level. On the one hand, the Court has struck down state rules that would even modestly discourage cross-state relocation, especially of needy people. At the same time, however, local residence requirements, in-locality purchasing, and exclusionary zoning are generally tolerated, even if the Court is sometimes suspicious of local hiring rules.

In the metropolitan region, these rules create barriers to economic integration. Consider the context in which Camden—a seriously depressed post-industrial city—adopted its in-locality hiring preference for city contractors. Camden's decision to adopt resident-favoring hiring policies was a product of the fact that its residents are limited in their ability to get to jobs that exist outside the city. One consequence of suburban land-use restrictions has been that, as employment has moved out of the central city and into the suburbs, residents of central cities have had difficulty finding and commuting to work. To the extent that labor follows employment, the de-concentration of industrial employment from the city center to the periphery should have been followed by the de-concentration of labor and residents. And indeed, this has happened: There has been a significant movement of employment and persons out of the central city and into the suburbs.

But many lower-income residents of the city have not been able to relocate in large part because of local land-use restrictions that prevent them from finding affordable places to live. Lower-income residents, hampered by physical distance and the costs of commuting, are thus at a significant disadvantage in the regional labor market. Urban economists have blamed this "spatial mismatch" between jobs and residents for the low employment prospects of those who continue to live in depressed areas of the central city.[32] Indeed, in one study of upward mobility, commuting time has emerged as "the single strongest factor in the odds of escaping poverty."[33]

The conventional objection to residents-only services and exclusionary land-use regimes is grounded in equality. As the New Jersey court observed in *Mount Laurel,* the problem of concentrated poverty in urban places is a function of mobility restrictions elsewhere. Potential reforms are targeted at redistributing resources across jurisdictional lines. School funding-equalization efforts and regional tax-base sharing are designed to remedy these kinds of structural inequalities, as was Camden's resident-favoring rule.

The proliferation of metropolitan-area boundaries and entrance controls, however, is also—and perhaps mainly—a problem of economic integration. For cities, the rules governing the mobility of labor are symmetrical: One cannot constitutionally prevent the entry or exit of labor without a very good reason. The rules governing residence, however, are effectively one way: Except in those few states that have barred exclusionary zoning, localities cannot prevent exit, but they can prevent entrance. Though they do so indirectly through their land-use policies, they nevertheless do so quite effectively.

The power to exclude is particularly useful to economically robust municipalities, especially high-income suburbs, which can assert some control over their fiscal health by restricting in-migration. Cities like Camden, which are trying to stem the outflow of tax-capable residents, have more limited options. Camden's attempt to funnel work to city residents through its contracting rules is a function of the significant barriers to obtaining work elsewhere in the region. The proliferation of metropolitan-area border controls is a real constraint on metropolitan-area economic integration.

Subsidizing Mobile Capital

Land-use-based border control strategies are one way local governments attempt to improve their fiscal conditions. Another way is to engage in costly inter-local subsidy battles for mobile capital. Two trade wars have emerged at the municipal level: the war to keep high-cost users out and the war to keep high-value capital in. In the context of the metropolitan area, the existing legal rules that govern cross-border relations between states have some predictable effects on cities. The dominant strategy adopted by any given municipality will turn on the municipality's economic health and its relationship to the wider metropolitan-area economy.

The Subsidy Battle

The subsidy battle is, of course, not new, nor are the political patholo-gies associated with the governmental promotion of, participation in, and subsidization of private commercial enterprise. As we have already seen, those pathologies were present at the very beginning of the in-dustrial city. Urban boosters, who came of age in the early nineteenth century, built American cities out of greed and optimism—the certain belief that local investments would reap rewards. As William Cronon observes, "Boosters sought to make their visions come true by convey-ing just this certainty to investors and merchants who might set up shop in the place being promoted."[34]

The idea was to take land and turn it into money through proximity—to natural resources, goods, and most of all, to other people and busi-nesses. As early boosters knew very well, there was sometimes no obvious reason that a given small settlement developed into a great metropolis when other small settlements did not. Natural advantages might have made some difference in urban growth. Proximity to trade routes and the availability of transportation lines also did—sometimes. But so did the simple belief that the city would prosper and the resul-tant self-reinforcing economic effects of in-migration and settlement. As I mentioned in chapter 1, early boosters seemed to intuit what the economic geographers have confirmed: that the city can be a self-fulfilling prophecy.[35]

Thus, seeking to attract mobile capital through direct or indirect sub-sidization has been of historical and continuing concern. Particularly in the mid-to-late-1800s, burgeoning towns and cities sought to attract outside investment—often in the form of railroad construction—and rushed to commit public monies to entice it to their respective ju-risdictions. A commentator in the September 1890 issue of *Scribner's Magazine* put it this way:

> A curious outgrowth of the rivalries of American cities, is the prac-tice that obtains so generally of offering bonuses and pecuniary in-ducements to manufacturers to move their plant. . . . Any factory or

established business employing labor can have its choice, nowadays, from a long list of cities, new and old, any one of which will give it a site for a factory, pay the expenses of moving, and perhaps contribute substantially toward the construction of a new building.[36]

The municipal bond default crisis that followed saw cities unable to pay off their debts when the promised investment did not materialize or when it failed to bring the promised benefits. Public monies were also committed to a raft of public works projects, again often to the benefit of business interests and often with poor returns to the general public. No doubt the nineteenth-century city brought significant public improvements as city services expanded to meet the needs of a growing populace. Nevertheless, the municipal defaults of the late 1800s led many to believe that cities could not be trusted with their finances.[37]

The modern equivalents of the nineteenth-century subsidies to railroad and public utilities are public subsidies to retail and industry. We see this at work in the deployment of tax subsidies to speed Walmart's entry into a community, in the building or improving of stadiums to retain or attract professional sports franchises, in the use of relocation subsidies and tax breaks to attract a new manufacturing plant, in the competition among local governments for major shopping malls, and in the use of public monies to underwrite mixed-use residential and commercial developments.

The costs of these efforts to attract relatively mobile capital often fall on the relatively immobile. Cities depend heavily on fixed assets for revenue (i.e., assets that are unlikely to flee from the jurisdiction). This is the reason that local governments rely on the property tax for the bulk of their local revenue—land cannot move across the city line.[38] But this means that cities might take advantage of place-dependent capital. That is, cities are inclined to extract as much as possible from less mobile capital while courting more mobile capital. Thus, the property tax can be a mechanism for cities to extract too much from relatively nonmobile taxpayers, particularly if politicians have short-term economic time horizons. In the context of a politics of capital attraction and retention through land-based development, the exploitation of place-dependent capital can be as much of a problem as the subsidization of more mobile capital.

Cities face limits on their ability to shift costs onto relatively immobile taxpayers—existing residents and businesses (if they have resources already) can ultimately flee if they are being taken advantage of.[39] Nevertheless, the siting of relatively permanent structures—homes, businesses, plants—entails risk. Local dependence—the need for spatial stability—is unavoidable,[40] the more so for those who are or will become attached to a particular location either out of commercial necessity, emotional or familial connections, or lack of alternatives. The more place-dependent an investor is, the more he or she is vulnerable. Undiversified owners of real property—the bulk of American homeowners—thus tend to worry a great deal about the tax and spending habits of municipal governments. Relatively place-dependent residents and firms have strong incentives to exercise influence in the local political process.[41]

The mobile/immobile distinction can be fluid. Any factor is highly mobile before it is transformed into a site-specific asset. After buildings, plants, or houses are constructed or individuals settle into a jurisdiction, however, capital may become relatively less mobile. That being said, when I refer to mobile capital, I am talking about individuals or firms that are relatively unconstrained geographically because transport costs and trade barriers are minimal, relocation costs are low relative to wealth, or skills are highly portable. These can be contrasted with individuals or firms that are poorly skilled, locked in place for some reason, or with limited resources. Capital mobility is a function of the elimination of geographic barriers to the movement of assets around the globe, whether those assets are currently fixed or not. Even when invested in site-specific assets, capital is mobile to the extent that it can still credibly raise the threat of exit and to the extent that it will and is able to exit if it is economically advantageous to do so.

Why should the subsidization of mobile capital be a problem? Competitive accounts of city growth and decline that treat the city as a product would suggest that local choices to pursue and perhaps subsidize mobile capital will simply reflect the invisible hand of the interlocal competitive marketplace. If cities are operating in a market where subsidies and taxes are the currency, then cities get exactly the amount of development they desire and will not give away too much. In an ideal Tieboutian local government market, cities would get exactly the amount of development they are willing to pay for.

In a world in which economic development is systematically and geographically uneven, however, such an equilibrium is never going to exist. The lumpiness of economic activity will invariably mean that many cities and regions will have less economic development than they want. But it also means that the standard Tieboutian response to underdevelopment (i.e., change the city's tax and spending bundle to attract the desirable residents or firms) is not likely to be very effective. Because of path dependence, it is very difficult for any given city to alter its relative spatial economic position merely by subsidizing new entrants.[42] No matter how low the taxes are in Anchorage, it is not going to become a banking center that can compete with New York.

Moreover, whether subsidies are welfare-enhancing in the short term does not solve the problem of the boom-and-bust cycle. Once mobile capital is attracted, it can then leave. This volatility has substantial negative effects given that the city is fixed in place and residents' ability to relocate lags or is limited. Because firms as well as residents are unequally mobile, cities will be inclined to redistribute from less mobile residents and firms to more mobile residents and firms. And that is what we have seen. According to some estimates, each year, states and local governments spend close to $80 billion, or roughly 7% of their total budgets, on tax incentives, breaks, and outright cash payments to induce corporate investment and relocation.[43]

How Law Encourages Cosmopolitan Capital

These location incentives have to be understood in the context of legal rules that continue to permit the heavy subsidization of mobile capital. Corporate capital is advantaged by two features of the existing constitutional regime. First, the legal rules mostly prevent states and local governments from raising barriers to entry in the form of discriminatory taxes. But, second, the rules permit local subsidies and incentives. Cities "compete" for private investment by subsidizing it, but cannot discriminatorily tax outsiders, though the lines between these two are not always so clear.

The basic contours of the U.S. common market were established in the late nineteenth century with the rise and ultimate dominance of the interstate business corporation. In the latter half of the nineteenth century, judicial decisions struck down absentee ownership laws and other state regulations discouraging multistate business operations or discriminating against out-of-state corporations.[44] Combined with the interstate competition for, and standardization of, corporate charters, the private business corporation soon gained the ability to operate relatively free of local interference throughout the nation. The chartering and regulation of corporations is still a state responsibility—states can and do set the conditions for entry. But the Commerce Clause of the U.S. Constitution prevents states from protecting locals from encroachment by out-of-state investment through obviously discriminatory rules. State and local governments cannot explicitly favor their own industries, businesses, or residents to the detriment of out-of-state competitors.

The current concern in the literature is not that states and cities will exclude out-of-state investment, but that they will be too eager to seek it. One of the most controversial and unsettled aspects of the law of the interstate common market is the extent to which states and localities can provide economic development incentives to attract or, more pointedly, to keep capital in-state.

Of course, any federal regime in which sub-federal governments can differently invest in infrastructure or adopt differential tax rates or regulatory rules will produce some distortions in the location of firms and residents. States or cities can have low or high taxes, can build roads or stadiums, can choose to provide housing or spend money on education. Thus, general economic regulation may cause some differences in the locational decisions of firms beyond a baseline in which only transport costs are taken into account, though those distortions are arguably quite minor.[45]

The constitutional doctrine of the common market is ostensibly intended to limit those distortions. At a minimum, it is supposed to allow persons, goods, and services to cross state and local borders and compete on equal terms with the persons, goods, and services that are already there. Location incentives, however, are often difficult to square with this general principle. Obviously, tax breaks or subsidies that favor resident industry, or industries that promise to become resident will have the economic effect of influencing the "geography of production"[46] and will undoubtedly tip the market to the benefit of the local producer (and thus to the detriment of the nonlocal producer). While the incentives to "come" into the state may not raise concerns about local protectionism, the incentives to "stay" in the state often do, and the two are difficult to disentangle.

The formal line that the Court has drawn, and that has come under significant criticism, is the line between subsidies and taxes, or between "[d]irect subsidization of domestic industry" (which is permitted) and "discriminatory taxation of out-of-state manufacturers" (which is not).[47] In *West Lynn Creamery v. Healy*, however, the Court fudged that line significantly, striking down a nondiscriminatory tax levied on milk dealers that was funneled back to Massachusetts milk producers in the form of a subsidy.[48] The combined tax and subsidy favored in-state dairy farmers over out-of-state dairy farmers, thus distorting the market in milk. Because it burdened out-of-state producers, the subsidy scheme was unconstitutional under the Commerce Clause. Since *Healy*, the status of locational subsidies and economic development incentives has been unsettled—the tax/subsidy distinction and the distinction between discriminatory and nondiscriminatory taxes are both unclear.[49]

Two Supreme Court decisions help illustrate the deep tensions in the doctrine: *DaimlerChrysler Corp. v. Cuno* and *Kelo v. New London*. *Cuno* involved a lawsuit brought by city and state taxpayers challenging a package of tax incentives offered by Toledo and Ohio officials to the car company to induce it to keep a Jeep assembly plant in Toledo rather than move it across the border to Michigan. That *Cuno* involved an effort to keep a large employer in Toledo was not incidental to the case. Much of the interstate competition for corporate investment is actually intercity competition. Toledo was competing with a neighboring Michigan city only fifteen miles away, and the particular circumstances of Toledo's declining economy obviously animated the push to keep the Jeep plant there.[50]

The Supreme Court held that city taxpayers did not have standing to contest the tax incentives. Generally, taxpayers who object to paying a certain tax can only bring lawsuits to declare such a tax unconstitutional under very narrowly defined conditions. The Court held that those conditions were not met in *Cuno*.[51]

What is notable, however, is that the lower courts had allowed the challenge to go forward and had invalidated at least some portion of the tax incentives. The locational incentives included a local property tax abatement and an investment tax credit—both commonly used tools for subsidizing industries in return for their remaining and investing in a particular jurisdiction. DaimlerChrysler argued that the Ohio tax abatement and credit were permissible subsidies, and in economic terms, they were. Both forms of tax relief could have easily been replicated by outright cash payments.[52]

The Sixth Circuit Court of Appeals acknowledged the difference between subsidies and discriminatory taxes and recognized that states and localities are permitted to encourage the intrastate development of commerce and industry. Nevertheless, it struck down the investment tax credit (but left the property tax abatement standing), citing a line of Supreme Court cases that had invalidated state statutes that gave instate business activity a tax advantage not shared by out-of-state business activity.[53]

As the Sixth Circuit observed, Ohio's investment tax credit put a burden on the cross-border movement of capital by putting a thumb on the tax scale. Businesses subject to the Ohio franchise tax could "reduce [their] existing tax liability by locating significant" capital investments within the state, but not if they invested outside the state.[54] The tax was a cross-border (or interstate) regulation of commerce in that it sought to displace business activity from one state to another, and it provided a direct commercial advantage to local or local-investing businesses as compared with nonlocal investing businesses. Though limited to the investment tax credit, the Sixth Circuit's decision seemed to call into question numerous tax incentives that states and localities had presumed to be constitutional, but which some commentators had argued were vulnerable if the Supreme Court took its own doctrine seriously.

Indeed, many commentators have observed that interstate and interlocal tax incentive competition is troubling. From a constitutional perspective, the Court's tolerance of local subsidies seems to undermine its common market jurisprudence. And from a policy perspective, tax subsidies seem to pit states and local governments against each other in wasteful races to provide corporate welfare.

The Supreme Court's decision in *Cuno*—that the taxpayers did not have standing to challenge the tax incentives—did not give the parties a chance to argue about either of these criticisms. Taxing local citizens to support corporate relocation does not excite Supreme Court attention. This form of subsidization has been going on for a long time. And indeed, the *Cuno* case faded away with little public or legal comment.

Other forms of local subsidization, however, have excited more attention, both from the Court and the public. Compare *Cuno* with *Kelo v. New London*.[55] In *Kelo*, the Court held that it was not a violation of the U.S. Constitution's Fifth Amendment Takings Clause for New London to condemn a non-blighted residence and transfer it to a private developer as part of a larger development parcel. The city's goal was to promote redevelopment by encouraging the drug-maker Pfizer to locate its headquarters in the city. As an inducement to the company, the city proposed developing a large, mixed-use residential and commercial project. Before condemning the property, New London had made the homeowner a market-based offer, and was willing and required to pay compensation for the home regardless. Nevertheless, the homeowner challenged the condemnation on grounds that it was impermissible because transferring the property to a private actor for economic development purposes was not a "public use." The text of the Takings Clause of the Fifth Amendment states: "nor shall private property be taken for public use, without just compensation."[56]

Kelo came to the Court as a property rights case—the Court was asked to decide whether a city could use eminent domain for economic development purposes. All the justices agreed that governments cannot seize the property of one owner and simply give it to another. The question in *Kelo* was whether "public use" included a city's economic development goals. Previous decisions of the Court had interpreted "public use" broadly—eminent domain need not be restricted to those properties that would be actually "used" by the public. In a number of cases, the Court had allowed transfers of property when cities had a legitimate public purpose. For example, in *Berman v. Parker*, decided in 1954, the Court ruled 8-0 that Washington, D.C.'s condemnation of a non-blighted department store that was located in an area set for redevelopment was a legitimate use of the takings power.[57]

Kelo is an urban redevelopment case. It is also a business incentives case. New London—like Toledo—was (and still is) facing the problem of disinvestment. The condemnation before the Court was just one element in the package of incentives designed to encourage large-scale redevelopment in the city. *Kelo*, like *Cuno*, is thus a case about the structured choices that cities encounter in attempting to alter and affect their economic circumstances. Economically distressed cities have few tools for attracting investment and jobs. The relatively free flow of capital puts old-line cities at a disadvantage.

The public's reaction to the two cases, however, could not have been more different. In *Cuno*, the Court easily rejected the taxpayers' standing to challenge the subsidies. The decision not only permits the incentives to stand, it also makes it difficult as a practical matter for parties to bring future challenges to such subsidies.

Kelo also upheld the city's exercise of power—the use of eminent domain in that case was permitted. But four justices argued vociferously that the local exercise of eminent domain for economic development purposes was constitutionally impermissible. And one justice—Anthony Kennedy—articulated some important limits on the exercise of that local power. Moreover, the public and many elected officials (though not often municipal ones) almost uniformly lambasted the decision. Legislators adopted laws to overturn it. And commentators continue to worry over it.

Critics of *Kelo* worry about the money. They worry about the fairness and legitimacy of sacrificing relatively immobile capital for relatively mobile capital. In his dissent, for example, Justice Clarence Thomas noted the sordid history of twentieth-century urban renewal: the forcible displacement of poor and working-class communities; the construction of highways through otherwise vibrant urban neighborhoods; the use of urban redevelopment funds to destroy small businesses and replace them with larger ones. For African Americans in the mid-twentieth century, urban renewal was known derisively and bitterly as "Negro removal." Jane Jacobs wrote *Death and Life* while she was a community activist resisting Robert Moses's efforts to build a highway through New York City's Greenwich Village, then a working-class ethnic neighborhood, where she lived.

There is a legitimate and longstanding concern about the political power of large-scale capital. A more economically valuable use for a particular piece of property can always be found, and local pro-development majorities tend to exercise outsized political power in the redevelopment process.[58]

Notably, however, that concern seems not to apply to the structure of inter-local economic competition for mobile capital itself. No one seems to blame mobile capital for abandoning New London in the first place.[59] Indeed, the context in which economic development takings were tested in *Kelo* obscured the precipitous decline of New London altogether. The plaintiff, Susette Kelo, was a white, middle-class homeowner occupying a well-tended and non-blighted residence. When African American residents of more distressed downtown locations across the country were being displaced in large numbers through urban renewal, neither the Court nor the public showed much restraint.

Moreover, critics of *Kelo* do not generally question the overall economic development project—even as it is the source of the political pathologies that they identify as requiring judicial oversight. Potential abuses of power can be seen across development processes, not just in the abuse of eminent domain. But few regard city efforts to reverse economic outflows by spending significant tax dollars to attract corporations to be as problematic as the isolated use of eminent domain. Incentive-based competition for productive firms is not only permitted, it is seemingly encouraged. The dominant competitive model of city growth and decline seems immune to criticism.

Thus, despite its similarities to the *Kelo* case, *Cuno* has not generated anything near the same level of popular or scholarly criticism. And yet, as in *Kelo*, the local taxpayers in *Cuno* are also worried about the money—the redistribution from resident property owners to corporate capital. They too argue that judicial oversight of local economic development incentives is required to prevent government from giving too much away.

In fact, to the extent one is worried about giveaways to mobile capital, the *Cuno* plaintiffs have a better argument. As a matter of public policy, economists have been fairly skeptical about the use of economic development incentives of the type used in *Cuno*. There is, in the words of one commentator, "little evidence to support their effectiveness."[60] Most appear to cost cities money without changing the actual locational choices of the corporations that demand them.

Moreover, the data suggest that the costs of attracting new industry or business through tax incentives are often not offset by local economic benefits. And commentators generally agree that locational incentives do not contribute to national prosperity because they are zero-sum. Toledo gains at the expense of the city where the plant would otherwise have located.[61]

Land assembly commitments, like the one used in *Kelo*, are also likely of limited efficacy, but at least an argument can be made that they might have more of an effect on corporate decision-making. One can make a colorable argument that cities need to attract the large-footprint industries, offices, and residential developments that firms desire. And so, regardless of the merits of any particular project, using eminent domain to solve land assembly problems seems obviously a "public use." Indeed, to the extent that the use of eminent domain to provide a parcel large enough is a plausible (even if high-risk) strategy for increasing the local tax base, it would be irresponsible for a city *not* to use it. The majority's holding then that "public use" encompasses takings for economic development is consistent with this view.[62]

If one is concerned about the influence of economic development dollars on the local political process, then *Cuno* is more problematic than *Kelo* in another way. Tax incentives of the kind offered in *Cuno* are somewhat invisible when compared to the public exercise of eminent domain. Takings for economic development are highly visible and arguably generate opposition from a well-motivated constituency—those whose property is being taken. Takings also have to be paid for. To the extent that they are not paid for using state money, condemnation funds are a local budget item and have to be accounted for by local political officials.[63]

In contrast, local and state tax incentives are much less visible because they do not constitute a direct charge to local budgets and are often paid for by future generations through municipal debt. This relative invisibility makes it much less probable that the local political process can be counted on to prevent bad incentive deals. Moreover, *Kelo*-style redistributions are generally compensated while *Cuno*-style redistributions are not. The property owner in *Kelo* was always going to receive compensation and did. The taxpayers in *Cuno* were not guaranteed anything, even if they might benefit indirectly in the future.

That mobile capital is not concerned is evident—in *Cuno*, the plaintiffs were the city and state taxpayers, not corporations seeking an even playing field on which to compete with Jeep. Corporations are more concerned about restrictions that limit their mobility, not incentives that assist it. Thus, the holding in the *Cuno* case—that city and state taxpayers do not have standing to challenge local and state locational tax incentives—means that those individuals or groups most inclined to bring such challenges cannot.

If one worries about the power of mobile capital in the local political process, then *Kelo* and *Cuno* should rise and fall together. Both cases are about cities' constitutional capacity to corral mobile capital. That capacity is defined by legal rules, not some inevitable economic logic.

Consider that following the *Kelo* case, state legislators enacted eminent domain reform in numerous cities and states. These laws restrict the local use of eminent domain for economic development purposes, limit eminent domain to blighted neighborhoods, or mandate that the locality pay above-market compensation to displaced homeowners. The idea once again—as in the nineteenth century—was to take power *away* from cities—to prevent the scramble for mobile capital that would result in the invasion of individual property rights.

But, as David Dana has observed, if eminent domain is taken off the table, cities will resort to other (currently) legal mechanisms to subsidize new development, including *Cuno*-style tax breaks, direct cash outlays, donations of public property, zoning exemptions, and infrastructure subsidies. These policies also shift monies from relatively immobile capital to mobile capital. It should be said that all these policies are unproven from the standpoint of long-term growth. But whether eminent domain is a significantly worse policy than these others is not at all apparent on its face.[64]

The Not-So-Free-Trade Constitution

The point is not the efficacy of any particular economic development practice—I have already expressed deep skepticism about the capacity for cities to *do* development, and I will say more in chapter 7 about the inadvisability of local industrial policy.

Here I am more concerned with the way law has structured the choices available to declining cities. The Court's treatment of *Kelo* and *Cuno*—and the whole panoply of metropolitan-area border-control activities—is not a function of a close examination of those policies' actual effects, but instead reflects the limitations of the existing legal regime.

Consider that the problem for old-line industrial cities like New London is private-side disinvestment, but the city has no legal or political right to economic self-sufficiency. It has little say over how property owners deploy their capital, even if those decisions undermine the city's welfare. The salient and legally cognizable act in the *Kelo* case was the city's use of eminent domain to seize private property—its invasion of the homeowner's property rights—not the abandonment of New London in the first place.[65] New London and Toledo did what struggling local economies often do—distribute monies from some group of local, relatively immobile property owners to mobile capital.

That kind of redistribution is only problematic, however, when it appears to invade a protected private right. The existing legal order has the necessary tools to prevent the public sphere from invading a protected private sphere. As in *Kelo*, the language of rights does most of this work (even if the outcome ultimately favored the city). Private property is extremely powerful—it protects both the homeowner's and Pfizer's rights to decide how to deploy their resources.

In contrast, we have more trouble understanding when the private sphere is invading the sphere of the public—we have more trouble preventing the distortion of public decision-making for private ends. Explicit corruption or capture of public processes can be guarded against, but the form of corruption that worries those concerned with capital's political power—the narrowing of the public sphere, the loss of political and economic independence, government policy driven by unaccountable and unelected economic actors—is more difficult to articulate. It is exhibited in the dependence of cities like New London on the grace of transnational corporations like Pfizer.

Our difficulty in articulating this concern reflects the pervasiveness of the negative conception of rights as trumps to be asserted against government invasions. But more so, it is a function of the conceptual rejection of public rights. The democratic public either does not exist or it has no interests that can be invaded by private-side rights-bearers. And yet both the public invasion of rights and the private corruption of the public good have been and continue to be the dominant concerns in the city-business relationship.

What are the relative vulnerabilities of city and capital, public and private? The conventional view is skeptical of government power on the ground that it will often be deployed to exploit unless there are some constraints. Liberty, on this account, is the exercise of rights against— and the operation of markets free from—direct government intervention or interference. One implication of this view is that where exit does not provide sufficient discipline, legal limits on city power are appropriate to prevent exploitation of property owners, corruption, and other political process flaws of local urban democracy. Courts and legislatures should step in to prevent local oppression of the vulnerable. City power is thus appropriately limited.

When one turns away from the dominant conception of rights and markets, however, a different idea of vulnerability emerges. A competing political tradition tells us that governments are also vulnerable to markets, though this vulnerability tends to be less visible. As we see in *Kelo*, the vulnerability of the city to mobile capital is often interpreted as something else: the vulnerability of private property to the city.[66]

In light of the dynamics of capital mobility, it is no surprise that a declining city like Toledo would tax its existing residents to subsidize the entry of a manufacturing plant and that New London would use eminent domain to assemble land to attract a large-scale residential/commercial development. These are rational responses to those respective cities' fiscal positions. The political dynamic, however, is one that pits relatively mobile against relatively immobile capital. Giveaways must be financed, and they are often financed by existing property taxpayers. Indeed, contrary to conventional political expectations, local jurisdictions often foist benefits on nonvoting outsiders and impose costs on voting insiders. Over-attentiveness to mobile capital explains this result.

Despite the expressed skepticism of the use of eminent domain in *Kelo*, however, current jurisprudence does little to challenge the primacy of mobile capital, even when local efforts to constrain it encroach upon individual property rights. Law dictates the structure under which local governments make their choices. The capacity for mobile capital to dictate terms to cities is a legal artifact, not an economic one.

To be sure, judges and courts are not ideally positioned to make local economic development policy. Nevertheless, the creation of a national common market has been to a significant degree a judicial project. Justice Oliver Wendell Holmes's famous (and oft-quoted) statement about the need for judicial oversight of state and local commercial favoritism captures this view. As Holmes observed:

> I do not think that the United States would come to an end if we lost our power to declare an Act of Congress void. I do think the Union would be imperiled if we could not make that declaration as to the laws of the several States. For one in my place sees how often a local policy prevails with those who are not trained to national views and how often action is taken that embodies what the Commerce Clause was meant to end.[67]

The Court continues to endorse the view that the Commerce Clause and other constitutional limits on local economic parochialism have prevented the republic from splintering into competing state or regional markets. The prosperity of the country is presented as the descriptive truth of this constitutional truism.

The presumptive success of the constitutional common market, however, has sometimes prevented close examination of its actual effects. The constitutional rules that govern cross-border mobility are not particularly attentive to intra-metropolitan cross-border dynamics. The rules are designed for states, not cities. But in an economy dominated by cities and the metropolitan areas that have grown up around them, judicial inattention to municipal borders has generated a set of inconsistent and incoherent constitutional commitments—a "(not so) free-trade" regime operating at the local level. There is no particular theory at work here; the city (and the wider metropolitan area) is mostly invisible to the doctrine. It emerges in the gaps between the rules.

In an urbanized national economy in which the status of municipalities is an ongoing economic preoccupation, however, those gaps are quite important. Currently, the Court's interstate mobility doctrines tend to enforce capital's mobility and the city's marginalization, favoring those local government jurisdictions with resources over those that have less. The result is some level of mismatch between those effects and the stated goal of preserving a common political and economic market. The stated commercial relationship between subnational governments in the United States holds that "the peoples of the several states must sink or swim together, and that in the long run prosperity and salvation are in union and not division."[68] That principle has not been honored at the metropolitan level.

Conclusion: Economic [Dis]integration

What should Toledo, Camden, and New London do in the face of economic restructuring? Toledo provided tax subsidies to keep a DaimlerChrysler plant in the city. Camden sought to direct municipal contracts to in-city firms. New London encouraged the Pfizer Corporation to relocate there by deploying eminent domain. Why any of these efforts to manipulate the local economy should be constitutionally more problematic than others, or more problematic than the entrance controls that suburban jurisdictions regularly employ, is unclear. In all cases, cities are trying to control the flow of persons, goods, and capital across their borders. These metropolitan-area borders *matter* even if, in constitutional terms, they are not supposed to. For the declining parts of the metropolitan region, the constitutional rules of horizontal state-based federalism are not helpful.

In fact, the constitutional rules of the common market drive predictable local government behaviors. That New London would resort to economic development takings is a rational strategy when understood in the context of a regime that encourages inter-local competition for mobile capital. Preventing New London's exercise of eminent domain for economic development purposes without addressing the subsidies that Toledo can offer DaimlerChrysler merely changes the form of inter-municipal tax-base competition. Preventing Camden from funneling work to city residents, while permitting the suburbs around Camden to exclude those residents altogether, does little to alter Camden's economic or political incentives. If one is concerned that mobile capital is distorting the legislative process, then one should adopt a broad-based doctrine that challenges the entire panoply of local development policies. Certainly, Congress could eliminate the inter-state subsidy race; it has been asked to do so repeatedly to little effect.

The problem is perennial. Recall that key features of laissez-faire or classical constitutionalism had their origins in the municipal debt crises of the 1860s and 1870s when, in a rush of boosterism, states and lo-calities overcommitted public monies to private enterprise and other-wise "devis[ed] techniques to abet their own self-exploitation."[69] Justice Stephen Field—the putative founder of laissez-faire constitutionalism—consistently railed against what one commentator has termed the "baneful effects of the private quest for special privileges."[70] Field's ju-risprudence was as skeptical of the local use of eminent domain on behalf of railroads as it was of public subsidies for mill owners. He arguably would have dissented from both *Kelo* and *Cuno*. That we have not gotten far from the turn-of-the-century concern about the use of public money for private purposes illustrates the timelessness of the local economic development project itself.

If a truly integrated national economy were a result, we might accept the downsides of a competitive inter-jurisdictional scramble for re-sources. But the assumption that we have a highly functional national common market obscures the fact that prosperity in the United States has been dramatically uneven—both in time and space. Regions and metropolitan areas have experienced significantly different levels of prosperity. Some places are economically ascendant while others are in decline. Thus, in a relatively short span of time, we have seen the rise and fall of the urban industrial metropolis, the shift of jobs and industry from northern industrial cities to the South and West, and the movement of capital and people out of older cities into the suburbs and exurbs. Recently, we have seen the decline of some of those suburbs and exurbs and a return to some central cities. Constitutional doctrine un-derstandably tends to focus on interstate economic relationships. But courts and commentators seem to miss the chief economic story of the twentieth century: the rise and fall of the great industrial cities and the economic balkanization of metropolitan-area economies.

The latter is often overlooked, but many U.S. metropolitan areas are less economically integrated than the national economy as a whole. Declining, decaying Detroit has almost no economic (and certainly no social) relationship to its wealthy suburbs only a few miles away. The social and economic connections between economically vibrant parts of the Detroit metropolitan region and economically vibrant parts of metropolitan regions in other parts of the country are far more robust.

This observation has been made internationally as well. Those metropolitan-area citizens who are integrated into the global economy often have more economic connections with similarly situated citizens around the world than with the unintegrated poor living right down the street. Despite physical proximity, local resource-poor jurisdictions are like foreign countries.

This state of affairs is not necessary. The constitutional rules that govern the cross-border movement of persons, goods, and capital could be quite different. As I have argued, there is ample evidence that the manipulation of local fiscal health through the use of economic development subsidies and land-use-based exclusion is unproductive.[71] That local governments resort to these policies appears to be a collective action problem that could be solved. Where local governments are engaged in such conduct, courts or legislatures could certainly play a role in containing the economic balkanization of the metropolitan region.

New London is a nice example. Pfizer did in fact relocate to New London. After years of development processes, litigation over eminent domain, and the use of public monies to condemn land, however, the proposed mixed-use development that had been promised never materialized. And in 2009, Pfizer decided to leave the city, moving 1,400 jobs to a suburban campus in nearby Groton as a cost-cutting measure. That New London chose to subsidize Pfizer's entry in the first place was predictable, as was the eventual failure of that project.

The metropolitan-area jurisdictional scramble for resources is a feature of our current horizontal federalism, but it is not a route to economic growth. Cities should be doing something other than manipulating their borders in an effort to "compete" for investment. Whether they can do so (and how) in light of the real constraints of American vertical and horizontal federalism is an important question that I turn to next.

5

The City Redistributes I: Policy

ACCOUNTS OF CITY POWER often begin with an "is" and end with an "ought"—conflating what cities are capable of doing with what they should be doing. The conventional account of what cities are capable of doing argues for a rather limited view of city possibilities in the face of mobile capital. These limits are presented as the inevitable outcome of economic markets, open borders, and the demands of economic growth.

I have drawn a distinction between false constraints and real constraints, however. The theoretical requirements of growth are a false constraint on city policies. The actual operation of state-based federalism is, in contrast, a real constraint. Nevertheless, the latter often assumes the former, making the dynamic of city competition and capital mobility self-fulfilling.

This is especially true with regard to social welfare spending, which is the subject of this chapter. I have thus far argued that city growth and decline cannot be explained by intercity competition for mobile capital, and I have urged that cities can and should therefore be doing things other than chasing it. One thing that cities could be doing is addressing economic inequality, even though doing so is also contrary to the standard assumptions about the city's capacities. Because capital can easily flee local efforts to tax it, "the conventional wisdom of urban finance is that municipalities should play little role in fulfilling the redistributive functions of government."[1]

Cities are not altogether cooperating, however. Despite the structural biases that favor mobile capital, cities are engaging in forms of regulation that defy conventional wisdom. This chapter describes some of these efforts, starting with municipal minimum wage laws, which have gained significant traction in cities across the country. Cities are also regulating incoming development in new ways, through the creation of local, project-specific labor laws, and through so-called community benefits agreements (CBAs).

That cities are adopting minimum wages and engaging in other forms of redistribution sharply undercuts the descriptive claim of the limited city—that the city is constrained to adopt developmental policies over redistributive ones. If growth is not an outcome of competitive inter-jurisdictional settings, and the mobility of capital is not an economic reality but an institutional one, then it is possible for cities to engage in more aggressive redistribution and regulation. And in fact, that is exactly what some cities are doing.

The fact of city redistribution suggests that cities can adopt policies that are not solely driven by the chase for mobile capital and that citizens normally marginalized by the politics of capital attraction can still assert influence over local economic policy. That influence is exercised in the context of a challenging political and economic environment, to be sure. Nevertheless, the scope of local decision-making in American cities is less constrained than has been commonly assumed. Cities are not converging on the same capital-friendly policies as conventional economic wisdom would predict. And the absence of convergence signals an enlarged realm for urban governance.

Moreover, the city's willingness to adopt redistributive policies that are political nonstarters at the state and federal levels suggests that cities may be able to recover some portion of the regulatory role that they enjoyed before the centralization of social welfare provision in the aftermath of the New Deal era. The form that the new urban regulation has taken in the United States is often partial and piecemeal—and it is limited by the features of U.S.-style vertical and horizontal federalism that I described in the previous chapters. That it is occurring at all, however, indicates that standard accounts of city power require fundamental revision.

The Limits of City Limits

We should start by first reviewing the conventional view of the city's "limits." The debate about the city's relative capacity to act is not new. In some ways, the last half-century of urban scholarship has been dedicated to elucidating the scope of city powerlessness. That the city is fundamentally constrained seems to be mostly taken for granted.

Recall again the basic claim, often attributed to Paul Peterson, that city policy is limited by the city's overriding need to attract capital and labor. Cities, being open economies, are not autonomous. They operate within a wider economy that requires them to compete for economic resources. The policies that are thus available to the city are "limited to those few which can plausibly be shown to be conducive to the community's economic prosperity."[2] City politics is developmental politics—and not much more. As Peterson writes, "the primary interest of cities [is] the maintenance and enhancement of their economic productivity. To their land area cities must attract productive labor and capital."[3] Local politics thus occurs on a relatively narrow stage: Cities have no choice but to privilege developmental policies over redistributive ones. To do otherwise is to precipitate the flight of mobile taxpayers to other jurisdictions.

This asserted constraint on city agency should be familiar by now. Douglas Rae's technological explanation for the decline of the industrial city is similarly pessimistic about the city's capacities in the face of shifting private-side decisions about where to invest. For those who have witnessed the decline of the great industrial cities over the last half-century, this basic point appears almost unremarkable. The twentieth-century city's dependence on mobile factors has seemed to be its defining feature.[4] The proof is in the rapid withdrawal of investment from some cities and its rapid deployment elsewhere.

We should hesitate to embrace the limited city, however—even on its own terms. Recall that Peterson begins with the notion that cities need to maximize their "market position, their attractiveness as a locale for economic activity." Further, he argues that doing so means having "a competitive edge in the production and distribution of desired commodities relative to other localities."[5] Indeed, as Peterson writes, "it is only a modest oversimplification to equate the interests of cities with the interests of their export industries."[6]

There is a great deal one could say about this claim, though here I will make just three relatively brief observations. First, it is important to note that equating a city's interests with its export industries is a fairly radical statement, embedding in it assumptions about the urban marketplace, the "truth" of intercity competition, the role that exports might play in the city's economic growth, and the relationship between exports and the general welfare. Only by narrowly defining the mechanics of the city's economic health—synonymous with the health of its export industries—can Peterson conclude that developmental spending will in fact contribute to the general welfare.

Second, even if we assume that the city's welfare is identical to the welfare of the city's export industries, the means for advancing the health of local export industries is not obvious. The term "redistribution" is normally associated with social welfarist policies—the shifting of money from rich to poor. But cities engage in large-scale activities that shift money from one taxpayer to another in the other direction. Economic development takings of the kind used in *Kelo*- and *Cuno*-style relocation incentives "redistribute" from current property owners to future businesses. The trick is figuring out which forms of redistribution contribute to the city's welfare and which do not—the "city's welfare" itself being an abstraction that can be defined by the inward or outward flow of capital, but need not be.[7]

In other words, distinguishing between redistributions that are benign and redistributions that are malign requires an account of how city policy affects economic growth. And, as I have been arguing, there is no reason to believe that development policy (or any other municipal policy) contributes to economic growth. One of my central claims is that so-called redistributive policies are no more inimical to the economic health of cities than so-called developmental policies are favorable to it.

Further, as we have seen in cases like *Cuno* and *Kelo*, the urban political contest is often a dispute about these very categories—about the justice or efficacy of particular city expenditures and who benefits or loses from them. Those conflicts cannot be defined away by choosing a particular side. "Redistribution" and "development" are not coherent categories except in some relation to an already given conclusion about the city's ends.

And finally, recall that the dependence of cities on private-side investment is a function of a particular legal structure. Those who assert that cities are constrained by development politics generally assume—whether they approve or not—that the broad outlines of the private, corporate capitalist economy are a given. Cities operate within a legal structure that privileges private ownership over public, that generally enforces private-side contract and property rights, and that makes possible large-scale enterprise and the accumulation of large-scale private wealth. In such a world, developmental policies seem like the only option. The dependence of the city on private business is over-determined.

As we saw in chapter 2, however, the division of the world into private corporations that engage in economic enterprises and municipal corporations that do not is a function of law, not nature. The division between corporations into those that exercise private power and those that exercise public power occurred in the mid-nineteenth century.[8] And while one would think that those exercising public power would be more powerful than those exercising "merely" private power, it turns out to be the opposite for cities. Because the city is a creature of private-side economic activity, the exercise of private power becomes crucial to the realization of the city's public functions. The primacy of development politics in the city is obviously a feature of such a regime.

At this point, we can see how "is" becomes "ought." That cities cannot engage in social welfare redistribution is often presented as a fact about the natural world. This "fact," however, assumes a relationship between city policy and a particular theory of economic growth that we have no reason to believe is true. It also assumes that we can figure out what constitutes "developmental" as opposed to "redistributive" policy. And finally, the bias toward development is a feature of a particular institutional structure—one that embodies a legally enforced division between state and market. If cities *are* in fact engaging in forms of redistribution that were heretofore thought impossible, then that fact may change our conceptions of what they *ought* to be doing going forward.

Mandating a Living Wage

Consider the municipal living and minimum wage movement, which on conventional economic accounts should be a nonstarter. Wage floors, it has been generally assumed, need to be set regionally or nationally. Otherwise, employers will flee across the border. And yet many cities have adopted wage floors that are significantly above the national or state level. The mere fact that municipal living and minimum wage laws exist is highly significant. Under the conventional view of the appropriate division of authority between levels of government and the standard theory of urban finance, they should not.

Nevertheless, city wage laws have steadily expanded, in the number of cities adopting them, the amount of the wage floor, and the businesses covered. The first local living wage campaign began in Baltimore in 1994. Approximately 140 cities have now adopted some version of a living wage or local minimum wage ordinance.[9] Many of these laws are limited to city employees and businesses that contract with the city. But that has been changing rapidly. Cities have begun to adopt broader business assistance ordinances that cover all businesses that receive some sort of aid from the city, that target all businesses in a particular industry, or that cover all employers (often exempting small businesses, however) in the jurisdiction.[10]

Indeed, citywide minimum wages in the largest cities, combined with new state-wide minimum wage laws, will eventually cover millions of employees. As of the beginning of 2016, San Francisco, Seattle, and Los Angeles had all adopted an hourly wage of $15, to be phased in over a number of years. Other examples include Buffalo, Rochester, Greensboro, Missoula, and Pittsburgh. Those cities are gradually raising their minimums to $15 for city workers. Albuquerque, San Jose, Santa Fe, San Diego, Oakland, Chicago, Portland, Maine, and Washington, D.C., have adopted somewhat lower minimums, though the coverage may be broader. In addition, spurred by municipal efforts, New York and California have adopted new statewide minimum wage laws. In New York City, the minimum will be raised to $15 by the end of 2018. Somewhat lower minimums will apply outside the city. In all cases, the wage floors are significantly higher than the national wage floor. Fifteen dollars an hour is more than double the current federal minimum wage.

Cities have also adopted other legislation favoring workers, especially low-wage ones. San Francisco has a paid sick leave ordinance, which guarantees all private sector workers up to seventy-two hours of paid sick leave. The city's health care security ordinance requires employers to provide health insurance to their workers or pay the city's Department of Public Health to do so. In Milwaukee, the city requires that contractors remain neutral in labor unionization efforts. A number of cities have also embraced wage theft ordinances in a bid to protect low-wage workers. In short, municipalities have become fertile sites for labor and employment policy.[11]

These wage and labor laws are components of a more comprehensive campaign to redefine the relationship between labor and capital at the municipal level. The labor movement's decline has paralleled the industrial city's decline. As the U.S. economy has moved away from heavy industry, both labor unions and the cities that relied on union members for their prosperity have experienced the same fate. Moreover, as labor power has dissipated, the shared interests of labor and urban politicians have dissipated as well. In the 1950s and '60s, big-city Democratic mayors supported the unionizing efforts of municipal workers. By the mid-1970s, however, this New Deal city-labor coalition had fractured as fiscally strapped cities faced escalating and increasingly militant public sector work actions.[12] Since then, the relationship between cities and municipal unions has been strained.

Outside the context of municipal unions, however, the new, smaller labor movement has found it productive to work for the adoption of labor-friendly legislation at the municipal level. And, to a surprising degree, sympathetic local officials have responded. The city-by-city approach is a function of the declining influence of—and hostility toward—labor on the federal level, the possibility of alliances with progressive mayors and city councils, and labor's new emphasis on organizing the low-wage service sector, which is heavily concentrated in large urban areas.

That cities have been the primary sites for minimum wage movements reflects the gap between local and national political opportunities. Living wage campaigns are examples of urban-based community-labor coalitions using the channels of municipal law-making to gain labor rights that would otherwise be political nonstarters at the federal level. The Seattle city council's vote in 2014 to raise the municipal minimum wage to $15 an hour came just weeks after Congress rejected a bill to increase the federal minimum wage from $7.25 to $10.10.[13] As Scott Cummings has observed, "Big cities . . . have become important sites for contesting low-wage service employment."[14]

Often these wage laws begin with a particular subset of workers: office janitors in Houston, low-wage garment workers in New York, and homecare workers/hotel employees in Los Angeles. Fast-food workers have organized across a number of cities, including New York, where the mayor favored a minimum wage increase that was eventually supported by the governor. These campaigns began with service workers because service workers are relatively "immune from the threat of exports used to discipline workers in the manufacturing context." Service industries must be provided in place—they are tied to local and regional economies.[15]

Labor's effort to support low-wage service workers also aligns with the city's interests. The working poor make up a significant percentage of central city populations. The services they provide in retail, hospitality, domestic service, cleaning, and security, however, are often heavily consumed by nonresidents—visitors who use the city's hotels, restaurants, hospitals, universities, and other locally-based and locally-dependent amenities; highly paid office workers who commute into the city; and suburbanites, who often purchase services from low-wage workers who reside in the city. Cities shoulder the burden of the large numbers of working poor who service the regional economy. Cities can assist them by shifting costs onto their employers, and in part, onto nonresidents.

Consider the evolution of Los Angeles's broad-based living wage law adopted in May 2015. The movement for a citywide living wage began with the regulation of the wages of hotel workers working near the Los Angeles International Airport (LAX). In 2008, the city adopted an ordinance that required that large hotels in the immediate vicinity of LAX pay a living wage. The ordinance was passed after coordination between the city and UNITE-HERE, a union representing many hotel and service-sector employees. The city's stated justification for the ordinance was that the hotels "not only derive significant and unique business benefits from their close proximity to LAX, a major public and City asset that produces numerous patrons of these hotels on a daily basis, but from the City's designation of the Corridor as an 'Airport Hospitality Enhancement Zone,'" with the added municipal services that come with that designation. In 2015, after a significant lobbying effort on the part of low-wage service workers, the city adopted a broader ordinance that phases in a $15.37 wage that applies to all hotels in the city. The extension of the minimum wage law to all low-wage workers followed soon thereafter.

The Los Angeles Alliance for a New Economy (LAANE), a non-union advocacy group, was instrumental in pursuing both the hotel wage law and the more comprehensive law. Hotels were an initially attractive target because they employ a significant population of low-income workers, many of whom are not unionized; they cannot readily move across the border to another city; and their costs can often be passed onto nonresident visitors to the city. LAX is an infrastructure anchor—hotels have little choice but to locate near the airport if they wish to gain access to their customer base. Those customers may be the ultimate bearers of the cost of the ordinance.

Who ultimately pays the costs of local minimum wage laws and other locally mandated employee benefits is relevant to the larger question of their efficacy. In Chicago, for example, the younger Mayor Daley vetoed a 2006 ordinance that would have required the payment of a living wage by all retail establishments over 90,000 square feet with revenue greater than $1 billion.[16] The purpose of the ordinance was to impose a living wage on big-box retailers, in particular the largest U.S. (and worldwide) employer Walmart. Walmart has long resisted efforts by its employees to unionize and has been frequently criticized for paying poverty wages. The city council's action was in response to significant organizing and agitation around that very issue. But Daley worried that the ordinance would "drive jobs and businesses from [the] city, penalizing neighborhoods that need additional economic activity the most."[17]

New York City's former mayor, Michael Bloomberg, objected in similar terms to a living wage proposal for his city. In 2010, a proposal was introduced to significantly expand New York City's narrow contractor-only living wage law to a broad "business assistance" ordinance covering all firms and real property owners receiving financial assistance from the city for economic development. The Bloomberg administration, however, shared Daley's fears regarding the detrimental effects on business. Mayor Bloomberg was quoted as saying: "We've got to attract jobs in this city, and the marketplace is going to set the compensation. . . . The last time people tried to set rates, basically, was in the Soviet Union, and that didn't work out very well. I don't think we want to go in that direction."[18] Bloomberg ultimately vetoed the provision in 2012.

The dynamics of city wage laws have been changing rapidly, however. In 2014, after the election of a new mayor, Rahm Emanuel, Chicago set a wage floor that will reach $13 an hour by 2019. And in New York City, Bloomberg's successor Bill de Blasio expanded by executive order a living wage law that applies to development projects that receive subsidies from the city, increasing coverage from 1,200 workers to possibly 18,000. New York's more comprehensive state minimum wage followed soon thereafter. Walmart itself raised its hourly wage for some workers in 2015,[19] in part because of pressure from city governments.

Nevertheless, Mayors Daley and Bloomberg both articulated a common objection to local minimum wage laws: that raising labor costs will reduce employment or limit business development. On a competitive theory of city growth and decline, this seems obviously true. Cities must compete to make themselves attractive to global capital, and competition is associated with lower costs.

But on a second look, this objection cannot be right, at least not in its sound-bite formulation. If labor costs were determinative, all of Manhattan's economic activities (where labor costs are high) would be taking place in nearby Jersey City or Newark—or in Camden or New London (where labor costs are low). Indeed, regardless of the mandated local minimum wage, labor costs are generally higher in economically robust cities and generally lower in economically depressed ones. Yet we do not see massive shifts of economic activity from one to the other.

In fact, as I observed in chapter 1, economic geographers have shown that richer places tend to get richer and poorer places tend to get poorer—at least as an initial matter. Despite significant differences in labor costs across metropolitan areas, states, nations, and continents, economic development seems to seek out other development, not solely or even predominantly lower labor costs. And to the chagrin of economists, the convergence in living standards across places that is a predicted outcome of conventional economic theory has not occurred. Despite higher labor costs, Manhattan's economy continues to flourish, Germany's economy continues to dominate, and Europe's economy continues to outperform Africa's. The cities that have adopted living wages tend to be places with higher wage scales. If they were already hampered by those wage rates, they do not appear to have suffered from it.

Perhaps that is why studies of local living wages do not conclude with what neoclassical economic theory would expect: decreases in employment or decreases in business development as firms locate elsewhere.[20] Indeed, there is some evidence that local increases in the minimum wage not only fail to cause more unemployment, but may in fact increase employment in some contexts.

In SeaTac, Washington, a Seattle suburb where the major employer is the region's international airport, the city voted to raise the hourly minimum wage to $15 for the 6,300 people who work at the airport, hotels, and nearby businesses. While companies expressed concern that the higher pay would force businesses to cut jobs, this has not been the case. One airport parking lot operator reported that while 140 of his employees have received raises, the company has not cut any job due to concerns that this would compromise their service and negatively impact their business. The cost has instead been spread to customers through the addition of a "living-wage surcharge" to daily parking prices.[21]

Similarly, a study by Michael Reich found no discernible impact on employment from San Jose's minimum wage, which primarily affected the restaurant industry. Data from 2013 show that unemployment fell in San Jose, and the San Jose Downtown Association reported that the number of restaurants in the district increased by 20%.[22] In a study of San Francisco's minimum wage, living wage, health care, and paid sick leave laws, researchers found that from 2004 to 2011, private-sector employment grew by 5.6% in San Francisco in comparison to a 4.4% decrease in other Bay Area counties that did not have a higher local wage.[23] Likewise, a study by T. William Lester that measures the actual impact of living wage laws, using a time-series analysis of employment and business establishment trends in large U.S. cities that have enacted these laws, found no evidence that ordinances mandating higher labor standards have an effect on aggregate economic development outcomes.[24]

The employment effect of the minimum wage is one of the most studied topics in all of economics, though consensus has proven to be elusive.[25] Disagreement among scholars can largely be traced to research methodology, differences in statistical framework, and publication bias. Standard state panel-data surveys that include all or a large sample of living wage cities tend to find a negative impact on employment, while case studies that examine employment in a particular city before and after an increase in the minimum wage tend to find minimal-to-no negative effects on employment levels.[26]

A recent monograph by Dale Belman and Paul J. Wolfson reviews the current varying opinions regarding the effects of living wages on business development and aggregate employment levels.[27] Belman and Wolfson's meta-analysis aggregates all of the employment and hours research from the past fifteen years, providing estimates of the effect of the minimum wage corrected for methodological differences and article-specific effects. They find that a 10% increase in the minimum wage is best estimated to reduce employment between 0.03 and 0.6%, but these effects are not statistically significant.[28] Their exhaustive analysis of minimum wage empirical data concludes that moderate increases in the minimum wage "raise the hourly wage and earnings of workers in the lower part of the wage distribution and have very modest or no effects on employment, hours, and other labor market outcomes."[29]

Despite some academic disagreement over the effect of minimum wage laws on business development and location decisions, there is less disagreement regarding their overall effectiveness in decreasing poverty. Even the strongest negative employment estimate is "a small drop in aggregate employment" compared to the number of beneficiaries of minimum wage increases.[30] A number of recent studies support the theory that living wage laws are successful in bringing about wage increases for low-income workers and a decrease in citywide poverty levels. One study examined the impact of citywide minimum wage in three cities: San Francisco, Santa Fe, and Washington, D.C. The report found that in San Francisco and Santa Fe, where the minimum wage was set sufficiently high to affect wages, there was a statistically significant increase in the average wage of low-wage establishments, and no statistically significant change in employment at these affected establishments.[31] In Washington, however, the increase in minimum wage was so minor and the compliance so weak that the findings did not yield any conclusive results of the effects of the city's minimum wage laws. The positive findings regarding the cities of Santa Fe and San

Francisco, though, are consistent with most of the recent literature on this topic.

A living wage ordinance that has small negative effects on employment but large positive effects on overall city poverty is likely a trade that most cities would make. The more important point, however, is that city growth and decline cannot be readily attributed to the cost structures of particular places. That economically struggling neighborhoods in Chicago or New York or Camden do not already benefit from their lower labor costs effectively undercuts the contrary assertion. These lower-cost neighborhoods are already "competing" in the way that Daley and Bloomberg urged them to—but to little avail. Lower labor costs have not fixed what ails them. And higher labor costs are not going to derail the economic activities already taking place in growing places. Those costs have not heretofore done so and, barring some extreme changes, they will not. Prospering cities will absorb these costs. And struggling ones will not be better competitors simply because they have lower wages.

To be sure, there are some concerns about races-to-the-bottom. The previous chapter noted how the distribution of existing wealth across metropolitan areas is affected by the existence of local government boundaries. Those boundaries define the taxable resources available to the jurisdiction and the residents who receive services there and can be excluded from receiving services elsewhere.

The combined effort by lawmakers in the Washington, D.C., metropolitan area to collectively raise the area's minimum wage can be understood as a response to this concern. In October 2013, lawmakers from Montgomery and Prince George counties and Washington, D.C., announced a "collaborative effort to lift the minimum wage to at least $11.50 an hour by 2016."[32] At the time, the minimum wage for the Maryland counties was set by federal law at $7.25, and in Washington, the minimum wage was $8.25. Local officials stated that this concerted, regional action was designed to increase the chances for success across all three jurisdictions, in large part by muting the concern about competitive races-to-the-bottom. Following a significant amount of local debate, particularly in the Maryland counties, minimum wage bills were eventually signed into law in all three localities creating a contiguous region with 2.5 million residents with a minimum wage higher than that of most states.

A metropolitan-area wage floor is an example of successful region-alism. As I argued in chapter 4, the jurisdictional boundaries in met-ropolitan areas like Washington's have little relationship to the area's economic boundaries. Metro regions are unified wage and labor mar-kets, but intraregional regulatory competition—despite its disconnect from economic growth or decline—creates perverse incentives. While regionalism is often understood as a way to share revenue across local governments, it should also be understood as a way of reducing regula-tory competition. A regional living wage undermines the incentive to "compete" for development through deregulation.

That being said, there is no compelling reason not to permit cities to adopt their own wage rates. And yet, a significant number of states bar municipalities from doing so. In New York, for example, the city cannot raise the minimum wage without state legislative approval. Proposals calling for the state to allow New York City to set its own minimum wage were rejected by state legislators, even as they eventually adopted a state-wide minimum wage that sets a higher floor for the city.

In other states, municipal wage and labor laws have been chal-lenged as falling outside of the authority of home rule jurisdictions. The Louisiana Supreme Court struck down the New Orleans living wage ordinance on these grounds. In New Mexico, however, the state court upheld Santa Fe's authority to institute a minimum wage. In New Jersey and California, courts have specifically held that local minimum wage ordinances are not preempted by federal law.[33]

As labor-community groups garner success at the municipal level, employers can shift scales. Even if they lose their preemption arguments based on existing law, employers can ask state legislatures to adopt newly preemptive legislation. In Wisconsin, the state legislature passed a law preventing municipalities from adopting a local minimum wage after the passage of such an ordinance in Madison. Alabama's legislature barred local minimum wages after Birmingham adopted a $10.10 wage floor. St. Louis's minimum wage law was struck down by a state judge. The Missouri legislature also affirmatively barred other cities in the state from adopting wage floors. North Carolina preempted all local wage laws even though it was not clear that cities had the authority to adopt them in the first place.

The success of minimum wage legislation in the cities depends not only on local political processes, but also on how immune local law-making is from contrary state intervention. In most cases, state legislatures can easily override local laws if there is the political desire. At least fifteen states now ban the adoption of local minimum wages, or otherwise restrict local efforts to regulate business.[34]

The municipal movement to adopt minimum wage laws, however, has influenced a number of states to *raise* their own wage floors. No doubt, municipal battles over fair wages have stimulated a wider national debate about inequality and labor standards. That cities have been the first movers is striking in light of the conventional economic wisdom. Though it would have been unheard of for cities to adopt minimum wages even a decade ago, we are now seeing cities with significant low-wage populations doing just that.

In turn, some states—including most prominently California and New York—have concluded that wage rates are too low and can be raised. As I observed in chapter 3, state officials take notice of their local political competitors. City officials' success in championing labor-friendly legislation can be leveraged by labor organizers into statewide campaigns. Success often breeds further success, as political entrepreneurs pave the way for later adopters.

Land-Use Unionism

Recent municipal minimum wage efforts have coincided with local efforts to hold specific developers or incoming industries to higher wage or labor standards. This is municipal regulation at the retail level, project-by-project, development-by-development.

An example is what I call "land-use unionism": organized labor's use of the local land development process to extract concessions from large employers, or prevent the entry of certain kinds of employers altogether. Here the city's authority over development can be harnessed to impose conditions on employers that are not required (or permitted) by general law, and to insulate those conditions from state or federal laws that would otherwise override them. In this way, the municipal economic development process can be used to pursue redistributive and labor-favoring agendas, even in the absence of state or national legislation—indeed, in the absence of any legislation at all.

The form that city regulation takes is shaped by the existing legal division of labor. Federal or state law often preempts direct local regulations of the labor and employment relationship. In the context of unionization efforts, the National Labor Relations Act governs labor-management disputes to the exclusion of any contrary laws at the state or local level. And so, municipal labor law has to be made in the interstices of the existing legal regime, through agreements between organized labor, the municipal government, and employers. Those agreements are enforceable under federal law, but they are not laws regulating labor directly—in which case, they would be preempted by federal law. Labor can thus pursue codes of organizing and bargaining rules that are—as Benjamin Sachs points out—"markedly different from the ones provided by federal statute" but that are also "invisible to preemption scrutiny."[35] In this way, locals can achieve labor rights that are often stymied at the national level, but through a mechanism that has nothing formally to do with labor regulation.

Sachs offers as an example the unionization efforts of hospital employees working for the Yale-New Haven Hospital system. As he observes, those efforts were regularly stalled until the hospital sought numerous city approvals in connection with its development of a new cancer center. The hospital needed permits for demolition and construction, but more importantly, it needed the city to modify its current zoning ordinance and transfer city land in order to proceed with construction. The New England Health Care Employees District 1199 union pressured the mayor and city council to condition the city's approvals on the hospital entering into a negotiated labor agreement outside the federal labor relations process. That process had been acrimonious for years and had produced little in the way of benefits for the health care workers.

The land-use process, along with favorable city politics and a sympathetic mayor, provided leverage in the union's negotiations. The hospital expansion required the support of the mayor and the city council, and they together exercised significant decision-making authority over city development processes. Faced with the political and practical reality of an intransigent municipal bureaucracy, which was moving slowly or not at all, the hospital eventually entered into two agreements that linked the development of the cancer center to a path for unionization of the health care workers.

The agreement with New Haven required the hospital to provide a direct payment to the city, several jobs programs, and a youth initiative. A separate side agreement between the hospital and Local 1199—brokered by the mayor—ensured that there would be a fair process for a secret ballot election on the question of unionization. The hospital agreed to allow union organizers access to hospital property, to disseminate only accurate information about the organizing campaign, to submit grievances about the process to an arbitrator selected by the parties, and not to hold one-on-one meetings with employees to discourage them from supporting unionization. Each of these conditions was a labor-favoring departure from baseline NLRA requirements. But each was enforceable under the NLRA, which requires enforcement of such labor-management contracts.[36]

Two features of the New Haven deal are notable, reflecting the legal context that both restrains and makes city power possible. First, New Haven was exercising its own property rights in a circumstance involving an employer that had already made substantial commitments to a particular location. The cancer center expansion required New Haven to transfer city-owned land to the hospital. When a city is providing subsidies or tax incentives to local developers, including its own land, it has more formal power to place conditions on how those subsidies will operate and who will receive them. Certainly in cases where a city subsidy is sought, the city can exercise more political influence over the deal. And in cases where the city is deciding how to dispose of its own land, municipal policy discretion is likely at its height.

This discretion reflects an intuition that exercises of the city's spending and contracting powers are different from exercises of the city's regulatory power. Consider the market participant exemption to labor preemption, which the courts have formally recognized, albeit with limitations. The exemption means that absent a state law to the contrary, cities can insist that contractors who enter into contracts with the city adopt certain labor standards. Those labor standards might also be incorporated into local procurement and investment policies—again, if state law permits.

These proprietary practices are still subject to some limits, both in the labor context and under other constitutional doctrines. The Supreme Court has been wary of too broad a reading of the market participant exception to the labor laws—it is aware that government can act by both putting conditions on spending and regulating directly.[37] And, as we saw in chapter 4, Camden's rule requiring that municipal contractors employ at least 40% city residents was challenged under the constitutional prohibition against cross-border employment discrimination. Nevertheless, the distinction between the city's regulatory and proprietary identity has concrete implications for the exercise of municipal power.

In contrast, the city's exercise of its land-use authority is obviously regulatory. But here too the fact that city land-use approvals were at issue helped insulate the city's labor-related conditions from preemption concerns. It is not contested that New Haven exercises authority over its own land and over the land-use process generally. Municipalities are not permitted to adopt labor regulations, but they can regulate land use in a way that affects labor rights. Put differently: There is no municipal labor law, but there is also no federal land-use law. Employers who have entered into agreements that alter the background rules of labor organizing cannot claim that municipal law is in conflict with federal law.

That land-use authority is being deployed in this way is the second notable feature of "local labor law." That city power can be brought to bear through the local development and land-use process is an artifact of the planning process itself. To the formalist's chagrin, the give and take of the local land-use process is shot full of ad hoc agreements, behind the scenes deal-making, and site-specific concessions. Land-use variances and other regulatory approvals are often contingent on developer acquiescence to government demands, whether or not those demands are explicitly articulated or would ultimately be permitted by law.

There are limits—judicial review ensures some regularity in the planning and development process—but litigation is costly. For this reason, the local land-use regulatory process is often criticized as unprincipled and extralegal.[38] But it is precisely the fact that the land-use process provides room for political considerations that gives labor and antipoverty groups leverage.

Consider laws regulating chain and big-box stores, which can be deployed to encourage unionization, gain wage concessions, and enforce health care mandates. Numerous cities have adopted anti-chain store laws, which may limit the square footage of particular retail outlets, impose specific conditions on large stores (as did the proposed Chicago ordinance), or exclude chain stores from particular areas of the city altogether. Some local jurisdictions have required that incoming big-box developers apply for a conditional-use permit or engage in a market impact study before proceeding.[39]

Additionally, some cities have embraced anti-chain store laws as a means for enforcing state and local environmental regulations. Similar to market impact analyses, certain cities require big-box stores that are seeking to locate in their jurisdiction to conduct an environmental impact survey (EIS) as a way "to slow down, to increase the cost of [construction], [or] . . . prevent the construction of a store." The ability to use laws requiring an EIS, regardless of motive, has been lauded as "a way for citizen activists to participate in the [local] decision-making process."[40]

Anti-chain regulations or EISs can simply represent another form of NIMBY-ism. As I argued in the previous chapter, land-use law can be used to erect boundaries that severely limit metro-wide economic integration. Consider that in some cases—such as affluent towns or suburbs—anti-chain sentiment is driven by aesthetics or class bias or by neighborhood concerns about traffic congestion and parking. Anti-chain ordinances in these settings serve the same purposes as other exclusionary or fiscal land-use regulations: preservation of neighborhood land values or exclusion of undesirable or costly land uses or users.

More interesting are the big-box site fights that occur in less affluent and more urban areas. The anti-big box store campaigns in these settings have a strong labor rights component. By erecting barriers to entry into valuable markets, labor-community groups hope to force Walmart (and other retailers) to pay higher wages, offer better health benefits, and, most significantly, succumb to unionization. Their bet is that urban markets are promising enough to leverage reforms in retailer employment practices.

As was the case with the New Haven hospital deal, the anti-chain store project is intended to gain indirectly what cannot be gained directly. As Catherine Fisk and Michael Oswalt have observed, "the strategies that would enable worker advocates to challenge Walmart's labor practices most directly are largely foreclosed by inadequate federal protection of the right to unionize."[41] Workers' rights advocates have thus turned to the municipal zoning and planning process. Even if cities cannot adopt labor laws, they can adopt land-use laws.

As I have previously noted, courts *do* oversee local land-use deals to prevent coercion of property owners. The Supreme Court has applied its unconstitutional conditions doctrine to local land-use practices. Thus, when a developer comes to the city seeking development approvals, the city cannot impose conditions unless those conditions have a "nexus" and are "proportionate" to the proposed development's negative effects. These constitutional requirements certainly place an outer limit on the exercise of the city's land-use authority and can influence local land-use practices—though how much in practice is uncertain. State courts often also place limits, statutory or constitutional, on the degree to which the municipal land-use process can be used to extract concessions from landowners.

The formal constitutional limits on the municipal land-use power, however, are less important than the political space that is opened up by the exercise of this power generally. Thus far, for example, courts have been almost uniformly deferential to chain store bans and other local barriers to entry (as they are to zoning generally). This is true despite the fact that these laws are often explicitly protectionist or have obvious protectionist effects. Indeed, exclusionary but facially neutral local land-use policies do not normally excite constitutional scrutiny. As the California Court of Appeal held: "so long as the primary purpose of the zoning ordinance is not to regulate economic competition, but to subserve a valid objective pursuant to the city's police powers, such ordinance is not invalid even though it might have an indirect impact on economic competition."[42] By utilizing the planning and zoning process, labor-community groups—operating through the instrument of local government—can exercise some influence over the forms of capital that enter the jurisdiction.

One could raise a democratic objection to the use of the land development process in this way. The local development process is often politically opaque. Normally, this lack of transparency favors repeat players who are more likely to have the resources and interests to monitor and advocate before local land-use authorities. In big cities, those players are usually developers and landowners. In smaller jurisdictions, local land-use authorities might defer to the loudest voices, like NIMBY homeowners, even if those interests are contrary to the public interest.

The solution to the problem of political capture in the development process, however, is not to foreclose its use by non-developer interests, but to have open political debates about the values animating a particular development decision. It was no secret in New Haven that the hospital's cancer center expansion was being held up because of the hospital's hostility to unionization. And so, though indirect, a discussion nominally about development became a discussion about unionization and the treatment of labor more generally.

So too, there is no reason that a local debate about an incoming Walmart cannot be both a debate about development patterns and a public discussion about the treatment of local workers. That the resulting municipal labor law can only be made in the shadows is a function of a legal regime that prevents cities from regulating directly.

Of course, imposing conditions on or excluding particular employers is only possible if local residents are willing to bear the costs, in taxes foregone or in reduced access to consumer goods or jobs. The effects of exclusion will be felt very differently in a declining city—where taxes are already prohibitive and consumer goods are difficult for locals to access—and a wealthy suburb—where property taxes are relatively low and residents can easily gain access to consumer goods located in a neighboring jurisdiction.

Indeed, as we have seen, suburban jurisdictions have been adept at using exclusionary land-use laws to manage their local tax base—mostly by excluding newcomers who would create a drain on local fiscal resources. That labor-friendly city-based movements are using similar tools to redistribute might raise some similar concerns. But as we saw in chapter 4, metropolitan-area boundaries and the rules of the intra-metro "free trade regime" encourage the employment of land-use-based strategies when they might work.

Regulating through Contract

Land-use-based strategies are an example of a more pervasive phenomenon: the direct deal-by-deal regulation of urban development. Cities have always put conditions on landowners and made development projects contingent on particular concessions. Increasingly, that process is becoming more formalized. In addition, the kinds of demands being made and the interest groups making them are expanding.

The rise of community benefits agreements (CBAs)—a tool used in the New Haven case—is a chief example. CBAs are agreements negotiated between prospective developers and community groups over the terms of specific development projects. In exchange for community political support, the developer might commit to limiting displacement of current residents or providing resettlement support or specified units of low-income housing. CBAs can also involve agreements for developers to provide certain neighborhood services such as parks, recreation, or childcare facilities, and they often involve developer commitments to pay a living wage, adopt local-favoring hiring preferences, embrace labor peace agreements, or provide for environmentally friendly or sustainable building or development practices.

There is no requirement that a CBA be connected to a project receiving public subsidies, but that has usually been the case. As in New Haven, community bargaining leverage is at its strongest when developers are seeking government subsidies or project approvals. Communities can create roadblocks in the zoning process to cause costly delays for developers.[43]

CBAs are relatively new—the first full-fledged CBA appeared in 2001.[44] But they are similar to clawback provisions, which require that industries or firms that receive government subsidies or other forms of assistance meet certain public interest goals. Clawback provisions have been used "with almost every form of industrial subsidy in ... European nations, including Italy, the Netherlands, Northern Ireland, Great Britain, Germany, Denmark, Luxemburg, and Belgium." One of the first of the modern American clawback provisions was adopted by New Haven over twenty years ago. Now twenty states and over one hundred cities have clawback provisions.[45] These provisions vary in their scope, triggers, and penalties, but they generally require subsidized firms to provide a specified public benefit. Often the primary requirement is that the firm remain in the community for a particular period of time or forfeit the subsidy. Clawback provisions are cousins to plant closing statutes. Those statutes require certain businesses to provide notice to local communities before ceasing operations and, in some cases, require businesses to make specified payments to affected employees or into a community assistance fund.

Unlike clawbacks, CBAs usually require developers to agree to some front-end conditions and are not necessarily enforced by the municipality. Nevertheless, both techniques seek to create accountability for publicly subsidized development—to link public approval to regulatory compliance. At their best, clawbacks and CBAs are efforts to ensure that public investments in private enterprise generate a concomitant public benefit, and that the costs of the project do not unduly burden particular neighborhoods.[46]

A number of features of CBAs make them an attractive tool in an otherwise limited regulatory environment. Because it is a site-specific private agreement, the CBA can bypass municipal officials or traditional federal grant-receiving housing or redevelopment agencies. This feature is attractive to community groups for a number of reasons. First, city council members, directors of the local housing authority, or the mayor's office may be too inclined to favor land-based developmental interests over other kinds of resident interests. To the extent city politics is dominated by developer interests, its public officials may not adequately represent the interests of residents who are negatively affected by those developmental policies.

Relatedly, the use of private enforcers is attractive because it does not depend on the political inclinations of a particular mayoral administration. Again, the politics of development in the city are oft-changing. There is no guarantee that particular development deals will be honored by incoming administrations. Giving community groups a stake in the development process may better ensure that the developer's commitments will be honored.

Second, the private nature of the agreement arguably insulates the bargain from constitutional takings or equal protection challenges. As I have already noted, federal and state constitutional law often frowns on "coercive" bargains that trade city approvals or permits for developer concessions, when those concessions are not directly related to the land-use-related costs of the project. But developer agreements with private groups do not constitute exactions subject to federal constitutional limitations.[47] CBA groups are not the city. They do not wield any formal authority over the development process. They can merely threaten political pressure.

A third benefit of CBAs is that they permit the city to regulate piece-meal what it could not otherwise regulate wholesale. Consider again the New Haven unionization effort. As we have already seen, because CBAs are not municipal law, they can "impose a host of standards on developers that federal preemption law would prohibit states and cities from imposing directly." Indeed, CBAs can be used to impose not only labor standards but other requirements on businesses, including health care requirements, and immigration and environmental standards. These requirements would typically be preempted by federal laws or regulatory standards.[48]

Of course, the existence of a CBA does not guarantee that it will be effective or in the public interest. The local political process, including the development process, can be used to enhance developers' power just as readily as it can be used to limit it. Developers have an interest in lim-iting or eliminating opposition to a project as early as possible and may use the CBA process to do so. In San Francisco, a regional CBA program gives companies that move to low-income areas of the city payroll tax breaks, but only if the company completes a number of tasks to help im-prove its new neighborhood. The program has been touted by some as largely successful in attracting business to economically depressed areas. Critics argue, however, that CBA companies are receiving much more in tax breaks than they return in community outreach. They further argue that, given the significant city subsidies, the companies' efforts have been too minimal and monetary donations far too low.[49]

A number of CBAs connected to redevelopment projects in New York City have been criticized on the grounds that the CBA process has been co-opted by the developers themselves. And certainly, the existence of a CBA in itself tells us nothing about the quality or purposes of the deal that was struck.[50] There is no formal mechanism or safeguard in place to ensure that CBAs are negotiated ethically and in the best interest of all affected parties and the greater community. At its worst, the CBA process is merely a different mechanism by which developer interests are advanced.

The advantages of CBAs are thus also what make them susceptible to possible abuse. First, because they are "private" agreements, CBAs may be contrary to the interests of the city or (some of) its residents, especially if the process of drafting the CBA lacks transparency. The worry is that CBA bargaining groups will not be representative, that the CBA process will be subject to political capture, or that the deal brokered will favor certain residents or community interests over others. The concern that CBAs may enhance developer power or the power of well-placed public officials or particular interest groups is fair. Private-side deal-making in the shadow of political mobilization can easily take on the character of extortion or a payoff, whether initiated by community groups, local public officials, or the developers themselves.[51]

Second, CBAs may be difficult to enforce. CBA terms might be vague or difficult to interpret, and ensuring compliance by developers of ongoing obligations is costly. Private enforcement is very time-consuming. Some critics argue that private regulation through a CBA is inferior to public regulation, that city officials are in a better position to adequately take into account the costs and benefits of any given development project, and that piecemeal regulation is inequitable and will favor certain developer interests over others.[52]

Skeptics of CBAs prefer an urban land-use process that is democratic, responsive to public needs, and enforced through transparent and fair public regulation. The reality is that such a process rarely exists. American-style urban development has never been particularly transparent, whether undertaken by city agencies or public-private groups. Private interests have long utilized the local development process for their own aims.

That community, labor, and poverty groups would take a more active role in city development decisions does not suddenly make that process any more suspect. There is no doubt that CBAs represent the outcome of a bargaining process between interested actors, and the outcome of that bargain will favor certain groups over others; but that CBAs formalize those deals should be viewed as a positive development. At their best, CBAs bring those groups that have traditionally been on the fringes of the development process into the discussion. And the process can serve as a check on the power of city officials when those officials are acting more in the private than in the public interest. CBAs can be understood as a second-best solution to the existing inequalities of business-friendly development policies.

Indeed, the move to connect public subsidy and private compliance must be understood in the context of the postwar history of urban redevelopment initiatives, most of which have been considered failures.[53] A thorough history of these programs is beyond this chapter, but the litany of criticisms is familiar: Urban redevelopment has relied too heavily on private-side investment; it has emphasized displacement and gentrification over reinvestment; it has lacked citizen participation or neighborhood input; and it has been riddled with patronage, incompetence, and distribution to favored groups.[54] Mostly, however, urban redevelopment policy has been unsuccessful—a conclusion that is not surprising if one is skeptical about the relationship between city policy and local economic growth.

Community groups' skepticism is more elemental, for they are wary—for good reason—of both the public and the private sectors. The older clawbacks and the newer CBA movement are responses to past promises made and not kept—private-side development that did not deliver economic benefits or that distributed economic burdens and benefits unfairly. Development policy has not just failed; it has also often exploited already marginalized citizens.

These failures might have been a product of a lack of foresight by government officials or a function of their outright collusion with downtown business interests—both are in evidence in the history of urban renewal and industrial subsidization. Public redevelopment funds have often benefited developers, downtown business interests, the construction trades, and other interest groups without demonstrably improving the condition of depressed urban neighborhoods, oftentimes making the residents of those neighborhoods markedly worse off.[55]

CBAs are both a response to these failures of urban policy and a function of the significant cutbacks in federal and state support for urban initiatives. Since the 1980s and the pullback in federal funds, urban infrastructure has been a thoroughly private-public enterprise; there simply is not sufficient government will or money to fund even traditional municipal infrastructure—like housing, schools, roads, or parks—absent private investment. In this environment, the traditional public routes for influencing local infrastructure development are diminished.

The rise of CBAs thus represents an entrepreneurial response to the increased privatization of the city's public functions, namely its regulatory and redistributive functions. On the regulatory side, cities face procedural and substantive limits on their authority to demand concessions from developers, even those it is subsidizing. And, as we have seen, city officials cannot directly require compliance with laws that are not within their province to adopt. The primacy of federal labor, environmental, securities, and other laws means that cities and their citizens are dependent on national actors for protection. The combination of federal under-enforcement and preemption of direct local regulation, however, produces a significant gap between citizen needs and the city's ability to respond. CBAs thus represent a way—albeit limited—for cities to regulate around their jurisdictional limits.

Conclusion: Exercising Urban Power

There is a historical analog to this form of urban regulation. As I observed in chapter 2, in the nineteenth century, the corporation of the City of New York regulated for the public good through the sale of its own property. Hendrik Hartog shows how the city's conditional land grants constituted a form of government regulation in an era when the taxing and regulatory capacities of the city were otherwise quite limited. New York City governed through individual land deals—by leveraging the conditions it could attach to the sale and lease of its private property.

CBAs and other ad hoc development processes can be seen in similar terms, though the reasons for the need to regulate through property are different. In the nineteenth century, the absence of a robust social welfare state and limits on the government's authority to tax and spend meant that cities had to do their work through private intermediaries. In the twenty-first century, cities enjoy taxing and spending powers, even if their taxing capacities are sometimes quite restrained. The presence of equally robust state and federal authority means, however, that city regulatory preferences are often marginalized and that local government regulation often cannot take place because of contrary state or federal commands.

Cities are thus seeking to exercise power in situations where there is an absence of policy consensus on the state and federal levels and a strong local desire for action in areas of significant citizen concern. That cities are adopting minimum wage laws suggests that they can engage in at least some kinds of redistribution that conventional models of urban finance and the administrative state would reject. Existing theories of competitive federalism do not anticipate that possibility—a signal that those theories need to be modified.

But what is also true is that a significant amount of that regulation will not come in the traditional form of ordinances adopted by the city council and signed by the mayor. Rather, the city, its agents, or neighborhood, community, and labor groups will turn to individualized contracts that require developers to do things that municipal law does not and cannot require of them. The negotiation over development in the city will continue to involve public officials, but increasingly also private actors, who will be tasked with enforcing the rules that govern specific projects.

And so we get piecemeal, somewhat haphazard regulation through city development processes. But not always—local minimum or living wage laws are straightforward exercises of local government authority. But even when the city regulates through municipal ordinance, it is highly susceptible to state overrides in those states that are hostile to the city's agenda. It might be more attractive to use individual development deals to extract concessions and thereby avoid attracting the attention of a hostile state legislature.

Invariably, the use of the development process in this way will excite opposition, as it did in the nineteenth century. The intermixing of public and private always raises concerns about fairness, coercion, and self-dealing. Recall that the drawing of a rigid jurisprudential line between public property and private property arose in part from these concerns.[56] Again, the purpose was to define the city's power in order to allow regulation for the public good while disallowing the use of public power to enhance private wealth—to prevent the redistribution of property from a disfavored interest to a favored one.

The city's public and private aspects are not so easily disentangled, however. And what constitutes a redistribution that is in the public interest is often in the eye of the beholder. What we can do is distinguish between those redistributions that aid and abet labor and relatively immobile low-wage workers and those that aid and abet landowners and relatively mobile corporations. Municipal minimum wage laws, land-use unionism, and labor-friendly CBAs represent the former. Industrial subsidies and location incentive packages represent the latter. In many instances, the city does and can engage in both kinds of redistributions simultaneously. But now, when it does so, we can no longer say that the city's social welfare spending is impossible and that the city's subsidization of mobile capital is inevitable.

6

The City Redistributes II: Politics

WHAT EXPLAINS THE RISE of a regulatory and redistributive urban politics that defies the conventional economic wisdom and finds ways around enduring political and legal constraints? Recall that the standard model does not merely assert that social welfare redistribution will have negative effects on growth in a competitive environment, but also that city politics generally will not allow it—that the city's political economy is invariably dominated by the forces of development. The first is a claim that urban politics is relatively uninteresting because local elected officials' policy options are by necessity limited. The second is a claim that because cities are so reliant on private-side investment, their politics will be dominated by business and other "growth-pursuing" interest groups.

In the previous chapter, I began to challenge both these claims. Municipal politics *is* interesting when separated from our theoretical preconceptions about what that politics can be about. That is not to say that municipal decision-making is politically autonomous. As I have shown, state and national officials limit the power of local officials, often quite significantly. Urban politics occurs against the backdrop of a state-based federalism that produces generally weak cities. These institutional constraints are real.

Nevertheless, city officials—and in particular, city officials in larger U.S. cities—have some leverage when seeking to pursue agendas other than those that are congenial to development capital. This does not mean those officials will pursue such agendas, but only that a different kind of politics is possible.[1]

This chapter describes some features of that politics—in some ways emerging and in some ways always dormant. The chapter begins by highlighting recent research suggesting that city politics *matters*—that citizen preferences concerning regulation and redistribution can be turned into local policy. This may be unsurprising to the layperson, but a significant and important strand of political theory asserts that the political party of the mayor or dominant coalition in a city makes little difference to municipal policy outcomes. If cities are limited by the economics of capital flight, then they will invariably converge on the same pro-developmental agenda. As we saw in the previous chapter, this is not what has happened.

The rest of the chapter discusses some features of an emerging regulatory politics. It considers the role that capital's relative immobility plays in opening space for redistributive policies; the ways in which urban political movements "shift scales" between local and nonlocal political actors and how these shifts can provide leverage for the pursuit of progressive policies; and the function that the rhetoric of local economic independence serves in advancing social welfare agendas.

As I argue, city efforts to redistribute and regulate are being driven by a decentralized labor movement, urban antipoverty organizations, political alliances with progressive city mayors, and the possibilities opened up by the recent urban resurgence. These efforts occur in a postindustrial context in which knowledge and service economy industries are now the norm. In this atmosphere, it may be possible for (some) cities— often the largest—to regulate in ways that nations and states cannot— to leverage place-dependent value and use it to challenge economic inequality. That cities might regulate in this way represents a renegotiation of the traditional terms of capital dependence and national supremacy. And it gives us reason to pay attention to city politics, both because city politics matters and because it is being newly contested.

Municipal Politics Matters

Does municipal politics matter? At one time, a preoccupation with city governance was at the core of the study of politics more generally.[2] But in more recent decades, political scientists have neglected the city in part because economic theory has made city politics seem mostly irrelevant.[3] If city policy is mostly dictated by external economic factors and those factors constrain cities to adopt the same or similar development-friendly policies, then city politics does not matter very much. The party identity of the mayor or the ideological preferences of the citizens play a limited role in municipal policymaking.

Indeed, the dominant twentieth-century accounts of urban politics tend to revolve (and understandably so) around the inevitable constraints of a business-centered orientation. Thus, Clarence Stone's regime theory asserts the inevitable and necessary alliance between city and business. "Given the weakness of governmental authority and the fragmentation of the nonprofit sector, the business elite are uniquely able to enhance the capacity of a local regime to govern."[4] Stephen Elkin similarly argues that,

[g]iven the manner in which officials get elected, the prerogatives of private controllers of assets, the limits on a city's ability to affect and exercise property rights, and the need for cities to raise money in the private credit markets, city officials will naturally gravitate toward an alliance with businessmen, particularly land interests, and such an alliance will naturally be devoted to creating institutional arrangements that will facilitate investment in the city.[5]

Harvey Molotch's image of the "city as growth machine"[6] captures the nature of this urban politics of capital attraction and retention. For Molotch, city politics pits those who seek to maximize land's "use" value against those who seek to maximize its "exchange" value. The growth machine thesis holds that "coalitions of land-based elites, tied to the economic possibilities of places, drive urban politics in their quest to expand the local economy and accumulate wealth."[7] The modern political players in the growth machine are heirs to the original city boosters: land developers and speculators, real estate agents, the local building trades, and local chambers of commerce.

To be sure, in many cities, the transnational corporation is the dominant economic (if not political) force, and global managerial elites often have different interests than local ones. The politics of development will differ depending on whether a city is dominated by global firms or regional ones. And there are many nuanced accounts of urban politics that recognize that other important interest groups play roles in policy outcomes. Nevertheless, to a significant degree, business-based urban development has been a defining feature of a city's political economy.[8]

That being said, recent scholarship has emphasized an enlarged realm for city politics—and not just one limited to the specific policies discussed in the previous chapter. Hank Savitch and Paul Kantor's *Cities in the International Marketplace* is an important example. Savitch and Kantor describe city politics in terms of bargaining leverage, arguing that cities are often able to make decisions about the contours of local economic development. In asserting control over local business development, cities can draw upon their relative economic position, their access to intergovernmental support, and the effectiveness of local political coalitions. These resources will vary by city, region, and nation. The background assumption that cities are operating in a competitive "international marketplace" for location, however, does not.[9]

Other scholarship has begun to emphasize the role of local governments in direct social welfare spending, suggesting that cities exhibit much more variance than has been conventionally assumed. Clayton Gillette notes that local governments spent $11.3 billion in direct, unreimbursed expenditures for public welfare in 2006/2007, plus an additional $20.8 billion for hospitals and health care. These expenditures do not include other forms of regulation—like the minimum wage or progressive income tax—that assist poorer residents.[10]

Michael Craw has observed that social welfare expenditures vary widely across local governments. In analyzing local social welfare policy, Craw finds that even when constrained by limited fiscal capacity, many local governments "still have a significant degree of independence in reacting to local policy preferences when it comes to decisions on providing social welfare services and participating in federal and state intergovernmental grants." He concludes that rather than "simply being 'junior partners' to federal and state governments, some local governments possess considerable autonomy in addressing local poverty."[11] And Chris Tausanovitch and Christopher Warshaw have recently found that "liberal" cities have higher taxes, less regressive tax systems, and spend over twice as much per capita than do "conservative" cities.[12]

In other words, for all the constraints on city officials, city dwellers have preferences that can be turned into policy. And the scope of political choice is much wider and more varied than theory would predict. "In contrast to previous work that emphasizes the constraints on city elected officials," writes Tausanovitch and Warshaw, "we find that city governments are responsive to the views of their citizens across a wide range of policy areas."[13]

Indeed, the city's regulatory aggressiveness is even more noteworthy because it is occurring against a backdrop in which governments generally, and nation-states in particular, appear to have *less* influence over capital flows. Scholars have argued that the rise of the transnational corporation, combined with large-scale free trade regimes, means that national boundaries are much less relevant for corporations, investors, and, to some extent, labor. In the face of mobile capital, governments generally enjoy less latitude to regulate. A central theme of late twentieth-century- and early twenty-first-century political theory is the nation-state's declining capacity to govern.

The relative weakness of the nation-state, however, has been accompanied by a return to the city. Urban theorists have been arguing that regulatory denationalization has coincided with the rise of the region or the global city as an important economic unit. Commentators claim that the locus of economic power has shifted both upward and downward. Large-scale firms and large-scale investments operate on the global scale where capital seems mostly unhindered by local and national borders. But economies are also highly geographically localized, with specialized industries or firms increasingly concentrated in particular metropolitan areas. The economy has become both global and local.[14]

From the perspective of democratic theory, the city's economic (if not regulatory) influence is notable. A defining political anxiety of our time is the real or perceived mismatch between our political institutions, geographically bounded as they are, and the scope of our policy problems—and further, the gap between democratic participation and policy effectiveness. The problem is that smaller political units allow for more participation, but only over a range of policies that are relatively inconsequential, while larger political units are much less participatory, but can actually do something about things that matter.

Robert Dahl considered this dilemma in his 1967 presidential address to the American Political Science Association. And though mostly forgotten now, the *city* was Dahl's antidote to this central problem of scale and democracy. As Dahl observed, there is no one level of government that can resolve the tension between participation and efficacy. But the city is the "optimum unit for democracy in the twenty-first century," he declared, because it is both small enough to engage the citizenry but important enough to matter. The city is where all of the basic tasks of the modern social welfare state are joined: education, public order, housing, poverty, health care, economic development, racial justice, and equality. For Dahl, writing in the mid-1960s, these were the chief challenges of governance, and they were the central challenges of the city.[15]

The 1960s city sometimes seemed to be on the verge of collapse. Dahl championed the city at a time when every major policy challenge seemed to involve a question of urban governance. Almost half a century later, the challenges remain, as does the city's potential. As the city reemerges as an economic entity, it also reemerges as an important site for democratic politics, even in an economy characterized by rapid flows of money and information. To be sure, the governors of declining postindustrial American cities do not experience themselves as exercising a great deal of agency. But in many cases, localized information economies are more susceptible to urban policy, not less. And the scale of city economies makes them fruitful and appropriate sites for negotiating the relationship between polity and economy. Recovering Dahl's "democratic city in the democratic nation-state," means recovering the relevance and importance of city politics.

That politics, of course, varies greatly city by city. One would rightly be skeptical of my claim that city politics matters if we could easily generalize about its content across times and places. Nevertheless, it is possible to identify some themes of an emerging regulatory urban politics, starting with the role that capital's relative mobility plays in enlarging urban agendas.

Immobile Capital

I begin with capital immobility—though I think it is less important than it appears to be at first. To be sure, a city cannot regulate or redistribute what is not there. For that reason, a regulatory or redistributive politics is most likely to occur in cities that are on the upsides of their economic cycles. It is important, however, to keep claims about the causes of city growth and decline separate from claims about what local policies are politically feasible. These are often conflated. The competitive model of city development assumes that capital is hyper-mobile, that cities have to solve the problem of capital flight in order to grow, and that solving the problem of capital flight requires policies that attract the right kinds of investments and residents.

As I have been arguing, however, there is no reason to believe that "solving capital flight" is possible or that adopting any particular attraction strategy will achieve it. Growing cities are ones in which new work is being added to old (to use Jane Jacobs's terminology), but that is not the same as saying that a city can only grow if it adopts policies aimed at attracting investments and residents. The origins of growth reside elsewhere.

The view that capital is always hyper-mobile is also incorrect. Cities form and grow when propinquity generates economic gains. Theoretically then, cities should be in a relatively good position to regulate when their locational advantages cannot be reproduced elsewhere. As I have already noted, the increasing localness of certain kinds of information-based economies suggests that cities are sometimes more relevant than their nation-states for the purposes of business location. And this means that cities may be able to leverage this more place-dependent capital toward regulatory ends.

Consider a global technology or financial services firm. As I observed in chapter 1, local agglomeration economies can assert a profound pull in certain economic sectors, especially those that depend substantially on the flow of information. Technology firms tend to locate in Silicon Valley or other equivalent, specialized economic regions. Finance firms tend to be located at the nodes of international finance and global capitalism—places like Tokyo, New York, or London. These addresses are often highly localized: Finance firms gather not just in New York, but in lower Manhattan. The firm's municipal address is thus both what makes the firm more valuable and what makes it susceptible to regulation. That the firm is also located in the United States is somewhat (though not entirely) incidental. In this way the administrative state is turned on its head: The fact that a nation can tax a resident firm is parasitic on the fact that the city can tax it.

Let's recall why this is so. First, firms might gain knowledge and informational benefits from being located close to other firms like them. Or they may require proximity to their client industries or contractors. Of course, those agglomeration or proximity benefits have to be available at short distances, otherwise businesses could locate just across the border. But a common claim is that in an economy increasingly based on knowledge transfers and face-to-face interactions, close proximity is a significant advantage.

Second, highly skilled laborers might have a preference for urban environments. Firm location depends a great deal on where the people are, and where the people are turns on their quality of life, their relative educational achievements, and their desires for specific amenities or architectural aesthetics. If potential employees desire an urban lifestyle and short commutes, the firms that employ them have to be located in the city.

Relatedly, it may be that cities provide consumption amenities that cannot be reproduced outside the city. The variety of goods and services, the urban atmosphere, the downtown street scene, the supply of warehouse, loft, or brownstone apartments or houses—these may be available only in the city. Certainly we know that in a number of metropolitan areas, residents are willing to pay significantly higher rents to access these amenities. Firms also seem willing to pay significantly higher rents, perhaps for the same reasons.

Third, industries are differently mobile. It is no surprise that local minimum wage and labor organizing movements have targeted relatively place-dependent service industries. Hospitals, hotels, universities, nursing homes, and government offices are relatively location-bound. Organizing local labor markets is an advisable strategy because it can take advantage of spatial dependence, particularly in large metropolitan areas. Service-based economies are heavily local and increasingly dominant. A steadily rising share of the urban workforce produces goods and services that are sold and consumed within the same metropolitan area. The increasing "localness" of metropolitan area economies provides space for local regulation.

In sum, place-specific characteristics can strongly influence location decisions and thereafter hold particular firms, because a specific location generates value for the firm, because labor is attracted to that place and the firm follows, or because the work and services are inherently local. The competitive model of city development assumes the hyper-mobility of capital and labor. But mobility is in fact often constrained. Location in particular parts of the metropolitan area still matters.[16]

If this is true, then our assumptions about capital mobility need to be revised, at least for some cities in some places. Once we begin cutting back on our assumption that capital is hyper-mobile, the city's capacity to regulate obviously becomes more robust. Indeed, for those who assume that the threat of exit is the primary mechanism by which firms and residents influence local policy, the implications of a shift in relative leverage are substantial. For better or for worse, cities can and will be able to regulate significantly, even in ways arguably unavailable to states or nations.

That being said, the relative mobility or immobility of capital cannot be the whole story, and we should be cautious about replacing one economically deterministic story with another one. If the presumption of capital flight has heretofore driven municipal policy, it is easy enough to reverse the presumption. In either case, however, economic necessity is still doing all the work; the range of city policies is a feature of either flight or the inability to flee.[17] On this account, local political factors still play significantly less of a role in policy than do economic factors, even if those factors operate in favor of city regulation rather than against it. The conventional account of capital mobility and a newly revised narrative of capital immobility both assume that exit drives municipal politics and policy away or toward redistribution.[18] But there are good reasons to question that assumption.

First, we should remember that political power in the city has long been exercised through mechanisms other than the threat or non-threat of capital flight. This fact has been underemphasized in recent urban theory. An emphasis on exit has dominated urban theory in part because it seems to be consistent with the late twentieth century's assumption that city failure was and is primarily a product of capital flight. Moreover, the emphasis on exit assumes that traditional political processes in the city are relatively impotent. How else can one explain the rapid flight from cities in the latter third of the twentieth century, except that those cities were being mismanaged? And how else can one explain the fact of mismanagement than the inability for otherwise rational city dwellers to actually govern through the ballot box?

The city, on this account, was "ungovernable" except through the discipline of citizens "voting with their feet" (i.e., exiting the jurisdiction). The processes of suburbanization that seemed to ravage twentieth-century cities appeared to confirm this directly. People were fleeing the cities. "Voting with your feet" perfectly captured the metropolitan politics of a suburban twentieth century.

This emphasis on exit (and the concomitant treatment of city politics as relatively uninteresting) has obscured the fact that the conventional way of expressing political will is through politics,[19] reflected as it is in the historical and traditional exercise of political influence by particular city interest groups, especially business groups. Business—especially large-scale business—exercises power whether or not it can flee, not solely *because* it can flee. And the city was never ungovernable, even if its politics has been or continues to be cacophonous and characterized by interest-group conflict and capture. If that is true, then the relative immobility of capital will not dramatically alter city politics unless local interest groups can translate that immobility into policy.

A second reason to hesitate in describing municipal policy and politics mainly in terms of relative capital mobility is that mobility does not have a predictable policy valence. As I observed in chapter 2, relying on Cai and Treisman, the fact of mobility can point in two directions. It can induce cities to overinvest in infrastructure and other amenities intended to attract mobile firms and residents. But mobility can also induce some cities to underinvest in capital-friendly policies on the ground that the city is unlikely to see any future benefits. It is somewhat risky for Buffalo's business incubator to invest in an innovative tech startup.[20] The chances that Buffalo will become a competitive tech center are somewhat low, while the chances that a new startup firm will eventually relocate to Silicon Valley are relatively high.

In contrast, there are certainly circumstances in which a city with an existing robust and relatively immobile industry will be inclined to invest in it, as it is reasonable for city officials to believe that future returns will benefit both. In this way, the relative mobility of capital has a policy effect that is the opposite of what is often predicted. The stickiness of capital could in fact make cities *more* inclined to adopt policies that are favorable to those relatively immobile industries it already has.

At a minimum, it seems that cities are unlikely to overregulate immobile industries, even independent of those industries' economic power. The cities of the upper Midwest were never going to overregulate the steel or automobile industries, despite the fact that both were relatively immobile during the middle part of the twentieth century. Nor would West Virginia mining towns over-regulate the coal industry, despite the fact that coal mines were obviously immoveable. Indeed, these places might have done better to diversify their economies by being less hospitable and more wary of their dominant immobile industries.

In fact, as I have noted before, the landscape of municipal social welfare redistribution and corporate subsidization is complex. New York City, for example, both actively distributes subsidies to attract business investment *and* actively distributes money to poor people. Many cities do likewise.

For theorists preoccupied with exit, these policies require explanation. The fact that both kinds of policies are taking place suggests that residents are not fleeing in the face of redistribution, as theory predicts. Thus, certain redistributions might be explained by the fact that the money is coming from elsewhere—from federal or state funds or through taxes on nonresidents. As for subsidies to business, some have argued that these kinds of policies are possible because what firms receive on the front end through subsidies is recouped on the back end through taxes (or vice versa).[21] Again, a theory of local political behavior that depends so dramatically on exit needs to explain how city spending that only benefits a subset of resident taxpayers can be possible without inducing flight.

A broader theory of political behavior that is not so focused on exit, however, has no difficulty explaining these kinds of policies as a reflection of the usual operation of interest-group politics or local political culture.[22] Only if one believes that capital flight *always* drives policy does the existence of a significant amount of municipal subsidization and redistribution become puzzling. But there is no reason to be so surprised if city politics looks a lot like other forms of politics.

My central point is that the possibilities for city regulation and redistribution are not dictated by an economic logic in either direction. When a city is popular among a certain type of resident or important to the viability of a particular industry, the city can leverage that popularity into public goods for the less fortunate. It can also spend money in the opposite direction, providing public or private goods for the already fortunate, or further subsidizing the dominant industry. These both occur. Certainly, the city's ability to regulate and redistribute turns on whether it has an economy within its borders. And the relative immobility of factors of production creates space for local redistributionist strategies. Whether cities will fill that space is a different question.

At one time, American industrial cities were willing to do so. Industrial investments of the early-to-mid-twentieth century were relatively fixed in place, and overseas production was limited, particularly in the wake of World War II, when European and Asian economies were in disarray. Those industrial cities produced the schools, hospitals, museums, subways, streetcars, and parks that disproportionately served the working and middle classes. What we may be witnessing in the first part of the twenty-first century is the reemergence of that capability (at least in some limited sense), and all to the good. But the fact of immobile capital in our cities does not represent a radical departure from what came before. Immobility is no more determinative than mobility. Sticky capital does not upend municipal politics, though it makes some redistributive regulation more feasible.

Translocal Networks

That it may be economically feasible to regulate locally despite economic globalization does not mean that it is politically feasible. Traditional urban power brokers are going to resist efforts to limit their influence. For this reason, reform efforts that seek to channel or regulate business are often dependent on alliances with progressive mayors. Alternatively, those efforts can seek to operate outside the traditional channels of local government altogether. Local living wage and community benefit agreement campaigns are emblematic of the latter. As I have noted, the purpose of CBAs is to bypass the traditional avenues of municipal decision-making and give neighborhood groups some regulatory authority over incoming development.[23]

But what is also abundantly clear is that municipal redistributive efforts are not merely local. Locals are often plugged into national political and labor networks—those networks provide leverage in local conflicts with incoming capital.[24] Municipal labor and antipoverty campaigns are not isolated; they are part of a larger cross-city effort to regulate using the tools of municipal government.

This nationalization of local politics should not be surprising. The chief targets of labor and living wage organizing—chains and big box stores—are not usually "local" either. And organized labor has always been involved in influencing city policy, often in competition with local business leaders, though sometimes—as with construction unions that support redevelopment efforts—in alliance with them. Certainly labor unions have always operated at the local level—contesting a plant closing in Detroit, for example, or organizing particular workers in the garment industry in New York or Los Angeles.

The use of municipal land use or municipal regulation as a means to bring pressure to bear on national firms, however, is somewhat novel. The political power being asserted by translocal antipoverty or labor networks at the neighborhood and municipal levels provides leverage to otherwise locally marginalized groups, but it also complicates our assumptions about the scale of political activity in the city.

Consider again community benefits agreements, discussed in the previous chapter. The CBA process disaggregates the city explicitly—not only do local groups seek to influence policy through lobbying or political resistance, they also make policy through private regulatory-side deals. In this way, as William Ho points out, business interests, city government, and "the community" are the three sides of urban development politics.[25] The privatizing of the regulatory function is purposeful: Community groups negotiate directly with the developer partially in order to sideline state and municipal officials. Animated in part by a distrust of local elected officials, the CBA structure seeks to localize the development process—the deals are site-specific—in order to maximize the neighborhood's political leverage. Progressive mayors, who may also find their influence limited by local business interests, may appreciate these efforts. The private character of the CBA deal means that the mayor need not expend political capital seeking concessions from developers herself.

These side deals are often negotiated by grassroots organizations, but increasingly with the aid or direct involvement of national labor unions. Thus, though site-specific deals are in some ways essentially "local," the involvement of large-scale, translocal antipoverty or labor networks situates them in the context of a national economic reform movement. Highly local land-use battles involving Walmart, for instance, are obviously and explicitly part of the nationwide fight against the chain, instigated by labor and antipoverty groups.[26] Local minimum and living wage movements are also part and parcel of a nationwide economic reform movement.

In these ways, local economic development politics is only geographically local; it otherwise occurs in the context of larger political and economic markets. And, in truth, city politics has never been autonomous. As we have already seen, in the nineteenth century, city politics was often state legislative politics. The city's legislative delegation made urban policy and dispensed political favors from the state capital. Local redevelopment politics in the New Deal and urban renewal eras was similarly a product of federal policy, and often reflected national political priorities—even if those priorities were to some degree decentralizing. And federal and state monies—mostly in the form of tax breaks—currently distort local decision-making. Economic development funds, enterprise zones, and other federal and state economic development incentives are targeted locally but can only be understood in the context of national and state politics: the interests of federal and state officials, the political demographics of the city and its influence in federal and state contests, and the money to be made in local development or redevelopment.

The lesson to take from this is that urban politics is always occurring against the backdrop of a competitive vertical political system. Economic development politics in the city is perpetually multi-tiered. Walmart site fights, local living wage campaigns, and CBAs illustrate how locals seek support from state and national networks and how national economic reform movements seek out opportunities at the local level.[27]

Consider an example: Chicago's 2006 big-box living wage ordinance. William Lester describes the ordinance's fate in his helpful treatment of the comparative municipal politics of living wage laws. As Lester notes, the ordinance had been pursued by local and national labor leaders and by the Association of Community Organizations for Reform Now (ACORN), a national progressive advocacy group. ACORN's

National Living Wage Resource Center and the Brennan Center for Justice (based in New Jersey) drafted the law. The coalition that pushed the ordinance included local and national labor and Chicago-based community-organizing and faith-based groups. The ordinance was also favored by a majority of city residents.[28]

National and local business groups, including the Illinois Retail Merchants Association, the U.S. Chamber of Commerce, and the big-box stores themselves fought the ordinance. A number of aldermen representing African American communities also opposed the ordinance on the grounds that it would undermine economic development efforts in their otherwise struggling neighborhoods. Some African American alderman "portrayed the big box ordinance and advocates as outsiders without connection to the economic reality of their wards, charging that the big box opponents were racist for trying to hold up development on the south and west sides but not on the (predominantly white) north side or in the suburbs." Mayor Daley argued that the ordinance would "deprive impoverished African-American communities of jobs, places to shop and revenues."[29]

These highly racialized claims were effective, at least in siphoning off support in some minority wards. Daley needed two aldermen to uphold his veto of the living wage ordinance. He got three. It is possible that the changed votes represented an honest grappling with the problems of South- and West-side poverty in Chicago. Other factors might also have been at play. As commentators note, Daley had appointed nineteen of the fifty sitting council members and had enormous political resources at his disposal. In either case, Daley got what he wanted (at least temporarily) and, though Chicago eventually adopted a minimum wage, Daley's initial success highlights the power of the pro-development coalition.

What the fight over the minimum wage in Chicago illustrates is how "local" interests are complicated along two dimensions. Within the city, the question of who benefits from and who is burdened by economic development is always being contested—it is here that business interests tend to exercise significant influence, as the Chicago example shows. There are also vertical conflicts between national, state, and local actors. What is good for local businesses may be bad for nationwide chain businesses; what is good for the national labor movement may not be consistent with the economic fortunes of local workers; what the mayor desires may not be consistent with what the state legislator from a particular urban district desires.

A local Walmart site fight, for instance, might be understood by national labor and antipoverty groups as a component of their larger project to unionize the chain. For neighborhood residents, however, the conflict is much less abstract: Mom and pop retailers might be concerned about competition; neighbors might be worried about noise; economic development officials might be worried about the tax base; and residents might want both the jobs (whatever their terms) and the inexpensive goods that Walmart provides. In opposing the Chicago ordinance, South-side aldermen used this disconnect to draw a distinction between outsiders and insiders: the unions pushing a national strategy of labor reform versus local residents whose lives might be improved by Walmart's entry.

A similar dynamic can be seen in the campaign to raise work and environmental standards related to trucking at the ports of Los Angeles and Long Beach. Scott Cummings describes how a diverse coalition of environmental, community, and labor organizations sought to raise environmental standards at the ports, reduce pollution and congestion in local neighborhoods, and improve economic conditions for port truck drivers. The coalition succeeded in passing a clean truck program in Los Angeles that required trucking companies to enter port property only if they converted their trucks from diesel to low-emission vehicles and only if they converted their truckers from independent contractors to employees who could be unionized. As Cummings describes it, "top-down labor planning intersected with bottom-up resistance to port activities at a moment of political opportunity to create a powerful coalition with the political leverage to make law." But that success was partial: The employee conversion was challenged on the ground that it was preempted by the federal law that regulates port facilities, and that portion of the law was struck down in the Ninth Circuit.[30]

The clean trucks campaign illustrates a number of themes in municipal regulation: the targeting of regionally immobile industries as a way to pursue citywide economic change; the leveraging of the city's property or proprietary rights to make law in areas that might otherwise be immune from the city's direct regulatory authority; the use of contracts to impose industry-wide standards that might otherwise be political nonstarters; and ultimately the vulnerability of local labor or environmental law to federal (or state) overrides. The federal law, in this case, was deregulatory. As Cummings describes it, "Organized labor attempted to re-regulate a sector of the globalized logistics industry—port trucking—tethered to the regional economy by *keeping law local*."[31]

That the city had the wherewithal to enforce rules for the Los Angeles port at all was and is a function of the port's legal status: The city council and mayor ultimately have the power and authority, operating through a city-chartered commission, to make policy for port operations. Moreover, the port's desire to expand operations gave neighborhood and environmental groups the opportunity to apply legal and political pressure at a moment when the port wanted something that the local community could resist. Aided by a pro-labor mayor, a local pro-labor coalition could therefore pursue city-level regulations to ameliorate the impacts of port growth. But, as Cummings also observes, "labor's local strategy is never entirely local." That the city's trucker conversion rules were stuck down illustrates how highly dependent municipal law-making is on existing state and federal law.[32]

The abstract forces of globalization are often said to make local regulation of labor and environmental conditions extremely difficult, if not impossible. But globalization occurs in specific geographical places and within regulatory frameworks that can be more or less hostile to the exercise of power by those places. Like municipal anti-chain store efforts, the municipal regulation of global supply chains is an effort to assert some control over local economic and labor conditions. Los Angeles happens to have some power over one of the central links in that supply chain—the port of Los Angeles is the largest in the United States. A local site fight over an incoming Walmart is similarly an attempt to disrupt or ameliorate the effects of global commerce on local communities. That these campaigns succeed or fail is not a result of inevitable economic forces, but of political interests and the existing distribution of regulatory authority.

As we have seen, city-business relations are negotiated at multiple levels. For my purpose, what is important is that the city can be the locus of political activity. Low-wage organizers are purposefully targeting urban employers and often relatively immovable infrastructure or industry—like hotels or ports. Local organizing is finding opportunities at the city level to try to create labor-friendly law. This is by its nature a necessity, but also a reality of current political organizing. As one leader of a leading worker's rights organization has stated, "Given the dysfunction of the federal government, our sense is, in a country as huge and complex as ours, cities should serve as laboratories for change."[33]

Localist rhetoric can be deployed by both proponents and opponents of municipal regulation. Mayor Daley defeated a push by national unions to raise wage levels in his city by declaring that it was not in the best interests of the city, or more to the point, certain neighborhoods in the city. The trucking companies operating out of the port of Los Angeles argued that more stringent environmental standards or unionization would cost local jobs. Their legal arguments, however, focused on local interference in the national market. The law regulating trucks explicitly prevents states or local governments from enacting laws "related to a price, route, or service of any motor carrier . . . with respect to the transportation of property."[34] This is a standard preemption provision, and it is presumably intended to prevent local economic protectionism—to preserve the benefits of a national free market. Its purpose and effect, however, are to destroy local law.

Nevertheless, that national labor and business organizations are fighting about local pro-labor ordinances and that those ordinances are appropriately debated in city councils are in themselves significant. They illustrate the multi-scalar nature of local economies, the entrepreneurial nature of local social movement groups, and the emerging role of the city as a regulatory agent. And they demonstrate how that role is shaped by the existing distribution of legal authority between local, state, and federal governments.

Economic Localism

Localist rhetoric can be deployed to push developmental agendas, as witnessed in Chicago. Localist arguments might also be deployed to *resist* those agendas. The resistance to large-scale mobile capital can be understood as democracy-reinforcing, both at the grassroots level where activists seek worker and neighborhood empowerment, and more broadly in the city as a whole, as citizens seek to assert control over their local economies. The goal is to protect communities, residents, and workers from the forces of global capitalism. Clawback provisions, plant closing laws, anti-chain store movements, community benefits agreements, and local labor and minimum wage laws need to be understood against a backdrop of the increasing dissatisfaction with a global, transnational, corporate economy.[35]

The rhetoric and ideology of economic localism are often underappreciated features of municipal politics, but they have a long pedigree. Republican political theory has long been skeptical of the concentration of capital. Corporate capital is threatening because it exercises power and authority over individuals and communities independent of political and constitutional constraints. Those concerns are apparent in the anti-corporatism of the classical jurists, the anti-monopolism of the Jacksonians, and the concern about the corporate "octopus" invoked by trust-busters, progressives, and agrarians.[36]

Modern anti-chain store activism, for example, has a precursor in the early twentieth-century resistance to large-scale retail. Before and during the Great Depression, the "chain store menace" was a topic of significant public interest. Between 1920 and 1940, a loose confederation of local merchants, independent merchant associations, agrarians, populists, and progressives sought to stem the chain expansion, and states rushed to adopt anti-chain store taxes. Chain opponents argued that the chain stores destroyed local businesses, took money out of the community, held down wages, turned tradesmen into clerks, and concentrated wealth in a few hands.[37] They believed, as Justice Louis Brandeis stated in his dissent in *Liggett v. Lee*, a case that struck down a state chain store tax, that the chain store

> by furthering the concentration of wealth and of power and by promoting absentee ownership, is thwarting American ideals; that it is making impossible equality of opportunity; that it is converting independent tradesmen into clerks; and that it is sapping the resources, the vigor and the hope of the smaller cities and towns.[38]

These kinds of claims were consistent with republican-inspired fears of corporate domination generally. Recall that Brandeis famously warned of the "curse of bigness." He and other progressive decentralists argued that large-scale private enterprise necessitates large-scale government regulation, and the combination of the two constitutes a threat to liberty, as that term is fully understood in its economic and political sense.[39] According to Brandeis, "the rapidly growing aggregation of capital through corporations constitutes an insidious menace to the liberty of the citizen." That is because "it tends to increase the subjection of labor to capital." Further, "because of the guidance and control necessarily exercised by great corporations upon those engaged in business, individual initiative is being impaired and creative power is being lessened."[40] Concentrated capital and centralized government regulation threaten individual and community economic and political self-sufficiency.

Brandeis made these arguments in the context of a Court that was suspicious of any form of government economic regulation, particularly regulations that appeared to favor one sort of property ownership over another. The conflict over chain store taxes occurred as the Court was protecting cross-border corporations from local discriminatory taxes using the Commerce Clause and the Equal Protection Clause. As I noted in chapter 4, the nineteenth and early part of the twentieth centuries witnessed the jurisprudential creation of an American free trade regime. And the increasing ability for national corporations to operate in every state of the union invited local protectionist legislation. Chain store taxes looked a lot like many other forms of discrimination against out-of-state corporations. They were thus contrary to the creation of a national marketplace.

Eventually, the Supreme Court would embrace Brandeis's deferential approach to local, state, and national economic regulations. It never came to share Brandeis's enthusiasm for economic and political decentralization, however. Even the anti-chain store regulations of the 1920s and '30s that survived Supreme Court review were eventually dismantled. And, as Lizabeth Cohen has argued, the progressives laid the groundwork for the "consumer's republic"—a regulatory state focused on price competition and consumer choice, rather than on regulations to protect the small businessman or independent tradesperson.[41] The New Deal mostly made peace with large-scale retail and production. Brandeis's argument against big government has been detached from his argument against big capital. Opposition to the New Deal state is now the province of pro-corporate libertarians, not progressive decentralists.

Nevertheless, the ideal of local economic self-sufficiency and a citizenship grounded in economic independence continues to resonate, even as it takes different forms. Consider the political philosopher Michael Sandel, who has invoked republican political theory in favor of a more robust economic and political localism. Sandel, like Brandeis before him, argues that political liberty requires some form of economic liberty—that citizenship requires not only the free exercise of political rights, but also the free exercise of economic ones. The rise of consumerism has signaled the end of a discourse in which the economy is viewed through a moral lens, as contributing or failing to contribute to the virtues of citizens, as encouraging or discouraging moral corruption, as promoting or failing to promote democracy and political independence. According to Sandel, rights-based liberalism does not have the intellectual resources to address the civic harm caused by a global, capitalist economy. A form of localist republicanism would do a better job.[42]

This kind of political argument, grounded as it is in republican sensibilities, is importantly different from the political arguments deployed by either the antipoverty or pro-labor movements. Antipoverty interests focus on the redistributive opportunities of urban economic development. This approach seeks to ensure that the city's economic gains are widely distributed throughout the urban population, that costs of municipal improvement do not fall on the least well off, and that attraction strategies do not lead to gentrification and displacement.

A labor-based approach sees an opportunity to advance worker rights and the labor movement more generally through urban-based organizing. The new labor takes the postindustrial landscape and the concomitant mobility of capital as a given, but shares with old labor the idea that collective action is the means for pushing workers' rights and economic advancement.[43]

Notably, the localness of both the antipoverty and labor movements is strategic. Nationwide, urban antipoverty efforts have largely dissipated over the last twenty-five years, particularly since the early '90s and the left-right consensus on welfare reform. Antipoverty efforts have thus become, by necessity, a city-by-city and project-by-project strategy. Similarly, urban-based labor organizing is a national movement operating at the local scale. As with the antipoverty movement, the decentralized nature of the labor movement is a product of the movement's decline at the federal level. It is not the result of an inherently localist agenda. The fact that post-New Deal welfare and labor efforts were centered in Washington may have precluded a robust economic localism. It may be that the dissipation of such efforts make local strategies more feasible.

In contrast to the antipoverty and labor movements, economic localism directly addresses the relationship between city and capital. The economic localist's response to the threat of mobile capital is not to ameliorate or redistribute it, but rather to reconstruct the economic order on a local and less vulnerable scale. Anti-Walmart campaigns may be spearheaded by labor groups seeking leverage in their unionization campaigns, but those fights often take advantage of the republican rhetoric of economic independence. In this, they benefit from an alliance with small retailers, who argue that protectionist legislation is necessary to defend their livelihoods, to secure good jobs for local workers, and to counter local economic and political dependence. As in the context of CBAs, minimum wage laws, and clawback provisions, activists worry about the vulnerability of the local economy to corporate control. Preserving space for an economically independent citizenry is a means for securing the community's economic stability and the community's capacity to assert local economic and political values.[44]

One of the attractions of this localist discourse is that it is not anti-business. Nor is the economic localist's program solely a redistributive one. The important distinction for economic localists is not between capital and labor or property owners and the poor. Rather, the important distinction is between relatively large-scale and relatively small-scale capital, and between relatively place-based businesses and relatively footloose ones. It is telling that the executive director of the Los Angeles Alliance for a New Economy—the pro-labor organization that has spearheaded minimum wage efforts in Los Angeles and elsewhere—states that LAANE is "pro-growth, not anti-business." Other LAANE officials describe their work on CBAs as ensuring that developers who receive the benefit of public investment should "give a return on that investment to the community."[45] The language is quite business-friendly—a reflection of LAANE's efforts to appeal to a wider constituency, no doubt, but also a reflection of a certain vision of local prosperity. The goal is local economic self-sufficiency, understood to be a precondition for political self-sufficiency.

The urban theorist David Imbroscio's work is an example of this approach. He calls his program the "ownership paradigm" to contrast it with a "redistributive paradigm." For Imbroscio, writing from the political left, the goal is to "restructure urban economies to make ownership of productive assets more widespread." Imbroscio advocates worker ownership to create "anchored jobs," micro-loans to foster small business development, consumer cooperatives, and community-owned corporations, and—like Progressive Era reformers—municipal ownership of local assets.[46] Sometimes grounded in an import substitution theory of local economic growth, the goal of these diverse efforts is to restrain capital in place.[47]

These policies—championed by a growing body of "progressive localists"—are animated by the reality of economic insecurity and instability. Deploying the republican language of civic independence, localists reject the "capture and redistribute" program, arguing that it is too weak to counter the forces of transnational capital mobility. Localists instead propose "efforts to build community-based development institutions, worker-owned firms, publicly controlled businesses, and webs of interdependent (locally networked) entrepreneurial enterprises"—all of which will "generate indigenous, stable, and balanced economic growth in local economies."[48]

Advocates admit that achieving indigenous, stable economic growth is a tall order, both economically and politically. The localists are relying on an extremely robust political countermovement to the excesses of global corporate capitalism. Nevertheless, the discourse of inequality and disenfranchisement—echoes of which can be heard in the rhetoric of national political campaigns[49]—has attained some level of political salience, especially in the aftermath of the 2008 recession.

Notably, George W. Bush's early 2000's invocation of the "ownership society" sounded a similar theme—though from the political right. Here the language of "dependence" was used to attack the social welfare state. Individual political responsibility is a byproduct of ownership of productive assets. Individual home ownership, minimal government redistribution, welfare for work, and deregulation to spur innovation are the hallmarks of this version of economic independence.

Its antiregulatory agenda has echoes in the progressive decentralists' original opposition to big government.

The cross-political appeal of a localist economics is notable. Economic localism has a left-leaning valence insofar as it champions a local regulatory role and favors communities over corporations. It is traditionally conservative, however, in that it emphasizes the importance of place, local practices, and economic self-sufficiency over cross-border markets, cosmopolitanism, national or global governance, and international finance. The anti-corporatist strand in American thought is evident in the opposition to free trade on both the right and the left. And the opposition to the bailouts of banks and other financial institutions in the aftermath of the 2008 recession is shared by both Occupy Wall Street (on the left) and the Tea Party (on the right)—by both Bernie Sanders (the socialist Senator) and Donald Trump (the conservative real estate magnate). This is no surprise. In the 1920s and '30s, anti-chain store sentiment was widely shared, by progressives like Brandeis and LaFollette, but also by populists like Huey Long, and reactionaries like the Ku Klux Klan.

These kinds of self-sufficiency arguments are not solely rhetorical. Consider the overwhelmingly negative reaction to the Court's decision in *Kelo v. New London*. Recall that in *Kelo*, the Court held that the "public use" provision of the Takings Clause did not prevent the condemnation and transfer of a private home from its owner to a redevelopment corporation for purposes of attracting a large corporate tenant. The *Kelo* case itself was brought by conservative property rights advocates seeking to limit the government's eminent domain power. But restrictions on eminent domain had long been endorsed by left-leaning neighborhood and minority rights organizations concerned about the displacement of poor and minority residents through urban renewal. As I have noted, the rise of CBAs has been in part a response to a history of local abuse of the development process.

Kelo's seeming endorsement of economic development takings is quite in line with the dominant redevelopment ideology—the use of eminent domain for economic development has and continues to be standard operating procedure in an environment that encourages industrial location subsidies. Yet *Kelo* met resistance from the white middle class and from small business owners, who might otherwise favor economic development more generally. *Kelo* elicited—using

Robert Johnston's terminology—a reaction from the "democratic, anti-capitalist middle class"—the petit bourgeoisie protecting their livelihoods against large-scale global capital.[50]

Commentators had not predicted the political backlash that followed the *Kelo* case. Perhaps they had underestimated how widely shared was the feeling of economic rootlessness at the turn of the twenty-first century. Or perhaps they shared the assumption at the heart of late-twentieth-century theories of municipal political economy that developmental spending is different from redistributive spending, and that the former is relatively uncontroversial while the latter is anathema.

But this preoccupation with developmental politics understates the fears and concerns of middle- and working-class residents, small business owners, and local, place-based institutions. It is too easy to conflate their preferences with the preferences of corporate capital, and pit both against a redistributive politics driven by the interests of national antipoverty groups, labor unions, racial minorities, and the poor. The reaction to *Kelo* illuminates a deep strain of anti-corporatism and a resistance to local developmental politics that aligns the middle class and the poor—one that crosses the predictable interest group lines.

Certainly, the discourse of individual property rights played a role in the public's reaction to *Kelo*. That reaction could be interpreted simply as anti-redistributionist. But *Kelo* also revealed a set of submerged but deeply held concerns about the current practice of corporate liberalism, with its emphasis on large-scale enterprise, free markets, and inter-local competition. These concerns have been in evidence since the plant closings of the 1970s and 1980s, and have only accelerated with the rapid pace of economic restructuring and the continued decline of postindustrial towns and cities. *Kelo*—and the broader issue of economic development takings—provided a point of entry into the anxiety associated with the increasing mobility of capital and the seeming threat it poses to local and individual economic stability. It elicited a normally quiescent resistance to the politics of development.

Conclusion: The Reemergence of the Regulatory City

Americans have few conceptual resources to address a deep source of democratic discontent: the loss of communal political autonomy that has accompanied the rise of the large-scale transnational corporation. And yet the city has often been a central (even if sometimes ineffectual) site for articulating these kinds of claims.

Indeed, city reformers have long sought to adopt policies to counter the vulnerability of the public to corporate capital. In part that is because cities do not have an effective response to the boom-and-bust cycle. Current municipal fiscal crises exacerbated by repeated recessions are evidence of this limitation. It thus makes sense for a city to try to reduce the volatility of capital flows, even if that means that its residents experience a lower level of economic well-being in the short term. Policies that mute the chase for highly mobile capital and promote local economic stability are going to be more feasible than those that pursue "growth."

The political movement to limit reliance on outside capital by producing it in-house is the most radical mechanism for restructuring capital-city relations. But while important conceptually, municipal ownership, city entrepreneurialism, and neighborhood-based capital formation are still very limited in size and impact.[51] Large-scale public or community ownership of the means of production is unlikely to make much serious headway.[52] And privatization efforts seem to be outpacing public ownership, as cities sell off traditional municipal services—like parking meters in Chicago—and state legislatures increasingly make efforts to dismantle public-sector unions. In short, as a matter of strategy, there is little doubt that cities remain highly dependent on large-scale, transnational capital.

Nevertheless, a progressive politics has emerged in cities across the country, even those with a long history of pro-development coalitions—and sometimes alongside those coalitions, as the CBA process illustrates. Progressive economic policies can be framed as a form of economic independence. Privileging relatively immobile, small-scale capital over relatively mobile, large-scale capital might be a better strategy for long-run economic stability.

Economic localists from Brandeis forward have long promoted such strategies. There is nothing new about them. But the politics of economic self-sufficiency is importantly perennial. The effort to strike better deals with incoming capital reflects this reality. If municipal officials are captured by development interests, then organizations and institutions that have an independent political base can act to ensure some balance. The backing of a progressive mayor or redevelopment agency chief, the support of labor unions, or the deployment of translocal networks can fill that political void. Developmental politics is still dominant in the city. But the rise of the regulatory city illustrates that it is not the only politics that matters.

7

Urban Resurgence

ANY ACCOUNT OF CITY power is a product of its time. In asking what cities are capable of at the beginning of the twenty-first century, we cannot ignore the fact that many central cities have seen their fortunes improve over the last fifteen to twenty years. As commentators have repeatedly observed, there has been a surprising "reversal of fortunes" as older industrial cities have stabilized or gained populations.[1] For a period beginning in the middle of the twentieth century, the trend toward Sunbelt cities and far-flung suburbs seemed inexorable. The old industrial cities did not appear to have a chance against newer, sunnier, and lower-cost places in the competition for residents and firms. Yet even taking into account the 2008 recession, parts of cities like New York and Chicago are increasingly desirable places to live, and cities like Pittsburgh and Philadelphia are seeing their populations and property values stabilize after a long period of relative decline. Many old downtown business districts are doing much better. Gentrification is fast occurring in places like Washington, D.C., and even—though to a lesser extent—places like Richmond and Baltimore.

One way to test our intuitions about the mechanics of city growth, the role of urban policy, and the scope of city agency is by considering the causes of this so-called urban resurgence. As I argued in the previous chapter, the relative popularity of urban living increases the city's capacity to regulate and redistribute. But the urban resurgence could also be taken as evidence for a different conclusion: that pro-development, capital-attraction policies work and redistributive policies do not. If growth can be induced through policy, it follows that cities can resurge by adopting good policies, and they can fail by adopting bad ones. If the city is a product, we might expect that it has resurged because it has been improved.

In fact, consistent with my argument throughout this book, scholars and policymakers are far from certain what has caused the urban resurgence, let alone what causes economic growth more generally. Indeed, in the last quarter-century, U.S. cities did not dramatically change what they had been doing from the quarter-century before. And so, though we sometimes attribute the urban resurgence to the smart choices made by wise city leaders, it is also fully possible (and seems likely) that "wise" city leaders are really just lucky.

At the least, any claim that cities have transformed themselves through better management or particular policies of capital attraction and retention are seriously overstated. That does not mean that urban policies do not matter, but it does mean that regulatory policies cannot be dismissed as obviously destined for failure and that "pro-growth" economic development policies can be obviously embraced as effective. Moreover, as I have been arguing, it again reaffirms that competitive accounts of city growth and decline are mistaken.

This chapter begins by assessing the conventional explanations for urban resurgence. Recall that the competitive federalism literature predicts that the appropriate fiscal discipline will lead to better economic outcomes. As cities become more efficient, innovative, and more growth-oriented, they will reap the gains of development and in-migration.

I have already questioned these theoretical claims. The urban resurgence provides further evidence that they are misplaced. It turns out that there is little evidence that improvement in local service provision, investment in infrastructure, or innovation in local policies has caused the recent growth in resurging places. More likely, as in the nineteenth century, the economic growth in these places has caused some improvement in local services.

The chapter then examines some common economic development policies. I argue that any claim that one policy or another does or will generate economic growth should be treated with a great deal of skepticism. I have already argued that cities can redistribute in ways that conventional economic wisdom thinks are impossible. Here I further argue that conventional urban economic development policies are likely unavailing. Cities should avoid trying to create growth through business attraction-and-retention strategies. Cities should instead get back to basics, through the improved provision of important municipal services to their citizens. City self-government needs to be redefined— away from chasing the elusive goal of growth and toward the provision of badly needed goods and services to citizens already in place.

Urban Policy and the Urban Resurgence

I start by examining the potential causes of the urban resurgence. Claims about the efficacy of urban policies have to be able to explain why cities have become more popular over the last two decades. If theory cannot explain the basic changes in urban fortunes, then we might reasonably be skeptical of the specific policy recommendations such a theory requires.

In fact, predicting city growth or decline is a hazardous business. Conventional wisdom has often been wrong. Few predicted the urban resurgence, for instance. And many would have predicted the opposite, arguing that with the revolution in information technology and the "death of distance," cities would become increasingly obsolete—the logical endpoint to a process of spatial de-concentration that has been occurring since at least the beginning of the twentieth century.

Consider also the oft-repeated claim that "sun and sprawl" always beats "old and cold." During the second half of the twentieth century, we were told, residents and businesses were acting on their preferences for warmer weather and a car-driven lifestyle, thus leading to the decline of the industrial cities of the Northeast in favor of the sprawling cities of the Sunbelt.[2] And even if people were not migrating south, they were migrating out of the cities to the suburbs. These preferences were allegedly made possible by technological innovations—relatively cheap transportation abetted by road-building, inexpensive communications, air conditioning, and the end of an era of industrial production, permitting firms to locate at a distance from suppliers and consumers.[3]

The puzzle is that while sun-and-sprawl cities have undoubtedly been gaining, northern industrial cities have also surged in recent years.

Moreover, none of the underlying technological factors have changed substantially. It is difficult to find a single explanation or set of explanations for why both these trends—continued growth in sunny, sprawling cities and resurgent growth in old, cold cities—are occurring. It is even more difficult to point to specific government policies that have led to the rise of certain cities, the decline of others, and the simultaneous growth of suburban and some central city locales.[4]

Formal Powers and Better Governance

One possibility is that there has been a change in the relative formal powers of cities and states, or, alternatively, that cities have simply done better at governing. Recall that competitive federalists believe that formal decentralization contributes to local and regional economic growth. Proponents of a competitive model of city development assert that mobile capital-friendly policies will be the outcome of inter-jurisdictional competition. Giving significant fiscal autonomy and responsibility to cities (and not bailing them out or backstopping their economies) will generate better policies everywhere. On this theory, if there had been a significant devolutionary movement in city-state relations, growth could be a result.

For this to be true, however, a change in city status would have had to predate improved economic circumstances. But most cities have either the same limited complement of powers they had at the turn of the century or considerably fewer powers because of state legislative tax-and-expenditure limitations. The most famous tax limitation of all is California's Proposition 13, which ushered in an era of state tax revolts starting in the 1970s. Proposition 13 has had significant and continuing negative effects on local governments' ability to raise and spend monies, as have many other states' tax-and-expenditure restrictions. That California cities have less fiscal authority seems not to be causally connected to their more recent popularity, however. San Francisco and Los Angeles, for instance, have both seen their popularity rise despite the limits on their taxing powers.

Another possible explanation is that the federalism revolution of the 1980s forced cities to fend for themselves. On this argument, the *reduction* in federal support for cities that characterized the Reagan era contributed to city independence. The city was forced to innovate or die. Arguably, the federalism revolution also gave the cities more room to maneuver by eliminating or reducing federal mandates.

This story seems similarly unlikely, however. The 1980s witnessed a significant decline in industrial cities' fiscal health, but one that had been occurring at least since the 1970s and, arguably, even twenty years before. With or without significant federal support, many cities experienced a half-century of decline. The federal government was hard-pressed to stem this decline, but it would be quite a feat to argue that its retreat from the field in the 1980s sparked an urban resurgence some fifteen or twenty years later.

Perhaps instead, the old, cold cities have simply gotten better at governing. If it is true that the competition with the Sunbelt cities and the suburbs has forced all cities to do better, then devolution has served a purpose. What constitutes "better governance" is difficult to capture. Certainly if we saw a notable reduction in city taxes with significant improvements in city services, then we might say that old, cold cities improved their position vis-à-vis the suburbs or the Sunbelt cities.

But the urban resurgence does not seem to be driven by tax rates or the more efficient provision of municipal services. First, tax rates in the old, cold cities remain higher than in the Sunbelt cities, which are growing even as tax rates increase. Second, it is quite difficult for any city to dramatically adjust its tax-and-spending bundle before an influx of new and wealthier taxpayers. City budgets are not particularly flexible. Public safety, education, pensions, and basic services take up most of a city budget, and while inefficient government does result in waste, it would be surprising if a worldwide urban resurgence were a product of effective cost-cutting. And third, it is very difficult, as Richard Deitz and Jaison Abel have argued, for any city to offer services or amenities that will dramatically change its *relative* position to other cities over the short term.[5]

More importantly, as I have been arguing throughout, the relationship between the efficient provision of municipal services and city growth is murky at best. In chapter 2, I observed that municipal corruption and municipal growth were both high in the early industrializing United States. In a more recent study of local government efficacy, the authors found little connection between the efficient provision of municipal government services by British local governments and job or population growth between 1995 and 2005. In answer to the question "Does government performance matter?" the authors concluded that it does not. Better services do not seem to *cause* city resurgence, though better services might be a result.[6]

What about improved education or public safety outcomes? Schools and crime (and tax rates) are conventionally invoked to explain the twentieth-century ascendance of the suburbs over the central city. And improvement along these dimensions is often claimed to be a necessary precondition for urban success.

But here too, the data do not support a direct connection between improved services and urban popularity. For example, education gains do not seem to have preceded the urban boom in places like New York, Chicago, or Boston.[7] At best, student achievement in the 1990s showed mixed results in these places. And more recent gains in urban student achievement have been relatively modest. New York City schools, for example, only showed some improvements starting in 2002, and even those gains have been questioned.[8]

More importantly, city-suburb gaps in educational outcomes across all major cities are still quite dramatic.[9] Those gaps occur in resurgent old, cold cities, as well as in growing Sunbelt cities. In Philadelphia, the school system is currently being starved of funds, but Center City continues to show dramatic gains in population and real estate values. Education gains cannot explain the boom in Las Vegas, as that city's schools have not dramatically improved over the last decade.[10] Indeed, it would not be a surprise if education outcomes *fell* in booming places, as often the influx of new residents adds burdens to already overburdened school systems.[11]

A different possibility is that the dramatic decrease in crime over the last twenty years or so has driven a return to the city. And, in fact, many cities (and indeed, the country as a whole) became dramatically safer in the 1990s.

Safer cities constitute a weak explanation for city resurgence, however. Ingrid Gould Ellen and Katherine O'Regan have analyzed the effects of the 1990s drop in crime on city population growth and have found little connection. They argue that if crime reduction is a cause of the urban resurgence, it is at best a minor one.[12] Consider also that even in cities where crime was not initially a problem or where crime did not fall, populations are increasing. Studies have shown that many European cities have also resurged despite not having experienced an American-style crime wave in the preceding decades.[13] Moreover, in growing Sunbelt cities, crime increases have *coincided* with urban growth—an outcome that often occurs as populations increase. In Las Vegas, crime stayed relatively constant through the 1990s but began to spike quite dramatically in 2002.

As criminologists have observed, crime has fallen everywhere in the last thirty years, in both resurgent and non-resurgent cities and regardless of what any particular city did. Broken-windows policies, aggressive stop-and-frisk policies, gun removal, mass incarceration, targeted policing, and community policing have all been given credit for the reduction. But many criminologists now reject a robust link between crime reduction and particular policing policies.[14] John Donohue and Steven Levitt famously attributed the crime decline to the legalization of abortion in the early 1970s. But for many social scientists, the reduction in crime still continues to be something of a mystery. As one commentator notes, it has made every policy intervention "look good."[15]

Cities are undoubtedly safer, but the decline in crime mostly coincided with the popularity of urbanized places. Moreover, though some policing policies certainly have an effect on crime rates, the overall trend seems to be driven by a complex set of factors, not directly related to municipal policy. It is notable that New York City's Mayor Bill de Blasio has deemphasized stop-and-frisk and other aggressive policing strategies. Critics predicted that his policies would contribute to a spike in crime. But crime has continued to decrease during de Blasio's mayoralty, even as the number of stop-and-frisks of New York citizens has also declined.[16]

To be sure, some suburban jurisdictions have experienced declining incomes and rising crime rates, so perhaps in certain cases, the central city looks better in comparison to a suburb in decline. Asking why some suburbs are declining, however, is no different than asking why some central cities are in ascendance. In general, suburbs still have lower tax rates, better schools, and generally less crime than most central cities. That certain suburbs are in decline does not explain urban rise. Indeed, suburban decline does not explain itself, at least not with reference to any particular policy or the overall quality of local government.

Agglomeration versus Amenities

If cities have not gotten dramatically better at providing basic munici-pal services, then something else might explain the urban resurgence. Two more general explanations have been offered. The first is that jobs have returned to the city because of the benefits of urban agglomera-tion. Cities are resurging, on this argument, because of the economic advantages for businesses of being in an urban place where there is a diversity of other firms, clients, suppliers, and deep labor pools.

The second is urban amenities. On this account, cities are resurging because young, skilled workers have a preference for a diversity of goods, services, and experiences that only urban environments can provide.[17]

These are related. As discussed in chapter 1, the argument from ag-glomeration asserts that firms want to be in cities because of the knowl-edge spillovers that propinquity to other firms and industries generates. As a result, cities have become preferred sites for knowledge-economy businesses. Moreover, deindustrialization has made cities more pleasant and amenable to these kinds of firms. Without heavy industry, cities are now cleaner, less noisy, and less polluted. Cities can thus recapture their historical role as centers of innovation, knowledge, learning, and skill-building.

To be sure, I share the view that cities are drivers of economic growth. Here as elsewhere, however, causation is a little tricky. Have city poli-cies encouraged either the agglomeration or amenities trends, or is it more accurate to say that cities are trying to take advantage of those trends? Whether cities create growth or capture it, the relevant ques-tion is whether the agglomeration benefits that cities provide and that seem to be sparking an urban resurgence can be attributed to actual city policies.

One should have doubts. Consider first the benefits of urban ag-glomeration to businesses. While cities may be taking advantage of those trends, few cities made long-term plans to become knowledge factories as the postindustrial future loomed. Most cities attempted to entice new industries as old ones faded. Others relied on one industry until it was too late. A number sought to reframe themselves as tourist and cultural destinations, or as corporate centers. Few cities explicitly diversified their economies—and it is not entirely clear how they would have done so in any case. City leaders did (often consciously) adopt economic development strategies in the postwar period—but deindustrialization was not a specific city policy. Moreover, any given city's choice to adopt policies geared toward manufacturing or downtown amenities or residential districts was time-bound, contingent, and often furthered the very decline that the interventions were intended to prevent. Much of postwar economic development policy failed badly, as I have previously noted.[18]

More importantly, while the agglomeration story helps explain why cities generally continue to exist, it cannot tell us why specific cities become the hosts of certain agglomerations, or why some cities succeed over time and some fail. As I observed in chapter 1, economic geographers argue that path dependence plays a large role in urban outcomes: New York City is currently a financial center because it has been a financial center since the founding of the market at Wall Street. New York's history of financial dominance ensures that it will continue to dominate.[19]

But how path dependence will be experienced is also hard to predict. Consider Detroit. A common story told about Detroit's decline is that its long history of dominating the automobile industry contributed to its downfall. Because it had an undiversified economy, Detroit could not weather the collapse of the U.S. car industry.

A different story could be told, however. In this one, Detroit's long engineering history is an asset. Having a deep bench of engineers, manufacturing plants, and specialized labor, Detroit could be well-placed to compete in the postindustrial knowledge economy, and it could now be a leader in spinoff industries. This story is no less plausible than New York's, yet Detroit's history of manufacturing works against it while New York's history of financial services works for it. The point is that these narratives cannot guide policymaking. Even if cities are thriving because of agglomeration advantages for businesses, it is very difficult to figure out what cities did in the past or should do in the future to pursue those advantages.

The second explanation for the urban resurgence is urban amenities. On this account, the reason that particular cities are thriving has to do with what amenities the city can provide, especially to the workers who provide the labor for the firms choosing city locations. Those theorists who favor an amenities explanation argue that the skilled labor necessary for knowledge industries has a special preference for cities.[20] Businesses then follow those individuals or, alternatively, a virtuous circle is generated whereby firm choices to locate in cities and labor choices to access certain amenities reinforce each other. The claim is that those cities that are now doing better invested in the right kind of infrastructure for an emerging urban class.

But this explanation also seems incomplete. Most cities did not anticipate the global restructuring that makes them more attractive places to live. Indeed, many cities thought that they needed to emulate the suburbs and adopted land-use strategies that were inconsistent with a preference for urban living.

Moreover, the infrastructure and amenity improvements of the late twentieth century and early twenty-first are comparatively modest. During industrialization, cities provided clean water, electricity, paved roads, subways, sewer systems, parks, schools, and streetlights. Cities have more recently invested in bike lanes, some transportation infrastructure, arts districts, and, in a number of cases, a reclaimed waterfront. In many cities, however, basic urban infrastructure is in decay, and massive new infrastructure or public goods projects akin to the Brooklyn Bridge or Central Park are a thing of the past. To attribute the urban resurgence to these relatively modest investments in making cities more walkable or pleasant seems to misalign the cause with the scale of the effect.

Indeed, cities have always tried to attract desirable residents by offering certain amenities. During the urban decline of the mid-twentieth century, cities built festival marketplaces, convention centers, museums, arts and entertainment venues, and stadiums. Urban renewal itself was a very costly effort to improve the urban product, and it, like many of these efforts, mostly failed at the time. The amenities brought in a few more suburbanites to the city, but those suburbanites did not stay.

Nevertheless, attracting skilled labor or individuals with high human capital continues to be a popular policy prescription.[21] The old recommendations were: Tear down slum housing, provide festival marketplaces, attract suburbanites by building roads into the downtown area, and subsidize manufacturing by providing location incentives. The new policies are: Go wireless or green, subsidize universities and hospitals ("eds and meds"), provide walkable downtowns, and offer prewar housing or relatively cheap housing.

Of course, some of these policy prescriptions are not in the city's control. A city has as much prewar housing as it will ever have. That a city did not tear down its housing might be an accident or a lucky break. Few observers thought that hundred-year-old industrial buildings would be desirable housing before those buildings became desirable. (Jane Jacobs is an exception—she argued that old buildings that can easily and cheaply be repurposed are an important feature of the city's regenerative capacity. But few city policymakers listened to her before oldness became chic.)

But even if old, cold cities are attractive in part because of their old buildings, we would be hard-pressed to attribute the preservation of old buildings to a conscious city policy. And not knowing what kinds of buildings will be attractive to future generations, we would be unable to advise the city about how to preserve or build them now. Even if the amenity explanation for urban resurgence is correct, predicting what will appeal to any given generation of metropolitan-area dwellers is extremely difficult.

We do know that cities with higher growth seem to have higher numbers of college-educated residents. Attracting such residents, famously labeled the "creative class" by Richard Florida, seems an obviously smart strategy.[22] Thus, much effort has been made to create the kinds of amenities that highly skilled people favor. Those amenities might include particular kinds of shops, cultural offerings, a vibrant urban street life, or a generally "bohemian, tolerant atmosphere."[23] The theory is that having more young college-educated people in a city will make it more successful. The idea is that if you build it, they will come, and the jobs will follow them. Indeed, one urban economist argues that the "best economic development strategy is to provide amenities that will attract smart people and then get out of their way."[24]

But here again causation is highly uncertain. As Mario Polèse observes, there is an inevitable chicken-and-egg problem: Which comes first, economic growth or an educated workforce? For some, employment is the chicken that gives birth to in-migration; for others, amenities come first, followed by jobs.[25]

Theorists who argue that jobs come first look to the *reasons* why young college-educated people are moving to cities. To be sure, Americans are marrying later, and the percentage of U.S. households with children has steadily decreased since the 1950s, when the suburban explosion began. Where those (single) people live, however, is not foreordained. Between 1995 and 2000, many old, cold cities saw a net in-migration of young college-educated people, thus supporting the theory that dense, urban cores were attracting this highly mobile group. But as Michael Storper points out, cities like Charlotte and Atlanta grew faster along this demographic, and Las Vegas experienced the greatest increase of all.[26]

To be fair, it is possible that certain preferences for amenities are still at work, and that different cities simply offer different advantages, depending on their circumstances. Cities are "bundled" goods: You have to take the weather in New York to get access to the Metropolitan Museum of Art; you can have an exciting nightlife in Las Vegas if you are willing to put up with the desert. Making sure that certain attractions are in place to the extent that a city can control them seems like a good bet.

The problem with this claim is that it is not at all clear whether high human capital individuals are migrating to Boston and Las Vegas because of the amenities or whether the amenities are there because of the high human capital individuals. Storper argues that the amenity story might have the causation exactly backward. He points to places like Silicon Valley, which had no preexisting amenities to offer before it became a technological center; Las Vegas, which was similarly devoid of the kinds of urban amenities that serve a growing permanent population; and Hollywood, which developed its amenities simultaneously with the development of the motion picture industry. Places like Atlanta and Charlotte have all seen their consumer amenities grow with the influx of a more skilled population. The old, cold cities may be able to attract some of the mobile educated with their urban charm, prewar architecture, and restaurants, but if there are no jobs, it is unlikely amenities alone will help them. People generally locate where they can maximize their access to work.[27]

For urban economists who emphasize jobs over amenities, cities are "workshops" not "playgrounds or amenity parks" and amenity-chasing is a bad strategy. In part this is because, even if amenities do drive growth, a city's relative amenity position is unlikely to change very

much. If each city is adopting similar strategies to make itself more attractive to a younger, educated demographic, it seems likely that none
will significantly rise above the pack.[28]

Amenity-chasing might also lead to wasteful spending. Consider
policy recommendations designed to attract highly mobile, skilled residents and prevent them from fleeing.[29] If the jobs-first story is more
accurate than the amenities-first story, then individual highly skilled,
educated amenity users are not particularly mobile. They follow the
businesses that employ them, and those businesses are likely to be located near other firms that are like them. This seems especially true of
creative enterprises like movie-making, fashion, arts, media, technology, and music; and also of knowledge industries like finance, law, and
accounting. These activities tend to take place in particular locations,
and going elsewhere to do them is not an option. It seems unlikely
that a city is going to attract those kinds of firms or kinds of people
by building a municipal Wi-Fi network or by developing a "cool" city
persona.

"Just So" Stories

Of course, cities do not have to concentrate on one strategy to the exclusion of another. Cities adopt policies intended to both attract an educated, urban-interested workforce and create a local business-friendly
atmosphere. As for the latter, policymakers often argue that cities should
use their fiscal and development policies to pursue certain aims. Even if
they cannot control the weather, the amount of prewar housing, or the
fact of deindustrialization, the city does have the ability to keep taxes low
or embrace policies that reduce labor or development costs, or the cost
of housing. Urban advisors have repeatedly asserted that cities should
"avoid redistributive policies that target the rich and drive them away";
that cities should "be responsive to the needs of developers and entrepreneurs"; and that cities should "fashion a pro-growth coalition."[30]

Whether such advice, pitched at such a high level of abstraction, can
be followed is an initial question. A further question is whether one
can ever generalize about the relationship between municipal fiscal and
tax policy and economic development. I have been arguing that one
cannot. A study of state economies finds little-to-no positive impact on
state-level economic indicators of a pro-business tax environment. Yet

another study finds no positive relationship between local economic development policies and employment center growth in the Los Angeles metropolitan region.[31]

Consider New York City again. In the 1970s, few would have predicted the kind of real estate appreciation that practically all of New York's boroughs have now experienced. But New York still has very high construction and development costs, relatively high taxes and regulatory burdens, and a significant amount of corruption.[32] And its housing costs are extremely high. Though crime declined during the city's ascendency, the schools did not improve dramatically—whatever education gains have been made are relatively recent. And while the city has attracted skilled workers, its advantage may actually be in its ready supply of low-wage workers, especially recent immigrants.

Moreover, the city redistributes from rich to poor relatively generously, and according to economic theory—which predicts that people will flee local redistributive activities—this should cause the city to decline. Indeed, despite Mayor de Blasio's progressive social policies, which his critics initially argued would "ruin the economy," New York was in excellent financial shape going into de Blasio's third year in office.[33] New York is also an example of how our stories about city resurgence can often be wildly off the mark. Consider the role of the financial services industry in the city's rebound. It is telling that urban economist Edward Glaeser, in explaining New York's resurgence, has argued that the financial sector has been an "innovation engine." In the 1960s, he argues, "the groundwork was being laid for New York's finance-based resurgence," after which "idea built on idea, as people in older, denser areas learned from each other" to create "ongoing improvements in the ability to assess the mispricing of assets."[34]

Of course, we now know that what we got was the opposite, a system of learning that reinforced mistake after mistake—a much different story about the actual operation of financial industry agglomerations. In 2008, the financial services sector was on the verge of collapse. Massive federal aid in the form of direct bailouts and favorable lending terms was required to shore up the country's banking system. Many of those banks and related financial services firms are located in New York. Thus, in backstopping the finance industry, the federal government also backstopped the city. To the extent that New York's economy was highly dependent on finance and related industries, the federal rescue of the banks was also a federal rescue of the city.

No doubt, New York City has benefited from its role as a center for financial innovation, but that path was set over 200 years ago, and municipal policy had little to do with it. Since the New Deal, the city has never had the power to regulate the financial industry, at least not directly, so the industry's location there cannot be said to arise out of any of the city's particular policy efforts.

Moreover, the city's reliance on the financial services industry turned out to be very risky. Regardless of how well the city was governed, this reliance would have had severe effects in the wake of the 2008 recession absent massive government intervention. The story that Glaeser tells about the origins of New York's resurgence is thus also the story of the city's potential undoing.

But there is a larger lesson to be learned, besides the fact that agglomeration economies do not always produce the best ideas. We now know that the urban boom of the last two decades was driven in part by what all urban booms have been driven by—land speculation. Land has always been the engine of spatial booms—land drives the urban political economy and is the initial basis for city wealth. Ultimately, the city has to be based on real productive activity, however—and that holds for the cities that profit from underwriting the creation of new cities. In the 1800s, New York money made Chicago; the New York financiers bet on that city and won.[35] More recently, New York money bet on Las Vegas, Miami, and thousands of other places. The financiers lost those bets, however, and the costs to the New York financial sector (and the New York-area economy) were significant, even if ultimately ameliorated.

The implications for policymakers are more important for our purposes. What should we have advised New York City in the 1990s about its dependence on the financial sector? Before 2008, many (though not all) urban theorists would have told a relatively positive story about New York's finance-based economy. And very few would have argued that the city—were it empowered to do so—should more heavily regulate or tax the financial sector. Indeed, even if city leaders had wanted to, they had limited authority to prevent the irresponsible lending and securitization practices that led to the economic crisis.[36]

New York was and is blessed with a money-making and innovation-making financial sector agglomeration that was and is the envy of every other city in the world; to regulate or tax it would be to precipitate its flight. But, of course, it turned out that the worst thing for New York was for it to be so heavily dependent on the financial sector. Without the federal bailout of the banking sector, the city's economy would have been in significant trouble. The best thing the city could have done ten years ago was to limit its exposure to that sector and deemphasize it, in the same way that the best thing for Detroit fifty years ago would have been to limit its exposure to the automobile industry and deemphasize it. But how would one have known?

Assessing Economic Development Strategies

That the causes of the urban resurgence are not easily ascertained reflects the larger difficulty of predicting and implementing long-term economic growth. Economists and policymakers have long struggled with this problem. If, as I observed in chapter 1, economic growth in cities is more akin to an ecological process, then how any policy intervention will affect a local economy is going to be highly uncertain. And if development is cyclical, one would need to predict not only the effect of any given intervention, but also its timing. Economic geographers have observed that a growing economy is often one in which one area is fading (rural America for instance), while other areas are growing (large metropolitan areas). Jane Jacobs similarly argued that in a system of cities, some would be creating new work at a rapid pace, while others would be in decline, and that these positions would change over time. Recall that for Jacobs, "Development cannot be given. It has to be *done*. It is a process, not a collection of capital goods."[37]

Two Strategies

The question I turn to next is whether local industrial policies can help cities *do* economic development. Consider two recent strategies. The examples are again drawn from New York City and again relate to the finance industry, but they could occur anywhere.

The first strategy is the standard location incentive. New York, like most cities, engages in ongoing economic development activities, and has done so with special regard to the financial industry. In 2004, the city provided $100 million worth of incentives to Goldman Sachs in response to its threat to relocate to New Jersey.[38] Goldman stayed in Manhattan, whether because of the subsidies or not is not known. Before the 2008 recession, paying Goldman to prevent its potential exit from the city seemed like a wise idea.

The second strategy also uses taxpayer money to subsidize economic activity. In 2009, following the collapse of the financial sector, the city proposed investing $45 million to retrain finance professionals and provide them with seed capital and office space for startup firms. The city's economic development corporation hoped to make small investments in new ventures with the aim of attracting additional private capital and keeping finance professionals in the city.[39]

How should we evaluate these two approaches to economic development? The first policy—location subsidies to large employers—has been and continues to be a standard tool of city economic development offices. As I observed in chapter 4, however, the economics literature is fairly uniform in questioning its efficacy. There is strong evidence that subsidies do not ultimately alter the location decisions of firms and that cities do not get back what they put in, either in the short or long term.[40]

The stories of failure are commonplace. Reporting that, five years after locating there, IBM fired most of its employees in Dubuque and Columbia despite a combined $84 million in tax breaks, the author of a Bloomberg News story noted that this scenario "has played out often across America: Big company comes to town, provides boost to the local economy and then leaves."[41] The *Kelo* case ended similarly: New London provided Pfizer with significant subsidies only to see the company depart a few years later.

Even if location subsidies enhance local welfare, they do not improve overall welfare—one city loses what another city gains. This is especially true if the firm relocates in the same economic region, as Goldman Sachs would have had it moved across the river to New Jersey. Moreover, if firms *are* ultimately influenced by subsidies, those subsidies distort firm location decisions. A move by Goldman Sachs to New Jersey is really a move from high rents to lower rents. But there is no reason that owners of commercial real estate in Manhattan should be subsidized; all location subsidies do is keep rents artificially high. Giving money to Goldman Sachs is the postindustrial version of smokestack-chasing: Businesses play one city or region against another, generating a subsidy race with dubious welfare effects.[42]

The city's incubator project took a different tack. Instead of giving money to a large, established firm to encourage it to stay, the city used taxpayer money to retrain finance professionals and subsidize startup firms. At the time, the city had no other choice; you cannot effectively subsidize the location choices of an industry that is in precipitous decline.

Nevertheless, advocates of a startup strategy assert that by investing in human capital, the city keeps and improves its labor force, which may be the key determinant for attracting new firms. And by backing small, entrepreneurial ventures, the city reduces its vulnerability to one employer or industry, which could leave or decline.

Moreover, smaller ventures have the capacity to grow and may be more attached and committed to their original locations. The hope is that by encouraging small-scale innovation, the city might help seed a homegrown agglomeration at low cost. Buffalo has backed this idea with real money: The city has dedicated up to $5 million in investment capital to promising startup ventures that agree to remain in or relocate to the city.

The idea that small, entrepreneurial ventures are necessary for economic growth in cities is popular. As we saw in chapter 1, Jane Jacobs argued that a growing city needs to generate new ideas, processes, and services, to—as we have seen—"add new work to old." She further argued that a developing city is one in which there are numerous small, entrepreneurial firms, and she claimed that in an unavoidably volatile economy, the city's most important "skill" is its ability to reset its product lifecycle by generating new startup firms. (Jacobs called them "breakaways.") According to Jacobs, large, vertically integrated multinationals have less ability to drive such a process. A more fluid and open local economy does better than one dependent on large firms.[43]

Whether city policy can generate breakaways is another question altogether. Consider a theory Ronald Gilson has offered for why growth in Silicon Valley has been stronger than a similar tech corridor along Route 128 outside of Boston. In the 1990s, AnnaLee Saxenian famously offered a cultural explanation for the difference, arguing that

California has a more open culture that favors mobility between firms among "job-hopping" engineers and that further disfavored large, vertically integrated companies.[44]

Gilson builds on Saxenian's observations, but instead of culture, he attributes the difference to a quirk in competition law. Gilson argues that a law adopted in the 1800s when California became a state helps explain the difference. For reasons mostly unrelated to competition policy, California does not enforce covenants not to compete, while Massachusetts does. The result, according to Gilson, is that Silicon Valley employees experience much higher rates of mobility across firms and to new startup ventures, and this fluidity has given Silicon Valley an innovation edge.

The conclusions Gilson draws are consistent with economic geography's emphasis on contingency. He argues that (1) happenstance plays an outsized role in development; (2) small policy interventions might make a huge difference in outcomes; but (3) it is very difficult to predict what those interventions should look like or where they should come from.[45]

This last point is important, and it can be applied with equal force to Gilson's own account. Gilson could just be wrong about the long-term effects of a serendipitous legal rule on the local economy. As of today—about fifteen years after Gilson's article—Route 128 is considered a highly successful technological agglomeration, admittedly second to Silicon Valley, but still robust despite the continued enforcement of non-compete clauses in Massachusetts.

Moreover, Gilson's theory is by his own admission highly industry-specific. It need not apply to other kinds of firms or industries. In addition, the facts on the ground may not quite align with the theory or may change over time. Consider more recent allegations that, during the mid-2000s, the largest Silicon Valley tech companies conspired not to poach each other's talent.[46] That these firms might have been conspiring to reduce employee mobility in the last decade does not necessarily undermine the argument that Silicon Valley had a fluid employment market previously. But it does raise questions about the long-term connection between growth, entrepreneurial culture, and employment law.

At a minimum, Gilson's story about Silicon Valley suggests that if government policy matters at all, it might matter more because of luck than any conscious policy decision. Location and business development subsidies of any kind are up against a complex economic geography that is not directly responsive to government inducements.

BIDs and TIFs

The important point is one that I have been asserting throughout: The causal relationship between municipal policy and growth is highly uncertain and unpredictable. This should have been one of the lessons learned from the mid-century failures of urban renewal, even as it was pursued on a scale that dwarfs current-day redevelopment efforts. Those current-day efforts look more successful, but only because causation and correlation are easily confused.

Consider another set of popular local policies that have been given some credit for the urban resurgence: business improvement districts (BIDs) and tax increment financing (TIF). Both have been lauded as examples of successful and indispensable public-private partnerships that have contributed to recent city success.

BIDs are well-known devices for providing enhanced municipal services in particular parts of the city. A BID is not the city, but it can collect assessments, issue bonds, make street improvements, hire security guards that augment the local police, and generally act within its sphere as a mini-municipality. BIDs arrived in the early 1990s and are now ubiquitous. They are a means of contracting out particular urban functions, targeting services to particular business constituencies, and arguably improving the city's delivery of those services.

TIF districts are similarly a form of privatization. State laws authorizing TIF districts permit a city to designate an area as one in need of redevelopment, either because it is blighted or at risk for blight. The TIF district's assessed property tax base is frozen for a set number of years, and any increase in valuation above that base level becomes an increment that is committed to financing development in the district. In other words, the potential increased tax revenues in the district are monetized and then used to back bonds for TIF district infrastructure, for subsidizing incoming businesses, and to finance a private developer's upfront and ongoing costs. TIF districts are not as ubiquitous as BIDs, but they have quickly gained significant traction in certain cities. As of 2005, TIF districts consumed nearly ten cents of every property tax dollar collected in Chicago and 26% of the city's total land mass. By the end of 2013, the city had 164 TIF districts.

Proponents of BIDs and TIF districts often assert that they are effective tools for promoting development in the city. But it is very difficult to figure out if this is so. Consider the argument that BIDs have been effective in part by reducing crime—a common purpose of BIDs in the early 1990s, and one that is often cited as a BID success and a cause of the urban resurgence more generally. As I have already observed, however, crime went down everywhere in the last decades, regardless of what policies were adopted. As for BIDs, the few studies that have been undertaken show at best a limited effect on crime—and one that could easily have been a function of the displacement of crime to other areas of the city.

These studies suffer from serious problems of causation. BIDs are not randomly assigned. They are a product of local social and political forces. Thus, "communities that adopt BIDs are likely to differ systematically from those that do not,"[47] and those differences may be more relevant than the BID itself. In fact, an examination of Philadelphia BIDs reveals that the biggest and most powerful BIDs have the backing of the biggest and most powerful economic and political actors: large universities, commercial real estate interests, and large corporations. BIDs on the Philadelphia periphery are only minimally effective, if at all. They have tiny budgets and spend most of their efforts trying to get local businesses to pay their assessments. More Philadelphia BIDs are failing than succeeding.[48]

Nevertheless, policymakers tout BIDs as an important tool in urban revitalization. But, as usual, they might have the causation exactly backward. Remember that BIDs are a form of taxation—paid for and targeted to the interests of a subset of the business community. Public officials would normally eschew raising taxes, but in the most successful BIDs, the most powerful political and economic actors voluntarily pay them. Why? Presumably these actors are pursuing their own self-interests and making a decision to invest in the downtown for a reason. That these businesses and landowners did not abandon the city, but chose instead to invest, could indicate that they had immobile assets that they wanted to protect, that they were taking a rational investment risk, or that they were anticipating the increasing value of downtowns.

In other words, the emergence of BIDs in the 1990s may have been an early indicator of the coming urban resurgence, not a cause of it. On this account, BIDs are a *symptom* of rising city wealth, not a generator of it. Those BIDs that succeeded were always going to succeed.

TIF districts' relationship to the urban resurgence is even more problematic, for the entire rationale for tax increment financing is that future economic growth can be harnessed to pay for infrastructure improvements today. TIF is the proverbial free lunch: Private developers are subsidized by future tax revenues that would not otherwise exist except for the development itself. No new taxes need to be raised to fund infrastructure improvements; monies for development are provided by the taxes that will accrue when development leads to higher assessments. In the meantime, those future monies can fund future debt. And eventually the district's tax revenues will return to the city budget, but with a more robust tax base in place.

The problem is that there is little evidence that TIF districts are a "but for" cause of development rather than merely subsidizing development that would have happened anyway. In Illinois, for example, the state statute authorizing TIF requires that it be used only in areas in which private development would otherwise not have occurred. But in Chicago, the most successful TIFs are in highly desirable downtown business districts. Summarizing the evidence, an influential report in 2007 by Cook County Commissioner Mike Quigley concluded that "a significant portion of the growth taking place inside TIF districts would have happened even without TIF, which means that the property tax revenues of local taxing bodies do in fact suffer because of TIF." The report further concluded that Chicago's taxpayers paid 4% more in property taxes than they would have paid without TIF, an indication that TIF districts simply shift or capture tax revenue but do not create it.[49]

TIFs are appealing for political reasons. Cities need revenue to build infrastructure, and state tax and debt limitations often restrict the city's fiscal options. There are also significant political reasons for Chicago city officials—especially the mayor—to keep monies in TIF districts instead of the general fund, where those monies would be susceptible to political dickering. Moreover, because TIF looks quite costless, it can serve as a subsidy to developers, banks, and other development interests without exciting the political attention that tax abatements or outright cash payments would. Critics of Chicago's TIF districts have long argued that TIF serves essentially as a slush fund available for the pursuit of the mayor's pet projects.

One need not assume that city officials have wholly malign motives, however. As Herbert Rubin reported in his classic article on the political economy of economic development: "Shoot anything that flies; claim anything that falls" captures the attitude of state and local politicians and development practitioners.[50] City officials feel the need to do something—anything—to prove that they are pursuing city growth. New York's creation of a relatively small business incubator in the midst of the largest worldwide fiscal meltdown since the Great Depression was likely motivated more by politics than economics. Likewise, BIDs and TIF districts—as well as other spatially targeted industrial development programs like enterprise zones—respond to a felt need on the part of city leaders to engage in economic development policy, even if unproven.

Uncertainty and Economic Development

As a practical matter, any economic development strategy that shifts money from taxpayers to private firms has to be measured against some other use of taxpayer money—say, providing schools, policing, or health care. And this again raises the question of what makes a city do better or worse economically. If the urban resurgence had a set of determinate causes, we might be confident that what a city is doing or not doing will have predictable effects. But urban economic policy is highly, even preternaturally, unproven, even if the politics of urban economic policy creates strong incentives for all involved to pretend otherwise. There are lots of reasons for this: Any given city policy will be mismatched to the metropolitan-wide scale of economic development; much is driven by chance or path dependency; larger economic and technological events will overshadow local interventions. Some of these problems can be overcome. But the biggest problem is that we do not really know enough about what works and what does not.[51]

The debate over the types of businesses that cities should encourage or subsidize is a good example. Economic base theory holds that cities can only grow economically by increasing exports to other places.[52] Fewer exports mean less money for local spending and less growth overall. This means that economic development strategy is unlikely to favor small businesses that service the local community, or businesses that are intended to substitute locally made goods for those that the city formerly imported. The export-based theory of local economic development tends to favor large transnational corporations or those corporations that can exploit local resources for cross-border sale. And it favors specialization (e.g., producing goods and services that cannot be imported).

Economic base theory has been the dominant approach to local (and international) economic development. Recall from chapter 5 how Paul Peterson equated the city's welfare with the welfare of its export industries.

This export orientation, however, has never been uncritically adopted. In the 1950s, it is worth noting, Charles Tiebout questioned whether exports were the only mechanism of city growth. Tiebout claimed that as a local economy grows, "its market becomes large enough to efficiently produce some goods and services that it had previously imported."[53] Jacobs also argued, even more strongly, that import substitution (she called it "import replacement") could drive city growth, as locals make for themselves what others had formerly made for them. A city can grow by providing more goods and services for itself, and by preventing money and resources from flowing outside the local economy. The implication is that self-sufficiency and leakage prevention should be a large part of economic development efforts. Though in the minority, those who advocate municipal import substitution point to the increasing localness of service-based economies, arguing that the local (non-export) share of the metropolitan-area economy can generate significant job growth.[54]

New York City's two interventions in the financial industry can be understood in the context of this wider debate. There is a significant shift in emphasis that is reflected in the decision to either support a large-scale multinational investment bank or fund local startups. Local economic development strategies can seek to enhance "global competitiveness"—an oft-used phrase in city development circles. Or a local economic development strategy might focus on supporting those firms and industries that mainly provide goods and services to locals. Though it is not always so, the startups that a local business incubator funds will most likely begin by providing services to local clients and producing goods for the local market. And the retraining of existing workers seems like a leakage-prevention strategy rather than an export-producing one.

Of course, growing your own is not inconsistent with exporting—Jacobs describes import substitution and export growth in cyclical terms. And we certainly know that having particular industrial agglomerations can be beneficial to the city as long as the city is not overly reliant on them. Paying Goldman Sachs to stay in Manhattan may have been a means of preventing the unraveling of New York's financial services agglomeration. The city surely feared that Goldman's move might trigger other firms to follow, though in the aftermath of the 2008 stock market crash, that fear looked a little foolish.

As I argued in chapter 6, the economic localist's argument for city economic self-sufficiency sounds in democratic theory—economic independence is a prerequisite for a free citizenry. A different argument for economic self-sufficiency is that relying too heavily on exports is risky because it makes a city vulnerable to global demand crashes. Proponents of municipal import substitution argue that the less self-sufficient one's economy is, the more global trends will affect it. They also point to data in the latter half of the twentieth century to support their argument that economies are becoming more local and that those economies are also growing.[55]

For example, in their examination of Canadian cities, the geographers Ted Rutland and Sean O'Hagan found that employment growth has mostly occurred in the local sector of the economy. Similarly, Joseph Persky, Marc Doussard, and Wim Wiewel have observed that as U.S. manufacturing declined during the second half of the twentieth century, the portion of the metropolitan-area economy that was produced and consumed locally rose.

This increasing localness has been attributed to the rise of the service sector economy in general. In larger cities, localness has increased as a bigger share of the local economy moved toward professional services. Producers of accounting, legal, marketing, and management consulting services tend to locate near their clients, within the same city or metropolitan area.[56] In an industrial era, it made sense to think of local economies as starting with exports, which would in turn generate a demand for local services as residents and workers flowed into the jurisdiction. But in a service economy, that story looks less plausible, and the causation might be reversed, as Michael Shuman, a current proponent of municipal import substitution, has argued.[57]

As always, however, there is the question of agency. An export-driven or import-substitution orientation implies different approaches to local economic development efforts. But it does not give us much purchase on the merits of specific, time-bound government decisions. That is because contingency is so hard to plan. New York's location incentives are misplaced, but the city's investment of public monies in startups also seems wrongheaded. Whatever theory of urban economic development one adopts, it is difficult to believe that municipal taxpayers need to provide investment capital to promising startup ventures in the very epicenter of global finance.

Conclusion: Back to Basics

Abandoning local economic development policies is almost politically impossible for local leaders. But it is the right thing to do. As I observed in chapter 2, economic geographers are skeptical of location subsidies, spatially targeted investments in infrastructure, or attempts to bring industry to lagging areas or spread it out among different jurisdictions. Those investments are unlikely to bear fruit, and they reinforce the misguided assumption that if the city could just get its local policies right, it could achieve economic lift-off.[58]

That mindset might actually be counterproductive. After repeated failures, it becomes quite rational for lagging areas to give up in such a race and fail to provide even minimally sufficient basic services. Growth happens in particular places because of the advantages that accrue when people and firms collect in a relatively circumscribed geographic place. The attempt to fight agglomeration by assuming that growth can happen everywhere is misguided and misunderstands the nature of economic development.[59]

The urban resurgence of the last few decades is a good example, as it does not seem to have been caused by any particular urban policies— and certainly not the ones that a competitive model of city growth and decline would favor. And yet popular efforts in economic development continue to revolve around competing for jobs. For much of the twentieth century, local economic development officials sought to attract industry and investment to underperforming areas and create incentive zones or other mechanisms to bring work to places without work. Inter-municipal tax base competition has been one result.

Unsurprisingly, this approach has had little success over time. In *The Problem of Jobs*, which recounts Philadelphia policymakers' attempts to deal with a looming postindustrial future, Guian McKee argues that prescience provides no advantage. As McKee describes it, Philadelphia city officials understood the problem of deindustrialization at mid-century. They took steps to address the problem and even experienced limited success, but ultimately they could do little about the emerging trends.[60] One possibility is that Philadelphia leaders adopted the wrong strategy, concentrating on manufacturing when they should have been looking at something else. In the 1950s, however, it would have been truly visionary for the city's managers to adopt a different approach.

Innovation is a characteristic of a flourishing urban economy, but it is not at all clear that policymakers can generate or sustain it through specific economic development policies. After repeated failures of policy, international developmental economists are also suitably modest about what industrial policy can achieve.[61]

Instead, it may be that in those jurisdictions or parts of jurisdictions that are lagging, the best policies are those that provide good basic services to those already there: health care, public safety, education, sanitation. Instead of treating lagging areas as deficient because they do not provide jobs, we should treat them as deficient because they do not provide a sufficient baseline of welfare. This means shifting the city's attention away from trying to attract the tech industry, the creative class, the middle class, or any other desirable demographic.

In other words, cities should not have a local development policy. The urban resurgence does not provide evidence that such a policy works—indeed, that any particular policy works—whatever its parameters. This change in emphasis counsels enhancing the city's capacity to provide basic services instead of charging it with fostering a good business environment or attracting investment.

8

Urban Crisis

THE URBAN RESURGENCE OF the last few decades should not blind us to the fact that many old-line U.S. cities have continued to struggle. During the second half of the twentieth century, as suburban and Sunbelt cities have boomed, many postindustrial U.S. cities have lurched from one fiscal crisis to another. I have mentioned New London, Toledo, and Camden—but there are many, many more.[1] The resurgence of core cities in some metropolitan areas has also coincided with the decline of some older inner-ring suburbs, a phenomenon that Bill Lucy and David Phillips have amply documented.[2] The 2008 recession precipitated the most recent handful of municipal fiscal crises, including Detroit's highly visible collapse, which resulted in the largest municipal bankruptcy in U.S. history.

Just as with the urban resurgence, the urban crisis allows us to test the relationship between city policy and economic outcomes—and test which constraints on cities are real and which are not. And as with the urban resurgence, the causes of city decline are not readily attributable to a particular city policy.

Nevertheless, the response to these crises has predictably been to urge cities to improve: to cut costs, lower taxes, and attract young, educated people and more industry. Whether a city can actually do any of these things is—as usual—assumed. City failure, like city success, has its presumed causes.

In the case of fiscally strapped cities, that cause is usually presumed to be a lack of fiscal discipline, and what we see in the context of urban

fiscal crisis is an effort to institutionally engineer that discipline. If profligacy is the problem, then constraining city power by imposing spending and debt limitations on cities at the front end and appointing state
receivers for distressed cities at the back end are legitimate and effective
policy responses.

These institutional mechanisms are going to be unsatisfying,
however—for reasons that have already been extensively described.
City growth and decline are not readily attributable to fiscal responsibility or the opposite. Moreover, the demand that cities attract and
subsidize capital is inevitably in tension with the requirement that cities
not become too complicit with it.

Thus, recent policy reactions to urban fiscal distress reprise the reaction to city and state defaults in the nineteenth and early twentieth centuries. As in the nineteenth century, the shifting of power away from
cities usually occurs in the aftermath of fiscal crises. But also as in the
nineteenth century, what we find is that the "disciplining" approach
to city power does not prevent urban decline. If one misdiagnoses the
causes of urban decline, then one will adopt institutional constraints
that are unresponsive to it. Those institutional constraints, however,
can dramatically undercut the capacity for cities to care for their citizens during times of economic distress.

Policymakers and scholars emphasize two structural mechanisms for
controlling local fiscal behavior: state constitutional constraints and
debt markets. Of course, representative democracy—citizens' power
to elect fiscally prudent agents and decline to elect fiscally imprudent
ones—is another way to control local fiscal behavior. But since the
nineteenth century, one of the central assumptions about the problem
of municipal fiscal policy is that local democracy—at least in its majori-
tarian and representative forms—has been a failure.

I discussed that assumption in chapter 3 and will say more about it
later in this chapter as well. Before I discuss the politics of fiscal failure,
however, we should look carefully at the efficacy of existing institutions.
It turns out that neither state constitutional constraints nor the debt
markets are effective in preventing local fiscal crises. As for state constitutional limits, they severely restrict the ability of states and localities
to respond to economic downturns; they lead governments to adopt
indirect and inefficient means of funding services; and they often fail

to depoliticize budgetary decisions, instead merely shifting ideological fights to the courts or other political arenas.

As for the market, it tends to reflect the underlying business cycle. In good times, cities are encouraged to take on debt. In bad times, greatly needed financing becomes unavailable. Furthermore, though cities may be inclined to follow market signals, they often have limited room to maneuver: Their hands are tied by constitutional constraints. This suggests that the problem of profligacy is itself a misdiagnosis. Indeed, government spending may be exactly what is needed in a downturn, but both market forces and constitutional constraints require municipalities to adopt pro-cyclical policies that undermine the city's fiscal stability.[3]

Debt and Discipline

The Fiscal Constitution

Consider first the "fiscal constitution" in the states. As I have discussed, constitutionalized fiscal policy is a product of a nineteenth-century reaction to state and municipal debt and a twentieth-century movement to restrict taxation. These two movements have led to state constitutional constraints designed to limit local fiscal flexibility. Forty-one state constitutions include balanced budget requirements. Forty-six states mandate the use of public monies only for public purposes. And three-quarters of the states limit the ability of state and local governments to acquire debt.[4]

Many states also have tax uniformity requirements intended to prevent subsidies through selective exemptions. Nineteen state constitutions and eleven state statutory codes contain tax and expenditure limitations (TELs) that can require legislative supermajorities (or supermajorities combined with a public referendum) to approve some or all new tax proposals. Moreover, at least forty-three states limit local governments by placing some restrictions on local property taxation.[5] Proposition 13 in California is again the most famous of these limitations. The result of a statewide property tax revolt, Proposition 13 spurred a national movement to restrict local taxation following its adoption in the late 1970s.

Like Proposition 13, all these fiscal constraints have been justified as responding to a perceived problem of overspending. We should be clear about the nature of that problem, however. One possibility is that public officials are engaged in profligate spending in contravention of the public interest because they are either corrupt or beholden to special interests. The main mission of nineteenth-century reformers was to eliminate subsidies to private enterprise—a goal consistent with classical jurisprudence's concern with economic favoritism.

Another possibility is that public officials are spending exactly as a majority of their constituents want, but current residents are foisting costs on future residents. This problem of shortsightedness is one that nineteenth-century reformers also sought to correct.

A final problem is that local tax and spending decisions might negatively affect outsiders—either neighboring jurisdictions or the state or country as a whole. At the turn of the twenty-first century, this worry is often voiced as a concern for the possibility of contagion—the potential knock-on effects of a default by a large city.

These are common agency or externality problems, and reformers have long debated how to solve them. Entrenching debt limits in constitutions, limiting the uses to which public monies could be put, and giving courts the role of enforcers were the nineteenth-century solutions. Limiting legislative authority to tax and spend by requiring extraordinary popular consent was the twentieth-century solution.

Scholars have been skeptical of all of these, arguing that the cure of the fiscal constitution has often been worse than the disease of overspending. An anti-debt and anti-tax fiscal structure sharply constrains the ways in which states and localities can raise and spend monies. It can have pernicious consequences because states and localities have to fund their services, and they will often find indirect ways to do so. The problem with constitutionalization is that it severely limits the ability of states and localities to respond to changes in economic circumstances.[6]

For example, states facing balanced budget requirements will seek to move as much spending "off-budget" as possible. The balanced budget requirement creates an incentive to put off costs or use accounting strategies to hide overruns. The underfunding of state employee pension funds, one of the chief problems animating current municipal crises, is one of these strategies. Constitutional or statutory rainy-day fund requirements are subject to similar manipulation.[7]

Consider also that in states with local property tax ceilings, cities compete for sales-tax-generating businesses and try to avoid housing. This "fiscalization of land use" induces local governments to zone in ways that distort regional property markets and generate high costs in terms of sprawl and the unequal provision of local public services.[8] Cities also increasingly depend on fees, intergovernmental transfers, or public/private schemes. Tax increment financing, discussed in the previous chapter, is an example. And taxation limitations force states and localities to depend to a greater degree on debt financing—an irony in light of constitutional debt limitations.

Meanwhile, those debt limitations induce states and cities to rely more heavily on special purpose districts or authorities that can issue debt outside of formal constitutional constraints. Cities need merely to create a special-purpose government, a quasi-public authority that can issue debt over and above the municipality's debt limitation. Significantly, this "non-debt" debt is often more expensive, and its issuance is less transparent.[9] The powers and management of special-purpose entities are often opaque as well and not subject to the conventional accountability associated with general-purpose local governments. As a constitutional matter, most special-purpose governments do not have to abide by the requirement of one-person-one-vote. And though sometimes justified on the basis that they will insulate directors from political pressure, often these entities serve as sites of political patronage.[10]

Courts have taken a realist position when it comes to the fiscal constitution, often reading constitutional restraints narrowly in order to allow the government to function, though not so narrowly as to obviate the need for local taxing authorities to think creatively. The result has been the judicialization of debt in some states (with judges making distinctions between "good" debt and "bad" debt), the routine avoidance of constitutional debt limitations, and the rise of new (and not always sensible) financing mechanisms. State legislatures generally endorse these avoidance mechanisms through regular legislation or by constitutionally entrenching exceptions to the general rules.[11]

Fiscal politics is thus state constitutional politics—oftentimes with a supermajority requirement, which gives minority interests effective vetoes. And, as interest groups well know, one can entrench both spending restrictions *and* spending commitments. Some states have constitutionalized their pension commitments or their education spending levels, for instance.[12] Especially in states with a robust initiative process, taxing restrictions coexist with spending requirements, thus limiting the range of revenue and spending options available to legislators. Plebiscitarian or supermajoritarian processes exacerbate that difficulty and are subject to all the usual critiques of such processes.[13] Of course, the purpose of constitutional entrenchment is to raise barriers to state and local fiscal decision-making. The result, however, has often been not less spending but constrained or distorted budget processes and perennial budget conflicts.[14]

The fiscal constitution has thus mostly been unavailing. This is not surprising. Almost immediately after nineteenth-century debt crises led to a restriction of city fiscal powers, institutional reformers initiated home rule movements to protect local fiscal autonomy—a reflection of their dissatisfaction with state legislatures' intermeddling. Similarly, the judicial avoidance of debt limitations and the dilution of public purpose requirements over the last eighty years signal a recognition that constitutional entrenchment makes for poor fiscal policymaking. More recent movements to remove tax and spending limitations in state constitutions reflect the same dissatisfaction.[15]

The Market

Can the markets—either the market in jurisdictions or the credit markets—do better? I will spend most of my time on the latter, as I have already argued at length that inter-local jurisdictional competition does not generate predictable local policy behaviors. Nevertheless, it is important to recall why theorists often argue that inter-local competition induces local fiscal responsibility. If residents and firms decide where to locate depending on the fiscal health of the jurisdiction, then they will punish (by exiting) those jurisdictions that are overextended. If a state or city wants to win in the intergovernmental jurisdictional competition, it must operate efficiently by providing good services at a low cost. Thus, fiscal federalism produces a race to the top: Interjurisdictional competition leads to good fiscal outcomes.[16]

The basic problems with the competitive model were described in chapter 2: It makes unrealistic assumptions about the motives and capabilities of public officials; it requires a link between the efficient provision of government services and economic growth that does not seem to exist; and it cannot explain the historic rise and decline of American cities. The market in jurisdictions is descriptively true, insofar as people and firms are by definition migrating out of declining cities and migrating into more prosperous ones. But as I have repeatedly emphasized, the market in jurisdictions does not explain what *caused* the struggling city to decline in the first place or what can be done about it.

The same can be said of the credit markets. Scholars have often argued that borrowing costs will create incentives for cities to exercise fiscal judgment. Assuming that credit rating agencies or the market as a whole can generate accurate predictions (and after the recent failures of rating agencies to correctly assess risk, one might have doubts about that), creditors—and more generally, the bond market—ensure that cities will make appropriate fiscal choices. The fiscal constitution in the states serves to reassure the bond market. Constitutional debt limitations and other constitutional and statutory constraints are ways for governments to credibly commit to exercise fiscal constraint. The theory is that by vocally asserting that it will limit its own borrowing and spending power, government lowers the current cost of credit.[17]

Certainly, the participants in the credit markets are capable of making sensible distinctions among government debtors. Thus, bond analysts know that the limits imposed by constitutional debt restrictions are not as important as tax limitations. For creditors, the revenue-raising capacity of the entity issuing the debt is the more important consideration. Moreover, cities and states obviously pay attention to market signals; they are justifiably wary of a poor credit rating. There is no question that the market "works" insofar as it induces the attention of state and local officials.

Nevertheless, the bond market is a fairly crude instrument for enforcing fiscal discipline. First, it is important to remember that the makers of the market—underwriters, banks, bond counsel, brokers—have an interest in promoting borrowing, especially in economically flush times.[18] Selling dubious products to both issuers and buyers of municipal debt— "trafficking in the shame of the cities," as A.M. Hillhouse wrote in his 1936 treatment of municipal bonds—has a long and sordid history.[19]

Questionable investment deals certainly contributed to a number of municipal fiscal crises that occurred after the 2008 stock market crash. Jefferson County, Alabama, for example, entered into interest rate swaps that helped swell its debt burden to $3 billion when interest rates collapsed. The county sued the lead underwriter, J.P. Morgan, on the grounds that it misled the county and investors. The Securities and Exchange Commission also imposed significant penalties on the underwriter in 2009. Detroit similarly entered swaps that the bankruptcy court ultimately settled for much less than their face value after the bankruptcy judge raised significant questions about the swaps' legality and enforceability.

Second, though the myth of perfect markets continues to hold sway in some quarters, it is fairly evident from the 2008 global downturn that markets do not price in all possible eventualities. By the time the bond market responds to an economic shock, it may be too late. Cities and states will have already taken on significant debt. And the short-term interests of market makers may also explain why cities and states can often return to the credit markets even after a default.

Third, even assuming that the debt markets are not exploitative and that debt can be priced correctly, it is not at all clear that those prices exercise real discipline. The short-term pressure of the debt market is real: Borrowing costs do increase as debt levels rise.[20] That being said, the reputational sanction for failing to pay is surprisingly muted. For example, commentators in the sovereign debt context have observed that creditors do not penalize defaulting governments with much stringency. Indeed, states that only partially repaid or never repaid their mid-nineteenth-century debts were still able to borrow at relatively reasonable rates within a decade. This raises the puzzle of why governments repay their debts at all. The evidence shows that they do, often by taking quite heroic measures.[21]

Scholars writing about sovereign debt have offered a number of theories for why this is so. Part of the challenge is determining how fiscal costs are (or, more pointedly, are not) translated into political ones. One possibility is that creditors participate directly in the policymaking process. No doubt, large debtholders have an interest in a jurisdiction's long-term budget decisions and may seek to influence policymakers, for better or for worse.[22] In mature credit markets, however, bondholders are more likely to express their preferences through their buy and sell orders, not through politics.

Thus, when scholars argue that creditors influence policy, they mostly mean that the price of debt influences policy. For the market to provide discipline, we must assume that local officials will pay a political price as debt service or the heightened cost of borrowing eats into the present provision of public services. Short of a default, however, the increased costs associated with a credit downgrade are unlikely to excite sustained public attention. Long-term debt presents a classic public choice dilemma. Interest payments are spread over time and across a large class of taxpayers. There is little incentive for any one taxpayer or even a group of taxpayers to expend political energy to contest the marginal increase.

Potential defaults or bankruptcies arguably raise different concerns, as a default is highly visible, tends to embarrass current public officials, and often has immediate fiscal repercussions. That being said, the mechanism for translating bad credit into political cost is still quite imperfect. Often, the public officials who pay the political costs of a default are not the ones responsible for the fiscal policies that led to it. And if defaulting governments can get back into the credit markets relatively quickly, the long-term political effects of a default will be relatively muted. The disciplining debt market has to turn borrowing costs into political costs, and those political costs in turn have to induce local officials to act.

This leads to a fourth reason that debt markets cannot be counted on to provide discipline: It is far from clear that even willing local officials can take any particular action in response to a rise in borrowing costs. Unlike private firms, cities cannot simply cut costs by restructuring their basic obligations. They cannot get out of the business of providing schools and minimum levels of public safety, health, and welfare to their citizens. The burgeoning costs of health care and education—which combined make up half of state budgets and a third of local budgets—are difficult for states and localities to manage or reduce.[23]

Meanwhile, on the revenue side, as we have seen, constitutionalized fiscal limits often restrict the ability of states and localities to make adjustments. State fiscal constitutions create only a partial fiscal federalism. In particular, localities cannot tax and spend as they wish. The fiscal constitution means that options that would otherwise be open to them (such as raising taxes) are often not.[24]

Asking governments to live with the consequences of their decisions is appropriate only when they have the full means to influence their fiscal fates. If the cost and revenue sides are mostly closed to them—as they are in states with significant restrictions on local taxation, for instance—governments are not capable of making the full range of tax and spending decisions. It is for this reason that some market-oriented scholars have criticized constitutional limitations on local taxation.[25] If market signals are to work, then you have to give cities the capacity to follow them.

And finally, the discipline of the market can only work if local tax and spending policies can materially affect city growth and decline. As I have been emphasizing, there is no reason to believe this is the case. On the ground, postindustrial cities are wrestling with economic restructuring as production has shifted away from old-line cities, regions, and nations. The processes of deindustrialization, suburbanization, and globalization operate on a large scale.

More importantly, boom and bust cycles continue to be a feature of modern economies. Those cycles unsurprisingly produce both business and government failures. Meanwhile, the fiscal constitution requires state and local budgets to be tightened in recessions—the very opposite of what a countercyclical economic strategy demands. The result is that state fiscal policy exacerbates downturns while cutting services to the most vulnerable. Scholars have suggested federal intervention to stabilize local budgets as a second-best solution to this problem. Others have argued for a wholesale rethinking of state fiscal constitutions.[26]

Of Bailouts and Bankruptcy

Despite the obvious failures of existing fiscal "constraints," the impulse to restrain city spending continues to be characteristic of the institutional response to municipal fiscal crisis. The approach to struggling cities seems always to focus on profligacy. The debate about whether to "bail out" cities and how and whether bankruptcy should apply to fiscally strapped municipalities reprises the long-running concerns about cities' fiscal irresponsibility.

Those concerns are predictably cyclical. After an economic crisis, institutional reformers shift power: from local governments to state

legislatures, from legislatures to the people, or from politically accountable actors to politically insulated ones. But those institutional reforms
are often found to be unsatisfactory, and then power is often shifted
again in the ongoing quest for an institutional solution. These cycles
of centralization and decentralization are animated by two themes: a
presumption of local mismanagement and a distrust of the local political process.

Of Bailouts

The allergy to giving financial assistance to fiscally strapped cities—to
"bailing them out"—encompasses both themes, as the main concern of
those who oppose bailouts of financially strapped cities is the so-called
"moral hazard." The conventional story is that local mismanagement
cannot be rewarded or else it will be repeated, and that local officials
and their citizens will act strategically to avoid their responsibilities. In
other words, the objection to bailouts assumes that state and federal
governments are not responsible for cities' fiscal difficulties, that local
leaders will regularly take advantage of the willingness of higher-level
governments to come to their rescue, and that backstopping local economies will send the wrong message to cities and investors.

All these assumptions are questionable. As I have already observed,
cities tend to pay their debts even in the absence of formal coercion.
There is no real mechanism to "foreclose" on defaulting governments
or force them into bankruptcy, and it is not possible to "liquidate" a
state or effectively attach municipal or state property. Even after governments have waived their sovereign immunity, creditors' remedies
are extremely limited. If moral hazard were such a pervasive problem,
we would expect to see much more opportunistic behavior and—more
importantly—much less lending to governmental entities. But we do
not. As scholars have noted, lenders continue to lend and governments
continue to pay back their debts "in spite of the lack of any severe or
coordinated debtor punishment."[27]

In fact, municipal bonds have always been viewed as conservative investments. There are approximately 40,000 general-purpose local governments in the United States. In the last decade, only a tiny fraction
have failed to pay their creditors, and, as I have noted, cities often cut
services significantly in order to meet their debt service. After declaring

bankruptcy, Orange County, California, continued to pay off its general obligation debt, as have many other cities. In Rhode Island, the bankrupt city of Central Falls continues to pay its general obligation debtholders, after the passage of a state law that gives bondholders a lien on the city's tax receipts. Municipal defaults are extremely rare and certainly less prevalent than bond defaults by corporations.[28]

The relative fiscal probity of local governments raises a conceptual puzzle for those who worry about local strategic behavior. What accounts for the low rates of municipal defaults? One answer may be that governments, unlike firms, do not raise revenue primarily through the sales of good and services, but rather through the collection of taxes. In a society in which the public generally complies with tax laws, taxes are a fairly stable source of revenue absent a large exogenous shock like a depression. The property tax, in particular, is a fairly stable source of revenue for local governments in most states.

Moreover, the paucity of full-scale municipal defaults—at least in the latter half of the twentieth century—can be attributed to the emergence of the federal government as a stabilizing force. The federal government plays an important regulatory role, policing the credit markets (even if that oversight sometimes falls short) and limiting (if not eliminating) corruption. More importantly, in addition to the direct aid that local governments receive, aid also flows to individuals through federal social welfare programs. The rise of the social welfare state means that economic downturns do not necessarily lead to economic collapse. The modern social welfare state seeks to ameliorate booms and busts with monetary policy, regulation of finance, large-scale tax and transfer programs, and nationwide social insurance. Cities do not have these kinds of tools at their disposal. But they benefit from them.

The concern that a specific bailout will encourage opportunistic behavior seems misplaced when local, state, and federal finances are already so intertwined. Cities are not even remotely fiscally autonomous, and certainly not autonomous in the way that idealized accounts of fiscal federalism presume. Intergovernmental transfers and direct federal outlays to state and local governments and state and local residents are the norm in our federalism. Those transfers are so significant as to make the worry about a one-time bailout seem odd. The federal government is already the primary fiscal backstop for individual citizens. It is not clear why we would see an increase in strategic behavior by cities if that fiscal intervention took the form of a bailout.

Moreover, the no-bailout view implicitly assumes that higher-level governments have little to no responsibility for local fiscal difficulties. But the federal government encourages municipalities to take on debt by providing a tax exemption for municipal bond interest. At the same time, federal and state policies shift costs downward via unfunded mandates or tax cuts—both of which require localities to assume a greater share of the fiscal burden. It stands to reason that state and federal officials have little incentive not to impose funding obligations on lower-level governments unless they have to take responsibility on the back end for the fiscal stresses they cause.

Again, a bailout is not particularly remarkable if the fiscal health of cities is already dependent on and vulnerable to central government fiscal decisions. Consider the perennially popular "property tax relief." State legislatures and governors are eager to adopt property tax ceilings, thus taking credit for reducing taxes. But the fact is that any state-level restriction requires local governments to find new revenue sources. State tax relief also begs the question of why local citizens are not capable of choosing their own tax rates. That property tax relief must come from above suggests that there is a problem with the political process at the municipal level. But in fact, it is likely the case that citizens are getting the tax rates that they prefer for the services they are receiving. Governor- or legislative-led tax relief is a chimera dangled in front of statewide voters. It promises something that cannot be delivered and that would be better pursued locally.

Indeed, the interrelated nature of national, state, and local finances means that solving a political process problem at one level of government might contribute to a different problem at another level of government. Elected officials have incentives to impose political externalities downward. If we treat local governments as fiscally autonomous in order to force local officials to make hard choices, other political actors in the system will be inclined to shift as many of those choices onto them as they can. And the last one holding the bag may be the least able to lift it. In other words, the strategic behavior of city officials might pale in comparison to the strategic behavior of state officials.[29]

That being said, it may be that opponents of bailouts are not worried about public officials' behavior at all. Perhaps the strategic behavior that we are trying to avoid is on the lender's side, not on the government's. A standard objection to bailouts is that investors anticipating a bailout will be too aggressive in extending credit. They too have a potential moral hazard that needs to be remedied.

Certainly, a bailout of bondholders can create perverse incentives to over-lend. But the uncertainty of any rescue and careful construction of its terms can mitigate those problems. The few bailouts of cities that have occurred have been accompanied by fairly severe terms—terms that can and should include pain for bondholders.

We sometimes forget for instance that New York City received significant federal support during its early-1970s financial crisis. It is easier to remember President Gerald Ford's initial objection to a bailout of the city, immortalized in the famous headline "Ford to City: Drop Dead."[30] Despite the President's objection, New York City did in fact receive $2.3 billion in short-term loans from the federal government to prevent the city from defaulting in 1975.[31]

No one would contend that New York's bailout signaled that investors should increase their exposure to city debt. In fact, the large banks holding the bulk of New York's notes had to accept far less favorable repayment terms. Nor did the bailout induce other cities to engage in "irresponsible" behaviors, in part because its terms were suitably stringent, but also because local elected officials are generally not inclined to lead their communities up to the edge of default. Forty years later, some commentators still think that Ford was correct to reject New York's original request for a bailout.[32] But their argument cannot be that federal funds induced future city dwellers or their governors to act irresponsibly, that banks suddenly went on a lending spree, or that other cities were led to assume that their fiscal decisions made no difference.

A more plausible objection to bailouts is a democratic one. When the fiscal choices made by one city affect the fiscal health of other cities, there must be some democratic justification. Assuming that higher-level governments are not contributors to local fiscal stress (and, as I have said, that is questionable), poorly run cities should not impose costs on better-run cities. That a city default might threaten the good credit of other cities perhaps makes bailouts inevitable, but also demo-cratically troubling.

This intuition might make sense with reference to private institu-tions that engage in risky investment activity, like the "too big to fail" Wall Street firms that were provided with massive infusions of cash in the immediate aftermath of the 2008 recession. In that case, a federal bailout might protect decision-makers from adverse consequences that are needed to prevent future bad behavior.

It is very different, however, to assert that a city that provides basic municipal services and has to be responsive to a local electorate has the same or a similar set of incentives as private firms. The city's agents may act irresponsibly at times, but the city as a whole does not have the same profit-maximizing goals as a private firm. It is unlikely to build into its very operations the protections afforded by a possible government backstop.

In any case, the federal government has not only injected cash into private enterprises to save the automobile, banking, and mortgage in-dustries, but has also in the past injected cash to stabilize foreign sov-ereigns.[33] The standard by which we judge the normative attractiveness of local bailouts should not be any higher. And again, there is nothing to prevent governments from imposing bailout terms that will induce caution. The existing institutional constraints thus seem well suited to minimize any objection to a municipal bailout.[34]

Of Bankruptcy

Some policymakers and scholars who have objected to bailouts favor municipal bankruptcy instead. There is certainly nothing wrong with deploying existing procedures to provide a fiscally strapped municipality with a "fresh start." But for policymakers who believe that cities need to be induced to exercise fiscal discipline, bankruptcy does not provide it—at least not on the debtor municipality's side. Like bailouts, bankruptcy erases debt without making a distinction between poor management and bad luck. It thus does little to counter the moral hazard objection, whatever its validity. The advantage of bankruptcy, according to those who advocate it, seems to be that it is *not* a bailout, and it can force fiscal decisions that would be politically unpalatable otherwise.[35]

In this way, the resort to bankruptcy replays the institutional move embodied in the fiscal constitution: shifting decision-making up the scale of government. In this case, a federal bankruptcy judge would have some authority to reorganize city debt at the near-default stage. Of course, the bankruptcy option at the back end will alter how power is exercised on the front end. Thus, depending on the structure of the bankruptcy law, bankruptcy may be an indirect way for Congress (through judges) to regulate local fiscal practices. Or the bankruptcy option will shift power within the state, possibly from legislatures to governors, depending on who is authorized to seek bankruptcy protection for a locality, who will negotiate its terms, and what kinds of legislative authorization might be required.[36]

Within this context, bankruptcy may provide strategic benefits for particular political actors. For example, state and city officials may use the threat of bankruptcy as a tool in their negotiations with public-sector unions or as a way of inducing higher-level governments to provide aid.[37] The politicians know this. As the recent Detroit bankruptcy process amply illustrated, policymakers understood that the bankruptcy question was really about the relative sanctity of existing and future municipal employee benefits and pension obligations.[38]

How costs will be allocated among bondholders, pensioners, and citizens is obviously the central question in municipal bankruptcies. And while the payment of bond interest appears to be a neutral, even unavoidable, expenditure, it is not. Forcing cities to pay their bondholders is a way of restricting a city's budgetary options. This explains why cities might favor bankruptcy, which allows them to seek protection from creditors and avoid painful cuts in public services or avoid a hostile state takeover.[39]

This effort may be resisted by state legislators who would rather control local fiscal outcomes through a state-appointed receiver. States, unlike localities, may also be more inclined to placate the credit markets, either because state officials worry about the state's overall credit rating or because bankers and bond investors exercise more power than do local citizens at the state level. Or the demand that fiscally strapped cities pay back bondholders in full might reflect political considerations: a general hostility toward public employee unions or to redistributive spending of any kind.

That bondholders should bear most of the risk of a municipal default seems obvious, however. Bondholders are in a better position than citizens or pensioners to monitor local fiscal behavior on the front-end. They have ample choices about where to invest. More importantly, bondholders can diversify. Citizens and pensioners cannot. Neither can readily hedge against downside risk at the back end.[40]

Kevin Kordana makes this point in an important article arguing that bankruptcy courts should approve reorganization plans that do not impose tax increases on citizens but do impose some loss on bondholders. Bondholders are more appropriate risk-bearers, he argues, because they have been paid ex ante to assume the risk.

As Kordana observes, it makes little sense to charge current residents for commitments that past residents may have undertaken. Local residents change over time and thus there is little relationship between risk-creators and risk-bearers. And raising taxes can be inefficient, as it may further strain local taxpayers and undermine the municipality's ability to recover from fiscal distress. Moreover, bondholders are better positioned to absorb economic shocks by pricing those eventualities into the interest rates they charge. Interest rates and diversification are the appropriate ways for creditors to protect against financial loss. There are no equivalent mechanisms for citizens. For that reason, it makes little sense to charge residents of fiscally strapped cities in order to pay off bondholders.[41]

But what about contagion? One repeatedly hears the claim that cities need to pay their debts because one city's default can reverberate across jurisdictions. State officials are eager to avoid local defaults or any whiff of municipal bankruptcy for fear that borrowing costs will rise for other localities and the state as a whole.

Like the worry about moral hazard, the worry about contagion is also overstated. The empirical literature is, in fact, quite mixed on whether contagion in capital markets exists at all. More specifically, while there is some evidence that there are some short-term interest rate increases for all borrowers in reaction to a default,[42] there is also evidence that municipalities are able to access the bond market relatively soon after a default and at reasonable rates. Indeed, as I have already observed, there is evidence more generally that the financial markets do not penalize sovereign defaulters very severely at all.[43]

Moreover, the bond market seems to be able to distinguish among municipal borrowers, even if crudely. Despite Detroit's filing of the largest municipal bankruptcy in U.S. history and some prominent predictions that the 2008 recession would trigger municipal defaults on a massive scale, the ten-year borrowing costs for states and local governments remained stable or actually went *down*. Neither Jefferson County's nor Detroit's bankruptcies had much impact on the wider bond market. Short of a panic, the bond market seems to be able to accommodate and domesticate municipal defaults just fine.[44]

When faced with a decision to protect bondholders or citizens, it is entirely appropriate as a matter of political morality for a public official to choose the latter over the former. As between pensioners and citizens, the calculus is slightly different. Pensioners are often as equally dependent and undiversified as current citizens, but it is possible that we might make a democratic argument for privileging citizens over pensioners (assuming there is not a great deal of overlap). What complicates matters is the possibility that pensioners might enjoy entrenched state constitutional entitlements. As I have observed, state fiscal constitutions can include spending requirements as well as limits, and courts have had to decide what those requirements mean in the context of modifying existing municipal pension commitments. These constitutional commitments should prevail over bondholders. But the choice between pensioners and citizens depends on the relative expectations and wealth of two dependent classes.

We can consider whether we want bankruptcy judges to make these choices. They are certainly capable of doing so and have done so repeatedly. But like other institutional fixes, the bankruptcy option will be unsatisfying over the long run. That is because the Bankruptcy Code does not provide for the structural reforms that might aid a distressed city. Indeed, currently, bankruptcy seems to be of limited use. Cities can already access bankruptcy if their states allow, but very few cities do so.[45]

Perhaps this is because the Bankruptcy Code does not contemplate the kinds of reorganizations that are possible on the private side and thus does not help cities grapple with underlying structural economic problems. For example, in many cases, redrawing municipal boundaries or reconfiguring the municipalities' status would be advisable. Disincorporation would allow fiscally strapped cities to become part of a larger taxing entity—in most cases, the surrounding county. But the law does not permit judges to order such involuntary dissolutions, nor would it appear to be consistent with state constitutional autonomy to permit them to do so. In truth, bankruptcy can provide debt relief, but it provides limited structural reform.[46]

Consider Detroit's bankruptcy resolution. The final deal involved three main components: the State Contribution Agreement, which required Michigan to contribute $194.8 million into Detroit's two main public pension systems; the Detroit Institute of Art settlement, which secured another $100 million for the pension system from private funders in exchange for transferring Detroit's art collection to a charitable foundation— a deal that also prevented the liquidation of the city's art collection; and a Global Pension Settlement, which restructured the city's pension liabilities in such a way as to mostly avoid cuts in pension benefits for retired city workers.[47]

Notably, the Detroit settlement also sharply limited the recovery of bond insurers who had entered into a number of complex deals with the city in 2005 to address its rising unfunded pension obligations. These deals—known as certificates of participation (COPs)—were necessitated in large part by state municipal debt limits, which limited Detroit's ability to issue more traditional forms of debt. The COPs structure allowed Detroit to characterize the payments that it made to creditors as contractual obligations for future services rather than as debt, thereby circumventing those limitations—a nice example of the perverse effects of the state's fiscal constitution.

When Detroit filed for bankruptcy, it had approximately $1.2 billion in outstanding COPs obligations. After the crash of 2008—which resulted in interest rate declines and triggered contractual changes in the underlying obligations—these obligations became unsupportable, and a precipitating cause of Detroit's fiscal spiral downward. In limiting the COPs holders' recovery, the bankruptcy court expressed skepticism about the legality of the COPs deals under Michigan law, observing that COPs holders "were aware that the structure of the COPs Transaction was precarious and that [Detroit] had reached its debt limit under state law."[48]

The combined effects of these settlements eliminated approximately $7 billion in city debt, preserved the city's pension system, and provided the city with some funds to improve services to existing residents and invest in badly needed municipal infrastructure. But the bankruptcy court did not and could not solve the city's ongoing structural dilemmas: continued population losses, an epidemic of abandonment, a shrinking city tax base, concentrated poverty, skyrocketing unemployment rates, and the lack of an industrial base. And as the bankruptcy judge observed, the calculations of future revenue and expenditures left Detroit with little room for error.

Eliminating municipal debt and voiding bad deals while preserving the city's ability to provide services and protect vulnerable pensioners certainly makes sense. But generally, the cities that have successfully come out of bankruptcy to full fiscal health are those that did not have significant structural problems to begin with. For struggling cities, bankruptcy can provide debt relief. It does so in part by giving unelected federal judges a great deal of authority to reorganize debts and pick winners and losers. Within this context, bankruptcy provides strategic benefits for particular political actors.

But institutionalized debt relief of whatever kind still leaves untouched the existing fiscal regime and the underlying institutions that have led to fiscal distress in the first place. Better to revisit the structural defects in the state's fiscal constitution on both the spending and revenue sides. In Detroit's case, this would mean revisiting state tax and debt limitations that constrain the city's revenue-raising capacity; fully funding city-state revenue sharing—which had been cut by the state legislature in the years immediately preceding Detroit's bankruptcy; and helping Detroit to better collect income taxes owed by those who work in the city but reside in the suburbs. It would be better to address the central problems of urban decline before cities enter into questionable financing deals. Detroit had been declining for over fifty years—the fiscal manipulations of the last decade were not to blame for Detroit's failure, and restructuring its finances going forward will not resolve them.

The Politics of Municipal Failure

And so we turn to the politics of municipal failure. One could treat city fiscal failure as an unavoidable feature of boom and bust economies, and one that is manageable through state or federal programs meant to even-out local economic volatility. Cities, like all organizational entities, sometimes need aid and assistance. Indeed, cities are in some ways more vulnerable than other kinds of economic entities because they are geographically fixed in place and thus subject to the vicissitudes of the spatial economy.

Urban fiscal crises are rarely approached in this manner, however, for they are political through-and-through. The causes of, and solutions to, fiscal crises are inseparable from questions about how power is allocated and exercised. And the discourse of fiscal crisis has itself been politicized: Local fiscal incompetence is inevitably tied to local political failure. A common view is that a city in fiscal crisis is a city whose politics is deeply deficient, and that solving the latter can solve the former.

The Relationship between Fiscal Failure and Political Failure

Consider two competing narratives of Detroit's descent into insolvency and bankruptcy. The dominant view, generally accepted by the media, described Detroit as being—in the words of its appointed financial manager—"dumb, lazy, happy, and rich."[49] Detroit failed to anticipate a looming fiscal crisis because it did not retool for the modern economy. The benefits it paid to municipal unions were too generous. And its elected officials were corrupt and self-dealing.

A counter-narrative, offered by critics, argues that the problem was giveaways to corporate capital. As David Sirota points out, the monies that Michigan and Detroit spent on corporate tax breaks and subsidies to the automobile industry would have more than made up for any underfunding of the city's pension system. The state and city governments were essentially held hostage to the auto industry, which, in the words of the attorney for the township of Ypsilanti, put "a stranglehold on the entire state of Michigan and other places across the country by just grabbing these tax abatements by the billions."[50] These subsidies and tax breaks were enormous and had dubious welfare effects.

In both these stories, Detroit's demise is tied to a political failure: the capture of city or state government by dominant interest groups. And the general response to a political failure is to adjust institutions. If municipal profligacy and cronyism—to benefit either unions or corporations—are the problem, then the solution is to create a system that avoids those pathologies. For Progressive Era reformers faced with similar concerns about corrupt city government, the failures could be remedied by fixing democratic institutions. And in large part, those fixes involved taking power out of the hands of locally elected officials.

The state takeover of a fiscally distressed city is the most radical version of this institutional fix. Consider that in 2016, Michigan had twelve municipalities and five school districts under some kind of emergency financial management process.[51] In Detroit's case, the state appointed a municipal receiver and dismissed the elected city council and mayor, who were essentially relieved of any legislative or executive functions. In light of the assumed links between fiscal failure and political failure, the necessity of imposing some external control over the city seemed obvious, even unavoidable.

That cities can be governed for extended periods of time by appointed officials, accountable only to the state's governor or legislature, is the logical outcome of the marginal constitutional status of American cities. There is no individual constitutional right to elect one's city leaders, nor is there a collective constitutional right to local self-government. The assumed political failure responsible for municipal fiscal failure can thus be remedied by treating the city as a failed business and changing its management—even as that change is defended on democratic grounds. Policymakers and politicians argue that takeovers are necessary to protect the city's citizens from mismanagement or to protect the state's citizens from the spillover effects of a large-scale municipal crisis.

Scholars too have justified state takeovers on democratic grounds. Consider Clayton Gillette's argument that appointed managers are essentially "dictatorships for democracy." Gillette argues that a state takeover of a city is not anti-democratic at all. Instead, it is a temporary measure designed to reinvigorate democracy by eliminating the local political machine (whatever its political valence) that does not represent the interests of the polity as a whole or actively acts against the wishes of the majority.[52]

To his credit, Gillette owns the "dictator" label, though surely he knows that few dictators in history have taken power without arguing that they better represent the people than do the "corrupt," "incompetent," or "captive" elected leaders whom the dictator is replacing. What is important about the rush to suspend municipal voting privileges is how often reformers assume that local political failure is at the root of local fiscal failure. The standard narrative assumes that local officials' incompetence, corruption, or inability to rule is a cause of fiscal failure, and not a symptom. This narrative further assumes that a dictator can actually adopt policies that will ameliorate the fiscal crisis over the medium and long term.

This seems implausible, especially in light of the long history of urban crisis in the United States. During the second half of the twentieth century, not only Detroit but many Rustbelt and older cities lurched from one fiscal crisis to another, while other, newer cities boomed. Deindustrialization, white flight, disinvestment, and concentrated poverty undermined many old-line cities as populations moved south and west. The process by which this occurred seems to have little to do with the relative fiscal discipline of particular cities or the relative effectiveness or ineffectiveness of local politics.

There are certainly examples when a municipal fiscal crisis has been precipitated by a single poor decision or a series of corrupt or incompetent decisions. Orange County is an example; so is the City of Bell, California. The questionable interest rate swaps that precipitated the immediate fiscal difficulties for Jefferson County and Detroit also fit into this category.

Those situations, while sometimes complicated, can be resolved with targeted interventions—electoral (throw the bums out), prosecutorial (jail the offending local officials), or substantive (revise the terms of the bad deal). These options are readily available to the local electorate, prosecutors, the state legislature, and state and federal courts, if they decide to act.

Indeed, in the nineteenth century, courts were often inclined to absolve cities of debt incurred in boom times. Ironically, they did so by using legal doctrines that read municipal powers narrowly. Judges invalidated agreements entered into by city officials on the ground that those officials never had the authority to enter into the agreements in the first place or on the basis that the agreement itself contravened state-imposed limits on city indebtedness.

These doctrinal "restrictions" on city power aided citizens. Releasing citizens from the burdens imposed on them by local officials acting in their private interests was a way for courts to warn both corrupt public actors and corrupt credit purveyors that they should be more circumspect about the commitments made in the city's name. Mismanagement could be solved by voiding bad deals on the back end.

The Detroit bankruptcy settlement looks something like this. By limiting recovery for holders of questionable municipal obligations, the bankruptcy court sent a message to past and future creditors that they should avoid taking advantage of cities that are otherwise in fiscal distress.

In contrast, for those cities facing the deeper problems of postindustrial decline, there is no good evidence that mismanagement, giveaways, incompetence, or laziness *caused* that decline, or that a dictator can resolve it. In a world of boom and bust, conditions unrelated to fiscal management are more relevant to the city's economic health. Of course, corrupt and venal city leaders should be pursued, and reformed government may be a good in itself. But municipal democracy might be working perfectly well and still the city will be in fiscal distress.

A municipal dictator can also get things badly wrong. Consider Flint, another Michigan city that was governed by an appointed emergency manager. In 2014, as a cost-cutting measure, officials determined that the city should obtain its water from the Flint River instead of continuing to rely on the Detroit water system. The water turned out to be contaminated with E. coli and other bacteria. It was also corroding the city's pipes, leaching high levels of lead into the city's water supply. Subsequent complaints about the quality of Flint's water were ignored by a series of appointed managers, who overrode city council efforts to remedy the problem. A similar, though less dramatic, failure has led the Detroit public school system—which has been governed by a series of unelected emergency managers since 2009—to the brink of collapse.[53]

Electoral accountability is at the core of responsive government. The assumption that municipal political failure is at the root of local fiscal failure, however, leads to the dismantling of those democratic institutions that would otherwise be responsive to local voters.

The relative ease with which this step is taken reflects a long-standing skepticism of urban democracy. Recall that, during the heyday of the urban machine in the nineteenth and early twentieth centuries, the perception that cities were abysmally managed was prevalent (even if unsupported by the facts). Institutional reformers found reasons to shift municipal power to experts or state administrators, leading Frederic Howe to complain in 1905 that

> [r]eform organizations have voted democracy a failure. Beginning with a conclusion, they have aimed to temper the failures of an experiment that has never yet been fully tried. They have petitioned State legislatures to relieve the overburdened city of the duty of self-government.[54]

To be sure, urban political machines can and do pursue interests that are contrary to the public interest. Breaking the political power of entrenched, corrupt, and sometimes incompetent regimes can be quite difficult. But as I have argued throughout, though local economic health is not impervious to bad government, it does not seem to turn on it. Corrupt local officials can preside over periods of robust city growth, and honest local officials can preside over periods of decline.

For Howe, the democratic institutions of the city were more than adequate to the task of policing city managers. He blamed mismanagement on corrupt special interests—a common view in the early nineteenth century. "Democracy has not failed by its own inherent weakness so much as by virtue of the privileged interests which have taken possession of our institutions for their own enrichment."[55] Cities needed *more* popular democracy—not *less*.

Howe was and still is in the minority, however. That we are so often unmoved when urban citizens are stripped of the ability to elect local leaders reflects the dominant skeptical approach. State takeovers of cities are pitched as pragmatic, procedural solutions to municipal mismanagement. They are understood as a technocratic solution to a political defect. The assumption is that constraining local elected officials so that they act consistently with the public good is the problem to be solved.

The Political Causes of Urban Distress

If we are going to look for the political causes of municipal fiscal failure, however, the deficiencies of a city's internal electoral politics are not the most obvious place to start. As the geography of urban fiscal crisis amply illustrates, the U.S. municipalities in the most severe financial trouble are predominantly postindustrial, extremely poor, and often heavily minority. Consider that emergency managers have mostly been appointed in predominantly African American cities or school districts—places like Detroit, Flint, or Newark. Atlantic City, New Jersey, on the verge of a state takeover, is 70% black or Hispanic.

These places—whether they are core cities or older suburbs—are often parts of larger declining regions: the Rustbelt or coal country, for instance. Alternatively, in some states, declining urban cores are surrounded by perfectly healthy (and heavily white) suburban jurisdictions, whose policies of racial and socioeconomic exclusion and inter-municipal tax competition have long exacerbated the core city's difficulties. In Detroit's case, for instance, the regional economy is strong, and the majority white suburbs immediately surrounding Detroit are some of the most prosperous in the country. New London, New Haven, Hartford, and Bridgeport are struggling Connecticut cities immediately adjacent to many of the wealthiest census districts in the country. Trenton, Newark, Camden, and Atlantic City are also similarly surrounded by wealthy New Jersey suburbs. That those suburbs exist apart from, and need not concern themselves with, cities' decimated black cores is a result of conscious decision-making. The political origins of municipal fiscal failure are written into the very geography of our metropolitan areas.

The essential features of this inequitable metropolitan geography are well established, and they are mostly a product of state and federal policy. While economic growth is and always has been geographically uneven, the fact that poor minorities are more often stuck in poor geographies is a function of political decisions: decisions that reinforce the jurisdictional separation between city and suburb; that make local property tax wealth the determinant of school quality; and that simply put poor and minority residents out of sight through discriminatory development, land-use, finance, housing, and zoning policies.[56]

Urban theorists and policymakers have long observed that there is nothing natural or foreordained about a metropolitan-area political structure that encourages white flight. As Peter Dreier, John Mollenkopf, and Todd Swanstrom have shown, economic segregation is increasing across and within metropolitan areas in significant part because of government policies that have encouraged "spatial inequalities and low-density suburban development."[57] Socioeconomic and racial exclusion were built into our metropolitan-area political arrangements from the start. These arrangements, as Stephen Macedo has argued, "make all of us into stakeholders in . . . the perpetuation of inequality."[58]

The second half of the twentieth century witnessed monumental efforts to dismantle those arrangements, but they have had limited success. After the riots of the 1960s, the Kerner Commission sought to promote an "urban Marshall Plan"—large, sustained federal investments in the city.[59] That plan never materialized. Racial integration, the promise of *Brown v. Board of Education*, was ultimately rejected and dismantled, even as the rhetorical commitment to integration displaced a competing commitment to substantive economic equality.[60] And, indeed, despite formal legal equality, our metropolitan regions continue to be riven by deep racial and economic divisions. The battles for fair housing, nondiscrimination in zoning and lending, and school funding equalization continue. But the surge of post-civil rights antipoverty and metropolitan reform efforts—in the courts and in the legislatures—has mostly been stalled or abandoned.

The experience of failing cities is thus an example of the intersection between economic geography and legal geography. Certainly, there are larger-scale economic forces at work in the rise and decline of any particular city in a wider system. Economic geographers have taught us that laggards and leaders are a feature of self-organizing economies in space. Economically lagging places will always exist.

There is no reason, however, that African Americans or other minority groups need to be overrepresented in such lagging places.[61] There is nothing about such places or such people that entails such a coincidence. Nevertheless, it is no surprise that economically lagging places tend to coincide with the locations of otherwise traditionally marginalized groups. The metropolitan-area geography of fiscal failure tends to map the metropolitan-area geography of race. This overlap of economic and legal geography is obviously a political failure—one of the starkest and least addressed in U.S. history.[62]

Conclusion: Marginal Cities

All of this is well known. Volumes have been written about it. And yet the standard tropes of elite skepticism of urban democracy are evident in the takeovers of fiscally distressed cities: the assumptions that local (often African American) citizens cannot adequately monitor and respond to fiscal failure; that state leaders will be more benign and responsible than local ones; and that fiscal mismanagement is to be expected absent coercive external authority. None of this is self-evident.

While we know that representative institutions in the city are far from perfect, fiscal responsibility has been more the norm than the exception. It is quite difficult on democratic grounds to justify allowing a judge to impose particular fiscal ends unless the political pathologies of the local and state budgeting process are so wide and deep that coercion outside elective politics is required. If it is true that cities will invariably engage in giveaways to vested interests, and rarely take into account future generations, then our ongoing efforts to design institutional checks on their authority would be warranted—even if that effort is likely to fail.

But, like Frederic Howe, I do not see an inevitable political failure. Our politics is characterized by an almost obsessive concern with excessive spending and debt. Elections are won and lost on the electorate's assessment of the relative fiscal probity of the candidates. Indeed, the reason that cities have paid their debts during normal economic times is not because the state fiscal constitution or the market has prevented profligacy, but because we have a mature decentralized political system that holds elected officials accountable more often than is sometimes assumed. The municipal bond market is fairly staid because cities occupy territory, have the power to tax, and provide basic government services. Local taxpayers are attentive to tax and spending decisions. And while municipal politics has traditionally fluctuated between machine and reform regimes, there is no reason to think that the local electorate is incapable of making informed political choices between them.

Nevertheless, policymakers often assert, even if implicitly, that fiscal failure and political failure are closely connected. The country's racial history is obviously implicated here—for it is an inescapable fact that poor cities are often black cities, and that their poverty and blackness are sometimes treated as both causes and results of failed local politics.

But city failure, like city success, has to be understood against the backdrop of an economic geography that is resistant to alteration. That does not mean, however, that our legal geography is similarly resistant. Our metropolitan areas do not have to be organized in order to exacerbate inequality. Indeed, revenue-sharing and other forms of metropolitanism have been around for a long time. Moreover, large-scale infrastructure and social insurance spending are now the province of the federal government, a government that has the capacity to engage in monetary policy. These features of our current federalism have been in place for some time. To the extent that there are "solutions" to municipal fiscal crises, they already exist. And none have to do with the democratic failures of cities.

What is evident from the history of city power is that political actors will deploy institutional reforms—like bankruptcy or state takeovers—as a means of pursuing substantive political ends. The city is vulnerable to this manipulation, even when pursued by well-meaning reformers. The state takeover of a city in fiscal crisis is simply the most dramatic example of how city power is always and easily effaced. And the relatively muted political reaction to such takeovers indicates how deeply our political culture has internalized the city's marginal status.

Conclusion

Can Cities Govern?

THIS BOOK BEGAN WITH the question "Can cities govern?" My short answer is "They can if we let them." My longer answer is less straightforward, for the relationship between economic growth, city agency, and legal institutions is more complicated than conventional wisdom asserts. At a minimum, I have argued that we assume too much about the city's economic constraints. Identifying profligacy as the reason for city failure and capital-favoring policies as recipes for success are too easy. The city's policy options are both less constrained and less determinative. That we do not know what causes local economic growth and decline should induce modesty in either attributing bad outcomes to bad governance or good outcomes to the opposite.

Nevertheless, we can draw some conclusions about the governing of cities. First, the notion that cities are actors in a marketplace for places is mistaken. The decentralization-growth thesis assumes that competition between local governments will induce government behaviors that will, in turn, favor economic growth. But this thesis finds little support in the history of municipal legal autonomy in the United States and even less support in current theories of economic development. Competitive inter-jurisdictional policymaking seems at best unproven, and at worst damaging.

Indeed, economic geography and the history of city rise and decline suggests that government policies that seek growth are up against a spatial economic structure that is difficult to manipulate. If geographically uneven economic development is a deep feature of economies on all scales, as economic geographers tell us, then the existence of leading and lagging economies will be a long-term feature of the landscape. And competition will merely exacerbate the shift of productive enterprise to leading places, generate unproductive races to the bottom, or induce lagging cities to give up altogether.

Second, economically lagging places do not exist because they are badly governed. The assumed connection between the efficient provision of public goods and economic growth is misguided. In fact, overly fragmented local government will more likely retard growth if it is anti-urban, impoverishes human capital, limits mobility, or increases the distance between workers and employers.

That does not mean that cities should give up on improving social welfare. Cities should do less of what they cannot do—induce economic growth through competitive local industrial policies—and more of what they can—provide quality basic services to their residents. While policy might have limited connection with inducing economic activity in a specific place, it is centrally relevant to the distribution of existing economic activity *across* places. Uneven economic development and booms and busts are a feature of spatial economies. But who benefits and who is burdened by the distribution of economic activity in a particular place are functions of policy. Despite the increasingly prevalent assumption that we live in a borderless world, the American postindustrial metropolitan-area landscape is still filled with boundaries. Racially and socioeconomically segregated, it is a place where one's life chances are often dictated by the neighborhood into which one happens to be born. Our economic geography might be relatively immoveable, but our legal geography is not.

This realization can liberate the city to pursue ends directed toward the health and welfare of its current citizens. The limited connection between governance and growth, the possibility of leveraging immobile capital, and the reality of municipal redistribution suggest that cities can pursue a fairer and more equal distribution of public goods. The emergence of local progressive or reformist regulatory efforts challenges the conventional view that local responses to economic restructuring are limited and likely to fail and that addressing economic inequality is primarily a national concern. Indeed, in our postindustrial world, it may be possible for cities to use their location-based advantages in ways that states and nations cannot.

Fixing Our Cities

Why does the city's power matter? The first reason is obvious. Despite the recent urban resurgence—often confined to already-wealthy parts of the metropolitan region—the American city continues to be badly abused: Its challenges are overwhelming, its resources limited, its citizens racially divided, its authority questioned, its capabilities undermined. Walk through the decaying neighborhoods of Detroit, Camden, Buffalo, or Baltimore, or the struggling neighborhoods in Chicago and Los Angeles, and consider the enormous political and fiscal response that would be required to revive those places and others just like them. Much of what policymakers do or can conceive of doing in this political environment to help the worst cities is, at best, partial.

Nevertheless, it is important not to mistake political limits for economic ones. A series of economic "truths" currently drive urban policy in the United States. These include the view that cities are relatively economically impotent, that redistribution at the local level is impossible, and that attracting or capturing wealth is the only way to improve urban lives.

These truths are somewhat odd in light of the urban resurgence of the recent decades. During this period, none of the postindustrial cities that have now seen their populations stabilize and their property values increase moved to reduce local tax rates or regulations substantially enough to eliminate the city-suburb differential. Indeed, those cities did not do anything starkly different from what they had been doing for thirty years to attract young people and suburbanites into the urban core. Those cities had already attempted to rebuild their downtowns, to create an attractive nightlife, and to create amenities that would appeal to the right kind of people.

All of which is to say that the causes of the urban resurgence are not at all self-evident. In many cases, both the initial decline and the more recent resurgence of particular cities has been overstated. To the extent that cities are doing better, however, the causes seem to turn on baby-boomer preferences, immigration trends, changes in global capital flows, and other factors that are not well understood. Or perhaps it was deindustrialization, ironically, that helped some cities by making them cleaner and more pleasant places to live and by opening up access to desirable waterfronts. Or possibly information industries and other creative technologies require agglomeration economies that only (certain) cities can provide.

These theories are speculative. The actual causes of city formation, rise, and decline are quite mysterious—as mysterious as any complex economic process. Without knowing what caused the resurgence in particular cities, we should be quite wary about proposing solutions—especially antiregulatory solutions—for those cities that have been less successful.

Where does this leave cities? If local economic development efforts are designed to help cities and their residents "productively fit into the global economy,"[1] one might adopt a particular set of strategies: redistribution at the national level to even-out the dislocations caused by large-scale economic restructuring, job training, assistance in internal migration, regionalism, encouraging urban entrepreneurialism, and market-based economic development. Reform of the relationship between mobile capital and the city can be directed toward improving the way cities operate within the constraints of private capital.

The problem is that many of these programs have either failed or not made much of a difference. Moreover, our goal might be more ambitious, directed toward restructuring capital's constraints altogether. Recall that the rejection of the corporatist medieval and early colonial city represented the end of monopoly, mercantilism, and autocracy in favor of open markets, democracy, and individual economic freedom. One may wish to reassert these same goals in the face of the power and authority of large, hierarchical corporate entities. The goal of the city would be to become less a passive recipient of global capital than a shaper of local capital in a direction more conducive to freedom.[2]

Consider income inequality. The basic assumption underlying competitive accounts of city development is that cities are competing for regional residents. Unless cities capture and keep rich people, they will experience a declining tax base, increased costs of services, and eventual ruin.

This argument has taken various forms over the last half-century. In the 1970s, James Buchanan observed that the city needs to attract and keep wealthier resident taxpayers. He recommended providing amenities that appealed to such residents: "art museums, symphony orchestras, theaters, and parks."[3] Douglas Rae has recently made a similar argument about inequality in the city. As he observes, the "healthiest central city economies ... turn out to have very unequal income structures." "Those of us who want better life chances for low earning households in major cities," Rae writes, "should set out to increase inequality by attracting and keeping high earners, now greatly underrepresented in central city populations."[4]

Buchanan's emphasis on the provision of urban amenities that appeal to wealthier people has echoes in Richard Florida's well-known strategies for bringing the "creative class"[5]—young entrepreneurial intellectuals—into the cities. Creative-class amenities might be different—young hipsters have preferences that do not necessarily align with those of the wealthy or middle-class suburbanites—yet the attraction strategy is identical. And in fact, the strategies of the 1970s—designed to lure suburbanites—have continued, just with an added emphasis on waterfront parks, arts districts, the creation of edgy urban streetscapes, and the repurposing of downtown turn-of-the-century industrial warehouses.

The mostly unrealized regionalist reform agenda of the last fifty years has been driven by this same impulse: namely, capturing and taxing the wealthy. Regionalism seeks to solve the problem of inequality between city and suburb by bringing the suburbs into the city, either via annexation rules that permit the city to absorb urbanizing areas or via regional governments that can redistribute across local jurisdictions.[6] The assumption here again is that the city needs to find a way to prevent flight. Regionalism simply moves the borders of the city so that it encompasses those who would have otherwise escaped. Creating the political will to generate a robust regionalism has always been difficult. But the theory is the same: Both the amenity and the regionalist policy prescriptions are efforts to tax the rich to help the poor.

This strategy assumes that cities are products that compete in the inter-jurisdictional location market. Certainly, the current extreme degree of income inequality in the United States is not something that cities can easily combat on their own. If we posit an existing background level of inequality, then cities should presumably compete—like all other jurisdictions—to obtain their share of the metropolitan area's richer people. And certainly changing the residential makeup of the city is by definition one path to a city's prosperity. If a city attracts talented, wealthy people, the city will be talented and wealthy.

But what if cities are not simply vessels to be filled with desirable populations? If cities are instead economic processes, then thinking in static terms about whom they should attract misunderstands their nature. For Jane Jacobs and the economic geographers, urbanization is a spatial economic process. Not all cities are prospering all the time. Nevertheless, cities drive economic development in important ways.

Cities attract the rich and the poor because both will prosper through the economic activity that accompanies urbanization. For the poor, especially the rural or small-town poor, the city may be the only conceivable path toward a better life. And indeed, incomes and educational attainments are higher in urban areas than in rural ones. For the rich, the healthy city is a massive generator of land-based wealth. On this account, income inequality should be understood as a *function* of the city itself, both something the city creates and something the city can solve. In other words, when working at its best, the city both creates inequality and ameliorates it.

This is why Jacobs argued that cities do not have to be passive jurisdictions competing for resident users of public services. The amenity-focused city is—by definition—a city for those who do not *need* resources. Such a city creates economic activity only incidentally. It is thus not really a city at all, but rather a free-market platform for already-resource-rich residents and visitors, only incidentally concerned with the production of urban public goods.

But Jacobs argued—consistent with the notion that cities are economic processes—that instead of *attracting* the middle class, cities "*grow* the middle class." She further argued that to keep the middle class "as it grows, to keep it as a stabilizing force in the form of a self-diversified population, means considering the city's people valuable and worth retaining, right where they are, before they become middle class."[7]

American cities have grown the middle class and can do so again by creating wealth and providing public goods. Consider that in a forty-year span in the middle of the twentieth century, industrial cities built thousands of units of working- and middle-class housing; hundreds of schools, libraries, and parks; and thousands of miles of roadways, bridges, tunnels, and subways.[8] The basic infrastructure built by the newly emergent industrial cities raised living standards for the rural and urban poor alike. And those goods helped produce a robust urban middle class at mid-century. In many places, these urban goods continue to provide the working class, the poor, and newly arrived immigrants with resources for upward mobility. Those resources are basic and obvious: security, education, transportation, health, and shelter. These forms of public provision can be understood as the mechanisms by which individuals access city-created wealth.

Using City Power

It is this wealth-generating capacity that makes the city so vulnerable to political manipulation—that induces private parties and public officials to pursue their interests through the strategic deployment and redeployment of city power. Recall that when institutional reformers shift power to the city or away from it, they are often attempting to address the political pathologies inherent in the relationship between city and capital, government and private enterprise. Dillon's Rule and the home rule movement that followed it were a response to local tax and spending efforts aimed at generating private economic activity. The fiscal constitution in the states, with its debt, spending, and taxation limitations, is similarly driven by a concern for limiting the use of city monies for private ends. Recent state takeovers of fiscally distressed cities and the debates over municipal bailouts and bankruptcy continue the pattern.

As I have argued, the institutional division of authority between cities and states—periphery and center—does not *precede* economic development. The mistake made by some institutional economists is to assume that institutions set the stage for economies, when they are constituted simultaneously. Markets and law are born together.[9] The city's oft-changing legal status—its sometimes private and sometimes public character and the cycles of centralization and decentralization—is a primary example. The division of legal authority between levels of government is shaped by and in turn shapes the local economy.

The important point is that institutional reform—the distribution of powers among and between governments—cannot substitute for a substantive account of the appropriate relationship between capital and the city. The decentralization of power is not a neutral institutional technology, even if it is often presented as such. Decentralization is not a good in itself; it must be measured against a set of ends. Any existing or proposed division of political authority between the local, state, and federal governments will reflect those ends.

In this book, I have argued that "growth" is not a proven justification for a competitive, decentralized intergovernmental system. "Disciplining" cities is not what institution-makers should be trying to do, either through constitutional constraints or an inter-local competitive marketplace. If the formal grant of power to local governments results in massive inequality in the provision of basic municipal goods and services, it should be avoided. If the formal grant of power to local governments enhances the provision of quality goods and services to citizens, however, it should be favored.

Much depends on the policy at issue. In the U.S., local governments' formal fiscal and land-use autonomy has often exacerbated inequality by permitting wealthier local governments to shut out poorer citizens. But local legal authority can also be used to ameliorate inequality. The municipal minimum wage movement is a good example.

At heart, urban politics is a contest over who controls access to the production and distribution of city wealth. This is arguably what theorists mean when they advocate for "spatial justice"—the recognition that land-based private development often limits and constrains the public's rights to the collective value of the city and that metropolitan-wide land-use and development processes regularly isolate, exclude, and restrict particular groups or classes of individuals.[10]

To make a claim on the city—as recent urban-based political movements do—is "to claim some kind of shaping power over the processes of urbanization."[11] "The aim, at least from the liberal egalitarian point of view," writes Edward Soja, "is to gain greater control over the forces shaping urban space ... to reclaim democracy from those who have been using it to maintain their advantaged positions."[12]

Municipal governance is about what constitutes the public good and who gets to use the city to pursue it. And what constitutes the public good is a question about ends, not means. "Fiscal discipline" is really a debate about what the public good requires. For some, all local redistributive spending is by definition "undisciplined": Taxing and spending should mimic what a private market in analogous goods would produce. For others, including myself, cities have a significant role to play in producing public goods and ameliorating economic inequality.

Reclaiming Urban Democracy

This brings me to a final reason for advocating city power. The increased wealth and dramatically expanded scope of the centralized social welfare state has—perhaps paradoxically—coincided with a loss of confidence in democratic institutions. In large part, this is a predictable outcome of the dilemma that Dahl identified in his 1967 presidential address. As policy problems become increasingly global, they outstrip the scale required for true democratic self-government. Citizens, acting in their local councils, feel democratically engaged, but they cannot actually do anything. Consequential decisions are made at a distance. The policy challenges of the twenty-first century do not appear to be susceptible to meaningful democratic governance.

This sense of democratic loss is accompanied by a concern that power is shifting away from democratic institutions to transnational corporations. Global shifts in industrial production, the off-shoring of jobs, cross-border migrant flows, and the concentration of wealth are all sources of local economic insecurity. The global corporation requires a global state to regulate it, but that global state is by definition undemocratic. Meanwhile, the nation-state does not seem to have the resources to address this basic source of citizens' contemporary discontent.

Does the city have these resources? Perhaps. The localization of economic regulation coincides with the rise of the region as an important economic unit and the relative decline of the nation-state as a central regulator of economic life. Even if there were the political will to generate a new relationship between transnational corporations and democracy, it is far from clear that the nation is in a better position than cities to deliver.

Indeed, cities have embarked on policy experiments that are political nonstarters at the state and federal level—where governance has often been stymied by partisanship or political capture. Cities are not only adopting minimum wage ordinances, but also regulating in other areas—embracing environmental, employment, health care, and anti-discrimination agendas that have been demanded and supported by broad-based municipal constituencies, but which have been less successful at the state or federal level.

This is not to say that capital's power has been overcome, not in the least. As I have been emphasizing throughout, cities and business are inextricably intertwined. The city is the physical manifestation of economic development; it exists and thrives when propinquity generates economic gains. And our legal institutions have been designed in significant part to manage the political pathologies that accompany the governmental promotion of, participation in, and subsidization of private commercial enterprise.

No doubt, local economic policy is going to be limited by the resources available to the often resource-constrained city. The reemergence of a progressive decentralist strand in our political economy nonetheless represents a renegotiation of the terms of capital dependence. That it may undermine and destabilize the conventional wisdom—the view that local efforts are always destined to fail—is itself useful.

How robust this movement is or will become is an open question. Regulatory localism might be a feature of globalization—that is the optimistic story for those who worry about the loss of local democratic control. The pessimists, by contrast, take the increasing mobility of capital to mean that cities have even less control over their economic fates. I choose the former story here, albeit cautiously. In reasserting the public's right and ability to control those large-scale corporate entities whose presence in the community is both a necessity and a threat, decentralized economic regulation suggests that city governance is still possible in an age of global capital flows.

The mid-century industrial city offers one possible model for what such a resurgent democratic city might look like. Mid-twentieth-century urban policy relied on the replacement of weak state welfare support with strong federal welfare support, significant federal dollars for urban public improvements, an immigrant-friendly agenda, and a focus on basic municipal services: housing, transportation, health care. This agenda collapsed with the shift of resources to suburban jurisdictions, though it may return with continued urbanization.

Reaffirming the importance of those goods and reviving a new form of urban politics will require a significant, though not impossible, political realignment. The dominance of city halls nationwide by adherents of the competitive model, the political weakness of American cities in our federal system, the fragmentation of urban political representation, and the national invisibility of urban leaders and urban issues are serious barriers to any new politics. But countertrends are beginning to emerge, including the migration back into the cities, the waning relative power of the suburbs, a rise in intercity progressive cooperation, and the localist backlash against globalization.

Indeed, it is important to observe that cities have not always lacked national influence. The New Deal coalition relied on urban ethnics and blacks, which made city mayors powerful political brokers at the national level. Starting with the New Deal and into the Great Society and the War on Poverty, mayors were able to garner funds and support from the federal government.[13] With the rise of suburbanization and the decline of urban economic and industrial power, the political landscape shifted. Cities are weak for structural political reasons. They are also weak because of changing spatial and demographic political alignments.

Those alignments can change, however. And some recent demographic shifts suggest that a nationally salient urban progressivism might be possible. First, scholars of urban America such as Myron Orfield and David Rusk have argued that cities and inner-ring suburbs can and should make political common cause as the problems of inequality, poverty, and economic stagnation become increasingly regional.[14] As already noted, the suburbs have not been immune to declining economic fortunes, and there is an increasing realization that they need relationships with healthy cities for regional prosperity. In some cases, as cities do better and suburbs do worse, regional agendas might be more palatable. Whether improving cities will find it in their interest to partner with declining suburbs, however, remains to be seen.

Second, local antipoverty and labor movements are increasingly receiving aid and support from larger cross-city, cross-state, and even cross-national networks. Occupy Wall Street is a recent example of a locally-based national movement gone international. Labor organizing across cities is another. International city-based environmental justice, labor, and housing movements have gained some traction, sometimes under the rubric of "the right to the city"—the theme of UN-HABITAT's 2010 World Urban Forum 5 in Rio de Janeiro. [15] These networks have some potential to alter both local and national political priorities, though battles over public-sector unions, collective bargaining, and right-to-work laws will continue to be waged statehouse-to-statehouse and city-to-city.[16] Indeed, with labor increasingly marginalized at the state and national levels, we should expect to see more city-specific efforts.

Third, as I have described previously, there is also the possibility of a revived vision of economic localism. The economic localist's response to the threat of globalization is to reconstruct the economy on a local and less vulnerable scale, to think of ways to resist the encroachments of transnational corporations by favoring small businesses, local employees, and municipal ownership. The localists are relying on an extremely robust political countermovement to the excesses of global corporate capitalism.

We have seen such a movement in response to the recent economic downturn, but it has taken multiple forms, from Occupy Wall Street to the Tea Party, which are not at all compatible. Nevertheless, the discourse of inequality and disenfranchisement—echoes of which were heard in the "ninety-nine percent" language of the 2012 presidential election—has obviously attained some level of political salience.[17]

Finally, the progressive electoral coalition that elected Barack Obama for a second term tends to be urban, ethnically diverse, and young.[18] If this coalition becomes a more permanent majority, then it can demand more responsiveness from national political leaders, though it will likely have to do so by framing those policies in non-geographical and non-city-specific terms. This may be appropriate as the sociological lines between cities and suburbs continue to dissolve.

Despite having become an urban nation in the last century, Americans still have yet to come to terms with the exercise of urban democratic power. To do so requires treating cities as something other than consumption preferences or as location providers for agglomeration-seeking firms, or as entities that are incompetent, corrupt, and in need of discipline. We have to think instead of the city as a process of economic development, as a generator of the middle class, and as the primary location for the exercise of robust self-government.

Many have imagined the city as such a place—for the city often serves as a political Rorschach test. "To the city, we are to look for a rebirth of democracy," wrote Frederic Howe at the beginning of the twentieth century, for "[h]ere life is free and eager and countless agencies cooperate to create a warmer sympathy, a broader sense of responsibility, and a more intelligent political sense."[19] The city, as Robert Dahl declared some sixty years later, "confronts us with a task worthy of our best efforts because of its urgency, its importance, its challenge, the extent of our failure up to now, and its promise for the good life lived jointly with fellow citizens."[20]

These perennial invocations of the democratic and social possibilities of the city should serve as both inspiration and caution. There are many reasons why the city might not be able to meet these high expectations. But these are political reasons, not economic ones. If politics drives our metropolitan arrangements and the distribution of resources across and within cities, then a political movement is what is required to change these arrangements. The first step is to identify accurately the sources of the city's constraints. The next step is to challenge them.

NOTES

Introduction

1. See generally Wallace E. Oates, *Fiscal Federalism* (1972).
2. The city limits model is most associated with Paul Peterson, see *City Limits* (1981), but the basic notion that cities are constrained by "the need to promote investment activity in an economic arena dominated by private ownership," Clarence Stone, *Regime Politics: Governing Atlanta 1946–1988*, 7 (1989), is common. See generally Stephen L. Elkin, *City and Regime in the American Republic* (1987); John R. Logan & Harvey L. Molotch, *Urban Fortunes: The Political Economy of Place* (1987); Susan S. Fainstein et al., *Restructuring the City: The Political Economy of Urban Development* (1983); Barbara Ferman, *Challenging the Growth Machine: Neighborhood Politics in Chicago and Pittsburgh* (1996); *The Politics of Urban Development* (Clarence N. Stone & Heywood T. Sanders eds., 1987); H.V. Savitch & Paul Kantor, *Cities in the International Marketplace: The Political Economy of Urban Development in North American and Western Europe* (2002); Todd Swanstrom, *The Crisis of Growth Politics: Cleveland, Kucinich, and the Challenge of Urban Populism* (1985).
3. But see Richard E. DeLeon, *Left Coast City: Progressive Politics in San Francisco, 1975–1991* (1992). For a recent discussion of urban progressivism, see Donald L. Rosdil, *The Cultural Contradictions of Progressive Politics: The Role of Cultural Change and the Global Economy in Local Policymaking* (2013).
4. Gerald E. Frug & David J. Barron, *City Bound: How States Stifle Urban Innovation* (2008).

5. "The exercise of civic free will takes place within the structural constraints of modern political economy," Swanstrom, 33.

6. The seminal works on the city and the public/private distinction are Gerald Frug, The City as a Legal Concept, 93 Harv. L. Rev. 1057 (1980), and Hendrik Hartog, *Public Property and Private Power: The Corporation of the City of New York in American Law, 1730–1870* (1989).

7. It is not possible to cite to the voluminous literature concerning the nature of the municipal corporation and its status in American law. Some examples include Gerald Frug, *City Making: Building Communities Without Building Walls* (1999); Richard Briffault, Our Localism: Part I—The Structure of Local Government Law, 90 Colum. L. Rev. 1 (1990); Richard Briffault, Our Localism: Part II—Localism and Legal Theory, 90 Colum. L. Rev. 346 (1990); David J. Barron, Reclaiming Home Rule, 116 Harv. L. Rev. 2255 (2003); Joan C. Williams, The Constitutional Vulnerability of American Local Government: The Politics of City Status in American Law, 1986 Wis. L. Rev. 83. For an introduction and additional sources, see Gerald E. Frug et al., *Local Government Law: Cases and Materials* (6th ed. 2015); and Richard Briffault & Laurie Reynolds, *Cases and Materials on State and Local Government Law* (7th ed. 2009).

8. See Robert Ellickson, Cities and Homeowners Associations, 130 U. Pa. L. Rev. 1519 (1982). Cf. Gerald E. Frug, Cities and Homeowners Associations: A Reply, 130 U. Pa. L. Rev. 1589 (1982).

9. Indeed, being in a particular neighborhood matters a great deal. See Robert J. Sampson, *Great American City: Chicago and the Enduring Neighborhood Effect* ch. 1 (2012) for a powerful indictment of the "distance is dead" thesis. Cf. Frances Cairncross, *The Death of Distance: How the Communications Revolution Will Change Our Lives* (1997).

10. These effects are often described in terms of "democracy deficits." Alfred C. Aman Jr., *The Democracy Deficit* (2004).

11. For a recent discussion, see Steven Conn, *Americans Against the City: Anti-Urbanism in the Twentieth Century* (2014).

12. Robert A. Dahl, The City in the Future of Democracy, 61 Am. Pol. Sci. Rev. 953, 964 (1967).

Chapter 1

1. Cf. Bruce Katz & Jennifer Bradley, *The Metropolitan Revolution: How Cities and Metros Are Fixing Our Broken Politics and Fragile Economy* (2013).

2. P.J. Taylor, Comment: On a Non-appraisal of the "Jacobs Hypothesis," 43 Urb. Stud. 1625 (2006) (summarizing his argument in Embedded Statism and the Social Sciences: Opening Up to New Spaces, 28 Env't. & Plan. 1917, 1919–1920 [1996]).

3. See, e.g., Jeb Brugmann, *Welcome to the Urban Revolution: How Cities Are Changing the World* (2010); Edward Glaeser, *Triumph of the City: How Our Greatest Invention Makes Us Richer, Smarter, Greener, Healthier, and*

Happier (2011); Benjamin R. Barber, *If Mayors Rules the World: Dysfunctional Nations, Rising Cities* (2013). See also Richard Harris, The City Resurgent, 49 Urb. Stud. 3233 (2012).

4. See, e.g., David Harvey, *Social Justice and the City* (1973).

5. Jane Jacobs, *Cities and the Wealth of Nations: Principles of Economic Life* 31–32 (1984).

6. Jacobs, *Cities and the Wealth of Nations* 32, 35–39.

7. Mario Polèse, *The Wealth and Poverty of Regions: Why Cities Matter* 149 (2009).

8. See, e.g., Mario Polèse, Cities and National Economic Growth: A Reappraisal, 42 Urb. Stud. 1429 (2005); Taylor; Mario Polèse, On the Non-city Foundations of Economic Growth and the Unverifiability of the "Jacobs Hypothesis": A Reply to Peter Taylor's Comment, 43 Urb. Stud. 1631 (2006).

9. Edward Soja, Beyond PostMetropolis, 32 Urb. Geography 451 (2011).

10. World Bank, *2009 World Development Report: Reshaping Economic Geography* 8 (2009). See also Pierre-Philippe Combes et al., *Economic Geography: The Integration of Regions and Nations* 365 (2008).

11. See Combes et al., 365; Polèse, *The Wealth and Poverty of Regions* 2–3; *2009 World Development Report* 8.

12. See Polèse, *The Wealth and Poverty of Regions* 16; Paul Krugman, *The Self-Organizing Economy* 3 (1996); see also Masahisa Fujita & Paul Krugman, The New Economic Geography: Past, Present and the Future, 83 Papers Reg. Sci. 139, 140 (2004); Masahisa Fujita et al., *The Spatial Economy: Cities, Regions and International Trade* 2 (1999).

13. *2009 World Development Report* 3.

14. Saskia Sassen, Introduction: Locating Cities on Global Circuits, in *Global Networks, Linked Cities* 1, 1 (Saskia Sassen ed., 2002).

15. Paul L. Knox, World Cities in a World-System, in *World Cities in a World-System* 3 (Paul L. Knox & Peter J. Taylor eds., 1995); Saskia Sassen, *The Global City: New York, London, Tokyo* (1991); Allen J. Scott, *Technopolis: High-Technology Industry and Regional Development in Southern California* (1993); Jeffrey Kentor, The Growth of Transnational Corporate Networks: 1962–1998, 11 J. World-Sys. Res. 263 (2005).

16. Randall W. Eberts & Daniel P. McMillen, Agglomeration Economies and Urban Public Infrastructure, in *Handbook of Regional and Urban Economics, Vol 3: Applied Urban Economics* 1457, 1461–1462 (Paul Cheshire & Edwin S. Mills eds., 1999).

17. See generally AnnaLee Saxenian, *Regional Advantage: Culture and Competition in Silicon Valley and Route 128* (1994); AnnaLee Saxenian, Inside-Out: Regional Networks and Industrial Adaptation in Silicon Valley and Route 128, 2 Cityscape 41 (1996); *On Competition* (Michael E. Porter ed., 1998); Michael E. Porter, Location, Competition, and Economic Development: Local Clusters in a Global Economy, 14 Econ.

Dev. Q. 15 (2000); Michael E. Porter, Regions and the New Economics of Competition, in *Global City-Regions. Trends, Theory, and Policy* 145 (Allen J. Scott ed., 2001).

18.   Eberts & McMillen, 1463 (citing G.S. Goldstein & T.J. Gronberg, Economies of Scope and Economies of Agglomeration, 16 J. Urb. Econ. 91 [1984]).

19.   Ibid.

20.   Jane Jacobs, *The Economy of Cities* 50 (1970).

21.   Ibid., 39, 49–51.

22.   Edward L. Glaeser et al., Growth in Cities, 100 J. Pol. Econ. 1126 (1992).

23.   Robert Lucas, On the Mechanics of Economic Development, J. Monetary Econ. 22, 38–39 (1988).

24.   Polèse, *The Wealth and Poverty of Regions* 2.

25.   Ibid.

26.   The city is also the chief agent of demographic change in the developing world. See National Research Council, *Cities Transformed: Demographic Change and Its Implications in the Developing World* 17–25, 76–95 (Mark R. Montgomery et al. eds., 2003).

27.   See Richard Moe & Carter Wilkie, *Changing Places: Rebuilding Community in the Age of Sprawl* 36–74 (1997); Alan Rabinowitz, *Urban Economics and Land Use in America: The Transformation of Cities in the Twentieth Century* (2004); Willem van Vliet, The United States, in *Sustainable Cities: Urbanization and the Environment in International Perspective* 169, 172–173 (Richard Stren et al. eds., 1992).

28.   U.S. Census Bureau, United States Summary 5 tbl. 4 (1993), http://www.census.gov/population/censusdata/table-4.pdf; U.S. Census Bureau, United States—Urban/Rural and Inside/Outside Metropolitan Area (2010), http://factfinder.census.gov/faces/tableservices/jsf/pages/productview.xhtml?pid=DEC_10_SF1_P2&prodType=table.

29.   See Rabinowitz; Jon C. Teaford, *The Metropolitan Revolution: The Rise of Post-Urban America* (2006).

30.   See Carl Abbot, Urbanization, in 8 *Dictionary of American History* 288–289 (Stanley I. Kutler ed., 3d ed. 2003).

31.   Ibid.

32.   William Cronon, *Nature's Metropolis: Chicago and the Great West* 120 (1991).

33.   Ibid., 82–83.

34.   Campbell Gibson, U.S. Census Bureau, *Population of the 100 Largest Cities and Other Urban Places in the United States: 1790 to 1990*, tbls. 13, 15 (1998), http://www.census.gov/population/www/documentation/twps0027.html.

35.   See Nicholas Lemann, *The Promised Land: The Great Black Migration and How It Changed America* (1991).

36.   U.S. Census Bureau, *Statistical Abstract of the United States: 2007*, 8, tbl. 5 (126th ed. 2006), http://www.census.gov/prod/2006pubs/07statab/pop.pdf.

37. Alexander von Hoffman & John Felkner, *The Historical Origins and Causes of Urban Decentralization in the United States* 17–18 (2002); Peter Mieszkowski & Edwin S. Mills, The Causes of Metropolitan Suburbanization, J. Econ. Perspectives, Summer 1993, 135 ("In the 1950s, 57 percent of MSA [Metropolitan Statistical Areas] residents and 70 percent of MSA jobs were located in central cities; in 1960, the percentages were 49 and 63; in 1970, they were 43 and 55; in 1980, they were 40 and 50; in 1990, they were about 37 and 45"). See also Brian J.L. Berry, Inner City Futures: An American Dilemma Revisited, 5 Transactions Inst. Brit. Geographers (n.s.) 1, 12–13 (1980); Allen C. Goodman, Central Cities and Housing Supply: Growth and Decline in US Cities, 14 J. Housing Econ. 315, 320–321 (2005).

38. Except where otherwise noted, all data cited in this paragraph can be found at U.S. Census Bureau, Ranking Tables for Metropolitan Areas: 1990 and 2000, tbl. 1, http://www.census.gov/population/cen2000/phc-t3/tab01.pdf.

39. Chicago is part of the Chicago-Joliet-Naperville, IL-IN-WI Metropolitan Statistical Area, which includes Kenosha to the north and Joliet to the south. See Office of Management and Budget, Update of Statistical Area Definitions and Guidance on Their Uses, OMB Bulletin No. 10-02 app. 28 (Dec. 1, 2009), https://www.whitehouse.gov/sites/default/files/omb/assets/bulletins/b10-02.pdf.

40. See, e.g., Daniel T. Lichter et al., Toward a New Macro-Segregation? Decomposing Segregation Within and Between Metropolitan Cities and Suburbs, 80 Am. Soc. Rev. 845 (2015). For data, see Alan Berube & Elizabeth Kneebone, *Confronting Suburban Poverty in America* (2013).

41. Bruce Katz & Jennifer Bradley, *The Metropolitan Revolution: How Cities and Metros are Fixing Our Broken Politics and Fragile Economy* (2013). See also *Global City-Regions*.

42. Richard Florida et al., Global Metropolis: The Role of Cities and Metropolitan Areas in the Global Economy 6 (Martin Prosperity Inst. Working Paper Series, March 2009), http://www.creativeclass.com/rfcgdb/articles/Global%20metropolis.pdf.

43. Global Insight, Inc., *The Role of Metro Areas in the U.S. Economy* 6 (2006), http://www.usmayors.org/74thwintermeeting/metroeconreport_january2006.pdf. Metro region statistics included in this paragraph can be found in app. 15 tbl. 3 and app. 40 tbl. 5.

44. William Thomas Bogart, *The Economics of Cities and Suburbs* 4–5 (1998).

45. See Bogart, 4; Jacobs, *Cities and the Wealth of Nations* 32; Paul Krugman, *Geography and Trade* 3 (1991).

46. Jacobs, *The Economy of Cities* 262.

47. But see ibid., ch. 1 (arguing that cities were a necessary precondition for increases in agricultural productivity).

48. See Douglas W. Rae, *City: Urbanism and Its End* 11, 215–216 (2003).

49. Ibid., 11, 216.
50. See Edward L. Glaeser, Growth: The Death and Life of Cities, in *Making Cities Work: Prospects and Policies for Urban America* 22, 25–26 (Robert P. Inman ed., 2009).
51. Ibid., 26–27.
52. See generally Charles M. Tiebout, A Pure Theory of Local Expenditures, 64 J. Pol. Econ. 416 (1956).
53. See Tiebout, 418–423; William A. Fischel, *The Homevoter Hypothesis: How Home Values Influence Local Government Taxation, School Finance, and Land-Use Policies* 58 (2001). See also Barry Weingast, The Economic Role of Political Institutions: Market-Preserving Federalism and Economic Development, 11 J.L., Econ. & Org. 1, 5 (1995) (noting that the mobility of capital gives rise to a diverse array of public goods packages); Wallace E. Oates, *Fiscal Federalism* 49–50 (1972). But see Hongbin Cai & Daniel Treisman, Does Competition for Capital Discipline Governments? Decentralization, Globalization, and Public Policy, 95 Am. Econ. Rev. 817–818 (2005) (arguing that competition has a polarizing effect, causing cities that are unable to attract mobile capital to abandon business-friendly policies in favor of predation or the interests of existing citizens).
54. See Paul E. Peterson, *City Limits* 25–27 (1981).
55. See, e.g., Richard C. Schragger, Can Strong Mayors Empower Weak Cities: On the Power of Local Executives in a Federal System, 115 Yale L.J. 2542, 2564 (2006). The seminal work along these lines is Gerald E. Frug, The City as a Legal Concept, 93 Harv. L. Rev. 1059 (1980).
56. See, e.g., Gerald E. Frug & David J. Barron, *City Bound: How States Stifle Urban Innovation* 50–51 (2009); David Rusk, *Cities Without Suburbs* 85 (1993); and *Southern Burlington County NAACP v. Township of Mount Laurel*, 336 A.2d 713, 724–725 (N.J. 1975) (holding that zoning restrictions may not be employed to eliminate low- and moderate-income housing). See generally Richard Briffault, Our Localism: Part II—Localism and Legal Theory, 90 Colum. L. Rev. 346 (1990) (criticizing local autonomy as insulating suburbs from the problems of urban poverty).
57. See Daniel B. Rodriguez & David Schleicher, The Location Market, 19 Geo. Mason L. Rev. 637 (2012).
58. See Robert P. Inman, Financing City Services, in *Making Cities Work* 328.
59. This is the causal problem that bedevils the international law and development literature and particularly the "new institutional economics." See Adam Przeworski, The Last Instance: Are Institutions the Primary Cause of Economic Development?, 45 Eur. J. Soc. 165, 165–168, 185 (2004) (arguing that it is incoherent to argue that institutions cause economic growth because institutions and economic growth have a reciprocal relationship).
60. See Jacobs, *The Economy of Cities* ch. 1.

61. See Barney Cohen, Urban Growth in Developing Countries: A Review of Current Trends and a Caution Regarding Existing Forecasts, 32 World Dev. 23, 48–49 (2003); *Cities Transformed* 362–384.

62. Jane Jacobs, *The Death and Life of Great American Cities* 440 (1961) (emphasis in original).

63. Ibid., 433; see also Jacobs, *The Economy of Cities* 125–126, 129.

64. Jacobs, *The Death and Life of Great American Cities* 443–444; Jacobs, *The Economy of Cities* 129; see also Luis Bettencourt et al, Growth, Innovation, Scaling, and the Pace of Life in Cities, 104 Proc. Nat'l Acad. Sci. 7301 (2007) (positing a predictive, quantitative model of urban development and organization).

65. Krugman, *The Self-Organizing Economy* 3. See also Fujita & Krugman, 140–141; Fujita et al., 1–4 (describing urban economic landscapes as "the result not of inherent differences among locations but of some set of cumulative processes, necessarily involving some form of increasing returns, whereby geographic concentration can be self-reinforcing").

66. Krugman, *The Self-Organizing Economy* 1, 49.

67. Ibid., 9, 22–30.

68. Ibid., 25.

69. Joel Garreau, *Edge City: Life on the New Frontier* ch. 1 (1991).

70. Krugman, *The Self-Organizing Economy* 37.

71. See Fujita & Krugman, 147.

72. See Thomas C. Schelling, *Micromotives and Macrobehavior* ch. 4 (1978).

73. Krugman, *The Self-Organizing Economy* 18–19.

74. See Jacobs, *The Death and Life of Great American Cities* 275–276, 279 (discussing the potential for "unslumming" in lively, diverse neighborhoods).

75. Krugman, *The Self-Organizing Economy* 39–43 (discussing the "spooky" consistency of the rank-size rule in U.S. cities). See also Xavier Gabaix, Zipf's Law for Cities: An Explanation, 114 Q.J. Econ. 739, 741–743 (1999).

76. See Krugman, *The Self-Organizing Economy* 43–46. But see Volker Nitsch, Zipf Zipped, 57 J. Urb. Econ. 86 (2005) (reviewing quantitatively the empirical literature on Zipf's law and suggesting that "cities are on average more evenly distributed than suggested by [a strict interpretation] of Zipf's law").

77. See generally Bettencourt et al. (describing additional regular, scalar relationships across urban systems).

78. See Combes et al., 130; Polèse, *The Wealth and Poverty of Regions* 74–75; *2009 World Development Report* 81.

79. Krugman, *The Self-Organizing Economy* 22–30.

80. Combes et al., 130; *2009 World Development Report* 82–83.

81. Combes et al., 14–15.

82. Paul Krugman, History versus Expectations, 106 Q.J. Econ. 651, 654 (1991).

83. See Krugman, *The Self-Organizing Economy* 43–46.

84. See Christian L. Redfearn, Persistence in Urban Form: The Long-Run Durability of Employment Centers in Metropolitan Areas, 39 Reg. Sci. & Urb. Econ. 224–225 (2009) (proposing that early fixed investments in an urban area partially explain the persistence of urban hierarchies). See generally Donald R. Davis & David E. Weinstein, Bones, Bombs and Break Points: The Geography of Economic Activity, 92 Am. Econ. Rev. 1269–1270 (2002) (describing increasing returns theories, which consider the effects of path dependence on the distribution of city sizes).

85. See *2009 World Development Report* 10–11; see also Combes et al., 157–159.

86. See Krugman, *The Self-Organizing Economy* 53, 61–73.

87. Ibid., 99–100.

88. Krugman, History versus Expectations 666.

89. This difficulty is noted by Edward L. Glaeser & Joshua D. Gottlieb, The Wealth of Cities: Agglomeration Economies and Spatial Equilibrium in the United States, 47 J. Econ. Lit. 983, 1014–1015 (2009) (observing that because small initial advantages can result in large outcomes, a "small push" could create big benefits, but that it is very difficult—if not impossible—to figure out what that small push should be).

90. But see Robert William Fogel, *Railroads and American Economic Growth: Essays in Econometric History* 10–16 (1964) (arguing that railroads were not essential prerequisites for economic growth).

91. For a discussion of the Chicago-St. Louis rivalry, see Jeffrey S. Adler, Capital and Entrepreneurship in the Great West, 25 J. Interdisc. Hist. 189–193 (1994) (arguing that Chicago emerged as the leading city of the West because it had more extensive connections to the Northeast marketplaces than St. Louis); Cronon, 295–309.

92. See Cronon, 296.

93. Ibid., 265, 297–309.

94. Jacobs, *The Economy of Cities* 140–142.

95. See, e.g., Kenneth W. Dam, *The Law-Growth Nexus: The Rule of Law and Economic Development* 38–39 (2006).

96. See ibid., 56: "Econometric results can be found to support any and all . . . categories of arguments. However, very little of this econometric work survives close scrutiny . . . or is able to sway the priors of anyone with strong convictions in other directions" (quoting Dani Rodrik, Introduction: What Do We Learn from Country Narratives?, in *In Search of Prosperity: Analytic Narratives on Economic Growth* 9–10 [Dani Rodrik ed., 2003]).

97. Michael Storper, *Keys to the City: How Economics, Institutions, Social Interactions, and Politics Shape Development* 1 (2013).

98. John Henry Schlegel does an excellent job of articulating this modest stance in his draft work in progress on the history of Buffalo tentatively entitled *While Waiting for Rain: Community, Economy, and Law in a Time of Change*.

Chapter 2

1. Consider as an example the subtitle of a recent prominent volume: *The Urban Imperative: Towards Competitive Cities* (Edward Glaeser & Abha Joshi-Ghani eds., 2015). Consider also Michael S. Greve, *The Upside-Down Constitution* 6–7, ch. 3 (2012) for an endorsement of "competitive federalism." On the incoherence of "competitiveness" as applied to cities, see Richard Shearmur, Editorial—Of Urban Competitiveness and Business Homelessness, 29 Urb. Geography 613 (2008).

2. The literature positing a connection between decentralization and growth is significant. See, e.g., Lars Feld et al., Fiscal Federalism, Decentralization and Economic Growth, in *Public Economics and Public Choice* 103 (Pio Baake & Rainald Borck eds., 2007) (collecting studies); Barry R. Weingast, Second Generation Fiscal Federalism: The Implications of Fiscal Incentives, 65 J. Urb. Econ. 281–282 (2009); Barry R. Weingast, The Economic Role of Political Institutions: Market-Preserving Federalism and Economic Development, 11 J.L. Econ. & Org. 1, 1–5 (1995); Jan K. Brueckner, Fiscal Federalism and Economic Growth, 90 J. Pub. Econ. 2107–2108 (2006); Wallace E. Oates, Fiscal Decentralization and Economic Development, 46 Nat'l Tax J. 237–238 (1993); Merilee S. Grindle, *Going Local: Decentralization, Democratization, and the Promise of Good Governance* 5–7 (2007).

3. The international development community has become quite enamored of decentralization. For example, see United Nations Development Programme, *Decentralised Governance for Development* (2004); U.S. Agency for International Development, Center for Democracy and Governance, *Decentralization and Democratic Local Governance Programming Handbook* (2000). The United Nations and the World Bank have been active in decentralization efforts. See United Nations Human Settlements Programme (U.N.-HABITAT), *International Guidelines on Decentralization and the Strengthening of Local Authorities* (2007); World Bank, *2004 World Development Report: Making Services Work for Poor People* (2004). For useful summaries of decentralization efforts, see *Decentralization and Local Governance in Developing Countries: A Comparative Perspective* (Pranab Bardhan & Dilip Mookherjee eds., 2006); Javed Burki et al., *Beyond the Center: Decentralizing the State* (1999); James Manor, *The Political Economy of Democratic Decentralization* (1999); Pranab Bardhan, Decentralization of Governance and Development, J. Econ. Perspectives, Autumn 2002, 185 ("All around the world in matters of governance, decentralization is the rage").

4. The argument that institutions are prerequisites for economic growth was pioneered by Douglass North, a founder of the "new institutional economics." Examples include Douglass C. North, *Institutions, Institutional Change and Economic Performance* 107–110 (1990); Douglass C. North, *Understanding the Process of Economic Change* (2005); Oliver Williamson, The New Institutional Economics: Taking Stock, Looking Ahead, 38 J.

Econ. Lit. 595, 598 (2000). Additional examples include Daron Acemoglu et al., Reversal of Fortune: Geography and Institutions in the Making of the Modern World Income Distribution, 117 Q. J. Econ. 1231 (2002); J. Bradford De Long & Andrei Shleifer, Princes and Merchants: Government and City Growth Before the Industrial Revolution, 36 J. L. & Econ. 671–674 (1993); Rafael La Porta et al., The Quality of Government, 15 J. L. Econ. & Org. 222 (1999). For a critical examination of this literature, see Adam Przewroski et al., *Democracy and Development: Political Institutions and Well-Being in the World 1950–1990*, 143–144 (2000); Edward Glaeser et al., Do Institutions Cause Growth?, 9 J. Econ. Growth 271 (2004).

The argument that law specifically affects economic development has been asserted in the legal origins literature, which holds that nations with a common law tradition have done better economically than nations that have inherited a civil law tradition. See, e.g., Rafael La Porta et al., Law and Finance, 106 J. Pol. Econ. 1113, 1116 (1998). For a summary and critique of this literature, see Kenneth W. Dam, *The Law-Growth Nexus: The Rule of Law and Economic Development* 31–32 (2006). The connection between law and development has been further asserted by those who argue that formal property rights are a necessary precondition for economic development. See, e.g., Hernando De Soto, *The Other Path: The Invisible Revolution in the Third World* 177–179 (1989). For a summary and critique of this literature, see, e.g., David Kennedy, Some Caution about Property Rights as a Recipe for Economic Development (Harvard Law School Public Law and Legal Theory Working Paper Series, Paper No. 09-59, 2009); Michael Trebilcock & Paul-Erik Veel, Property Rights and Development: The Contingent Case for Formalization, 30 U. Pa. J. Int'l L. 397 (2008).

5. See Weingast, The Economic Role of Political Institutions, 8–9; John Joseph Wallis & Barry R. Weingast, Equilibrium Impotence: Why the States and Not the American National Government Financed Economic Development in the Antebellum Era 23–26, NBER Working Paper 11397 (June 2005). See also Greve, 11.

6. Weingast, Second Generation Fiscal Federalism, 281–282.

7. Roderick M. Hills Jr., Federalism and Public Choice, in *Research Handbook on Public Choice and Public Law* 211 (Daniel A. Farber & Anne Joseph O'Connell eds., 2010). A further assumption is that economic growth will actually maximize land values, revenues, or tax base. A suburban jurisdiction dominated by homeowners, however, might reasonably favor stable home values over economic growth. See generally William A. Fischel, *The Homevoter Hypothesis: How Home Values Influence Local Government Taxation, School Finance, and Land-Use Policies* (2001).

8. See Oliver Blanchard & Andrei Shleifer, Federalism With and Without Political Centralization: China Versus Russia, 48 IMF Staff Papers 171, 172

(2001) (observing that decentralization to local governments in Russia led to the capture of local governments by existing firms).

9. Max Weber, The City (Don Martindale & Gertrude Neuwirth trans., 1958); see De Long & Shleifer, 674, 700.

10. See David Stasavage, Was Weber Right? The Role of Urban Autonomy in Europe's Rise, 108 Am. Pol. Sci. Rev. 337–354 (2014).

11. See Susan Rose-Ackerman, Risk Taking and Reelection: Does Federalism Promote Innovation?, 9 J. Legal Stud. 593–594 (1980); see also Brian Galle & Joseph Leahy, Laboratories of Democracy? Policy Innovation in Decentralized Governments, 58 Emory L.J. 1333, 1337 (2009).

12. Sebastian Heilmann, Policy Experimentation in China's Economic Rise, 43 Stud. Comp. Int'l Dev. 1, 21 (2008).

13. For additional critiques of the relationship between federalism and growth in China, see Daniel Treisman, The Architecture of Government: Rethinking Political Decentralization 93 (2007); Hehui Jin et al., Regional Decentralization and Fiscal Incentives: Federalism, Chinese Style, 89 J. Pub. Econ. 1719 (2005). But see Ronald J. Gilson & Curtis J. Milhaupt, Economically Benevolent Dictators: Lessons for Developing Democracies, 59 Am. J. Comp. L. 227, 269 (2011). For a general critique of the law and development project in China, see Jedidiah J. Kroncke, The Futility of Law and Development: China and the Dangers of Exporting American Law (2016).

14. See Hongbin Cai & Daniel Treisman, Does Competition for Capital Discipline Governments? Decentralization, Globalization, and Public Policy, 95 Am. Econ. Rev. 817 (2005).

15. Ibid., 818.

16. See Richard Schragger, Consuming Government, 101 Mich. L. Rev. 1824 (2003). A deeper critique of the methodological individualism that underlies Tiebout and other theories of residential mobility is offered by Robert Sampson, who has argued that "neighborhoods choose people" rather than the reverse—that one cannot assume individual choice-making divorced from the context of community. Robert J. Sampson, Great American City: Chicago and the Enduring Neighborhood Effect 327 (2012). For a discussion, see Kenneth A. Stahl, Mobility and Community in Urban Policy, Chapman University Fowler School of Law Legal Studies Research Paper No. 14-2 (2014).

17. See Charles Tiebout, A Pure Theory of Local Expenditures, 64 J. Pol. Econ. 416, 418 (1956). Of course, many scholars believe that inter-local competition produces inefficient outcomes. For a description of the debate, see Keith Dowding & Richard Feiock, Intralocal Competition and Cooperation, in The Oxford Handbook of Urban Politics 29 (Karen Mossberger et al. eds., 2012). Some of these inefficiencies are identified in Stephen Ross & John Yinger, Sorting and Voting: A Review of the Literature on Urban Public Finance, in Handbook of Regional and Urban Economics 2001 (Paul Cheshire & Edwin S. Mills eds. 1999).

18. See Oates, 237–240.

19. Tiebout wrote about local economic growth, but in the context of the debate between economic base theory and import substitution. See Charles M. Tiebout, The Urban Economic Base Reconsidered, 32 Land Econ. 95, 98–99 (1956); Charles M. Tiebout, Exports and Regional Economic Growth, 64 J. Pol. Econ. 160 (1956). I discuss these further in chapter 7.

20. See Jan K. Brueckner, Fiscal Federalism and Economic Growth, 90 J. Pub. Econ. 2107–2109 (2006).

21. See World Bank, *2009 World Development Report: Reshaping Economic Geography* 147, 167–168 (2009). See also David Schleicher, The City as a Law and Economic Subject, 2010 U. Ill. L. Rev. 1507.

22. See Raj Chetty & Nathaniel Hendren, The Impacts of Neighborhoods on Intergenerational Mobility: Childhood Exposure Effects and County-Level Estimates (2015), http://scholar.harvard.edu/files/hendren/files/nbhds_paper.pdf. See also Mikayla Bouchard, Transportation Emerges as Key to Escaping Poverty, N.Y. Times, May 7, 2015, A3.

23. See *2009 World Development Report*.

24. See Jane Jacobs, *The Economy of Cities* ch. 3 (1970).

25. See Jon C. Teaford, *The Municipal Revolution in America* 25, 30 (1975).

26. One of the most important accounts of this transformation, with particular emphasis on New York City, is Hendrik Hartog, *Public Property and Private Power: The Corporation of the City of New York in American Law, 1730–1870* (1983).

27. See Teaford, 29–34, 57–59.

28. Relatively early on, legal thinkers began bifurcating the corporation into public and private—the former corresponding to the state and thus subject to democratic control; the latter corresponding to the market and thus relatively immune from it. See Gerald E. Frug, *City Making: Building Communities Without Building Walls* 39–45 (1999).

29. See generally Howard Gillman, *The Constitution Besieged: The Rise and Demise of Lochner Era Police Powers Jurisprudence* (1993); G. Edward White, *The Constitution and the New Deal* (2000).

30. See Frug, *City Making* 40–45; Hartog, 1–5.

31. Hartog, 8.

32. *Hunter v. City of Pittsburgh*, 207 U.S. 161, 178–179 (1907).

33. John F. Dillon, *Commentaries on the Law of Municipal Corporations* 449–450 (5th ed. 1911).

34. See Gerald E. Frug, The City as a Legal Concept, 93 Harv. L. Rev. 1057, 1118 (1980).

35. Richard L. McCormick, The Discovery That Business Corrupts Politics: A Reappraisal of the Origins of Progressivism, 86 Am. Hist. Rev. 247, 255 (1981).

36. Frug, *City Making* 46.
37. See David J. Barron, Reclaiming Home Rule, 116 Harv. L. Rev. 2255 (2003).
38. Ibid., 2286–2288 (2003) (quoting Howard Lee McBain, *The Law and Practice of Municipal Home Rule* 6 [1916]).
39. Jon C. Teaford, *The Unheralded Triumph: City Government in America, 1870–1900*, 103–104 (1984).
40. See Teaford, *The Rise of the States: Evolution of American State Government* 21, 24 (2002).
41. See Barron, 2292–2293; Teaford, *The Unheralded Triumph* 103–105.
42. See Barron, 2292–2293.
43. Teaford, *The Unheralded Triumph* 1, 308.
44. Rebecca Menes, Limiting the Reach of the Grabbing Hand: Graft and Growth in American Cities, 1880 to 1930, in *Corruption and Reform: Lessons from America's Economic History* 63 (Edward L. Glaeser & Claudia Goldin eds., 2006).
45. Teaford, *The Unheralded Triumph* 111.
46. Ibid.
47. See Frug, *City Making* 50–51.
48. This point is not uncontroversial. William Fischel, e.g., has offered a competing explanation. See William A. Fischel, *The Homevoter Hypothesis: How Home Values Influence Local Government Taxation, School Finance, and Land-Use Policies* chs. 5–6 (2001) (arguing that school finance equalization led to Proposition 13). For my view, see generally Consuming Government, 1842–1847.
49. For a discussion of tax and expenditure limitations by state, see generally Michael A. Pagano & Christopher W. Hoene, States and the Fiscal Policy Space of Cities, in *The Property Tax and Local Autonomy* 243 (Michael E. Bell et al. eds., 2010).
50. Forcible annexation was the general rule in the nineteenth and early twentieth centuries. See, e.g., *Hunter v. City of Pittsburgh*, 207 U.S. at 161–164. See, e.g., *Holt Civic Club v. City of Tuscaloosa*, 439 U.S. 60, 60 (1978); Merchants' Association of New York, *An Inquiry into the Conditions Relating to the Water-Supply of the City of New York* 508–509 (1900) (citing statutes related to the extraterritorial use of eminent domain by New York City).
51. See generally Richard Briffault, Our Localism: Part I—The Structure of Local Government Law, 90 Colum. L. Rev. 1 (1990); Richard Briffault, Our Localism: Part II—Localism and Legal Theory, 90 Colum. L. Rev. 346 (1990).
52. See Joan C. Williams, The Constitutional Vulnerability of American Local Government: The Politics of City Status in American Law, 1986 Wis. L. Rev. 83.
53. For a discussion of these studies, see Feld et al., 115–126 (noting one study of state or local decentralization found no effect on U.S. GDP

but another study did find a relationship). Two studies that found some relationship are Dean Stansel, Local Decentralization and Local Economic Growth: A Cross-Sectional Examination of U.S. Metropolitan Areas, 57 J. Urb. Econ. 55, 56 (2005); Nobuo Akai & Masayo Sakata, Fiscal Decentralization Contributes to Economic Growth: Evidence from State-Level Cross-Section Data for the United States, 52 J. Urb. Econ. 93, 94 (2002). Both studies note that their findings contradict prior studies' empirical results.

54. George W. Hammond & Mehmet S. Tosun, The Impact of Local Decentralization on Economic Growth: Evidence from U.S. Counties, 51 J. Regional Sci. 47, 48 (2011).

55. Andrew Haughwout & Robert P. Inman, *Should Suburbs Help Their Central City?* (2002), https://www.newyorkfed.org/medialibrary/media/research/economists/haughwout/citysubbrookings.pdf.

56. *2009 World Development Report* 141–142. See also Nestor Davidson & Sheila Foster, The Mobility Case for Regionalism, 47 U.C. Davis L. Rev. 63 (2013) (arguing that the intra-metropolitan competition for residents is being replaced with inter-metropolitan competition and that this should induce local governments in any given region to work together).

57. Between 1930 and 2000, those cities' populations shrank by 39%, 49%, and 47% respectively; Menes, 90.

58. Treisman, *The Architecture of Government* 6.

59. Roberto Mangabeira Unger, *False Necessity: Anti-necessitarian Social Theory in the Service of Radical Democracy: From Politics, a Work in Constructive Social Theory* xvii (2001).

Chapter 3

1. See Richard C. Schragger, Cities as Constitutional Actors: The Case of Same-Sex Marriage, 21 J.L. & Pol. 147, 174, 176 (2005).

2. See Mike Goldsmith, Autonomy and City Limits, in *Theories of Urban Politics* 228 (David Judge et al. eds., 1995) (discussing the fluid nature of scholarly attempts to create a typology or schema of comparative local autonomy). The ongoing debates in the legal literature concerning the relative power or powerlessness of the city reflect this dual status. Those who emphasize city power argue that certain localities, especially suburban ones, exercise significant local autonomy in areas in which they are deemed locally sovereign, mostly those activities that implicate land use, education, and local health and welfare. See Richard Briffault, Our Localism: Part I—The Structure of Local Government Law, 90 Colum. L. Rev. 1 (1990); Richard Briffault, Our Localism: Part II—Localism and Legal Theory, 90 Colum. L. Rev. 346 (1990). Scholars who emphasize city powerlessness point to the fact that municipal corporations exercise power at the state's sufferance. See Gerald E. Frug, *City Making: Building Communities Without Building Walls* 17–25 (1999). See generally *Comparing Local*

Governance: Trends and Developments (Bas Denters & Lawrence E. Rose eds., 2005) (comparing local autonomy across countries).

3. See Richard Thompson Ford, Law's Territory (A History of Jurisdiction), 97 Mich. L. Rev. 843 (1999), for a theoretical discussion of this point.

4. See Sidney Tarrow, *Between Center and Periphery: Grassroots Politicians in Italy and France* ch. 1 (1977). For discussion of federalism and political decentralization—or lack thereof—see, e.g., Richard Briffault, "What About the 'Ism'?": Normative and Formal Concerns in Contemporary Federalism, 47 Vand. L. Rev. 1303 (1994).

5. See Edward C. Page, *Localism and Centralism in Europe: The Political and Legal Bases of Local Self-Government* 142–143 (1991).

6. See Vivien A. Schmidt, *Democratizing France: The Political and Administrative History of Decentralization* 66–104 (1990). Reforms have given cities their own "competencies," though much financial authority is still derived from the center. See French Constitution Amended to Allow Decentralization, Agence France-Presse, Mar. 17, 2003.

7. Walter J. Nicholls, Power and Governance: Metropolitan Governance in France, 42 Urb. Stud. 783, 788–789 (2005). See generally Tarrow.

8. Mike Goldsmith, Cities in an Intergovernmental System, in *The Oxford Handbook of Urban Politics* 133, 138 (Karen Mossberger et al. eds., 2012).

9. *Printz v. United States*, 521 U.S. 898 (1997).

10. *United States v. Lopez*, 514 U.S. 549, 568 (1995).

11. Justice Breyer, articulating "the implied answer to a question Justice Stevens asks." *Printz v. United States*, 521 U.S. at 977 (Breyer, J., dissenting).

12. Ibid., 976 (Breyer, J., dissenting).

13. See Frank B. Cross, The Folly of Federalism, 24 Cardozo L. Rev. 1 (2002); see also Edward L. Rubin & Malcolm Feeley, Federalism: Some Notes on a National Neurosis, 41 UCLA L. Rev. 903 (1994); Pradeep Chhibber & E. Somanathan, Are Federal Nations Decentralized? Provincial Governments and the Devolution of Authority to Local Government (May 2002), http://web.stanford.edu/class/polisci313/papers/ChhibberJune 03.pdf. But see generally Roderick M. Hills Jr., Is Federalism Good for Localism? The Localist Case for Federal Regimes, 21 J.L. & Pol. 187, 215 (2005) (criticizing Cross, Rubin, and Feeley).

14. See Daniel Treisman, *The Architecture of Government: Rethinking Political Decentralization* 251–258 (2007); Arthur A. Goldsmith, Slapping the Grasping Hand: Correlates of Political Corruption in Emerging Markets, 58 Am. J. Econ. & Soc. 865 (1999). See also Pranab Bardhan & Dilip Mookherjee, Decentralization, Corruption, and Government Accountability: An Overview, in *International Handbook of Economic Corruption* 161–188 (Susan Rose-Ackerman ed. 2006).

15. Elisabeth R. Gerber & Daniel J. Hopkins, When Mayors Matter: Estimating the Impact of Mayoral Partisanship on City Policy, 55 Am. J. Pol. Sci. 326, 327 (2011).

16. See James H. Svara, The Embattled Mayors and Local Executives, in *American State and Local Politics: Directions for the 21st Century* 139, 140–142 (Ronald E. Weber & Paul Brace eds., 1999) (describing the imbalance between city responsibilities and city resources).

17. Alan Greenblatt, Beyond North Carolina's LGBT Battle: States' War on Cities, Governing, March 25, 2016, http://www.governing.com/topics/politics/gov-states-cities-preemption-laws.html.

18. In the education context, however, a number of state courts have ruled that significant inter-local variations in education spending violate state constitutional guarantees. See, e.g., *Edgewood Indep. Sch. Dist. v. Kirby*, 777 S.W.2d 391, 397 (Tex. 1989).

19. Cross, 40 (quoting Rubin & Feeley, 941).

20. See Pietro S. Nivola, *Tense Commandments: Federal Prescriptions and City Problems* (2002); James E. Ryan, The Perverse Incentives of the No Child Left Behind Act, 79 N.Y.U. L. Rev. 932 (2004); Gordon Morse, Virginia Must Learn the Car-Tax Lesson Over and Over, Daily Press (Newport News, Va.), Dec. 11, 2005, H1.

21. This is a simplification. Reformers did urge "home rule" as a means of protecting cities from state interference, but they also urged other reforms that would have the effect of limiting city power. See David J. Barron, Reclaiming Home Rule, 116 Harv. L. Rev. 2255, 2289–2333 (2003).

    Whether state legislatures were in fact hostile to city concerns is the subject of some debate. Compare Robert H. Wiebe, *The Search for Order, 1877–1920*, 176 (1967), and Robert Brooks, Metropolitan Free Cities, 30 Pol. Sci. Q. 222 (1915) with Scott Allard et al., Representing Urban Interests: The Local Politics of State Legislatures, 12 Stud. Am. Pol. Dev. 267 (1998) (studying Alabama, Massachusetts, and Michigan), and Nancy Burns & Gerald Gamm, Creatures of the State: State Politics and Local Government, 1871–1921, 33 Urb. Aff. Rev. 59 (1997).

22. Gerald Gamm & Thad Kousser, No Strength in Numbers: The Failure of Big-City Bills in American State Legislatures, 1880–2000, 107 Am. Pol. Sci. Rev. 663–664 (2013).

23. See ch. 6 for further, more detailed discussion of local minimum wage ordinances.

24. Matt Flegenheimer & Michael M. Grynbaum, De Blasio Takes a Businesslike Approach as Ebola Arrives in New York, N.Y. Times, Oct. 28, 2014, A17.

25. See Errol A. Cockfield Jr., Stadium Plan Gets Sacked, Newsday, June 7, 2005, A7.

26. David Nice and Patricia Fredericksen tell a similar story of state and federal intervention in the construction of the Battery Tunnel between Manhattan and Brooklyn. See David C. Nice & Patricia Fredericksen, *The Politics of Intergovernmental Relations* 192 (1995). For a description of how Robert Moses became the most influential public official in

New York City through his control of state-created public authorities, see generally Robert A. Caro, *The Power Broker: Robert Moses and the Fall of New York* (1974).

27. See Donald H. Haider, *When Governments Come to Washington: Governors, Mayors, and Intergovernmental Lobbying* 4–5, 35–38, 48–75 (1974); see also Suzanne Farkas, *Urban Lobbying: Mayors in the Federal Arena* 35–38, 66–67 (1971) (discussing the influence of the USCM during the New Deal). See generally F. Richard Ciccone, *Daley: Power and Presidential Politics* (1996) (describing Mayor Richard J. Daley's national political influence).

28. See Margaret Weir, Central Cities' Loss of Power in State Politics, Cityscape, May 1996, 23.

29. See Jeanne Becquart-Leclercq, Local Political Recruitment in France and the United States: A Study of Mayors, 8 Eur. J. Pol. Res. 407 (1980).

30. Haider, 300 (internal quotations omitted).

31. Only Andrew Johnson, Grover Cleveland, and Calvin Coolidge had been mayors. See *Guide to the Presidency and the Executive Branch* 406, 417, 507, 1718 (Michael Nelson ed., 5th ed. 2013). Nineteen of the 1,528 presidential appointees covered in a leading biographical database had served as mayor or as a city or local administrator. See G. Calvin Mackenzie & Paul Light, *Presidential Appointees, 1964–1984* (1987).

32. See Anne Marie Cammisa, *Governments as Interest Groups: Intergovernmental Lobbying and the Federal System* 6–7 (1995); John Shannon, The Return to Fend-For-Yourself Federalism: The Reagan Mark, Intergovernmental Persp., Summer-Fall 1987, 34–37.

33. See *Obergefell v. Hodges*, 135 S. Ct. 2071, 576 U.S.—(2015).

34. See *Lockyer v. City and County of San Francisco*, 95 P.3d 459 (Cal. 2004).

35. Ibid., 463, 499.

36. See Patrick McGeehan, De Blasio's City Feels Effect of Recovery, Silencing Business Leaders, N.Y. Times, March 7, 2016, A1.

37. See Jon C. Teaford, *The Unheralded Triumph: City Government in America, 1879–1900* (1984); Russell D. Murphy, The Mayoralty and the Democratic Creed: The Evolution of an Ideology and an Institution, 22 Urb. Aff. Q. 3 (1986).

38. Frederic C. Howe, *The City: The Hope of Democracy* 1–2 (1905).

39. Ibid., 185.

40. Ibid., 180.

41. See National Municipal League, *A Municipal Program: Report of a Committee of the National Municipal League, Adopted by the League, November 17, 1899, Together with Explanatory and Other Certain Papers* (1900).

42. See Murphy, 16.

43. See National Municipal League, *A Model City Charter and Municipal Home Rule* (1916).

44. Harold Wolman, Local Government Institutions and Democratic Governance, in *Theories of Urban Politics* 135, 138–139 (David Judge

et al. eds., 1995) (quoting R.J. Stillman, *Rise of the City Manager* 8 [1974]).

45. See Wolman, 138–139.

46. See generally Gerald E. Frug & David J. Barron, *City Bound: How States Stifle Urban Innovation* (2008).

47. Murphy, 3.

48. Troubled Cities—and Their Mayors, Newsweek, Nov. 13, 1967, 38.

49. See Megan Mullin et al., City Caesars?: Institutional Structure and Mayoral Success in Three California Cities, 40 Urb. Aff. Rev. 19 (2004).

Chapter 4

1. Raj Chetty & Nathaniel Hendren, The Impacts of Neighborhoods on Intergenerational Mobility: Childhood Exposure Effects and County-Level Estimates (2015), http://scholar.harvard.edu/files/hendren/files/nbhds_paper.pdf.

  See also Peter Dreier et al., *Place Matters: Metropolitics for the Twenty-First Century* (2001); Robert J. Sampson, *Great American City: Chicago and the Enduring Neighborhood Effect* (2012).

2. Global Insight, Inc., *The Role of Metro Areas in the U.S. Economy* 6 (2006), http://www.usmayors.org/74thwintermeeting/metroeconreport_january2006.pdf.

3. Paul Krugman, *Pop Internationalism* 211 (1996).

4. *United States v. Guest*, 383 U.S. 745, 757–758 (1966).

5. *Corfield v. Coryell*, 6 F. Cas. 546, 551–552 (C.C.E.D. Pa. 1823) (No. 3230).

6. *Edwards v. California*, 314 U.S. 160, 174 (1941).

7. *Shapiro v. Thompson*, 394 U.S. 618, 627 (1969); see also *Dunn v. Blumstein*, 405 U.S. 330, 332–333 (1972); *Hicklin v. Orbeck*, 437 U.S. 518 (1978).

8. *Saenz v. Roe*, 526 U.S. 489, 503–504 (1999).

9. *Edwards v. California*, 314 U.S. at 173; see also *Crandall v. Nevada*, 73 U.S. 35, 49 (1867) (striking down a tax on every person leaving the state by common carrier).

10. *Shapiro v. Thompson*, 394 U.S. at 629; *Saenz v. Roe*, 526 U.S. at 499.

11. *Saenz v. Roe*, 526 U.S. at 502. In-state residents cannot bring challenges under the Privileges and Immunities Clause, and the Court has yet to determine if there is a right to intrastate travel. Nevertheless, some courts have found such a right. See Harry Simon, Towns Without Pity: A Constitutional and Historical Analysis of Official Efforts to Drive Homeless Persons from American Cities, 66 Tul. L. Rev. 631, 651–653 (1992).

12. See, e.g., *Zobel v. Williams*, 457 U.S. 55, 68 (1982) (observing that if a state is able to limit or discourage interstate migration, "the mobility so essential to the economic progress of our Nation, and so commonly accepted as a fundamental aspect of our social order, would not long survive"). While there are still some interstate restrictions on labor mobility that

have anticompetitive effects, rules that explicitly seek to prevent out-of-staters from working in-state by requiring residency as a prerequisite for employment or statutes that discriminate against in-state employees who live out of state have repeatedly been struck down on Commerce Clause grounds. See, e.g., *Austin v. New Hampshire*, 420 U.S. 656–657 (1975) (striking down state tax on income earned by nonresidents); cf. *McCarthy v. Philadelphia Civil Serv. Comm'n.*, 424 U.S. 645–647 (1976) (upholding a continual residency requirement for municipally employed firefighters). Moreover, states cannot discriminate against out-of-staters if the purpose appears to be protectionist in nature. This doctrine does not prevent states from requiring that a person become a resident in order to access some non-fundamental benefits of state citizenship, such as welfare benefits, but it does require that states not raise outright barriers or significant disincentives to obtaining state citizenship. See, e.g., *Vlandis v. Kline*, 412 U.S. 441, 452 (1973) (upholding residency requirements for in-state college tuition breaks as long as a residency decision can be challenged).

13. *Village of Euclid v. Ambler Realty Co.*, 272 U.S. 365 (1926).
14. *Ambler Realty Co. v. Village of Euclid*, 297 F. 307, 316 (N.D. Ohio 1924).
15. *Warth v. Seldin*, 422 U.S. 490, 504–506 (1975). See, e.g., *Village of Arlington Heights v. Metro. Housing Dev. Corp.*, 429 U.S. 252 (1977); *City of Eastlake v. Forest City Enters.*, 426 U.S. 668 (1976); *Village of Belle Terre v. Boraas*, 416 U.S. 1 (1974); *James v. Valtierra*, 402 U.S. 137 (1971); see also *Construction Ind. Ass'n, Sonoma County v. City of Petaluma*, 522 F.2d 897, 904 (9th Cir. 1975) (rejecting challenge to local growth-control ordinances based on a right to travel).
16. *Village of Belle Terre v. Boraas*, 416 U.S. at 7. The Court sidestepped a right-to-travel claim in a case that upheld a California property tax scheme that favored long-time homeowners over more recent ones. *Nordlinger v. Hahn*, 505 U.S. 1, 10–11 (1992) (holding that the petitioner did not have standing to assert a right to travel because she lived in California).
17. William A. Fischel, *The Homevoter Hypothesis: How Home Values Influence Local Government Taxation, School Finance, and Land-Use Policies* 54 (2001) ("[T]he U.S. Constitution . . . does not permit states to restrict immigration from other states . . . [l]ocal government regulations, however, get pretty much a free pass on the same issue"); John R. Logan & Harvey L. Molotch, *Urban Fortunes: The Political Economy of Place* 41 (2001) ("Whereas the courts have frequently overturned local legislation that interferes with 'interstate commerce,' they have allowed many constraints on residential migration to stand"); see also William T. Bogart, "Trading Places": The Role of Zoning in Promoting and Discouraging Intrametropolitan Trade, 51 Case W. Res. L. Rev. 697, 709 (2001) (observing that though it is illegal for municipalities to set a minimum house value, they can achieve the same goal through fiscal zoning); Roderick M. Hills Jr., Poverty, Residency, and Federalism: States' Duty of

Impartiality Toward Newcomers, 1999 Sup. Ct. Rev. 277–278 (observing the disjuncture between the rhetoric in *Saenz* and the Court's tolerance of access controls at the local level).

18.   *S. Burlington County N.A.A.C.P. v. Twp. of Mount Laurel*, 336 A.2d 713, 724–725 (N.J. 1975); *S. Burlington County N.A.A.C.P. v. Twp. of Mount Laurel*, 456 A.2d 390, 418–419 (N.J. 1983).

19.   *S. Burlington County N.A.A.C.P. v. Twp. of Mount Laurel*, 336 A.2d at 723; see also Stewart E. Sterk, Competition Among Municipalities as a Constraint on Land Use Exactions, 45 Vand. L. Rev. 831, 839–841 (1992); Keith R. Ihlanfeldt, Introduction: Exclusionary Land Use Regulations, 41 Urb. Stud. 255–257 (2004).

20.   See Fischel, *The Homevoter Hypothesis* 54. See Robert C. Ellickson, Suburban Growth Controls: An Economic and Legal Analysis, 86 Yale L.J. 385, 390–392 (1977); William A. Fischel, An Economic History of Zoning and a Cure for Its Exclusionary Effects, 41 Urb. Stud. 317–318 (2004); John M. Baker & Mehmet K. Konar-Steenberg, "Drawn from Local Knowledge . . . And Conformed to Local Wants": Zoning and Incremental Reform of Dormant Commerce Clause Doctrine, 38 Loy. U. Chi. L.J. 1, 16–19 (2006).

21.   See Edward L. Glaeser & Joseph Gyourko, The Impact of Zoning on Housing Affordability, Econ. Pol'y Rev., June 2003, 21, 23; see also Edward L. Glaeser & Bryce A. Ward, The Causes and Consequences of Land Use Regulation: Evidence from Greater Boston, 65 J. Urb. Econ. 265 (2009) (noting that land-use regulations and not a shortage of land have made it more difficult to construct new housing); Ellickson, 404–407; see also Jonathan Levine, *Zoned Out: Regulation, Markets, and Choices in Transportation and Metropolitan Land Use* (2006).

22.   William Thomas Bogart, *The Economics of Cities and Suburbs* 85, 212–214 (1998); William T. Bogart, "Trading Places": The Role of Zoning in Promoting and Discouraging Intrametropolitan Trade, 51 Case W. Res. L. Rev. 697, 715–718 (2001).

23.   *San Antonio Ind. School Dist. v. Rodriguez*, 411 U.S. 1 (1973).

24.   *Milliken v. Bradley*, 418 U.S. 717 (1974).

25.   Myron Orfield, *Milliken, Meredith*, and Metropolitan Segregation, 62 UCLA L. Rev. 364, 452 (2015).

26.   Indeed, some economists have argued that fiscal zoning is efficient insofar as it prevents lower-income newcomers from free-riding on the public service expenditures of current residents. Zoning ensures that new development will "pay its own way" by indirectly mandating a minimum property value, thus ensuring that all residents will pay roughly the same amount in property taxes for services received. See Fischel, *The Homevoter Hypothesis* 65–67; Bruce W. Hamilton, Zoning and Property Taxation in a System of Local Governments, 12 Urb. Stud. 205–206 (1975).

27.   *Saenz v. Roe*, 526 U.S. at 506; see also Joan M. Crouse, Precedents from the Past: The Evolution of Laws and Attitudes Pertinent to the "Welcome"

Accorded to the Indigent Transient During the Great Depression, in *An American Historian: Essays to Honor Selig Adler* 191 (Milton Pleseur ed., 1980); Stephen Loffredo, "If You Ain't Got the Do, Re, Mi": The Commerce Clause and State Residence Restrictions on Welfare, 11 Yale L. & Pol'y Rev. 147, 165–166 (1993); Note, Depression Migrants and the States, 53 Harv. L. Rev. 1031, 1033–1034 (1940). But see Hills, Poverty, Residency, and Federalism, 311–312, which argues that the Court could distinguish local from state restrictions on mobility on the ground that such restrictions might be appropriate for those communities tied together by bonds of mutual affection or trust, like neighborhoods, but not appropriate for larger communities, like states.

28. *United Bldg. & Constr. Trades Council v. Camden*, 465 U.S. 208, 210–211, 215–216 (1984).

29. Ibid., 217 (quoting *Toomer v. Witsell*, 334 U.S. 385, 395 [1948]).

30. *McCarthy v. Philadelphia Civil Serv. Comm'n*, 424 U.S. 645–647 (1976) (upholding a continual residency requirement for municipally employed firefighters).

31. Donald H. Regan, The Supreme Court and State Protectionism: Making Sense of the Dormant Commerce Clause, 84 Mich L. Rev. 1091, 1240–1241 (1986).

32. Michael H. Schill, Deconcentrating the Inner City Poor, 67 Chi.-Kent. L. Rev. 795, 799–804 (1991). See also Laurent Gobillon et al., The Mechanisms of Spatial Mismatch, 12 Urb. Stud. 2401, 2403–2404 (2007); John F. Kain, A Pioneer's Perspective on the Spatial Mismatch Literature, 41 Urb. Stud. 7, 20–24 (2004).

33. Mikayla Bouchard, Transportation Emerges as Crucial to Escaping Poverty, N.Y. Times, May 7, 2015, A3.

34. William Cronon, *Nature's Metropolis: Chicago and the Great West* 35 (1991).

35. See Paul Krugman, History versus Expectations, 106 Q.J. Econ. 651, 666 (1991).

36. The Point of View, Scribner's Magazine, Sept. 1890, 396.

37. See Jon C. Teaford, *The Unheralded Triumph: City Government in America, 1870–1900*, 103 (1984).

38. For other advantages of a (reformed) property tax system, see Darien Shanske, Revitalizing Local Political Economy Through Modernizing the Property Tax, 68 Tax L. Rev. 143 (2014).

39. Vicki Been, "Exit" as a Restraint on Land Use Exactions: Rethinking the Unconstitutional Conditions Doctrine, 91 Colum. L. Rev. 473, 513–514 (1991).

40. See Kevin R. Cox, The Local and Global in the New Urban Politics: A Critical View, 11 Env't & Plan. D: Soc'y & Space 433, 437 (1993); Sterk, 859–863 (arguing that firms are less mobile than theory provides).

41. Fischel, *The Homevoter Hypothesis*.

42. See Hans Jarle Kind et al., Competing for Capital in a "Lumpy" World, 78 J. Pub. Econ. 253 (2000).

43. Edward Alden & Rebecca Strauss, How to End State Subsidies, N.Y. Times, May 10, 2014, A23.

44. See Charles W. McCurdy, American Law and the Marketing Structure of the Large Corporation, 1875–1890, 38 J. Econ. Hist. 631, 638–643 (1978).

45. Paul Krugman, *Development, Geography, and Economic Theory* 52–55 (1995).

46. *West Lynn Creamery v. Healy*, 512 U.S. 186, 193 (1994).

47. *New Energy Co. v. Limbach*, 486 U.S. 269, 278 (1988).

48. *West Lynn Creamery v. Healy*, 512 U.S. 186, 189, 194 (1994).

49. See See Walter Hellerstein & Dan T. Coenen, Commerce Clause Restraints on State Business Development Incentives, 81 Cornell L. Rev. 789–792 (1996); Daniel Shaviro, An Economic and Political Look at Federalism in Taxation, 90 Mich. L. Rev. 895, 931–932 (1992).

50. Robyn Meredith, Chrysler Wins Incentives from Toledo, N.Y. Times, Aug. 12, 1997, D3.

51. *DaimlerChrysler Corp. v. Cuno*, 547 U.S. 332, 338 (2006).

52. *Cuno v. DaimlerChrysler, Inc.*, 386 F.3d 738, 746 (6th Cir. 2004); see also Edward A. Zelinsky, *Cuno*: The Property Tax Issue, 4 Geo. J.L. & Pub. Pol'y 119, 131 (2006) (concluding that "[t]he economic result Ohio achieved by granting property tax exemption to DaimlerChrysler could alternatively have been accomplished by comparable direct expenditures, whether in the form of grants, loans or in-kind services to DaimlerChrysler").

53. *Cuno v. DaimlerChrysler, Inc.*, 386 F.3d at 742, 746.

54. Ibid., 743.

55. *Kelo v. City of New London*, 545 U.S. 469 (2005).

56. U.S. Const. Amend. V.

57. *Berman v. Parker*, 348 U.S. 26 (1954).

58. See generally Charles E. Cohen, Eminent Domain After *Kelo v. City of New London*: An Argument for Banning Economic Development Takings, 29 Harv. J.L. & Pub. Pol'y 491 (2006); Orlando E. Delogu, *Kelo v. City of New London*—Wrongly Decided and a Missed Opportunity for Principled Line Drawing with Respect to Eminent Domain Takings, 58 Me. L. Rev. 18 (2006); Dean Allen Floyd II, Irrational Basis: The Supreme Court, Inner Cities, and the New "Manifest Destiny," 23 Harv. BlackLetter L.J. 55 (2007); Timothy Sandefur, The "Backlash" So Far: Will Americans Get Meaningful Eminent Domain Reform?, 2006 Mich. St. L. Rev. 709; Laura S. Underkuffler, *Kelo*'s Moral Failure, 15 Wm. & Mary Bill Rts. J. 377 (2006); Eric L. Silkwood, Note, The Downlow on *Kelo*: How an Expansive Interpretation of the Public Use Clause Has Opened the Floodgates for Eminent Domain Abuse, 109 W. Va. L. Rev. 493 (2007). See also Tresa Baldas, States Ride Post-*Kelo* Wave of Legislation, Nat'l L.J., Aug. 2, 2005, 1 (describing movements in several states to prevent the use of eminent domain for private development).

59. But see Joseph William Singer, The Reliance Interest in Property, 40 Stan. L. Rev. 611, 657–659 (1988) (arguing that mobile capital owes duties to

local communities that can be vindicated through property law). On the tensions between neoliberal development policies and property rights, see Nicholas Blomley, Legal Geographies—*Kelo*, Contradiction, and Capitalism, 28 Urb. Geography 198, 202 (2007).

60. Michael R. Betz et al., Why Do Localities Provide Economic Development Incentives? Geographic Competition, Political Constituencies, and Government Capacity, 43 Growth & Change 361–362 (2012). See also Amy Liu, *Remaking Economic Development* 8, notes 10 & 11 (Brookings 2016) for the consensus view.

61. See Bogart, *The Economics of Cities and Suburbs* 236; Peter D. Enrich, Saving the States from Themselves: Commerce Clause Constraints on State Tax Incentives for Business, 110 Harv. L. Rev. 377, 391–392 (1996); Terry F. Buss, The Effect of State Tax Incentives on Economic Growth and Firm Location Decisions: An Overview of the Literature, 15 Econ. Dev. Q. 90 (2001); Carlos F. Liard-Muriente, U.S. and E.U. Experiences of Tax Incentives, 39 Area 186, 189–190 (2007) (reviewing literature). But see Clayton P. Gillette, Business Incentives, Interstate Competition, and the Commerce Clause, 82 Minn. L. Rev. 447, 453–455 (1997); Roderick M. Hills Jr., Compared to What? Tiebout and the Comparative Merits of Congress and the States in Constitutional Federalism, in *The Tiebout Model at Fifty: Essays in Public Economics in Honor of Wallace Oates* 239, 260 (William A. Fischel ed. 2006). Some cities and states have sought to enter into voluntary "anti-poaching" compacts but these have generally been unsuccessful. Thad Williamson et al., *Making a Place for Community: Local Democracy in a Global Era* 140–142 (2002). Congress has on occasion considered legislation that would address this competition, but continually fails to adopt it. See, e.g., Distorting Subsidies Limitation Act of 1997, H.R. 3044, 105th Cong. (1997).

62. See generally Clayton P. Gillette, *Kelo* and the Local Political Process, 34 Hofstra L. Rev. 13–16 (2005) (arguing that eminent domain power is necessary to solve another political problem—that of individual landowners who hold out against the majority will).

63. See generally David A. Dana, Reframing Eminent Domain: Unsupported Advocacy, Ambiguous Economics, and the Case for a New Public Use Test, 32 Vt. L. Rev. 129 (2007).

64. See ibid. Thanks also to Lee Fennell for this point.

65. But see Singer, The Reliance Interest in Property, 40 Stan. L. Rev. 611, 657–659 (1988) for one effort to articulate the social harm of abandonment in legal terms.

66. Ibid.

67. Oliver Wendell Holmes, *Collected Legal Papers* 295–296 (1921).

68. *Baldwin v. G.A.F. Seelig, Inc.*, 294 U.S. 511, 523 (1935).

69. Charles W. McCurdy, Justice Field and the Jurisprudence of Government-Business Relations: Some Parameters of Laissez-Faire Constitutionalism,

1863–1897, 61 J. Am. Hist. 970, 982 (1975) (quoting Gene M. Gressley, *West by East: The American West in the Gilded Age* 12 [1972]).

70. Ibid., 989.

71. See, e.g., Mark Schneider, *The Competitive City: The Political Economy of Suburbia* 210–211 (1989); see also Bogart, *The Economics of Cities and Suburbs* 220–223, 237–238; Enrich, 380.

Chapter 5

1. Clayton P. Gillette, *Local Redistribution and Local Democracy: Interest Groups and the Courts* 8 (2011).

2. Paul E. Peterson, *City Limits* 30 (1981).

3. Ibid., 15.

4. See Kevin R. Cox, The Local and Global in the New Urban Politics: A Critical View, 11 Env't & Plan. D: Soc'y & Space 433 (1993) (describing this literature); William J. Grimshaw, Revisiting the Urban Classics: Political Order, Economic Development, and Social Justice, 24 Pol'y Stud. J. 230 (1996) (same).

5. Peterson, 22. As he writes: "cities, like all structured social systems, seek to improve their position in all three of the systems of stratification—economic, social, and political—characteristic of industrial societies."

6. Ibid., 23.

7. See generally Kevin R. Cox, Globalization, Competition and the Politics of Local Economic Development, 32 Urb. Stud. 213 (1995).

8. Gerald E. Frug, *City Making: Building Communities Without Building Walls* 17–19 (1999).

9. Heidi Swarts & Ion Bogdan Vasi, Which U.S. Cities Adopt Living Wage Ordinances? Predictors of Adoption of a New Labor Tactic, 1994–2006, 47 Urb. Aff. Rev. 743–744, 748 (2011).

10. T. William Lester, Labor Standards and Local Economic Development—Do Living Wage Provisions Harm Economic Growth? 32 J. Plan. Educ. & Res. 331–332 (2012).

11. See Benjamin I. Sachs, Labor Law Renewal, 1 Harv. L & Pol'y Rev. 375 (2007); see also Miriam J. Wells, When Urban Policy Becomes Labor Policy: State Structures, Local Initiatives, and Union Representations at the Turn of the Century, 31 Theory & Soc'y 115 (2002).

12. See Joseph A. McCartin, "A Wagner Act for Public Employees": Labor's Deferred Dream and the Rise of Conservatism, 1970–1976, 95 J. Am. Hist. 123 (2008).

13. Wesley Lowery, Senate Republicans Block Minimum Wage Increase Bill, Wash. Post, Apr. 30, 2014, http://www.washingtonpost.com/blogs/post-politics/wp/2014/04/30/senate-republicans-block-minimum-wage-increase-bill/.

14. Scott L. Cummings, Law in the Labor Movement's Challenge to Walmart: A Case Study of the Inglewood Site Fight, 95 Cal. L. Rev. 1927, 1943 (2007).

15. Ibid., 1942–1943.
16. Fran Spielman, Daley's Big-Box Veto Holds Up: Backers Vow to Target Firms with 1,000 Employees, Chi. Sun-Times, Sept. 14, 2006, 8.
17. Fran Spielman, Aldermen: Big-Box Veto Will Stand, Chi. Sun-Times, Sept. 12, 2006, 6.
18. Kate Taylor, Quinn, Pulled 2 Ways on Wage Bill, Delays Taking a Stand, N.Y. Times, Oct. 6, 2011, A28.
19. Walmart Gives a Raise, N.Y. Times, Feb. 25, 2015, A18. See also Hiroko Tabuchi, Walmart to Raise Starting Pay for Some Managers, N.Y. Times, June 3, 2015, B8.
20. See Dale Belman & Paul J. Wolfson, *What Does the Minimum Wage Do?* (2013), for a thorough review of the literature. For an excellent (albeit early) summary of the two main trends in minimum wage research methodologies, see David Card & Alan B. Krueger, *Myth and Measurement: The New Economics of the Minimum Wage* (1995).
21. Victoria Stilwell et al., Highest Minimum-Wage State Washington Beats U.S. in Job Creation, Bloomberg Business, Mar. 5, 2014, http://www.bloomberg.com/news/2014-03-05/washington-shows-highest-minimum-wage-state-beats-u-s-with-jobs.html; Kelly Phillips Erb, Seattle Area Biz Tacks "Living Wage Surcharge" onto Receipts in Response to $15/Hour Minimum Wage, Forbes, June 12, 2014, http://www.forbes.com/sites/kellyphillipserb/2014/06/12/seattle-biz-tacks-living-wage-surcharge-onto-receipts-in-response-to-15hour-minimum-wage/.
22. Michael Reich, Increasing the Minimum Wage in San Jose: Benefits and Costs, Policy Brief, Oct. 2012, Center on Wage and Employment Dynamics, Institute for Research on Labor and Employment, UC-Berkeley, http://www.irle.berkeley.edu/cwed/briefs/2012-01.pdf.
23. *When Mandates Work: Raising Labor Standards at the Local Level* (Michael Reich et al. eds., 2014), http://irle.berkeley.edu/publications/when-mandates-work.
24. T. William Lester, Labor Standards and Local Economic Development: Do Living Wage Provisions Harm Economic Growth? 32 J. Plan. Educ. & Res. 331 (2012). Compare Aaron S. Yelowitz, Employment Policies Institute, Santa Fe's Living Wage Ordinance and the Labor Market 7 (2005), http://epionline.org/studies/yelowitz_09-2005.pdf, with Mark D. Brenner, Political Economy Research Institute, The Economic Impact of Living Wage Ordinances 29 (2004), http://www.peri.umass.edu/fileadmin/pdf/working_papers/working_papers_51-100/WP80.pdf. Some scholars have cited evidence that firms do not simply cut employment in response to minimum wage laws but will respond in other ways. Namely, they will raise prices, increase productivity, or redistribute income throughout the firm as the lower-level wage earners are required to make more. John Schmitt, Why Does the Minimum Wage Have No Discernible Effect of Employment? 22 (2013), https://cepr.net/documents/publications/

min-wage-2013-02.pdf (explaining why measured employment effects of minimum wage increases are so consistently small); Brenner, 29. Any given firm's "ability to pass along higher costs will ultimately be governed by demand elasticities." Brenner, 25.

Modest increases in the minimum wage do not appear to have an impact on bid prices for government contracts, for example. John A. Rehfuss, *Contracting Out in Government: A Guide to Working with Outside Contractors to Supply Public Services* (1989). Firms' responses to higher labor costs will turn on the relative mobility of the industry, the geographical location of the employees, the location of customers, and the competitiveness of the market. Given that firms do not rush to raise prices, the key consideration is what other means of offsetting the increased costs of wages are at their disposal. The two most significant ways are through increases in productivity and internal cost-shifting. There is both theoretical and empirical evidence that improving wages increases the efficiency of workers. For a theoretical analysis, see *Efficiency Wage Models of the Labor Market* (George A. Akerlof & Janet L. Yellin eds., 1986); Joseph E. Stiglitz, The Causes and Consequences of the Dependence of Quality on Price, 25 J. Econ. Lit. 1, 5 (1987). For empirical data, see Carl M. Campbell III, Do Firms Pay Efficiency Wages? Evidence with Data at the Firm Level, 11 J. Lab. Econ. 442 (1993); Peter Cappelli & Keith Chauvin, An Interplant Test of the Efficiency Wage Hypothesis, 106 Q.J. Econ. 769 (1991); David I. Levine, Can Wage Increases Pay for Themselves? Tests with a Production Function, 102 Econ. J. 1102 (1992).

Recent studies of localities where living wage ordinances have been enacted show stark declines in turnover. See Michael Reich et al., Living Wage Policies at San Francisco Airport: Impacts on Workers and Businesses, 44 Indus. Rel. 106 (2005) (showing an 80% decline in turnover in low-wage jobs at the San Francisco Airport after a living wage was put into effect); see also Candace Howes, The Impact of a Large Wage Increase on the Workforce Stability of IHSS Home Care Workers in San Francisco County 2 (Working Paper), http://laborcenter.berkeley.edu/homecare/Howes.pdf (showing a 20% decline in turnover for home health care workers covered by a San Francisco ordinance). As a result, firms will save money in hiring and recruiting costs, which will help to offset wage increases.

25. Compare David Neumark, The Effects of Minimum Wages on Employment, FRBSF Economic Letter, Dec. 21, 2015, with Jared Bernstein, Did Minimum Wage Increases Really Kill 200K Jobs? Nope, Huffington Post, Dec. 24, 2015, http://www.huffingtonpost.com/jared-bernstein/minimum-wage-job-numbers_b_8869518.html. For reviews of the literature and conflicts in research methodologies, see generally Schmitt.

26. Lester, Labor Standards, 334–335. Compare David Neumark, How Living Wage Laws Affect Low-Wage Workers and Low-Income Families (Public Policy Institute of California, 2002), http://www.ppic.org/content/pubs/

report/R_302DNR.pdf; Scott Adams & David Neumark, The Effects of Living Wage Laws: Evidence from Failed and Derailed Living Wage Campaigns, 58 J. Urb. Econ. 177 (2005) with David Fairris, The Impact of Living Wages on Employers: A Control Group Analysis of the Los Angeles Ordinance, 44 Indus. Rel. 84 (2005).

Panel studies' large, negative elasticities are due primarily to regional and local differences in employment trends, and single case-study analyses are difficult to generalize, as they represent only one result from a distribution of possible outcomes. Compare Arindrajit Dube et al., Minimum Wage Effects Across State Borders: Estimates Using Contiguous Counties, 92 Rev. Econ. & Stat., 945, 961–962 (2010) (critiquing panel surveys) with David Neumark & William L. Wascher, Minimum Wages and Employment, 3 Foundations & Trends in Microecon. 1 (2007) (using panel survey data); Schmitt, 7–8.

27. Belman & Wolfson. Compare with David Neumark & William L. Wascher, *Minimum Wages* 104 (2008) (arguing that "the preponderance of evidence supports the view that minimum wages reduce the employment of low-wage workers").

28. Belman & Wolfson, 178.

29. Ibid., 406. They are careful to note that more than two-thirds of the eighty studies dedicated to U.S. minimum wage effects could not be used in their analysis because they did not have a common measure to compare. Ibid., 178. Also, current research does not speak to the effects of large increases in the minimum wage.

30. Neumark, The Effects of Minimum Wages on Employment, 4.

31. John Schmitt & David Rosnick, The Wage and Employment Impact of Minimum-Wage Laws in Three Cities (2011), http://reimaginerpe.org/files/min-wage-2011-03.pdf.

32. Bill Turque, Maryland Jurisdictions Tackle the Minimum Wage, Wash. Post, Nov. 17, 2013, http://www.washingtonpost.com/local/maryland-jurisdictions-tackle-the-minimum-wage/2013/11/17/4263ad98-4f99-11e3-9fe0-fd2ca728e67c_story.html.

33. Darin M. Dalmat, Note, Bringing Economic Justice Closer to Home: The Legal Viability of Local Minimum Wage Laws Under Home Rule, 39 Colum. J.L. & Soc. Probs. 93, 93 (2005). Compare *New Orleans Campaign for a Living Wage v. City of New Orleans*, 825 So.2d 1098 (La. 2002) (striking down a living wage ordinance) with *New Mexicans for Free Enterprise v. City of Santa Fe*, 126 P.3d 1149 (N.M. Ct. App. 2005) (upholding a local minimum wage statute as falling within the city's home rule powers). See also *Visiting Homemaker Service of Hudson County v. Bd. of Chosen Freeholders*, 883 A.2d 1074, 1076–1077 (N.J. Super Ct. App. Div. 2005); RUI One Corp. v. City of Berkeley, 371 F.3d 1137 (9th Cir. 2004); *Golden Gate Restaurant Ass'n v. City & County of San Francisco*, 558 F.3d 1000 (9th Cir. 2008) (en banc).

34. Jenni Bergal, Cities Forge Policy Apart From States, PEW Charitable Trusts, Jan. 15, 2015, http://www.pewtrusts.org/en/research-and-analysis/blogs/stateline/2015/1/15/cities-forge-policy-apart-from-states (listing the fifteen states that have laws preventing cities from regulating wages). See also When States Fight to Overturn Good Local Labor Laws, N.Y. Times, Feb. 19, 2016, A30.

35. Benjamin I. Sachs, Despite Preemption: Making Labor Law in Cities and States, 124 Harv. L. Rev. 1153, 1155–1156 (2011).

36. Ibid., 1178.

37. Ibid., 1168.

38. See Robert C. Ellickson et al., *Land Use Controls: Cases and Materials* 304, 308–309 (3d ed. 2005).

39. George Lefcoe, The Regulation of Superstores: The Legality of Zoning Ordinances Emerging from the Skirmishes Between Walmart and the United Food and Commercial Workers Union, 58 Ark. L. Rev. 833, 841–847 (2006).

40. Catherine J. LaCroix, SEPAs, Climate Change and Corporate Responsibility: The Contribution of Local Government, 58 Case W. Res. L. Rev. 1289, 1294–1296, 1312–1313 (2008).

41. See Catherine L. Fisk & Michael M. Oswalt, Preemption and Civic Democracy in the Battle over Walmart, 92 Minn L. Rev. 1502, 1507 (2008); see also Cummings, Law in the Labor Movement's Challenge to Walmart (discussing the Inglewood site fight over Walmart's entry).

42. *Van Sicklen v. Browne*, 92 Cal. Rptr. 786, 790 (Cal. Ct. App. 1971); see Lefcoe, 891.

43. Patricia Salkin, Understanding Community Benefit Agreements: Opportunities and Traps for Developers, Municipalities and Community Organizations, 2007 Land Use Inst.: Plan., Reg., Litig., Eminent Domain, & Compensation 1407, 1409; Scott L. Cummings, Mobilization Lawyering: Community Economic Development in the Figueroa Corridor, in *Cause Lawyers and Social Movements* 302, 319 (Austin Sarat & Stuart A. Scheingold eds., 2006).

44. Julian Gross et al., *Community Benefits Agreements: Making Development Projects Accountable* 3 (2005), http://www.goodjobsfirst.org/sites/default/files/docs/pdf/cba2005final.pdf.

45. Greg LeRoy, *No More Candy Store: States and Cities Making Job Subsidies Accountable* 34 (1997), http://www.goodjobsfirst.org/sites/default/files/docs/pdf/nmcs.pdf; Greg LeRoy & Sara Hinkley, *No More Secret Candy Store: A Grassroots Guide to Investigating Development Subsidies* 146 (2002), http://www.goodjobsfirst.org/sites/default/files/docs/pdf/nmscs.pdf; Good Jobs First, Key Reforms: Clawbacks, http://www.goodjobsfirst.org/accountable-development/key-reforms-clawbacks; specifically the chart Examples of Clawback Provisions in State Subsidy Programs, http://www.goodjobsfirst.org/sites/default/files/docs/pdf/clawbacks_chart.pdf.

46. See Virginia Parks & Dorian Warren, The Politics and Practice of Economic Justice: Community Benefits Agreements as a Tactic of the New Accountable Development Movement, 17 J. Community Prac. 88 (2009).

47. Julian Gross, Community Benefits Agreements: Definitions, Values, and Legal Enforceability, 17 J. Affordable Housing & Community Dev. L. 35, 47–48 (2007/ 2008).

48. Sachs, Despite Preemption, 1153.

49. Nick Bilton, A Tax Break to Anchor Tech in San Francisco, N.Y. Times, Mar. 31, 2014, B6.

50. See Salkin, Understanding Community Benefit Agreements, 1407, 1418; Patricia E. Salkin & Amy Lavine, Negotiating for Social Justice and the Promise of Community Benefits Agreements: Case Studies of Current and Developing Agreements, 17 J. Affordable Housing & Community Dev. L. 113, 121 (2008) (discussing problems with New York City CBAs). See also Comments by Bettina Damiani, Project Director, Good Jobs New York, http://www.goodjobsny.org/sites/default/files/docs/baytestimony.pdf (criticizing the Atlantic Yards, Brooklyn CBA).

51. See Vicki Been, Community Benefits Agreements: A New Local Government Tool or Another Variation on the Exactions Theme?, 77 U. Chi. L. Rev. 5 (2010).

52. Ibid.

53. See generally William H. Simon, The Community Economic Development Movement: Law, Business, and the New Social Policy 8–9 (2001).

54. Audrey G. McFarlane, Local Economic Development Incentives in an Era of Globalization: The Exploitation of Decentralization and Mobility, 35 Urb. Law. 305 (2003); Audrey G. McFarlane, Race, Space, and Place: The Geography of Economic Development, 36 San Diego L. Rev. 295, 298 (1999).

55. See Scott L. Cummings, Community Economic Development as Progressive Politics: Toward a Grassroots Movement for Economic Justice, 54 Stan. L. Rev. 399, 455 (2001).

56. See Hendrik Hartog, Public Property and Private Power: The Corporation of the City of New York in American Law, 1730–1870 (1983).

Chapter 6

1. There have always been "progressive cities" that seemed to depart from the standard developmental agenda. See, e.g., Pierre Clavel, The Progressive City: Planning and Participation, 1969–1984 (1986); Richard E. DeLeon, Left Coast City: Progressive Politics in San Francisco, 1975–1991 (1992); Donald L. Rosdil, The Cultural Contradictions of Progressive Politics: The Role of Cultural Change and the Global Economy in Local Policymaking (2013).

2. See Robert Dahl, Who Governs? Democracy and Power in an American City (1961); Jessica Trounstine, All Politics Is Local: The Reemergence of the Study of Local Politics, 7 Perspectives on Pol. 611 (2009) (urging renewed attention to local politics).

3. See Trounstine, noting how urban politics has been marginalized within political science for at least twenty-five years.

4. Clarence N. Stone, *Regime Politics: Governing Atlanta 1946–1988*, 233 (1989).

5. See Stephen L. Elkin, *City and Regime in the American Republic* 42 (1987).

6. Harvey Molotch, The City as a Growth Machine: Toward a Political Economy of Place, 82 Am. J. Soc. 309 (1976); see generally John R. Logan & Harvey L. Molotch, *Urban Fortunes: The Political Economy of Place* (1987).

7. Andrew E.G. Jonas & David Wilson, The City as a Growth Machine: Critical Reflections Two Decades Later, in *The Urban Growth Machine: Critical Perspectives, Two Decades Later* 3 (Andrew E.G. Jonas & David Wilson eds., 1999).

8. See Elkin; Susan S. Fainstein et al., *Restructuring the City: The Political Economy of Urban Development* (1983); Barbara Ferman, *Challenging the Growth Machine: Neighborhood Politics in Chicago and Pittsburgh* (1996); Logan & Molotch; Paul E. Peterson, *City Limits* (1981); *The Politics of Urban Development* (Clarence N. Stone & Heywood T. Sanders eds., 1987); Douglas W. Rae, *City: Urbanism and Its End* (2003); H.V. Savitch & Paul Kantor, *Cities in the International Marketplace; The Political Economy of Urban Development in North American and Western Europe* (2002); Stone.

9. See Savitch & Kantor.

10. Clayton P. Gillette, *Local Redistribution and Local Democracy* 10 (2011).

11. Michael Craw, Deciding to Provide: Local Decisions on Providing Social Welfare, 54 Am. J. Pol. Sci. 906–907 (2010); see generally Michael Craw, Overcoming City Limits, 87 Soc. Sci. Q. 361 (2006).

12. Chris Tausanovitch & Christopher Warshaw, Representation in Municipal Government, 108 Am. Pol. Sci. Rev. 605 (2014).

13. Ibid. See also Katherine Levine Einstein & Vladimir Kogan, Pushing the City Limits: Policy Responsiveness in Municipal Government 52 Urb. Aff. Rev. 3 (2016) (finding that as cities become more liberal, they increase spending across a number of service areas, and concluding—consistent with Tausanovitch and Warshaw—that politics matters).

14. See Saskia Sassen, Globalization or Denationalization?, 10 Rev. Int'l Pol. Econ. 1–2 (2003); See Kevin R. Cox, Globalization and the Politics of Local and Regional Development, 29 Transactions Inst. Brit. Geographers 179 (2004); Kevin R. Cox, The Local and Global in the New Urban Politics: A Critical View, 11 Env't & Plan. D: Soc'y & Space 433–434 (1993); see generally Saskia Sassen, *The Global City: New York, London, Tokyo* (1991).

15. Robert Dahl, The City in the Future of Democracy, 61 Am. Pol. Sci. Rev. 953, 964 (1967).

16. Discussed further in ch. 7. See Ted Rutland & Sean O'Hagan, The Growing Localness of the Canadian City, or, On the Continued (Ir)relevance of Economic Base Theory, 22 Local Econ. 163 (2007); see Joseph Persky et al., Export Orientation and the Limits to Local Sovereignty, 46 Urb. Stud. 519 (2009) (arguing that as metropolitan economies have

become more local in orientation, local governments have been able to exercise more regulatory leverage); see also Ann Markusen & Greg Schrock, Consumption-Driven Urban Development, 30 Urb. Geography 344 (2009) (arguing that locally consumed services and goods can be a source of regional growth and stability).

17. Consider David Schleicher, I Would, But I Need the Eggs: Why Neither Exit or Voice Substantially Limits Big City Corruption, 42 Loy. U. Chi. L.J. 277 (2011) (arguing that corruption is higher in big cities because of the inability of residents to exit).

18. Thus, e.g., Paul Peterson admits that some cities may be able to redistribute but only because they enjoy a natural monopoly (i.e., that there is some constraint on exit); Paul Peterson, *The Price of Federalism* 29 (1995).

19. Albert O. Hirschman, *Exit, Voice, and Loyalty: Responses to Decline in Firms, Organizations, and States* (1970).

20. Buffalo has tried anyway. See Stacy Cowley, Buffalo Entices Start-Ups to Relocate with $5 Million Contest, N.Y. Times, Nov. 4, 2015, B4.

21. See Gillette, 1084.

22. Consider, e.g., Donald L. Rosdil, *The Cultural Contradictions of Progressive Politics: The Role of Cultural Change and the Global Economy in Local Policymaking* (2013).

23. See Patricia Salkin, Understanding Community Benefit Agreements: Opportunities and Traps for Developers, Municipalities and Community Organizations, in *Land Use Institute: Planning, Regulation, Litigation, Eminent Domain, and Compensation* 1407, 1409 (2007).

24. See Judith Resnik et al., Ratifying Kyoto at the Local Level: Sovereigntism, Federalism, and Translocal Organizations of Government Actors (TOGAs), 50 Ariz. L. Rev. 709 (2008).

25. William Ho, Community Benefits Agreements: An Evolution in Public Benefits Negotiation Processes, 17 J. Affordable Housing & Community Dev. Law 7–8 (2007/2008).

26. See Making Change at Walmart, http://makingchangeatwalmart.com. See also Scott L. Cummings, Law in the Labor Movement's Challenge to Walmart: A Case Study of the Inglewood Site Fight, 95 Cal. L. Rev. 1927, 1933 (2007).

27. For a discussion of how shifting scales can produce successful reformist outcomes, see Marc Doussard, Equity Planning Outside City Hall: Rescaling Advocacy to Confront the Sources of Urban Problems, 33 J. Plan. Educ. & Res. 296 (2015); Marc Doussard & Ahmad Gamal, The Rise of Wage Theft Laws: Can Community-Labor Coalitions Win Victories in State Houses?, Urb. Aff. Rev. (forthcoming 2016).

28. T. William Lester, The Role of History in Redistributional Policy Discourse; Evidence From Living Wage Campaigns in Chicago and San Francisco, 36 J. Urb. Aff. 783, 794–796 (2013).

29. Ibid., 794.

30. Scott L. Cummings, Preemptive Strike: Law in the Campaign for Clean Trucks, 4 U.C. Irvine L. Rev. 939, 943 (2015).
31. Ibid., 942.
32. Ibid., 942, 945.
33. Quoted in Steven Greenhouse, The Fight for $15.37 an Hour, N.Y. Times, Nov. 23, 2014, BU1.
34. 49 U.S.C. § 14501(c)(1).
35. See, e.g., Michael J. Sandel, *Democracy's Discontent: America in Search of a Public Philosophy* 201–249 (1996); James DeFilippis, *Unmaking Goliath: Community Control in the Face of Global Capital* (2004).
36. See Richard L. McCormick, The Discovery That Business Corrupts Politics: A Reappraisal of the Origins of Progressivism, 86 Am. Hist. Rev. 247, 252–253 (1981); William E. Forbath, Caste, Class, and Equal Citizenship, 98 Mich. L. Rev. 1, 39–40 (1999); Richard C. Schragger, The Anti-Chain Store Movement, Localist Ideology, and the Remnants of the Progressive Constitution, 1920–1940, 90 Iowa L. Rev. 1011 (2005); Edward S. Shapiro, Decentralist Intellectuals and the New Deal, 58 J. Am. Hist. 938–939 (1972).
37. See Schragger, 1025.
38. *Louis K. Liggett Co. v. Lee*, 288 U.S. 517, 568–569 (1933) (Brandeis, J., dissenting).
39. See Louis Brandeis, *The Curse of Bigness: Miscellaneous Papers* (1934); E.E. Steiner, A Progressive Creed: The Experimental Federalism of Justice Brandeis, 2 Yale L. & Pol'y Rev. 1 (1983).
40. *Louis K. Liggett Co. v. Lee*, 288 U.S. at 580.
41. Lizabeth Cohen, *A Consumers' Republic* (2003).
42. Sandel, 224–225; see also Christopher Lasch, *The True and Only Heaven: Progress and Its Critics* 78–81 (1991). Undoubtedly, Sandel romanticizes the small dealers and "worthy men" who were the chief constituents of the early twentieth-century localist ideology. To those who tend to be skeptical of the exercise of local power because it has traditionally been used to exclude marginalized groups, Sandel's politics of local "small-holders" will appear retrograde. See, e.g., Mary Lyndon Shanley, Liberalism and the Future of Democracy, 49 Stan. L. Rev. 1271, 1276, 1291 (1997). And to those who believe that one cannot effectively protect local economies from the expansion of global markets without serious social welfare losses, the protectionist economic policy that Sandel celebrates will appear naïve. See Schragger, The Anti-Chain Store Movement 1084–1094.

   Practical theorists working in this vein, however, seem to be aware of these limitations. See David Imbroscio, *Urban America Reconsidered: Alternatives for Governance and Policy* 9 (2010); Gar Alperovitz, *America Beyond Capitalism: Reclaiming Our Wealth, Our Liberty, and Our Democracy* (2005); Michael H. Shuman, *Going Local: Creating*

Self-Reliant Communities in a Global Age (1998); Thad Williamson et al., *Making a Place for Community: Local Democracy in a Global Era* (2002).

43. See Benjamin I. Sachs, Labor Law Renewal, 1 Harv. L. & Pol'y Rev. 375–376 (2007).

44. See, e.g., Justin Sean Myers & Joshua Sbicca, Bridging Good Food and Good Jobs: From Secession to Confrontation Within Alternative Food Movement Politics, 61 Geoforum 17–26 (2015).

45. Quoted in Greenhouse.

46. See David Imbroscio, From Redistribution to Ownership: Toward an Alternative Urban Policy for America's Cities, 49 Urb. Aff. Rev. 787–788 (2013).

47. See Mark Pendras, Confronting Capital Mobility, 31 Urb. Geography 479, 487 (2010).

48. David Imbroscio, *Urban America Reconsidered: Alternatives for Governance and Policy* 9 (2010); see also Gar Alperovitz, *America Beyond Capitalism: Reclaiming Our Wealth, Our Liberty, and Our Democracy* (2005); Michael H. Shuman, *Going Local: Creating Self-Reliant Communities in a Global Age* (1998); Thad Williamson et al., *Making a Place for Community: Local Democracy in a Global Era* (2002).

49. See The 99 Percent Project, Occupy Wall Street, Aug. 29, 2011, http://occupywallst.org/article/99Percent/; see also Chuck Collins, A Voting Guide for the 99 Percent, Huffington Post, Oct. 3, 2012, http://www.huffingtonpost.com/chuck-collins/a-voting-guide-for-the-99_b_1935222.html.

50. Robert D. Johnston, *The Radical Middle Class: Populist Democracy and the Question of Capitalism in Progressive Era Portland, Oregon* (2003).

51. See generally David Osborne & Ted Gaebler, *Reinventing Government: How the Entrepreneurial Spirit Is Transforming the Public Sector* (1992). As already noted, turn-of-the-century progressives favored municipal ownership of city services and utilities. Those who champion entrepreneurial government have advocated municipal ownership of more traditional moneymaking ventures, services, and businesses as well. The community economic development literature has emphasized local economic self-sufficiency through worker- and neighborhood-owned enterprises, community credit unions, housing cooperatives, community land trusts, local procurement and purchasing cooperatives, and local currencies. More importantly, they have long advocated city-owned banks and insurance companies—efforts to keep finance in the city. In Detroit, e.g., the mayor has advocated a city-sponsored insurance company that would offer city residents lower rates for automobile insurance.

52. That being said, there are important examples of public ownership of productive assets, even in conservative states and cities. See, e.g., Gar Alperovitz & Thomas Hanna, Socialism, American-Style, N.Y. Times, July 23, 2015, A27.

Chapter 7

1. For a description, see Alan Ehrenhalt, *The Great Inversion and the Future of the American City* (2012); Michael Storper & Michael Manville, Behaviour, Preferences, and Cities: Urban Theory and Urban Resurgence, 43 Urb. Stud. 1247 (2006); Edward L. Glaeser & Joshua Gottlieb, Urban Resurgence and the Consumer City, 43 Urb. Stud. 1275 (2006); Ingrid Gould Ellen & Katherine O'Regan, Reversal of Fortunes? Lower-income Urban Neighborhoods in the U.S. in the 1990s, 45 Urb. Stud. 845, 866 (2008).

2. Storper & Manville, 1249, 1251.

3. See Douglas W. Rae, *City: Urbanism and Its End* 361–363 (2003).

4. See Storper & Manville, 1251, 1269 (noting that none of the major explanations adequately explain the increasing popularity of both types of cities).

5. See Richard Deitz & Jaison R. Abel, Have Amenities Become Relatively More Important Than Firm Productivity Advantages in Metropolitan Areas? 17, Federal Reserve Bank of New York, Staff Report No. 344, Sept. 2008, http://www.newyorkfed.org/research/staff_reports/sr344.pdf (observing that it is difficult for any region to change its relative amenity position over a decade).

6. Stephen Greasley, Peter John & Harold Wolman, Does Government Performance Matter? The Effects of Local Government on Urban Outcomes in England, 48 Urb. Stud. 1835 (2011).

7. See G. Alfred Hess Jr., Understanding Achievement (and Other) Changes under Chicago School Reform, 21 Educ. Eval. & Pol'y Analysis 67, 79–80 (1999); Diane Ravitch & Joseph P. Viteritti, Introduction, in *City Schools: Lessons from New York* 1, 3–5 (Diane Ravitch & Joseph P. Viteritti eds., 2000); *A Decade of Urban School Reform: Persistence and Progress in the Boston Public Schools* 133–134 (S. Paul Reville & Celine Coggins eds., 2007).

8. As for New York City, the data arguably show some gains starting in 2002. See generally Grover Whitehurst & Sarah Whitfield, Executive Summary, School Choice and School Performance in the New York City Public Schools—Will the Past Be Prologue? Brown Center on Education Policy, Oct. 2013, http://www.brookings.edu/~/media/research/files/reports/2013/10/08-school-choice-in-new-york-city-whitehurst/school-choice-and-school-performance-in-nyc-public-schools.pdf; National Assessment of Educational Progress, 2007 Trial Urban District Assessment: New York City Highlights (2007), http://schools.nyc.gov/daa/reports/2007_NAEP_TUDA_Results.pdf (detailing the standardized test results of fourth and eighth graders in New York City and comparing the results to 2002–2003 levels). But see Diane Ravitch, Mayor Bloomberg's Crib Sheet, N.Y. Times, Apr. 10, 2009, A23 (arguing that any gains in the New York City schools have been overstated).

9. *Closing the Graduation Gap: Educational and Economic Conditions in America's Largest Cities* (Christopher Swanson ed., 2009) (comparing

graduation rates in the principal school systems of the country's fifty largest cities with nearby suburban communities for the period 1995–2005); Sam Dillon, Large Urban-Suburban Gap Seen in Graduation Rates, N.Y. Times, Apr. 22, 2009, A14.

10. For a summary of Las Vegas's progress, see Gibson Consulting Group, Educational and Operational Efficiency Study of the Clark County School District, Executive Summary of the Clark County School District (2011), http://ccsd.net/district/gibson-report/gibson2011/Executive_Summary-Stand_alone.pdf; Roberta Furger; Full House: The Las Vegas Building Boom Has Stretched the Creativity and Resources of the Fastest-Growing School District in the Nation, Edutopia, Sept./Oct. 2004, 31, 33–34.

11. Even if education gains did not precede the urban resurgence, the urban resurgence could lead to education gains. The evidence, however, is not encouraging. Micere Keels et al., The Effects of Gentrification on Neighborhood Public Schools, 12 City & Community 238 (2013), provides a thorough review of the literature on urban resurgence and public school education, finding no aggregate academic benefit from gentrification, with possible negative effects on underprivileged children in Chicago. According to some studies, a clear negative relationship exists between the process of gentrification and the overall experience of local public school students. See, e.g., Tomeka Davis & Deirdre Oakley, Linking Charter School Emergence to Urban Revitalization and Gentrification, 35 J. Urb. Aff. 81, 85 (2013) (finding the incorporation of education reform into Chicago's urban renewal agenda concomitant with, not precursor to, gentrification). See Pauline Lipman, Contesting the City: Neoliberal Urbanism and the Cultural Politics of Education Reform in Chicago, 32 Discourse 217 (2011), for a particularly incisive critique of Chicago's school reform and urban policies. For an account of the link between urban renewal and urban school revitalization in Philadelphia, see Maia Cucchiara, Re-branding Urban Schools: Urban Revitalization, Social Status, and Marketing Public Schools to the Upper Middle Class, 23 J. Educ. Pol'y 165 (2008); see also Kristen A. Graham, Near-broke Phila. Schools Must Borrow to Make Payroll, Phila. Inquirer, Oct. 22, 2015, A1; Joshua Rosenblat & Tanner Howard, How Gentrification Is Leaving Public Schools Behind, U.S. News, Feb. 20, 2015, http://www.usnews.com/news/articles/2015/02/20/how-gentrification-is-leaving-public-schools-behind.

12. See Ingrid Gould Ellen & Katherine O'Regan, Crime and Urban Flight Revisited: The Effect of the 1990s Drop in Crime on Cities, 68 J. Urb. Econ. 247, 257 (2010) (finding that the decline in crime in the United States during the 1990s had little positive effect on overall city growth and that while the crime decline did abate some amount of urban flight, it did not reverse it).

13. For evidence of resurgence in European cities, see Ivan Turok & Vlad Mykhnenko, Resurgent European Cities?, 1 Urb. Res. & Prac. 54, 58 (2008). For crime statistics showing a slight uptick in crime in Europe

in the mid-1990s, see Martin Killias & Marcelo F. Aebi, Crime Trends in Europe from 1990 to 1996: How Europe Illustrates the Limits of the American Experience, 8 Eur. J. Crim. Pol'y & Res. 43, 54–55 (2000).

14. Steven D. Levitt, Understanding Why Crime Fell in the 1990s: Four Factors that Explain the Decline and Six that Do Not, J. Econ. Perspectives, Winter 2004, 163–164; Philip J. Cook, Crime in the City, in *Making Cities Work: Prospects and Policies for Urban America* 297, 301 (Robert P. Inman ed., 2009). For a summary of the literature, see Vanessa Barker, Explaining the Great American Crime Decline: A Review of Blumstein and Wallman, Goldberger and Rosenfeld, and Zimring, 35 Law & Soc. Inquiry 489–492 (2010) (observing that "researchers have had a difficult time explaining the [crime] decline . . . there is no consensus, no single most important cause").

15. Cook, 297, 301.

16. See New York City Policing, By the Numbers, N.Y. Times, Dec. 28, 2015, A18.

17. Storper & Manville, 1247.

18. For a case study of Philadelphia, see Guian A. McKee, *The Problem of Jobs: Liberalism, Race, and Deindustrialization in Philadelphia* (2008). Joel Rast, *Remaking Chicago: The Political Origins of Urban Industrial Change* (1999), argues that postwar Chicago had a choice between a developer-based downtown redevelopment strategy and a manufacturer-based working-class neighborhood redevelopment strategy and that it mostly choose the former. Joel Schwartz, *The New York Approach: Robert Moses, Urban Liberals, and Redevelopment in the Inner City* (1993), argues that one of the detrimental effects of Moses-style redevelopment was the demolition of factories. On deindustrialization in the Progressive Era, see Domenic Vitiello, Machine Building and City Building: Urban Planning and Industrial Restructuring in Philadelphia, 1894–1928, 34 J. Urb. Hist. 399 (2008).

19. Storper & Manville, 1254:

> The disadvantage of emphasizing agglomeration economies is the great weakness we discussed before: the inability to explain the where question, and therefore the inability to draw policy-relevant conclusions. The firms may attract (or create) the labour and a virtuous circle may begin from there, but why do the firms end up where they do?

20. See Glaeser & Gottlieb, 1275.

21. See Edward L. Glaeser, Growth: The Death and Life of Cities, in *Making Cities Work* 22, 50.

22. Richard Florida, *The Rise of the Creative Class: And How It's Transforming Work, Leisure, Community and Everyday Life* (2002). Theorists distinguish between "creative class" and "human capital" theories of urban growth. The former emphasizes technology clusters, talented populations, and tolerance. The latter emphasizes high concentrations of educated

individuals. See Michele Hoyman & Christopher Faricy, It Takes a Village: A Test of the Creative Class, Social Capital, and Human Capital Theories, 44 Urb. Aff. Rev. 311 (2009). Obviously, these categories overlap, even if the specific policies that each theory suggests might not. For an approach that emphasizes both creativity and education, see Enrico Moretti, *The New Geography of Jobs* (2012).

23. Storper & Manville, 1252.

24. Edward L. Glaeser, Growth: The Death and Life of Cities, 58; see also Glaeser & Gottlieb, 1297.

25. Mario Polèse, *The Wealth and Poverty of Regions: Why Cities Matter* 16 (2009). Michael Storper, *Keys to the City: How Economics, Institutions, Social Interactions, and Politics Shape Development* 23, 27, 70–71 (2013) argues for jobs first, while Glaeser favors amenities; see Edward L. Glaeser, Growth: The Death and Life of Cities, 49.

26. Storper & Manville, 1253.

27. Ibid., 1254.

28. See Storper, 31, 224–225; Polèse, 206.

29. For the clearest statement of this view, see Edward Glaeser, Will "Millionaire Tax" Cause an Exodus of Talent?, N.Y. Times Economic Blog, Apr. 27, 2009, http://economix.blogs.nytimes.com/2009/04/27/will-a-millionaire-tax-cause-an-exodus-of-talent.

30. See, e.g., Robert P. Inman, Financing City Services in *Making Cities Work* 328, 349–352; Joseph Gyourko, Urban Housing Markets in *Making Cities Work* 123, 147–151; Glaeser, The Death and Life of Cities, 59; Robert P. Inman, City Prospects, City Policies, in *Making Cities Work* 1, 17–18.

31. Soledad Artiz Prillaman & Kenneth J. Meier, Taxes, Incentives, and Economic Growth: Assessing the Impact of Pro-business Taxes on U.S. State Economies, 76 J. Pol. 364 (2014); Ajay Agarwal, An Examination of the Determinants of Employment Center Growth: Do Local Policies Play a Role?, 37 Urb. Aff. Q. 192 (2014).

32. New York Building Congress & New York Building Foundation, New York's Rising Construction Costs: Issues and Solutions 1–2 (2008), http://www.buildingcongress.com/research/costs/01.html (reporting that nonresidential construction costs in New York City average 60% more than in Dallas, 50% more than in Atlanta, and that total construction costs for high-rise office towers can exceed $400 per square foot ("psf") in New York, compared to $180 psf in Chicago). New York's overall tax burden places it in the top fourth of big cities. See Government of District of Columbia, *Tax Rates and Tax Burdens in the District of Columbia—A Nationwide Comparison 2013*, 8–12 (2014), http://cfo.dc.gov/page/tax-burdens-comparison. New York City residents pay the highest income tax rate in the country. See Josh Barro, NYC Income Taxes Going from Ridiculous to Ridiculouser, Tax Policy Blog, Tax Foundation, Dec. 5, 2008, http://www.taxfoundation.org/blog/show/24013.html. One commentator observes

that New York City's Department of Investigation—the chief corruption investigator for the city—arrested half the city's building inspectors, half its plumbing inspectors, and a substantial number of elevator inspectors in the 1990s. Larissa MacFarquhar, Busted, New Yorker, Feb. 1, 2010, 57.

33. Patrick McGeehan, De Blasio's City Feels Effects of Recovery, Silencing Business Leaders, N.Y. Times, March 7, 2016, A1.

34. Glaeser, Growth: The Death and Life of Cities, 49.

35. See William Cronon, *Nature's Metropolis: Chicago and the Great West* 297–307 (1991).

36. The collapse of the U.S. financial industry nicely illustrates the mismatch between regulatory scale and effects—national regulation seems both too large and too small considering both the disproportionate local effects of the collapse and its global reach. The gap between local and national effects is endemic. Consider the controversy over the payment of bonuses to financial industry employees immediately in the aftermath of the 2008 crash and federal bailout. For the city, the bonuses were considered a tax boon. For the nation, however, the bonuses looked like the redistribution of federal tax dollars to the undeserving rich. See David W. Chen, Much Vilified, Financial Titans Find a Friend in Bloomberg, N.Y. Times, Apr. 14, 2009, A17; David W. Chen, Economist's Forecast: Chance of Change 100%, N.Y. Times, Feb. 16, 2009, A17.

37. See Jane Jacobs, *Cities and the Wealth of Nations: Principles of Economic Life* 119, 209–210 (1984).

38. See Patrick McGeehan, After Reversal of Fortunes, City Takes a New Look at Wall Street, N.Y. Times, Feb. 23, 2009, A19.

39. Ibid. Other cities have promised cash investments to new and promising startup ventures that agree to relocate or stay in the city. Buffalo has one of the largest programs of this kind; see Stacy Cowley, Buffalo Entices Start-Ups to Relocate with $5 Million Contest, N.Y. Times, Nov. 4, 2015, B4.

40. See Yoonsoo Lee, Geographical Redistribution of U.S. Manufacturing and the Role of State Development Policy, 64 J. Urb. Econ. 436–447, 445 (2008); see also Terry F. Buss, The Effect of State Tax Incentives on Economic Growth and Firm Location Decisions: An Overview of the Literature, 15 Econ. Dev. Q. 90, 97–99 (2001); Carlos F. Liard-Muriente, U.S. and E.U. Experiences of Tax Incentives, 39 Area 186, 189–190 (2007) (reviewing literature). But see Teresa Garcia-Mila & Therese J. McGuire, Tax Incentives and the City, Brookings-Wharton Papers on Urban Affairs (2012) (observing that though under existing theories, it is difficult to justify tax incentives, on a theory of concentration externalities, they might be justified in certain circumstances).

41. Alex Barinka, Iowa Spent $50 Million to Lure IBM. Then the Firings Started, Bloomberg News, May 19, 2015, http://www.bloomberg.com/news/articles/2015-05-19/iowa-spent-50-million-to-lure-ibm-then-the-firings-started.

42. See William Thomas Bogart, *The Economics of Cities and Suburbs* 237–239
     (1998) (comparing competition among cities to the "prisoner's dilemma"
     problem and arguing that while the overall situation would be improved
     if cities did not invest resources competing with one another, any given
     city has good reasons to offer location subsidies); Peter D. Enrich, Saving
     the States from Themselves: Commerce Clause Constraints on State Tax
     Incentives for Business, 110 Harv. L. Rev. 377, 397–398 (1996) (arguing
     that state tax incentives may provide a benefit to the states if these states
     are able to attract more businesses, but that incentives do not create a net
     benefit to the country as a whole, because businesses choose one state to the
     detriment of others). Jacobs thought that "transfer economies"—economies
     that grow by relocating assets from elsewhere—were a weak basis for
     ongoing economic development; see Jacobs, *Cities and the Wealth of Nations*
     208–210.

43. Jane Jacobs, *The Economy of Cities* 50, 59, 67, 71–79, 97–98 (1970).

44. See AnnaLee Saxenian, *Regional Advantage: Culture and Competition in
     Silicon Valley and Route* 128 (1994).

45. Ronald Gilson, The Legal Infrastructure of High Technology Districts:
     Silicon Valley, Route 128, and Covenants Not to Compete, 74 N.Y.U.
     L. Rev. 575 (1999).

46. See Howard Mintz, Silicon Valley's $415 Million Poaching Settlement Finalized,
     San Jose Mercury News, Sept. 3, 2015, http://www.mercurynews.com/crime-
     courts/ci_28751080/silicon-valleys-415-million-poaching-settlement-final.

47. Amy Ellen Schwartz & Joan Voicu, The Impact of Business Improvement
     Districts and the Extra-Governmental Provisions of Public Safety 3–6
     (N.Y.U. Furman Center for Real Estate & Pub. Pol'y, Working Paper No.
     07-01, 2007.)

48. See generally Richard Schragger, Does Governance Matter? The Case
     of Business Improvement Districts and the Urban Resurgence, 3 Drexel
     L. Rev. 49 (2010).

49. Mike Quigley, *A Tale of Two Cities: Reinventing Tax Increment Financing*
     12 (2007); see also T. William Lester, Does Chicago's Tax Increment
     Financing Programme Pass the "But-For" Test Job Creation and Economic
     Development Impacts Using Time-series Data, 51 Urb. Stud. 655 (2014).

50. Quoted in Timothy Bartik & Randall Ebberts, The Roles of Tax Incentives
     and Other Business Incentives in Local Economic Development, in *The
     Oxford Handbook of Urban Economics and Planning* 634, 648 (Nancy
     Brooks et al. eds., 2012).

51. In answer to the question "How much does urban policy matter?" Harold
     Wolman replies: "the brutal answer to the question . . . is 'we don't really
     know' or, perhaps a bit more accurately, 'we know very little.'" Harold
     Wolman, What Cities Do: How Much Does Urban Policy Matter?, in *The
     Oxford Handbook of Urban Politics* 415, 436 (Karen Mossberger et al. eds.,
     2012).

52. See Douglass C. North, Location Theory and Regional Economic Growth, 63 J. Pol. Econ. 243, 251 (1955); for an overview, see generally Ted Rutland & Sean O'Hagan, The Growing Localness of the Canadian City, or, On the Continued (Ir)relevance of Economic Base Theory, 22 Local Econ. 163 (2007); see also John Adams, Editorial, 29 Urb. Geography 741–742 (2008) (providing a synopsis of economic base theory and asserting that the approach does not account for large and increasingly self-sufficient metropolitan economies).

53. Charles M. Tiebout, Exports and Regional Economic Growth: Rejoinder, 64 J. Pol. Econ. 169 (1956); see Charles M. Tiebout, Exports and Regional Economic Growth, 64 J Pol. Econ. 160, 161 (1956) ("There is no reason to assume that exports are the sole or even the most important autonomous variable determining regional income"); see also Charles M. Tiebout, The Urban Economic Base Reconsidered, 32 Land Econ. 95, 97 (1956); Rutland & O'Hagan, 165–166.

54. See Jacobs, The Economy of Cities 145 (discussing, e.g., how Tokyo's imported bicycle trade gave rise to a market for locally made bicycle parts, which in turn led to the domestic manufacture of complete bicycles); see also ibid., 169. For advocacy of this strategy, see Michael H. Shuman, Going Local: Creating Self-Reliant Communities in a Global Age 52–58 (2000). Import substitution has been generally rejected in the international arena, but it has made something of a comeback at the municipal level. For a review of the import-substitution debate in the context of international economic development, see Henry J. Bruton, A Reconsideration of Import Substitution, 36 J. Econ. Lit. 903–904 (1998).

55. Joseph J. Persky et al., Export Orientation and the Limits to Local Sovereignty, 46 Urb. Stud. 519, 525 (2009); see Rutland & O'Hagan, 179–183.

56. Persky et al., 522–523; Michael Thomas Power, Lost Landscapes and Failed Economies: The Search for a Value of Place 37 (1996); Paul Krugman, Pop Internationalism 211 (1996); see also Saskia Sassen, The Global City: New York, London, Tokyo 20–22 (1991).

57. See Shuman, 52–58. See Jacobs, The Economy of Cities 245–246 (asserting that "services will become the predominant organizational work" in cities); see also Persky et al., 519–520. Current-day import-substitution advocates do not argue that making your own is sufficient—as Jacobs and Tiebout recognized, export growth is still needed. But current advocates do point to trends in the latter half of the twentieth century to support their argument that economies are becoming more local and that those economies are also growing. See also Sassen, 20–22; Richard Schramm, The Interface of Urban Economics and Urban Planning in Local Economic Development Practice, in The Oxford Handbook of Urban Economics and Planning 655, 668–669 (Nancy Brooks et al. eds., 2012).

    Whether the local share of productive activity will continue to increase is an open question. Some scholars have indicated that the trend is starting to move in the opposite direction, as service firms begin to export more of what they do; Persky et al., 523–524. This is not surprising. Indeed, it seems consistent with Jacobs's argument that once cities begin to replace exports with homegrown goods and services, they are more likely to become proficient to the point of creating a new export market for those services; Jacobs, *The Economy of Cities* ch. 5.

58.	See World Bank, *2009 World Development Report: Reshaping Economic Geography* 25 (2009) ("spatially targeted interventions should be used least and last").

59.	See Hongbin Cai & Daniel Treisman, Does Competition for Capital Discipline Governments? Decentralization, Globalization, and Public Policy, 95 Am. Econ. Rev. 817–818 (2005); *2009 World Development Report* 5–6.

60.	McKee, 15–16.

61.	One well-known development theorist puts it this way:

> [I]t is not clear that the best way to get growth is to do growth policy of any form. Perhaps making growth happen is ultimately beyond our control. . . . Perhaps we will never learn where it will start or what will make it continue. The best we can do in that world is to hold the fort until that initial spark arrives: make sure that there is not too much human misery, maintain the social equilibrium, and try to make sure that there is enough human capital around to take advantage of the spark when it arrives.

> Abhijit V. Banerjee, Big Answers for Big Questions: The Presumption of Growth Policy, in *What Works in Development? Thinking Big and Thinking Small* 207, 219–220 (Jessica Cohen & William Easterly eds., 2009). For an argument that growth in the United States is inevitably slowing after a burst of technological progress in the century after the Civil War, see Robert J. Gordon, *The Rise and Fall of American Growth* (2016). Gordon suggests that in this new low-growth environment governments should focus on ameliorating inequality rather than pursuing growth. Ibid. at 641-652.

Chapter 8

1.	Consider that one study of Pennsylvania local governments found that 39 out of 56 cities and 288 out of 906 boroughs were suffering from a loss of tax base and the onset of significant financial distress, and that another approximately 600 localities were experiencing insufficient tax bases and reductions in core services; Pennsylvania Economy League, Inc., *Structuring Healthy Communities* (2009). See also Josef Konvitz, *Cities and Crisis* 3–4 (2016) (observing significant problems and structural deficiencies in cities throughout the world).

2. See William H. Lucy & David L. Phillips, *Tomorrow's Cities, Tomorrow's Suburbs* (2006); William H. Lucy & David L. Phillips, *Confronting Suburban Decline: Strategic Planning for Urban Renewal* (2000); see also Alan Berube & Elizabeth Kneebone, *Confronting Suburban Poverty in America* (2013).

3. David A. Super, Rethinking Fiscal Federalism, 118 Harv. L. Rev. 2544, 2609–2611 (2005); David Gamage, Preventing State Budget Crises: Managing the Fiscal Volatility Problem, 98 Cal. L. Rev. 749, 766–769 (2010).

4. Nat'l Conf. of State Legislatures, NCSL Fiscal Brief: State Balanced Budget Provisions 3 (Oct. 2010), http://www.ncsl.org/documents/fiscal/StateBalancedBudgetProvisions2010.pdf. This is the number of states that have either constitutional or statutory requirements that the legislature pass a balanced budget. Other definitions, such as the requirement that the governor submit a balanced budget, lead to a different number of total state provisions. Dale F. Rubin, Constitutional Aid Limitation Provisions and the Public Purpose Doctrine, 12 St. Louis U. Pub. L. Rev. 143, n.1 (1993); Stewart E. Sterk & Elizabeth S. Goldman, Controlling Legislative Shortsightedness: The Effectiveness of Constitutional Debt Limitations, 1991 Wis. L. Rev. 1301, 1315.

5. Sterk & Goldman, 1318–1319; see Richard Briffault & Laurie Reynolds, *Cases and Materials on State and Local Government Law* 667–68, 699–700 (7th ed. 2009); Bert Waisanen, Nat'l Conference of State Legislatures, State Tax and Expenditure Limits—2010, http://www.ncsl.org/research/fiscal-policy/state-tax-and-expenditure-limits-2010.aspx.

6. Susan P. Fino, A Cure Worse than the Disease? Taxation and Finance Provisions in State Constitutions, 34 Rutgers L.J. 959–960 (2003); see also David Gamage & Darien Shanske, The Trouble with Tax Increase Limitations, 6 Alb. L. Rev. 50 (2012).

7. Gamage, 765–768.

8. Jonathan Schwartz, Note, Prisoners of Proposition 13: Sales Taxes, Property Taxes, and the Fiscalization of Municipal Land Use Decisions, 71 S. Cal. L. Rev. 183, 201–204 (1997).

9. Briffault & Reynolds, 790, 872–877 (noting "the many legal techniques state and local governments have developed to avoid those limitations"); ibid., 919–920.

10. See Robert A. Caro, *The Power Broker: Robert Moses and the Fall of New York* (1974) for the most compelling account of how power can be exercised through unelected special-purpose governments.

11. For instance, although the Alabama Constitution bars state debt, it contains numerous amendments allowing bonds to be issued for specific projects; James H. White III, Constitutional Authority to Issue Debt, 33 Cumb. L. Rev. 561, 565–567 (2003).

12. California is one state that has constitutionalized education spending. Cal. Const. Art. IX, § 6. For constitutional commitments regarding retirement plans, see Amy B. Monahan, Public Pension Plan Reform: The Legal Framework, 5 Educ. Fin. & Pol'y 617, 638–639 (2010).

13. See Julian N. Eule, Judicial Review of Direct Democracy, 99 Yale L.J. 1503, 1513–1522, 1557–1558 (1990); Derrick A. Bell Jr., The Referendum: Democracy's Barrier to Racial Equality, 54 Wash. L. Rev. 1 (1978).

14. California had been the poster child for these failures, at least in the recent past. See Joe Mathews & Mark Paul, *California Crackup: How Reform Broke the Golden State and How We Can Fix It* (2010). For discussion of the failures of state debt limitations, see D. Roderick Kiewiet & Kristin Szakaly, Constitutional Limitations on Borrowing: An Analysis of State Bonded Indebtedness, 12 J.L. Econ. & Org. 62, 66 (1996). For discussion of the failures of state balanced budget amendments, see Richard Briffault, *Balancing Acts: The Reality Behind State Balanced Budget Requirements* 63–65 (1996).

15. See Richard Briffault, Foreword: The Disfavored Constitution: State Fiscal Limits and State Constitutional Law, 34 Rutgers L.J. 907, 910–914 (2003).

16. See Clayton P. Gillette, Fiscal Home Rule, 86 Denv. U. L. Rev. 1241, 1242 (2009).

17. See Kiewiet & Szakaly, 66 ("it is the discipline of the credit market that is the real constraint on issuing debt, not the state constitution"); Clayton P. Gillette, Fiscal Federalism, Political Will, and Strategic Use of Municipal Bankruptcy, 79 U. Chi. L. Rev. 281, 290 n.34 (2012) ("any locality refusing to make payments would have difficulty in subsequent borrowings").

18. Thanks to Richard Briffault for this observation. For discussion of problems in the municipal debt markets, see, e.g., Gretchen Morgenson, Wall Street's Tax on Main Street, N.Y. Times, Aug. 7, 2011, BU1; Kelly Shea, Transparency Problems in the Municipal Debt Markets and Their Effect on Fiscal Condition, Public Purpose, Spring 2010, http://www.american.edu/spa/publicpurpose/upload/Transparency-Problems-in-the-Municipal.pdf.

19. A.M. Hillhouse, *Municipal Bonds* (1936).

20. See Tamim Bayoumi et al., Do Credit Markets Discipline Sovereign Borrowers? Evidence from U.S. States, 27 J. Money, Credit & Banking 1046, 1057 (1995).

21. William B. English, Understanding the Costs of Sovereign Default: American State Debts in the 1840s, 86 Am. Econ. Rev. 259, 269–270 (1996); Kevin A. Kordana, Tax Increases in Municipal Bankruptcies, 83 Va. L. Rev. 1035, 1074–1077 (1997).

22. Compare Gillette, Fiscal Home Rule, 1261 (arguing that creditors enhance democratic responsiveness), with Paul Krugman, Rule by Rentiers, N.Y. Times, June 10, 2011, A35 (arguing that interest-group pressure from creditors has undermined democratic processes).

23. See Iris J. Lav & Elizabeth McNichol, Center on Budget and Policy Priorities, Misunderstandings Regarding State Debt, Pensions, and Retiree Health Costs Create Unnecessary Alarm 19–20 (2011), http://www.cbpp.org/files/1-20-11sfp.pdf.

24. See Gillette, Fiscal Home Rule, 1243–1244; Gerald E. Frug & David J. Barron, *City Bound: How States Stifle Urban Innovation* 75–98 (2008).

25. See generally Gillette, Fiscal Home Rule.

26. See generally Super; see, e.g., Brian Galle & Jonathan Klick, Recessions and the Social Safety Net: The Alternative Minimum Tax as a Countercyclical Fiscal Stabilizer, 63 Stan. L. Rev. 187 (2010).

27. Kordana, 1085.

28. Paul Sullivan, The Risks and Returns of Municipal Bonds, N.Y. Times, Apr. 9, 2010, http://www.nytimes.com/2010/04/10/your-money/ 10wealth.html ("The reality is that municipal bonds have a historically minuscule default rate"); see also Joel Seligman, The Obsolescence of Wall Street: A Contextual Approach to the Evolving Structure of Federal Securities Regulation, 93 Mich. L. Rev. 649, 699 (1995) (noting that between 1983 and 1988, the municipal bond default rate was 0.7%, while the corporate bond default rate was 1.1%).

29. Consider state-mandated property tax caps that diminish the ability of local governments to raise revenue. See, e.g., Thomas Kaplan, Senate Passes Cuomo's Property-Tax Cap, Adding Pressure on Assembly to Follow, N.Y. Times, Feb. 1, 2011, A25.

30. Frank Van Riper, Ford to City: Drop Dead, N.Y. Daily News, Oct. 30, 1975, 1; see also Richard Pérez-Peña, Hugh Carey, Who Led Fiscal Rescue of New York, Is Dead at 92, N.Y. Times, Aug. 8, 2011, A1.

31. Roger Dunstan, California Research Bureau, Overview of New York City's Fiscal Crisis 5–6 (1995), http://www.library.ca.gov/crb/95/notes/V3N1.pdf.

32. Alex J. Pollock, The 40th Anniversary of Gerald Ford Disciplining a Profligate New York, American Enterprise Institute, Oct. 29, 2015, https:// www.aei.org/publication/the-40th-anniversary-of-gerald-ford-disciplining- a-profligate-new-york/; Henry S. Rowen, A New York Solution for Bailing Out California, Wall St. J., July 8, 2009, A17; Rick Hills, Obama to States: Drop Dead? PrawfsBlawg, April 8, 2010, http://prawfsblawg.blogs. com/prawfsblawg/2010/04/obama-to-states-drop-dead.html.

33. Anna Gelpern & Mitu Gulati, Public Symbol in Private Contract: A Case Study, 84 Wash. U. L. Rev. 1627, 1638 (2006) (discussing the "$50 billion U.S.-led rescue package" of Mexico).

34. Indeed, a more significant concern from the perspective of democratic theory is that the conditions of assistance will be so onerous as to undermine local self-government. See Monica Davey, Michigan Residents Sue over Law on Emergency Management of Struggling Cities, N.Y. Times, June 23, 2011, A15.

35. See Steven L. Schwarcz, A Minimalist Approach to State "Bankruptcy," 59 UCLA L. Rev. 322, 326 (2011) ("bankruptcy law is an obvious mechanism of debt relief"); David A. Skeel Jr., States of Bankruptcy, 79 U. Chi. L. Rev. 677 (2012).

36. Advocates of a federal law of state bankruptcy are unabashed about this intention. See Skeel, 694–701 (describing how a federal bankruptcy law would alter state officials' and political actors' incentives and help to

"establish more coherent" state budgetary priorities); ibid., 716 (proposing that Congress vest the authority to propose a restructuring plan directly in the governor).

37. For a sympathetic account of the city's use of bankruptcy in this way, see Dorothy A. Brown, Fiscal Distress and Politics: The Bankruptcy Filing of Bridgeport as a Case Study in Reclaiming Local Sovereignty, 11 Bankr. Dev. J. 625–626 (1995). For a skeptical account, see Gillette, Fiscal Federalism 281. Gillette's proposal to permit bankruptcy judges to impose tax increases to "neutralize the strategic behavior of local officials" has been rejected by Kordana, 1096–1106.

38. E.J. McMahon, State Bankruptcy Is a Bad Idea, Wall St. J., Jan. 24, 2011, A17; see also Mary Williams Walsh & Abby Goodnough, Edging Toward Default, N.Y. Times, July 12, 2011, B1. For a discussion of the politics of a federal law of state bankruptcy, see Adam J. Levitin, Bankrupt Politics and the Politics of Bankruptcy, 97 Cornell L. Rev. 1399, 1446 (2012).

39. See generally Brown; see, e.g., Sabrina Tavernise, Judge Rejects Bankruptcy in Harrisburg, N.Y. Times, Nov. 24, 2011, A27.

40. Lee Anne Fennell has written at length about this problem and has suggested mechanisms to solve it; see Lee Anne Fennell, Controlling Residential Stakes, 77 U. Chi. L. Rev. 143 (2010).

41. Kordana, 1099–1101.

42. See Bayoumi et al., 1046.

43. English, 269; see also Kordana, 1074–1077. For a summary of contagion literature, see John M. Halstead et al., Orange County Bankruptcy: Financial Contagion in the Municipal Bond and Bank Equity Markets, 39 Fin. Rev. 293, 297 (2004). See also Ken Cyree & Philip Tew, Is Financial Distress Risk Systematic? A Look at the Short Sells (under review, Rev. Econ. & Fin.).

44. See Center on Budget and Policy Priorities, Policy Basics: State and Local Borrowing (Jan. 15, 2015), http://www.cbpp.org/research/policy-basics-state-and-local-borrowing ("Interest payments on debt averaged just 4 percent of current spending in 2011, the lowest level since Census began tracking this data in 1977"); United States Census Bureau, State Government Finances Summary: 2013, 5 (Feb. 2015), http://www2.census.gov/govs/state/g13-asfin.pdf ("Interest payments on general long-term debt decreased by 2.4 percent in 2013 to $46.1 billion, compared to $47.3 billion in 2012"); State and Local Governments—Summary of Finances: 1990 to 2011, *ProQuest Statistical Abstract of the United States* (2015 online ed.), table 456; See Michael McDonald, Banks Cash In on Whitney's Muni-Default Scare, Bloomberg News, Dec. 14, 2011; Brian Chappatta, Detroit's Bankruptcy Doesn't Faze the Municipal Bond Market, Bloomberg BusinessWeek, Aug. 8, 2013, http://www.businessweek.com/articles/2013-08-08/detroits-bankruptcy-doesnt-faze-the-municipal-bond-market.

45. Omer Kimhi, Chapter 9 of the Bankruptcy Code: A Solution in Search of a Problem, 27 Yale J. Reg. 351, 359 (2010).

46. Michael W. McConnell & Randal C. Picker, When Cities Go Broke: A Conceptual Introduction to Municipal Bankruptcy, 60 U. Chi. L. Rev. 425, 481–485 (1993).

47. See In re City of Detroit Bankruptcy, 524 B.R. 147, 162, 169–170, 175–181 (Bankr. E.D. Mich. 2014).

48. Ibid., 193.

49. As quoted in William K. Tabb, If Detroit Is Dead, Some Things Need to Be Said at the Funeral, 37 J. Urb. Aff. 1, 6 (2015).

50. Ibid., 5. For a more personal and journalistic approach to Detroit's demise, see Charlie LeDuff, Detroit: An American Autopsy (2014).

51. See generally Michelle Wilde Anderson, The New Minimal Cities, 123 Yale L.J. 1118 (2014).

52. Clayton P. Gillette, Dictatorships for Democracy, 114 Colum. L. Rev. 1373 (2014).

53. See Josh Sanburn, The Poisoning of an American City, Time Magazine, 33, February 1, 2016; Julie Bosman and Monica Davey, Anger in Michigan Over Appointing Emergency Managers, N.Y. Times, January 23, 2016, A9.

54. Frederic C. Howe, The City: The Hope of Democracy 1 (1905).

55. Ibid.

56. An enormous literature describes this history. For a sampling, see Thomas Sugrue, The Origins of the Urban Crisis: Race and Inequality in Postwar Detroit (1996); Beryl Satter, Family Properties: Race, Real Estate, and the Exploitation of Black Urban America (2009) (Chicago); David Kirp, John Dwyer, Larry Rosenthal, Our Town: Race, Housing, and the Soul of Suburbia (1995) (Mount Laurel, NJ); Kevin M. Kruse, White Flight: Atlanta and the Making of Modern Conservatism (2005).

57. Peter Dreier et al., Place Matters: Metropolitics for the Twenty-First Century 27–28 (2001).

58. Stephen Macedo, Property-Owning Plutocracy: Inequality and American Localism, in Justice and the American Metropolis 33, 50 (Clarissa Rile Hayward & Todd Swanstrom eds., 2011); see also Richard Briffault, Our Localism: Part II—Localism and Legal Theory, 90 Colum. L. Rev. 346, 415–416 (1990); Gerald E. Frug, City Making: Building Communities Without Building Walls (1999).

59. See Richard C. Leone, Foreword, in Rethinking the Urban Agenda: Reinvigorating the Liberal Tradition in New York City and Urban America v (John Mollenkopf & Ken Emerson eds., 2001).

60. How this occurred is described in Risa L. Goluboff, The Lost Promise of Civil Rights (2007).

61. As Robert Sampson observes, "blacks, more than whites or Latinos, have historically borne the brunt of differential exposure to concentrated poverty. Unfortunately, as I have shown, they continue to do so to this day." Robert J. Sampson, Individual and Community Economic Mobility in the Great Recession Era: The Spatial Foundations of Persistent Inequality (draft presented at the Federal Reserve Conference on Economic Mobility, April

2–3, 2015, Washington, D.C.). For a comparison of Canadian and American Rustbelt cities that attributes the high levels of inner-city abandonment in U.S. cities to racial discrimination, see Jason Hackworth, Why There Is No Detroit in Canada, 37 Urb. Geography 272, 288-290 (2016).

62. Classic discussions of this failure include William Julius Wilson, *The Truly Disadvantaged: The Inner City, the Underclass, and Public Policy* (1987); and Douglas Massey & Nancy Denton, *American Apartheid: Segregation and the Making of the Underclass* (1993).

Conclusion

1. James DeFilippis, *Unmaking Goliath: Community Control in the Face of Global Capital* 24 (2004).

2. The debate about market-based community economic development (CED) can be understood in these terms. See Scott L. Cummings, Community Economic Development as Progressive Politics: Toward a Grassroots Movement for Economic Justice, 54 Stan. L. Rev. 399, 408 (2001) (poverty lawyers must move away from the current emphasis on "injecting capital into geographically discrete, racially homogenous communities, and instead embrace a politically engaged conception of CED that . . . creates greater equity for workers").

3. James M. Buchanan, Principles of Urban Fiscal Strategy, Pub. Choice, Fall 1971, 14.

4. Douglas Rae, Two Cheers for Very Unequal Incomes, in *Justice and the American Metropolis* 105–106 (Clarissa Rile Hayward & Todd Swanstrom eds., 2011).

5. See Richard Florida, *The Rise of the Creative Class and How It's Transforming Work, Leisure, Community and Everyday Life* (2002).

6. See Margaret Weir, Coalition Building for Regionalism, in *Reflections on Regionalism* 127 (Bruce Katz ed., 2000); see also John A. Powell, Addressing Regional Dilemmas for Minority Communities, in *Reflections on Regionalism*, 218–222.

7. Jane Jacobs, *The Death and Life of Great American Cities* 281 (1961).

8. See John Mollenkopf & Ken Emerson, Introduction, in *Rethinking the Urban Agenda: Reinvigorating the Liberal Tradition in New York City and Urban America* 1 (John Mollenkopf & Ken Emerson eds., 2001).

9. See Adam Przeworski, The Last Instance: Are Institutions the Primary Cause of Economic Development?, 45 Eur. J. Soc. 165, 185 (2004).

10. Edward W. Soja, *Seeking Spatial Justice* (2010); see also Richard Thompson Ford, The Boundaries of Race: Political Geography in Legal Analysis, 107 Harv. L. Rev. 1841, 1844–1847 (1994); David Harvey, *Rebel Cities: From the Right to the City to the Urban Revolution* 22–23 (2012) ("Since the urban process is a major channel of [surplus] use, then the right to the city is constituted by establishing democratic control over the deployment of the surpluses through urbanization").

11. Harvey, 5.
12. Soja, 96.
13. See Int'l Econ. Dev. Council, *Forty Years of Urban Economic Development: A Retrospective* 12 (2008), http://www.iedconline.org/clientuploads/Downloads/history/Forty_Years_Urban_Economic_Development.pdf.
14. See Myron Orfield, *American Metropolitics: The New Suburban Reality* 3–4 (2002); David Rusk, *Inside Game/Outside Game: Winning Strategies for Urban America* 10–11 (1999).
15. *World Charter for the Right to the City* (Jodi Grahl trans., 2005), http://www.urbanreinventors.net/3/wsf.pdf.
16. See, e.g., Monica Davey, Limits on Unions Pass in Michigan, Once a Mainstay, N.Y. Times, Dec. 12, 2012, A1.
17. See The 99 Percent Project, Occupy Wall Street, Aug. 29, 2011, http://occupywallst.org/article/99Percent/; see also Chuck Collins, A Voting Guide to the 99 Percent, Huffington Post, Oct. 3, 2012, http://www.huffingtonpost.com/chuck-collins/a-voting-guide-for-the-99_b_1935222.html; Robert Kuttner, Sanders, Trump, and Economic Populism, Am. Prospect, Jan. 12, 2016, http://prospect.org/article/sanders-trump-and-economic-populism.
18. See Ruy Teixeira & John Halpin, The Return of the Obama Coalition, Center for Am. Progress, Nov. 8, 2012, http://www.americanprogress.org/issues/progressive-movement/news/2012/11/08/44348/the-return-of-the-obama-coalition/; Harold Meyerson, The Revolt of the Cities, Am. Prospect 30 (May/June 2014).
19. Frederic C. Howe, *The City: The Hope of Democracy* 280 (1905).
20. Robert A. Dahl, The City in the Future of Democracy, 61 Am. Pol. Sci. Rev. 953, 964 (1967).

INDEX

Abel, Jaison R., 195, 294n5
abortion, legalization of, 197
ACORN (Association
    of Community
    Organizations for Reform
    Now), 177–78
Adams, John, 300n52
administrative entity, belief in
    city as, 96–102
African Americans
    Chicago big-box living wage
        ordinance and, 178
    urban crisis and, 243–44,
        245, 306–7n61
    urban renewal and, 125, 126
    urbanization and
        immigration north after
        WWI, 27
agglomeration effects
    decentralization-growth
        thesis and, 54–55
    economic activities of cities
        and, 18, 23–25, 28
    in specific economic sectors,
        22, 170
    urban resurgence attributed
        to, 198–99
air conditioning, explanation
    for Sunbelt city growth, 41

Alabama
    Birmingham minimum
        wage law and, 147
    constitution, fiscal
        provisions in, 302n11
    Jefferson County, urban
        crisis in, 224, 240
    minimum wage law
        restriction in, 148
Albuquerque, NM, minimum
    wage law in, 140
amenities in cities, 171,
    198–203, 251, 252
    as cause of economic growth,
        199–203
American Political Science
    Association, 169
anti-capitalist middle class, 188
anti-chain store movement. See
    big-box and chain stores
anti-growth policies,
    53–54, 270n7
"anti-poaching" compacts
    between states, 283n60
antipoverty movement
    democracy,
        reclaiming, 257–58
    economic localism and,
        184–85, 188

land-use unionism and, 152
significance of city politics
    in, 165
translocal networks in, 176,
    177, 179
urban crisis and, 244
Association of Community
    Organizations for Reform
    Now (ACORN), 177–78
Atlanta, GA, 16, 27,
    202, 297n32
Atlantic City, NJ, 243
Austin v. New Hampshire
    (1975), 279n12
automobile culture,
    development of, 19,
    29, 30, 41
automobile industry, 174, 199,
    206, 232, 238
automobile insurance in
    Detroit, 293n51

bailouts
    in 2008 recession, 187, 204,
        206, 232
    of cities, 228–32
balanced budget requirements,
    221, 302n4
Baldas, Tresa, 282n58

309